WHEN BIBLE MEETS HISTORY

Ancient Voices Tell Their Version

By Stephen Lee Crane

WORDS OF PRAISE

*W*hy Secular US Jews Like Me Should Read When Bible Meets History: 'After years of 'intellectual rebellion,' successful American Jewish author and businessman Steve Crane entered weekly Torah study at a Reform congregation, and began recording his weekly reflections and intense research. This book, traversing a year's Torah cycle, affords secular US Jews like me as well as my orthodox friends a unique vista upon modern liberal Diaspora interpretation of The Five Books of Moses, the distillation of our people's view of the world and most fundamental beliefs. We're One People. We on the secular side can appreciate our unity more fully through insights gleaned from following Steve on this year of his journey.   --- Jerome R. Verlin, book and column author, media critic

----

I'm overwhelmed! The book is so comprehensive it takes my breath away! There is so much fine work in it. When Bible Meets History is very interesting and I loved the photos and other illustrations. It is an amazing body of work. As for who would use the book, I think anyone studying Torah, Biblical history, archeology, geology or linguistics would benefit.

■ Bonnie Freundlich, founder of Dona Gracia Hadassah Chapter

When Steve first approached us with the idea to add a layer of history to our weekly congregational Torah study, we were intrigued, to say the least! Typically our Torah study focused on traditional commentaries (parshanut) as well as some modern academic scholarship but rarely looked at the historical underpinnings of our weekly parsha.

Each week, Steve, along with other members of our Torah study group, presented a historical analysis of the weekly portion that enhanced our understanding of the text in light of Bronze Age archaeological findings. While the historical record was sometimes in conflict with the

Torah narrative, this did not create a dilemma, but in fact, added to the nuanced understanding on our origins as a people

This book is a labor of love and community. While there are many books about biblical history, this book is unique in that it presents the history through the lens of the weekly parshiot, making it a perfect companion for congregational or personal Torah study. Torah is sparse and not written as a history, thus understanding the context of each parsha, provides new understanding for the reader to gain better insights into their own lives.

We hope that you enjoy this perspective as much as our own Torah study group did and that it brings new meanings and insight into your study of our sacred texts.

Rabbi Jill Maderer, Rabbi Eli Freedman, Cantor Bradley Hyman, Rodeph Shalom Clergy

----

When Bible Meets History is a wonderful model for reaching a brand new audience for Torah study. By connecting each week's parshah with what is known historically about the events described and practices and settings depicted, Steve Crane's approach brings a freshness to the topic, and makes an important contribution that will help keep Torah relevant for many years to come and for wide range of people.   --- Jonathan Broder, President of Congregation Rodeph Shalom, Philadelphia, Temple University professor

----

When Bible Meets History represents a very significant work of scholarship, pulling together a coherent argument that hopefully will help to restore the Old Testament and Hebrew culture of the Old Testament as a leading, and a very significant basis for the American Republic's founding. It is a perspective long overdue and long lacking in American historical thinking that needs to be restored, and urgently so in my opinion.

In a sense, When Bible Meets History is a prequel to Crane's previous book Jewish German Revolution, which I hope will be re-issued. That is also a very important contribution to historical knowledge for other reasons and in other areas. For one, it helps to bridge the gap between history and modern religious thought. The history of the many Near East peoples cannot be entirely separated by ethnicity or faith, for as Crane documents in this new work, the interactions among these peoples, especially with the Egyptian dynasties of pharaoh, cannot really be separated from the leadership of many Hebrews we know from the Old Testament. There is no question that this attempt to integrate the history and culture lays a stepping-stone for forging a more complete understanding of their intermingling co-development.

Crane has now opened the door wide for both the Old World and the New to rethink the contributions of Hebrews to universal human history and economy, in the quest to overcome our collective amnesia about our past

 --- Edward Carl, Mid-Atlantic author, journalist, and editor, Bah'a'l Faith Spiritual Assembly member, specialist in early American history

----

Steve Crane's book <u>When Bible Meets History</u> takes its place as required reading for people captivated by the secrets hidden in the Bible. It is written in plain, easy to understand language and is a perfect resource for both Bible teachers and serious students.

--- Susan Warner, Lecturer, Writer, Activist, Co-founder of the Christian Olive Tree Ministries

----

The convergence of well-researched fact with biblical imagery in "When Bible Meets History" creates a flowing and relatable story line that is designed to produce a comfort level with the religious text that may be absent for those who are not Torah scholars. For casual readers of the Five Books of Moses, "When Bible Meets History" is a perfect accompaniment.

—Paula Joffe, retired MidAtlantic Executive Director for StandWithUs, an international organization that fights antisemitism, past Executive Director of the America-Israel Chamber of commerce, MidAtlantic Region, and independent advocate to Congress for the US-Israel alliance.

As someone who received most of his religious education from MGM and 20th Century Fox (mostly New Testament), "When Bible Meets History" was a revelation. Of course there are the familiar boxes to check — Abraham and Moses and Ruth — but for non Biblical readers, author Steve Crane peels back history like the skin of an onion to uncover facts about a unique people — the Jews — before they were even known as that.
With patience and persistence, he demonstrates that the laws handed down to Moses, The Torah, became the foundation for the governance of all of Western Civilization. Happily, the book is written in plain English, free of religious preaching, and when it gets a bit deep for the reader like me, the next chapter is just a few pages away.

- Stu Bykofsky, Longtime columnist, the Philadelphia Daily News, author, now blogging at StuBykofsky.com

<u>Comments from Torah Study participants at Congregation Rodeph Shalom:</u>

In modern times, the dialogue concerning historicity of biblical accounts has grown intense, leading many to dig in, rejecting archaeological records and contemporaneous historical accounts that don't align with a traditional understanding of the Torah, and leading many others to wholeheartedly reject the Torah as a fiction. The middle ground is hard to find, and can be a struggle for those of us who find deep meaning in the Torah, and are interested in viewing it from a historical perspective. Steve Crane's book is a real resource to people like us.

It is full of fascinating information and valuable perspectives, and it's been a real pleasure for us to read! We always enjoy hearing what Steve brings to the table in Torah study, and this book is a treasure-trove of biblical scholarship and historical facts that make for an interesting discussion of the weekly parashah. --- Olivia and Luke Brown

----

We have always wondered if there is any historical truth behind the stories of the Torah. Did these things really happen? And if so, what else was going on at the time of these events? Steve Crane has done extensive research and brings together findings in archeology, geography and ancient history to try to answer these questions. His book is beautifully illustrated with maps and archeological findings. He skillfully traces the contribution of the Hebrews to our modern understanding of law and justice. It's a fascinating study and offers a new understanding of the five books of Moses! --- Alice & Len Sayles

----

Holy smoke! 400 footnotes plus 200 pix, maps and charts! Steve's incredible devotion to this topic is overwhelmingly impressive to me. Being a lifelong scholar of Hebrew and Jewish studies, I find myself feeling wholly inadequate after listening to and perusing Steve's weekly scholarship. Though I have for years questioned the premise that Torah closely parallels history, I must admit that Steve has actually given me pause and an opportunity to re-think my opinions. Mazel tov on an amazing achievement! --- Jerry Silverman

----

My close friends and family describe me as a "born-again Jew." Throughout my youth, my Jewishness was defined by long Passover seders at my nana and grandpa's and dancing the hora at weddings or bene mitzvahs. My spiritual awakening began when I had children of my own. Now, by choice, I attend services and get involved. Torah study has become an important addition to my spiritual practice. Stephen Crane's book When Bible Meets History brings a historic context to lessons learned from Torah; an understanding of how Torah evolved; and its relevance to contemporary Jews. It should be required reading for both Biblical scholars and "born-again" Jews like me. --- Lynn Edelman

----

In When Bible Meets History, Steve Crane has written a highly readable account of the Hebrew Movement set against the socioeconomic and political development of the Middle East. It is a fascinating exploration of the traditions, practices, beliefs, and historical foundations of Judaism. --- Heshi Zinman

WHEN BIBLE MEETS HISTORY

ANCIENT VOICES TELL THEIR VERSION

By Stephen Lee Crane

The history behind The Five Books of Moses

Front cover – Hebrew immigrants Escorted into Egypt (Tomb at Beni Hasan, sas.upenn.edu, and in The Procession of "Asiatics" at Beni Hasan by Janice Kamrin)

Rear cover - Hebrew Warriors of the Shosu tribes (Belzoni sketch from Theban Tomb)

Books by Stephen Lee Crane

Survivor from an Unknown War

Jewish German Revolution

Treasury of Jane Austen Illustrations (ed.)

When Bible Meets History

With deep appreciation to Elaine

Wife, Friend, Study Partner, Soulmate

PAVILION PRESS

ISBN: HARDCOPY 978-1-4145-0488-9

E BOOK 978-1-4145-0489-6

Library of Congress Control Number: 2024906861

Copyright © 2023 Stephen Lee Crane

Publication date: June, 2024 pavilionpress.com

pavilionbooks@gmail.com   1232 Ridge Ave. # 101 Philadelphia, PA

Disclaimer: This book contains the independent research of the author(s) and represents opinions, recognizing that other opinions and research exist. Care has been taken for appropriate citations, and any mistakes discovered or notified of will be corrected in the next printing.

TABLE OF CONTENTS

PREFACE

Stephen Crane has written a delightful, well-researched book that guides the curious reader through the Pentateuch's rich complexity. As Crane points out in his prologue, the Bible sells some 100 million copies a year. No other text comes even close. And still, although nearly half of humanity is familiar with (and to varying degrees, believes in the truth of) the Bible's basic teachings, there is so much the lay reader doesn't know about the historical, archeological and moral context in which the Bible's books were composed.

Crane makes clear that the Bible is not teaching us history, but rather "aims to teach a moral life respectful of an involved Creator." To help us navigate this timeless wisdom, Crane introduces us to the rich and complex worlds of Biblical commentary and scholarship and summarizes essential findings in clear prose and with personal insight.

"When Bible Meets History" is a book for everyone who is curious about the Bible, the context in which it was composed, and the values which it continues to teach us today.

- *Rabbi Joshua Weisberg, Talmudic scholar at Jeanie Schottenstein Center for Advanced Torah Study for Women and documentarian at Fuchsberg Jerusalem Center*

PROLOGUE

When Bible Meets History grew out of my conviction that knowing the historical backdrop of the Five Books of Moses — *Torah* — can support and enhance religious or secular understanding of this great work. The book addresses the largely unresolved question of whether history is compatible with *The Five Books* or at odds with the patriarchal story. The scholarly divisiveness over this issue has not helped Torah study. However, an even-handed search of extra-Biblical sources including archeology and an understanding of the differences between patriarchal scripture and modern historicity provide the tools to reconcile Torah with history both for skeptics and devoted Torah students. The result is displayed in 54 chapters that allow for coordination with weekly study or a direct read. The path to this end is both surprising and gratifying.

When Bible Meets History is compatible with the belief that Torah is a divine gift. It avoids theological opinions but does quote a few. It discloses that modern historicity is not in lock-step with Torah and explains that "differences" are due to different purposes, writing style, and some 3000 years of separation. The book's narrative implies that divine interventions would not have abrogated laws of nature, in line with Maimonides, Berachot 60a, Nachmanides, Nachman, Levi, and Mendelssohn (See chapter 54).

There I was, after years of intellectual rebellion, attending Torah study, with my wife -- and loving it. Study of Torah, i.e. the five books of Moses, confirmed the idea I formed in my later life that our modern civil society is a direct descendent of ancient Hebrew holy innovations. The spirited discussion and the insightful leadership of clergy at Philadelphia's Rodeph Shalom, deep as it was, led to ever-more questions rather than answering them: Did that really happen? Did the Hebrews really do that? Were they truly slaves? Were there actual plagues? I took these questions seriously and investigated what, in fact, we know about ancient events. Opinions abounded:

-Stanley Giannet and Von Rad called the Joseph story a "novella."
-William Albright wrote that Torah has a "basic authenticity in the events and situations described."
-Israel Finkelstein called it a "literary masterpiece that has exerted an unparalleled impact on world civilization as both sacred scripture and history."
-Thomas Thompson claimed that "The Bible is not a history of anyone's past."
-Rashi suggested that there is "no earlier or later in Torah."
-Maimonides proposed that Torah was divinely given to Moses.
-Tzvi Freeman of Chabad observed that "Torah is how the Creator shares the purpose, intent, and desire behind all that exists."

The purpose of Torah, as explained in *When Bible Meets History,* is instruction about God, morality, law, the narrative of the Hebrew people, and religion. When Bible Meets History, however, is only concerned with history. In doing so, Bible is one of the references, but not the only. We leave theological interpretations to clergy.

Some 100 million copies of the Bible are sold each year, with various opinions on the veracity of its historic content. Torah is not a modern, academic history of the sort published today. Rather, its principal purpose is to teach a moral way of life consistent with an involved Creator. Specifically, it presents a revolutionary concept of God, the origin and development of a people, studies of patriarchs, laws both spiritual and secular, new ideas about governance – all infused with a humanistic morality. The beneficiaries of laws and ethics in Torah are the wide swath of humanity rather than the narrow stem of autarchy. Many techniques are employed in delivering instructions on morality including narrative, chronology, law, metaphor, eponyms, allegory, symbolism, hyperbole, and didactics.

Torah has led to a profound change in the course of humanity and its values. Modern minds, however, including my own, prefer not to study Torah in a vacuum. We ask -- what was the context from which these pivotal ideas emerged?

The Five Books of Moses contain a deep coherence and resolve that earn its place in guiding religion and civil society. Without aids to interpret the ancient language in those books, misinterpretation is understandable. What became clear to me was that a history for readers – corresponding to each portion of Torah – is needed; a history that gives background and clarification of events.

When Bible Meets History attempts to delineate actual history from the moral framework of Torah, and in so doing, to expand the understanding of Torah. This goal requires a basic recognition that Torah holds a unique view rooted in the world of 1000 BCE yet still instructive today. *When Bible Meets History* respects a separation between what history is interested in and what the guidance of Torah is interested in. Because it endeavors to present the history side, it does not comment on Divine authorship or Divine inspiration of Torah, yet fully recognizes the Divine connection. Furthermore, the subject of Divine intervention is not addressed in these pages. That is the province of theology and clergy.

Some of the ways in which history departs from Torah are given to us by sages, such as "There is no absolute chronological order in the Torah" (Pesachim 6b), or "Torah only tells us what we need to know" (Ben-Bezazel the Maharal). However, descriptions of Biblical personalities such as Joseph and Moses and events such as the plagues in Exodus or manna in the desert suggest that religion and history are compatible, but described from different viewpoints. The pioneer biblical archeologist William Albright referred to "the rapid accumulation of data supporting the substantial historicity of patriarchal tradition." (Albright,

Biblical Period, p. 2) Indeed, archeology points to floods of Noah dimensions, volcanic eruptions as per the plagues, and movements of people in and out of Egypt. Torah did not influence the course of history because of its references to wondrous events, but rather because of its blueprint for monotheism and humanistic moral laws. This book endeavors to show how the patriarchal history evolved into the patriarchal masterpiece of Torah.

We view Biblical writing as a style with a purpose all its own and deserving of its own particular understanding and appreciation. There is one opinion that the *Five Books of Moses*, being delivered from God, are not subject to review or comments from non-Biblical sources. This book does not attempt to subject the Torah to review or judgment, but rather seeks to look at the history associated with early Biblical events. Is the manna growing in the Sinai the same manna eaten by Israelites in the desert? There is little, if any, historiography in the ancient Near East and Egypt (Hoffmeier, Israel in Egypt, p. 11). We do not render an opinion, but only state that the manna event has roots in fact. The attempt is to "examine the linguistic, historical, and social setting of the Hebrew writings in the light of cognate literature (and other evidence) of Israel's neighbors (Hoffmeier, Israel in Egypt, p. 16). Hebrews and other peoples witnessed natural phenomenon from volcanoes to floods; starvation; oppression; the wonders of life; a vast universe; the devastation of war; and the benefits of trade. Only Hebrews concluded that the place of humanity in our world should be respect for the morality of one God and given moral laws.

I am fully cognizant of the fact that patriarchal historicity is anything but settled, and also aware that more recent history, such as that of the United States and even the post WWII world is still evolving, pending research and discovery. *When Bible Meets History* merges a logical history of the debated Hebrew chronology with Torah, the ancient and modern guide for human co-existence and explains the compatibility of one with the other. Suggestions and constructive modifications are welcome.

It is my hope that this book will aid in understanding the religion of Abraham and Moses and its contribution to modern civil society. The opinions and interpretations in this book that are not documented are my own. Differences of opinion will lead to further discussion and study, it is hoped. Care has been taken to avoid mistakes.

Stephen Lee Crane 5784

ACKNOWLEDGEMENTS

All of these listed are dear friends and partners in Torah Study who I gratefully thank for their support, help, and encouragement

Congregation Rodeph Shalom in Philadelphia

Joel Eichen of Blessed Memory – Linguistic Advisor

Ellen Poster – Author of Chapters 15 & 20

Elaine Crane – Copy Editor, Advisor, and Critic

Senior Rabbi Jill Maderer

Rabbi Eli Freedman

Cantor Brad Hyman

Rodeph Shalom Torah Study Group

Edward Carl and Michele Green, copy editors

Steve Feldman, editor and advisor

Jerome R. Verlin, technical advisor

INTRODUCTION

For serious students of the Torah, we must often differentiate between a multiplicity of approaches in reading the text. The Bible, or Tanakh, is the 24-book corpus made up of the Torah, Prophets, and Writings, and is the greatest gift of the Jewish people to the entire world. The stories, laws, and wisdom literature of the Hebrew Bible have impacted, influenced, and shaped the foundation of Western society from the Axial Age to the present, and have shaped our legal systems, cultural norms, and expressions of religiosity and spirituality to become what they are today. With our particularist lens, there is no question that the Tanakh lies at the heart and soul of Judaism. The evolution of Jewish literature – what we commonly refer to as 'the Jewish bookshelf' - from the Talmud and Midrash and the world of rabbinic literature to Jewish philosophy and mysticism, to modern Jewish thought, all find their deepest roots in the Bible. For millennia, Jews and other faith communities have been transformed by this formative collection of manuscripts formulating the basis of our collective narrative and as the religion of ethical nationhood[1]. Tanakh is accessible and can benefit both young children and the most sophisticated scholars and thinkers. I believe that it is a unique privilege to encounter its sacred words, to engage with its eternal messages, and to be galvanized to greater ethical and social action and spiritual growth as a result of our study. *When Bible Meets History* is an important tool for understanding the historicity behind the patriarchal story.

There is no one right way to approach the Bible. Each reader and each student brings their unique lens to the text, and often we wear different "hats" in our study. One could wear the hat of the philosopher who searches for meaning and truth. Another of the poet, who looks to feel the author's emotions and intentions focusing on specific words aimed at conveying a specific meaning through nuance. One could approach the Bible as a detective with the hopes of solving the mysteries of the plot line and understanding the motivation and underlying personalities of the various characters.

The archaeologist might read the Tanakh as a guidebook to the ancient biblical landscape seeking out the physical evidence of the Jewish people's indigeneity and its continual presence in the Land.

---

[1] This is a reference to the 1970 book of the same title by Mordecai Kaplan.

The theologian or believer reads the text as the written word of God and its very study fulfills one of God's commandments, as it is written: *"Let not this Book of the Teaching cease from your lips, but recite it day and night, so that you may observe faithfully all that is written in it."* (Joshua 1:8)

And it is the historian who provides us with the essential knowledge of context in our Biblical exploration. The historian reminds us that child sacrifice was the norm, and that Avraham's refusal was the aberration of societal expectations in Genesis 22, or that it was a common practice for a man to meet a future courtier at the desert watering hole and kiss her as Jacob does with Rachel (Genesis 29:11). Although "history" is a much-used term, it is not easily defined. Is history the sum total of past people and events? Or does it include only those people and events whose memory is preserved in written records? The challenge with the biblical record is that the ancient documents provide very selective information, which is often ambivalent, and sometimes the ancient sources make unlikely or uncredible and even conflicting claims. To wade through this often murky and potentially confusing material, the author, Stephen Crane, looks to support the readers making their way through the narrative of the Torah with an aggregated history that touches on and discusses developments such as the emergence of Hebrews, ancient Assyriology, and the early desert worshippers of the ancient God YHVH. It is critical to understand the emergence of the Hebrews as our familial dynasty and tribal clanship-turned-nation through the lens of our land being decidedly at the crossroads of civilizations between two major ancient empires – Egypt and Mesopotamia.

The importance of reading the Bible cannot be underestimated and the understanding of the historical context provides us with a window to our origin story as a people and an understanding of the context in which our civilization rose. This contribution to the study of Torah and the Hebrew bible will prove to be a valuable addition to understanding the *Five Books of Moses* and to all those who continue to 'turn it etc."

Rabbi Josh Weinberg, 5784

VP Union for Reform Judaism; Executive Director, Association of Reform Zionists of America

A beginning: The Bible and the History

1 Bereishit Gen. 1-6:8 בראשית In a Beginning

We embark on a search for events behind the most influential book the world has known, and by looking at history, discover why that book   is so misunderstood today and at the same time, so crucial to the development of our modern civil society. The reputation of the Bible is so great that hundreds of millions look to it for inspiration, but today another large number have questioned its relevancy. By coupling the words of Bible with a chronicle of causal events behind the scripture, an extra-clear understanding will emerge of its relevance to both ancient and current eras.

In a beginning God created the heaven and the earth (Gen 1:1). This statement made thousands of years ago was meant for a small group of Hebrews. Those words initiated the end of idolatry in the world and recognition that the universe conforms to one set of natural laws.   A couple of thousand years passed before that concept was widely accepted. And a thousand more years passed before the sun, moon, and stars were relegated in the minds of humans to being parts of creation rather than being gods.

A revolution in religion, law, human dignity, and morality began, certainly with determined opposition, but with a truth and logic so strong that the people of the world took notice despite ruthless attempts by an elite, privileged establishment to put an end to the democratization of worship, knowledge, and power. A new social order came about through the efforts of the Hebrew people, the actions of inspired leaders we know of as Abraham, Moses, and others, and the anguish of isolation and slavery. While respecting the Divine aspect of Hebrew history, this book concentrates on following a wide range of documents and archeology in places like Egyptian tombs and ancient desert encampments. The crucial period for *When Bible Meets History* extends from what we know as "Torah, Five Books of Moses, Pentateuch, Chumash," through "Joshua" and "Judges" because of their relevance to early Israel.

In determining the historicity of the earliest Hebrew people, many clues exist within the words of Torah, but Torah was not written as a modern history. Rather its purpose is for instruction or law. A distinct writing style was introduced, which can only be called "Biblical." The history being sought can be found by identifying relevant clues from the genre of Biblical writing and reconciling them with known discoveries in archeology.

One example of the Biblical writing genre is prose. In the opening pages of Genesis, powerful poetry is introduced, speaking volumes in a few words:

And God said: 'Let there be light,' and there was light.
And God saw the light, that it was good;
And God divided the light from the darkness.
And God called the light Day

And the darkness He called Night. And there was evening and there was morning, one day. (Gen. 1;3-1;5)

Stock image >>>

"This is now bone of my bones, and flesh of my flesh; she shall be called Woman because she was taken out of Man. (Gen 2:23)

Biblical writing, as introduced in *Genesis*, relies on non-fiction, theology, biography, history, geography, poetry, didacticism, parody, adventure, mystery, metaphor, condensation (compressing events from different times and place into one event), or representation (describing a place or a group as a person). It uses techniques from alliteration and adage to innuendo and hyperbole. The marvel is that this literary masterpiece was composed in Hebrew when Hebrew was paleo or proto and immediately afterward.

The words, "In a beginning, God created the heaven and the earth," presents a solid creation story; and suggests a start of the universe in line with modern astrophysics and versions of the "Big Bang" theory. It does not rely on celestial beings marrying each other or such superstition. It is a powerful opening statement using very few words.

NASA visualization >>>>

Hence, Torah quickly establishes itself as an intellectual and religious paragon. It is not interested in recording history as modern readers know it. However, as the Five Books unfold, it is possible to sift between the concise words and the message in order to determine historicity. A simple time line is not followed but some logic is followed. For example, the first day, for instance, could not have been 24 hours because earth was not formed until the third day.

Genesis gives clues not only about where to look for history, but also reveals much about the literary methodology. We explore how to peel back the scripture, with the help of available extra-biblical exhibits, in order to write history. If Torah had been concerned with history only, its influence and popularity would be greatly diminished. In the story of Eden it can be concluded that Adam and Eve is a teaching parable about good and evil (see chapter 30 comments). Eden also tells about the geography important to Hebrews.

The reference to Eden provides a connection to present-day geography and archeology by naming rivers flowing out of the garden. These rivers represent actual rivers because the descriptions reflect known facts about ancient valleys that hosted the beginning of organized civilization. One of the rivers is the Tigris and we accept the translation of "חדקל Chdekal" to be Tigris. Another river, the Euphrates, is translated from the Hebrew "פרת Perat" aka Purattu. Its attested ancient name appears in Genesis 2:14. In looking for other mentions of "Perat," the blessings of Jacob come to mind, blessings in which Joseph is referred to as the "son of פרת," or son of the Euphrates. We dwell on this because the blessing of Jacob to his son Joseph is usually mistranslated as fruit פרי of the vine rather than Perat – Euphrates (*Gen.* 49:22; Albright, *Patriarchs from Abraham*). This blessing shows that the tribe of Joseph originated from the upper Euphrates, adding to evidence we will consider that the sons of Jacob are eponymous names for actual tribes that later assembled into the Hebrew nation. We will present evidence that the tribe of Benjamin came from further south on the Euphrates and that names of descendents of Noah are actually geographical places. By this literary technique, Torah has transformed the history of Israel into an exciting drama rather than dry recitation. By reversing the process and adding current antiquarianism, history is revealed.

Another river is Pishon which encompassed the land of Havilah with gold and onyx. Much commentary on this river and the land of Havilah appears in Torah and elsewhere, also as the name of a person, with heavy emphasis on Egypt as place of reference. The last river, Gihon, is less certain - with suggestions ranging from rivers everywhere from Egypt to India. (Gen 2:10-14, 49:22, Albright, *Patriarchs from Abraham* p. 27, Albright *Yahweh, p.* 79-80, Har-El)

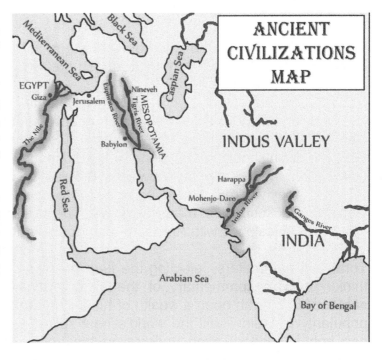

Ancient important rivers >>>>
Glimmercadeducation.com

An investigation of the Gihon River points to India as a likely source. Mention of primeval rivers in Torah would have to include those of Indian origin, either the Indus, the Ganges, or the dried-up Sarasvati. In Genesis, this river is mentioned together with Cush, which usually means Ethiopia, but the Pishon already claims identity with the Nile and so there are other alternatives to consider, namely in India. Since India has Dravidian dark-skinned inhabitants, (DNA similarity with Africans) and was so important in ancient times, it is a strong candidate for hosting a river out of Eden. India had relations with the city of Abraham, Ur, from the third millennium BCE, and lent Tamil and

Sanskrit words to the Bible such as orez for rice and koph for monkey. The history of pre-Vedic India corresponding to the time of Abraham is poorly understood, but there are a few similarities between the culture of Abraham and later India that lend some credence to a cultural, as well as trade, relationship.

Torah	Vedas
Means to "teach"	Means to "know"
Abraham & Sarah	Brahma & Sarasvati
Adam	Adityam, Yama
Noah was righteous.	Manu was a sage.
Make yourself an ark.	Build a strong massive ark.
Only Noah was left	Manu alone remained
Noah built an altar.	Manu made a paku sacrifice.
Earth was unformed and void.	Darkness and unperceived void
God said, "Let there be..."	The world arises from the word.
God, "I am that I am."	Brahman-Atman is reality, alone at the beginning
God is One	God is One

(Hays; Radday; Jhujhunwala; Stavig; Jewishvirtuallibrary; Werner; Holdrege, pp. 63-64, 126 & throughout; Dudhane)

In addition to setting the geographical stage for the Hebrew story, Genesis, before introducing Hebrew patriarchs, introduced the One God and proceeded to plant seeds of future Laws of Moses.

Gen1:27 God created man in His own image...male and female, or, we are all equal under God. Kings are not special under God, leading to equal votes.

Gen 2:2 God rested on the 7th day. Later, God commanded Hebrews to do the same.

Gen 2:18 Man should not be alone, reflected in family-friendly laws of Moses.

Gen 3:19 In the sweat of thy brow shall thou eat bread. Humans were not to eat unless they worked (See chapter 30 for the wisdom of Eve).

Gen 6:5 Wickedness of man was great. The struggle for morality begins, reaching milestones with Abraham and Moses, but still continuing.

Torah set parameters, rejecting the idea of "might is right" and replacing it with moral thinking. This commentary of the history behind Torah demonstrates how a few sentences of Torah open a wealth of historic information. Notwithstanding the continual popularity of Bible – still the world's best selling work – modern tools of interpretation can help a modern mind understand the ancient writing genre. Many sages have contributed explanations throughout the ages via writings, sermons, pilgrimages, and art.

The painter Marc Chagall can be considered an interpreter of the Bible and an example of the artistic expression therein. He used paintings to explain inspiration from the Bible, "the greatest source of poetry of all time," as he said. Chagall shows many metaphoric interpretations in his painting of Adam and Eve being expelled from the Garden of Eden. They fly out on the back of a rooster-like bird, symbol of fertility, vitality, and perhaps the future of humanity. They fly over a maternity scene. (picture and quote from Chagall Musee in Nice, by Crane; also see chapter 30 re: Eve)

Hence it can be seen that lessons derived from the ancient Torah have modern implications. In addition to religious revelation, there is everything from laws on justice, theft, and business ethics to modern suggestions for government and morality. The effort to place Torah in its modern context is helped by relatively recent extra-Biblical discoveries and acknowledgements in archeology, ancient documents, and linguistic studies. The following chapters will explore a multidiscipline approach.

Art inspired by Torah leaders: *Noah's Ark* by Edward Hicks 1846; *Crossing the Red Sea by Nichlas Poussin 1634;* and *March of Abraham* by Jozsef Molnar 1850

Noah and who were Hebrews before they were Hebrews?

2 Noah Gen 6:9-11:32 נֹחַ Noah

As the history of civilization proceeded with natural disasters and the formation of city-states, so does the story rendered in Torah with recitation of a great flood and the separation of peoples geographically and linguistically in the chapters on Noah and the tower of Babel.

In this continuing probe of the history behind the Torah, the goals are two-fold: The obvious one is to understand the actual events that occurred. The other goal is to determine the imprint of Torah on our civilization and what impact is still to come.

Consider three quotes below and one suggestion on the subject of Torah influence:

1. *A series of spectacular discoveries and decades of steady archaeological excavation and interpretation suggested to many that the Bible's accounts were basically trustworthy in regard to the main outlines of the story of ancient Israel.*
2. *And yet this land was the birthplace of a literary masterpiece that has exerted an unparalleled impact of world civilization as both sacred scripture and history.*
3. *Also unlike the histories and royal chronicles of other ancient Near Eastern nations, it does not merely celebrate the power of tradition and ruling dynasties. It offers a complex yet clear vision of why history has unfolded for the people of Israel – and indeed for the entire world – in a pattern directly connected with the demands and promises of God.*
4. As advocated by Abraham in Torah, the elimination of idol worship has been a success as virtually the entire world either believes in God or in a centrality for the laws of nature. Successful, but not as much, are the laws of Moses. The recognition of God and the laws of Moses are the largest miracles and contributions of the Hebrew experience. Unfortunately, some states and groups bemoan murder, theft, dishonesty, jealously, hatred, ignorance, and slander – to name a few laws - but still practice those heinous acts.
   (1, 2, 3, are from Finkelstein and Silberman, *The Bible Unearthed*, pp. 4,8,15.)

map from freeman inst >>

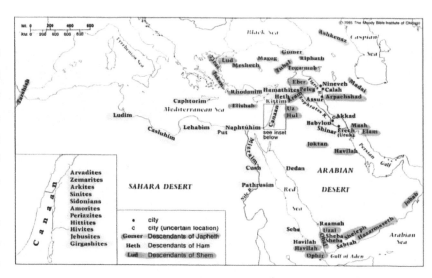

The saga of the Hebrew people takes place in the general area of the Eastern Mediterranean. In the story of Noah, God brings a flood upon the earth in an attempt to eliminate wickedness. Noah and his sons survived that flood. An enumeration of descendents from Noah's family represents both the geography and the ethnicities of the areas that entered Hebrew history. The literary idea of using a name to identify both a person and a location is used in various Torah chapters.

The Sons' of Noah - Shem, Ham, and Japheth

List of Nations Descended from **Noah's 3 Sons** Grandsons Greatgrandsons		
Shem (Semitic Race)	Ham (Turanian Race)	Japheth (Aryan Race)
Elam (Elamites)	**Cush (Ethiopia or India)**	**Gomer (Celts)**
Asshur (Assyrians)	Seba (Meroe E. of Red Sea)	Ashkenaz S.Russia,Crimea
Arphaxad (Chaldeans)	Havilah(Arabia,Egypt,India?)	Riphath (Riphaean (Russia)
Shelah	Sabtah (part of Arabia)	Togarmah (Armenia)
Lud (Lydians)	Raamah (Persian Gulf)	Magog (Scythians)
Aram (Syrians)	Sheba(Africa or Arabia)	Madai (Medians, Persians)
Uz (Land of Job)	Dedan (NW Persian Gulf)	Javan (Greeks)
Hul		Elishah (Aeolians)
Gether	Nimrod (Mesopotamia)	Tarshish (Tartessians)
Meshach (Babylon area)	**Mizraim (Egypt)**	Kittim (Cypriots)
	Ludim (Nubia)	Dodanim (Trojans)
	Anamites	Tubal (Black Sea)
	Lehabim (Libya)	Meshech (Moscovites)
	Naphtuhitim (Napetu)	Tiras (Thracians)
	Pathrusim (Pathros)	
	Casluhites (Philistia)	
	Philistines (Mediterranean)	
	Caphtorites (Crete)	
	Phut (Libya)	
	Canaan (Canaanites)	
	Sidonites Arkites	
	Hittites Sinites	
	Jebusites Arvadites	
	Amorites Zemarites	
	Girgashites Hamathites	
	Hivites	

Long before Abraham, the hierarchy of the day consisted of kings, slaves, and gods. His hometown of Ur in Sumer stood out with inventions, irrigation plans, a written word, and an agricultural economy. For all its sophistication, Sumerian civilization possessed an inflated view of itself. Rulers declared themselves gods but had no power over even the closest neighbors. The world 4000 or 5000 years ago included many city-states, each with its own god or gods, king, customs, and laws. Only a few people travelled between these centers and therefore could compare them to see how parochial they actually were.

One group did travel the routes between these power centers as well as to less inhabited regions. They were called "Apiru." In the early days, certain tribes, together with numbers of disparate groups, lived on the outside of organized cities as shepherds, guards for hire, and wanderers. Respectable aristocrats referred to them as "Apiru" or the cognate "Habiru" or outcasts or nomads on the other side. As reflected in contracts or treaties that some Apiru signed with rulers, it can be said that Apiru reached respectability in a number of quarters. The word "Apiru" sounds like the English word "Hebrew," or the Hebrew word Ivri. The name described a disparate, unrelated group that did not own land, did not belong to an aristocracy, were not enslaved or pledged to a temple or king, but rather insisted on independence. That included merchants and displaced people from Mesopotamia to Egypt such as laborers, mercenaries, brigands, runaway peasants or slaves, and stateless individuals. They needed quick wits to survive in a world where kings ruled everyone from privileged classes to slaves. (Wolfe, 14-20; Thompson, Gary pp. 24-37 & 104-105; Coote, p. 549, McLaughlin p. 36; Finkelstein & Silberman p. 44; Rainey p. 51; Albright, *Biblical pp.* 4-7; Pritchard, pp. 261, 275,)

In general, Apiru paid scant respect to all the local gods and god-king traditions. They did not respect the tradition of primogeniture as did local aristocracies. The mighty god-king of Sumer, Shulgi, from his capital of Ur, the early home of Abraham, took notice of Apiru, and was not happy. His advisers reported on the Apiru and said:

> *...As for their men and women, their men go where they please. Their women carry spindle and spinning bowl. Their encampments are wherever they pitch them, the decrees of Shulgi, my king, they do not obey.* (In earliest days they sold textiles)((William Albright, *Patriarch to Moses I,* pp 5-33, esp. 6-7).

<<< Modern replication of Apiru caravans
Some of these Apiru figured out how to retain their culture as outsiders and at the same time make a stable living. They used knowledge of the routes between city-states and knowledge of where minerals,

foodstuffs, and manufactured goods could be bought and sold. Certain of the Apiru organized donkey caravans and developed sophisticated trade organizations. The trick was to convince powerful war lords and kings to trade for goods or to purchase goods rather than to plunder for goods. Apiru learned to negotiate, to deal with tyrants, to make contracts or covenants, to manage finances, and to adopt sensible laws among themselves if not their clients. They formed trading centers like Haran and generally joined the Semitic migrations into Syria and Israel (then Canaan, Mendenhall p. 122; Noth p. 3;, Albright, *Biblical* 3-5; Albright, *From Patriarchs 1,* p. 7).

Texts from early dynasties far and wide referenced Apiru, with the appellation at varience depending on the language used. Early Egypt called them Amu but Ramesis II used the word "Apiru." Early dynasties of Ur and, later, Hammurapi, used the cognate "Hapiru" or the designation SA.GAS while writing about payments or about culinary items. Hittite treaties and Akkadian empire records use the terms interchangeably, as do later 14th Century BCE correspondences between pharaoh and Canaanite vassals. The majority of documents concern business transactions around trade or military arrangements. Apiru made contracts directly with kings of the powerful Mitanni empire. Greenberg offers original Babylonian, Ur, Akkadian, Mari, Alalab, Nuzi, Egyptian, Hittite, Syrian, texts that refer to Apiru.

Although they ventured far, their deepest roots were in Syria around Haran, the onetime home of Abraham, by the Habur River, which empties into the Euphrates. Many of the Apiru/Habiru trading centers and commercial courts were in that area. Wool, metals including Haburatean copper, Lebanese timber, and textiles changed hands at the mercantile centers. The question can be asked, did the group attain the name Apiru/Habiru early on because of the Habur River = Habiru? Did the definition of Apiru/Habiru take on connotations of wanderer, dusty caravan driver, and ruffian after or before the group was identified as associated with the Habur River? Places were often named after people and visa versa. Apiru manned royal garrisons, had their pre-Israel gods cited, and partnered with rulers, and so achieved respectability in many circles. (Gray; Gwaltney, 90-91, 6-121; Greenberg, 6, 3-96; Layton, pp. 1-18)

Not until Israel did the Apiru – thereafter called Hebrews – obtain their own permanent land, although the short-lived country of Amurru was dominated by Apiru.

One trading item that established the Apiru as desirable merchandisers was the invention of glass, probably by themselves or close relations in Ur. Glass, textiles, metal products, and

 jewelry were items of the trade caravans. (Kurinsky, *Glassmakers*). The Apiru acquired another appellation, namely the "dusty ones" because of the dust kicked up by their donkey caravans. Also, not surprisingly, the *<< Glass products from Ur*

Apiru were disdained for welcoming runaway slaves and other outcasts.

The Apiru merchants of necessity added related types of expertise to their activities. They acquired a certain military proficiency to resist brigands. It was the Apiru who invented aspects of trade and markets such as contracts, finance, and partnerships to satisfy those who had copper but wanted wood, had textiles but wanted ceramics, or had gems but wanted spices, all the while providing an environment of safe travel.

Caravans traversed routes from Egypt to Ur to Turkey to China and to India, with many donkeys or camels in each entourage. Managers selected which animals to use and which routes to take. Donkeys were best suited for hard roads and camels for sandy ground. Each animal could carry a few hundred pounds of spices, gems, tools, metals or metal objects, pottery, or weapons. The merchant organizers knew how to use those weapons. A slow-moving line of valuable goods and costly animals attracted many schemes of theft. Sometimes a merchant might make payments to local warlords either for protection or to prevent an attack. A large caravan could consist of 1,000 donkeys, 400 armed escorts, various animal handlers, managers, passengers, and translators. Financiers and suppliers waited at each end of the journey. (Wolfe, pp. vi-20; Gary Thompson, 31-34; Bottero, 145-159; Albright, *Patriarch to Moses p.6; Gary Thomson, 33.*) They promoted trade by establishing "port authorities" with colleges of judges to solve disputes. (Albright, *From Patriarch to Moses, p.12;* Burke, pp. 328-336)

Although largely Semitic, the Apiru attracted into their caravans, encampments, and military escorts, many kinds of adventurers, drifters, escaped slaves, and misfits. They enforced a morality necessary to their work that forbade theft or murder as bad for business. (Thomson, pp. xi, 32). Military kings depicted themselves riding horses and driving chariots with arrows and spears. Hebrews evoked an image of men leading a train of donkeys loaded with objects of trade. Sacrifice of a donkey was sometimes used to validate agreements (Milevski).

Because of their position as outsiders to any one city-state, the Apiru inspired combinations of admiration and fear. A king might like the exotic goods and passage fees brought by caravans, but fear the sheer numbers of armed men and outside influences accompanying them. Yet, more than a few times, when those same kings found themselves in a precarious military situation, they would hire those armed Apiru as guards.

Even though at the fringes of society, Apiru were not to be trifled with. For instance, Idrimi, the son of a deposed king of a small province in the north of Syria (now Aleppo), was forced into exile. That northern area, where the headwaters of the Tigris and Euphrates began, served as home for a number of Apiru. Idrimi joined an Apiru group and became a celebrity among them. Apiru leaders assembled a small army, defeated the usurper, and put Idrimi back on the throne (DeMagistris, 27; Albright, Patriarchs I, p. 28, Pritchard, Ancient Vol. II pp.

96-99).   Numerous Apiru, their successor Hebrews, then further successors called Jews lived in that area until the twentieth century .

Idrimi of Alalakh – Apiru king
British Museum (author)

Abraham's alliance with Egypt

3 Lech Lecha Genesis 12.1-17.27 לך לך Go Forth

We again view the history associated with Torah to show consistency between Bible and actual events. Lech Lecha begins with our founders, matriarch and patriarch, Sarai and Avram, just after 2000 BCE. They were living in the trading city of Haran, and apparently were financially successful, for they had "wealth and souls." Later events suggest that the substance was wealth from caravan trading and "souls" were followers, including his nephew Lot. At the behest of God, they departed Haran and travelled to the hill country of Lebanon, Syria and Israel then called Canaan.

Names are important here. Eber Nari in the old Akkadian and Assyrian languages designates the land across the Euphrates known today as Syria (Sanmartin, p. 116; Abraham & Sokoloff p. 30). Eber also was an ancestor of Abraham and the name means "cross over." (Gen. 10:24)   A cluster of ancient cities, some still in existence, lie in the area of the Tigris and Euphrates in southwest Turkey and northeast Syria. These include cities Serug, Nahor, Terach, places where Apiru resided and could have been named after Avram's brother, father, grandfather, and great-grandfather. Avram and his brothers Nahor and Haran are also represented. (S. Feldman; Bodi 27; Malamat, *King p. 166*).

The area surrounding these Biblical cities lies between the upper Tigris and Euphrates Rivers including the tributary Habur River. In their various forms, the Habur River is a cognate of names given to early proto-Hebrews, namely Apiru and Habiru. Economically speaking, these early Amorites cultivated grains, pastured livestock, mined salt, participated in logging, and provided military protection: all in conformance with the commercial activities described in the previous chapter and later in this book. This part of Syria between the rivers was known as Padan Aram, the plain of Aram and home of the Amorite people whose later iteration was as Aramaic, the lingua franca of later Mideast international trade and is still the language of the Jewish Kaddish prayer that praises God and is said for the deceased. Hence we can consider that the tradition of Israel is related to the ancient peoples of Syria (Fleming, *Mari* pp. 42-61, Golinets, pp. 185-186).

<<< City of Haran from Trip Advisor

A look at the name of patriarch Avram reveals possible derivation from the location known as the Plain of Aram in Syria. Today's city of Aleppo was once called Aram by Hebrews.   Aram is from the root Rom רמ or רום and means "from a high place" the Taurus Mountains are located there. "Av" of course means "father." So Avram then could be "father of the high place" or "father of the Aramaens." He is described as such in *Deuteronomy* 26:5.

In addition to considering the names of cities near the Haran residence of Avram, the ethnic composition of Hebrews influenced their history.   Important Hebrew Syrian tribes such as Benjamin and Joseph were distilled from a larger group of Syrians called Amorites, whose various factions conquered Babylon – with the Amorite Hammurabi - to Ashkelon in Israel. 4000 years ago nations like Egypt referred to the areas and people controlled by Syrian Amorites as "Amu" or "Amurru" meaning west of Babylon. Hebrews and other minorities were submerged in the designation of "Amu." Some Amu, especially Hebrews, were friends of Egypt, while others, especially Ashkelon and Babylon, were rivals and enemies. In the time of Joseph, a small kingdom called "Amurru" along the northern coast of Syria developed a distinctly Apiru tendency. Before this group of Apiru focused on Israel and adopted One God, the State of Amurru signed treaties with the surrounding great powers. The treaties invoked the Apiru god(s) among others. The Hebrew language retains the word "Amu" in the word "Am," which means people, as in the people of Israel Am Israel עם ישראל. (Burke, Amorites, pp. 40-177, 361; DeBoer, pp. 16-208; Pritchard, pp. 205-206 re: treaties)

Hebrew history differed from that of other Amorites, what Egyptians called "Amu" and various other groups by their divergent language, religion, dress, personal names, geology, scripture. For example, the name for the ancient Apiru traders is a cognate of Ivri, עברי, or Hebrew. (Saretta, pp. 13 – 108; Wolfe, pp. 15-21; Gary Thompson, pp. xi, 32, 105; Gelb, Computer-Aided, deBoer, 283-424).

Thus, Avram was likely a leader of the group of Apiru who concentrated, as previously mentioned, on trade using donkey caravans for transportation. Haran caravans provided employment for all sorts of outsiders and wanderers such as herdsmen, guards, inventory personnel, financiers, and, at the top of the hierarchy, trade masters and caravan operators. Products included wine, olives, grain, meat, textiles, metalwork, fish, bitumen from the Dead Sea, pottery, honey, dyed cloth, and wood products. These products fostered trade and even banking (Thompson, pp. 115-129, Lemche 91-117). It is probable that Avram gained wealth described in *Genesis* 12:5 as a caravan master, trading from as far away as India. As such, he would have visited the financier Eliezer of Damascus, sixty miles south of Haran, referred to in Genesis 15:2 (Snell 56-60; Albright, *Patriarch to Moses, pp.* 11-14; Albright, *Yahweh, pp.* 64,107-109; Wolfe, pp. vi-20; Gary Thompson, pp. 31-34; Bottero, pp. 145-159, Albright, *From Patriarch to Moses p.6*). Avram journeyed from Mamre near Hebron between Kadesh, Shur, and then Gerar, which is an ancient caravan route (Gen 20.1). Apiru were not quiet in Haran, but inflamed uprisings against the king (https://www.jewishvirtuallibrary.org/mari). See map of trade routes in chapter 4.

Extra-Biblical references to Abraham do abound, often with viewpoints different from the Torah, but with later dates rather than contemporaneous. Well over a dozen Egyptian, Babylonian, Greek, Roman, and Jewish authors wrote about Avram/Abraham/Abrahamos. Some repeated the Biblical story, but others extended available commentary. Accounts are uniformly positive in commending his wisdom, political leadership, knowledge of astronomy or astrology, practice of theurgy or sacrifice, travel, and formation of the Hebrew movement. Amulets and papyri invoke the name and powers of Abraham to ward off enemies and to help the petitioner achieve desired results. The writers include Emperor Julian, the Babylonian Berossus, Valens, and Nicolaus of Damascus, who wrote that Abraham came, "with an army from the country beyond Babylon called the land of the Chaldees. He reigned in Damascus for a while, after which he left with his people for the land of Canaan, where he settled." (Siker)

A mixed group of peoples occupied Canaan, but the ruling structure had been altered a few hundred years before Avram from marauding Amorite bands from the East (Albright, *Patriarchs from Abraham*). Along the Mediterranean coast from Egypt all the way to Lebanon and Syria the various Amorites lived in cities as rulers. Semitic Amorites had already settled in alluvial plains inland and coast such as Ashkelon and Jerusalem. Avram headed for the hill country, largely unpopulated and left to nomads (Albright, *Egyptian Empire;* Sethe p. 45; Burke, Amorites 236, 265-270)

According to Torah, Avram's first stop was Shechem, today's Nablus (from the Roman "Neoplis"), a city that became very important to Hebrews, and other caravan stops. (Albright, *Archaeology, p.* 80; Albright, Abram the Hebrew; Thomson, Gary, p. 17). Then he visited Egypt with Sarai and was well-received. They departed with even more riches and with an official escort. The actual history regarding a possible trip of Avram to Egypt is more complicated. There are several reasons a leader of Apiru from Israel would have visited Egypt:

First, proto-Hebrew tribes helped to install the new Pharaoh Amenemhat I on the throne during a civil war. The new pharaoh's Count Nehry expressed his thanks:

> It is I who acted as a fortress when there were no people with me except for my retainers, the Medjay (Sudan tribes later royal police and guards), Wawat (Nubians), and the Asiatics. Upper Egypt and Lower Egypt being united against me, I emerged the affair as a success, my entire city being with me without a loss

(Mourad *Rise* 94; Redford 73; Stephen Cross, p. 136; Kelder, p. 6; Tyldesley, Stories, pp.78-86).

Amenemhat I at the Met >>>

A number of indicators point to early Hebrew speaking Asiatics forming an alliance with the 12th dynasty.   Ongoing conflict occurred between Egypt and other Asiatics, specifically those along the coast and in Jordan rather than those in the Hebrew highlands. As will be outlined, Hebrew speaking Asiatics worked closely with several Egyptian dynasties beginning with the 12th and its first pharaoh, Amenemhat I, around 2000 BCE. The tomb of Prince Khnumhotep I (after 2000 BCE) shows Amorite auxiliary troops. His grandson's tomb shows depiction of Amu entering Egypt following the Hebrew named leader Abishai dressed in multi-colored tunics like Joseph. (Redford, pp. 69-93; Bietak, Der ubergang…; Mourad, Foreigners; chapter 23,24).

Egypt encountered a number of "Asiatics," "Amorites", in the context of Egyptian neighbors to the North, either as friends and allies or as adversaries. The adversaries are usually referred to as miserable, wretched, or defeated, while friends do not have such descriptive adjectives or are given bland suffixes.

While Asiatics/Amorites we identify as proto-Hebrews fought with the incoming Amenemhat I of the new 12th Dynasty, other Asiatics fought to preserve the 11th. Seige scenes in the tombs of rebel nobles show Asiatics on both sides (Mourad, Rise, 81-85 tombs of Noblemen Khety and Khnumhotep I). Subsequent history shows friendship with the Hebrew faction and continuous friction with other Amorites.

References to wretched or miserable enemy Asiatics at the time of Abraham and Amenemhet I include the "Instruction for Merikare," "The Prophecy of Nerferti," and a general who defeated the "Asiatic Troglodytes." At the same time, the Egyptian noble Sinuhe travelled to Byblos and was welcomed by the friendly presumably Hebrew Asiatic leader Ammunenshi – name built around the word "Ammu," who had visited Egypt. Other probable Hebrew Asiatics are mentioned often with simple suffixes like "I" or "t" when they are described as clerks, butlers, craftspeople, revered friends, sailors, or those "may they live eternally." (Saretta, pp. 16-17, 2-21; Redford, p. 68; the name Ammunenshi comprises "Ammu," home of Hebrews and nenshi as in Ex. 17:15, Num.21:8 & 26:10, Jer. 51:12, Is 49:22; Mourad, Asiatics and Abydos; Nielsen; Genesis 25:30, 32:4, 36:5,14; Breasted Vol. 1, pp. 227-239 # 486-497: ch. 3; Tobin). Subsequent chapters will also separate Hebrews from other Amorites/Asiatics.

Shortly after the beginning of the 12th Dynasty, a military general identifiably proto-Hebrew was referred to at the bustling desert highway way station at Wadi el-Hol south of Thebes. That was Bebi, (or Bebe) general of the Asiatics and royal messenger. (Darnell, p, 74-75; ch. 23 this book) Bebi is a Hebrew name and also is in ch. 23.

By allying with the winning side, "Asiatics," in this case proto-Hebrews, gained friendship with the new 12th dynasty (Mourad, *Rise, p.* 94). Those Asiatics left messages in the then newly discovered paleo-Hebrew language alphabet, including military conversation. (Goldwasser, *How the Alphabet*, Petrovich; Darnell, *Early Alphabetic*; Darnell, *Wadi el-Hol*). "The Egyptian administration was allied with Asiatics." (Mourad *Rise* 124). This new 12th dynasty appointed a "General of Asiatics" (Himelfarb). Hebrews were the Asiatics referenced by Amenenhat I, which can also be deduced because of an ongoing Egyptian enmity with other Canaanites and ongoing friendship with Hebrews.

Israelites distanced themselves from the major force in Syria, namely the Amorites, and they made it very clear.

And they shall return here in the fourth generation, for the iniquity of the Amorites is not yet complete. Gen 15:16
You sulked in your tents and said, "It is out of hatred for us that יהוה *brought us out of the land of Egypt, to hand us over to the Amorites to wipe us out. Deu 1:27*
Then the Amorites who lived in those hills came out against you like so many bees and chased you, and they crushed you at Hormah in Seir. Deu 1:44
Therefore the five kings of the Amorites, the king of Jerusalem, the king of Hebron, the king of Jarmuth, the king of Lachish, the king of Eglon, gathered themselves together, and went up, they and all their hosts, and encamped against Gibeon, and made war against it. Joshua 10:5
And elsewhere…

Second, an ambitious king from Elam threatened both Egypt and Israel by subduing city-states around the Dead Sea. This was described in the *Genesis* 14 war of foreign King Chedorlaomer against five Dead Sea area kings who were friends of Avram. Elam thus threatened Egyptian trade. There is evidence of Apiru and Egyptian cooperation in confronting an Elamite thrust into Israel.

Third, there may have been a drought in Israel.

Statue possibly of Sarah in tomb of Amenenhat's advisor >>>

Genesis 12 makes it clear that Sarai created quite a stir in the court of pharaoh. This is possible. A statue seemingly of Sara, with the pose of an honorary offering bearer, found in the tomb of Amenemhat I's advisor, is an example of a rare occurrence: an Apiru or Canaanite in this high position, identifiable as such by her clothing. Other Egyptian bearers wore Egyptian linen and a royal wig and circulated with at least one other bearer. (Glueck, 77; Gertoux, *Avraham and Chedorlaomer*.)

History asks the question, "What were the results of collaboration between Abraham and Egypt?" *Genesis* 13-14 provides the Biblical answer, namely that the five Dead Sea area kings rebelled and King Chedorlaomer ruthlessly crushed them, whereupon Avram tracked Chedorlaomer and killed him.

History is consistent with Genesis, but the event was more complicated. Both Amenemhat I's and Avram's followers faced the same problem: King Chedorlaomer. (Chedorlaomer is his Biblical name, Kudur-Lagamar his historic name). The situation observed by Avram included some hard facts. The army of Elam was on the move. King Chedorlaomer collected forced tribute from several cities along the Jordan River Valley. He set his sights on controlling the main trading routes enjoyed by the pharaoh of Egypt along Israel's coastline, as well as routes through the hill country. His vassal communities could provide stepping stones to control of trading routes to Egypt (Albright, Abram the Hebrew, p. 49; Gertoux, Abraham; Bodi, p. 408).

Then Avram returned to Israel with an Egyptian military escort. "Pharaoh put men in charge of him and sent him off with his wife and all that he possessed." (*Gen* 12.20) An Egyptian General cooperated with Avram to defeat Chedorlaomer. The general wrote:

> *Year 24, month 4 of Shemu, under the majesty of Life to the Horus.... Son of Re, Amenemhat.... I destroyed the Asiatic nomads, the Bedouin* (In this case, the Elam contingent)*, I overthrew their strongholds, creeping like the desert fox on the desert margin. I came and went through their streets without an equal therein by command of Monty, he who is victorious, through the plan of the one who puts his oppression and terror upon the foreigners Hr.yw-s [presumably Elamites] for him, the one who pacifies the St.(t)yw* (Gee, p. 24; Mourad, *Asiatics* 33; also trans from Kurt *Sethe, Agyptische Lesestuck;, Gertoux Avraham, pp. 45-58).

Avram became Abraham the Hebrew (Albright Patriarchs From V. 1 p. 15, Gen 14.13). With friendship sealed between Egypt and Abraham, new immigrants from Hebrew parts of Canaan were permitted, and they poured into the Delta, aka Goshen. The border wall of Egypt opened to Hebrews. Due to the Egyptian that wall, only the invited could enter (Beitak, Harbor, p.212)

<< *Immigrants shown in the Egyptian tomb of Khnumhotep II They wore clothing with stripes of many colors similar to that described as belonging to Joseph. Their leader Abishai had the same name as was later the name of King David's nephew, reasons for concluding that this group was Apiru.*

Allowing such numbers of immigrants into Egypt changed a long-lasting policy, possibly because of the close cooperation with Abraham. Just before Amenemhat came to power, a previous pharaoh proclaimed: *The Asiatic is a crocodile on its shore, It snatches from a lonely road,*

It cannot seize from a populous town. (Saretta, 18-39; Pharaoh Khety's *Teachings*)

Over the next 800 years, in several dynasties, Egypt held a close friendship with Hebrews.
Avram formed this friendship.

Sarah and Abraham by Lars Justinen

That Abraham was an important figure in his day seems probable.... The narrative in *Genesis 14,* describing Abraham's triumph over the four kings of the East, has long been recognized as containing very archaic features.... References to places in Trans-Jordan and the Negev of western Palestine fit in extremely well with the nineteenth century BCE. (Albright, *Biblical, pp.* 4-9)

Rabbi Jonathan Sacks, said this of Avram:

> *He began life as Avram, performed no miracles, commanded no armies, ruled no kingdom, gathered no mass of disciples and made no spectacular prophecies. Yet there can be no serious doubt that he is the most influential person who ever lived (Sacks, Great Partnership, p. 12).*

Abraham: Man of God, caravan trade, teaching, and a moral leader

4 Vayeira Genesis 18.1-22.24 וירא *(vision of God) appeared*

It is written how Abraham followed the dictates of God, and that his wife Sarai, even though advanced in age - would have a child and therefore the Hebrew experience would go forward. After their service to Hebrews and to Israel, *Genesis* states that God changed Avram's name to Abraham and Sarai's to Sarah. Bible referred to Abraham as "the Hebrew."

The righteousness of Abraham was recognized in extra-Biblical writing in later years. "He excelled all men in nobility of birth and wisdom.... Because he was eager in his pursuit of piety, he was well pleasing to God" (Polyhistor ~ 75 BCE) "Hebrews, thus are called Jews after Abraham." (Claudius Charax ~ 125 CE)

The era of Abraham was interesting, which is to say it was a disruptive time across the developed and connected world from the Pacific across Asia and Africa to the Atlantic. For one thing, drought encompassed northern Africa and the Mideast, causing migration, such as the trek of a small Hebrew group to Egypt. The world was connected as never before because of the routes that brokers such as Apiru used to conduct the business of trading products across those continents and even into Europe. Routes like the Silk Road and its numerous connections gave wealth to clever caravan merchants like Abraham. The trade disrupted the isolation of the emerging societies and in the time of Abraham moved seeds, azaleas, grapes, figs, spices, glass, jade, silk, and metalwork along with with raw metals.

public domain map>>

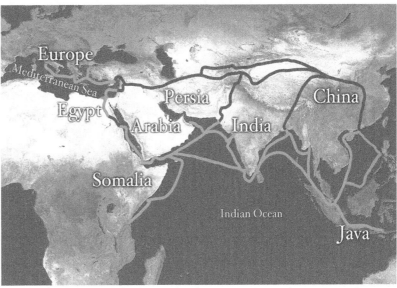

A Mesopotamian trader gave instructions to his caravan master (Frank & Brownstone, pp. 26-40; Christian, 1- 14):

> *This silver belongs to the trust of Kudatum... buy goods of the city for half of our silver buy linen cloths, and for half the silver buy tin* (Frank & Brownstone, p. 41).

Trade was not the only disruptor to follow the ancient routes. Invaders realized which areas were rich and vulnerable. At this time, centralized government came to China in the form of the Xia Dynasty. Indian civilization, already over 1,000 years old and very advanced, collapsed under exterior pressure.

Invaders also pressed the empire of Babylon making for a violent world, the world encountered by Avram. Apiru/Hebrew Traders had to be alert and pay attention to global events, as reported by one trader from the Persian plateau:

Since I arrived here I am in trouble and the whole land is in trouble. Do not come here this year… till I send you a dispatch, do not come! Better return to Susa (Frank & Brownstone, 40).

In those "interesting times," Abraham served his budding community well by concentrating his trade from the Euphrates to Egypt, which brought wealth and stability, rather than from the Euphrates to India and China, besieged with turmoil. Trading westward worked especially well since Hebrews had ingratiated themselves with the new Egyptian dynasty by sending armed forces to help put the new dynasty in power (see ch. 3 of this book). Another drama of a personal nature unfolds in this chapter with a long-sought birth of a son to Sarah, the preparation of that son for sacrifice on a burning pyre, and the destruction of Sodom due to wickedness. These events and others provide windows into important events and traditions of the era.

For instance, the birth of Isaac concludes a drama that began in the previous chapter when

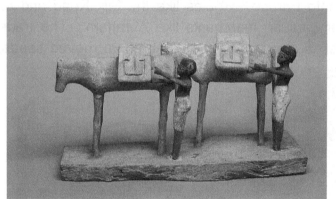

Abraham, in his old age, bemoaned a lack of heirs. This would affect both his Hebrew legacy and his material wealth, At this time, no god kings, no peasant group, and no war lords were willing to give up their divine powers or their state-controlled system of priests and temples.

(from Metropolitan Museum of Art showing the commercial transport of the era)

Without an heir to carry on Abraham's teaching, monotheism could have ended. None of the extended family of Abraham was preaching the idea of one God. Torah acknowledged this, and lists tribes that went their own way . Semites who could have allied with the Hebrew culture but chose not to included; the children of Lot, Ammonites (Gen. 19:36-38), and brother Nahor who remained in Aram (Gen. 22:20-24), and later progeny of Abraham (Gen. 25). These family members represent tribes or groups.

Before the birth of Isaac, Abraham fretted about dangers to his fortune. Genesis and history explain Abraham's borrowing for business in the days before stocks, bonds, and mortgages. This is presented indirectly though the problems of inheritance. Torah relates that Abraham experienced great distress and worry about his lack of an heir, "Oh, Lord God, what can You give me, seeing that I shall die childless, and the one in charge of my household is Damascus Eliezer." Who was Eliezer from Damascus?

Eliezer was probably an investment banker. Caravan traders like Abraham required funds for their business pursuits. Traders had no real estate or available collateral since donkeys could be moved quickly and ownership could be hidden. Therefore, the practice used in financial centers like Damascus was for the banker to become heir to the caravan operator. Then, the investment banker of Avraham could claim his estate in order to settle unfinished business unless an heir assumed the debt. This implies a large amount of trade, and, rather than have traders carry gold bars, letters of credit and banks could accommodate money transactions. (Albright, From Patriarchs Abraham)

And still another problem, according to Torah, evolved. The cities of Sodom and Gomorrah by the Dead Sea, rulers of which were befriended by Abraham, behaved immorally and had to be destroyed by God (Gen 18.20-19.20). History records conflagration in Sodom, as the early historian Strabo wrote:

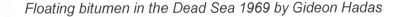

Floating bitumen in the Dead Sea 1969 by Gideon Hadas

Lake Sirbonis [the Dead Sea or Asphalt Lake] *is very large. Some have said it is 1,000 stadia in circumference. It extends along the seacoast, having a length of a little bit more than 200 stadia. It is deep and has extremely heavy water so that one doesn't need to swim to stay afloat, rather, when someone wades into it, even just up to the waist, he is immediately buoyed up. The lake is full of asphalt. At random times, it rises with bubbles like boiling water from the middle of its depths. The surface bulges and has the appearance of a ridge. A great amount of soot is also carried up, which is smoky but invisible to the eye. Copper, silver, and anything shiny--even gold--is tarnished by it. ... The source of fire is in the middle, as is the majority of the asphalt.* (Strabo here refers to the Dead Sea, but errors in calling it Lake Sirbonis, confusing it with a similar named Dead Sea district – see Falconer, Strabo 16.2.42)

Other proofs that the area of the Dead Sea was fiery have been offered. For instance, there are some ragged rocks around Masada that have been scorched; caves are numerous [where Lot presumably hid]; *the soil is ashes; drops of pitch that fall from the cliffs and that rivers that boil with a far-reaching stench; and that there are scattered dwellings in ruins. Thus, we believe the rumors spread by the local inhabitants, that there were once cities situated here, one of which was the metropolis Sodom: an area of about 60 stadia, suffered earthquakes and eruptions of fire and hot water filled with asphalt and sulfur. This caused the lake to burst its banks and the rocks to be seized by fire; while some of the cities were swallowed by*

the earthquake, others were abandoned by those who were able to flee.
(Strabo.,*Geography, Book XVI,* Chapter 2:44; Clapp)

*Sulpher balls that cause fire and brimstone
from Wyatt Museum*

Jonathan Sacks wrote that Abraham is the most important person in history (Sachs, *Great*, p. 8). Extra-Biblical references to Abraham exist. They were written after the time of Abraham, but they do show a different memory than that of Torah.

> **Eupolemus** in his book *Concerning the Jews of Assyria* states that Abraham was born, who surpassed all men in nobility and wisdom, who was also the inventor of astronomy and the Chaldaic art, and pleased God well by his zeal towards religion.
>
> **Artabanus** in his *Jewish History* says that the Jews were called Ermiuth, which when interpreted after the Greek language means Judaeans, and that they were called Hebrews from Abraham.
>
> **Molon**, the author of the collection *Against the Jews,* said that Abraham was born, by interpretation "Father's friend," and that he became a wise man.

Another subject brought up in this chapter on Abraham was morality. As a trader and partner with foreign governments, he needed contracts and honesty. As a father, his actions eliminated the common practice of child sacrifice as far as Hebrews were concerned. Canaanite gods demanded too much, often including the life of a firstborn. Great furnaces consumed the children (Hoerth, pp. 179, 203-4). One such place, a narrow shadowy valley by Jerusalem, gave rise to *Psalm* 23:4, "Yea, though I walk through the valley of the shadow of death...." Canaanites also used slaves extensively and maintained a strong aristocracy. Hebrews were collecting laws such as no murder, obey God, no stealing, refer disputes to courts, control sexuality, and respect our Creator. These are foundations leading to the Laws of Moses. Abraham set in motion a universal morality from one God.

What is in the Tomb of the Patriarchs?

5 Chayyei Sarah Gen 23.1-25.18 חיי שרה Life of Sarah

The matriarch Sarah was unique among the Hebrew founders, and not only because she lived in the first generation. She is the only early founder with a possible statue of herself, found in an Egyptian tomb. She had a part in the two most successful friendships developed by those early Hebrews, namely the close understandings with Egypt and with Abimelech. It is easy to suspect that she was a celebrity, ambassador, and politician *par excellence.*

In Torah, *Chayyei Sarah* actually starts with the death of Sarah and with Abraham declaring himself still an alien resident in the land. He approaches those who control one particular parcel of land, Hittites, to purchase a resting place for Sarah. In an indication of his mercantile roots, Abraham bought the land with silver, "at the going merchant's rate."

Historically speaking, however, Abraham's Hebrew experiment was on the verge of extinction. No larger community of Hebrews existed. Hebrews controlled no notable land area. No assemblage worshipped one God. Hebrews were only one of a multitude of clans and mini-states that came and went in the land called Canaan.

In addition to the Hebrews, many different peoples occupied the land called Canaan in

ancient times. The first hunter-gatherers 12,000 years ago settled in Jericho, a rich oasis that could support a village or even a city. Other groups joined those early inhabitants, including people from the Caucasus, and later, Semites. The mixture resulted in what we call Canaanites, and it is notable that Canaan represents a geographical area and not a single ethnic group. Those with original genes from very ancient Canaan were defeated and absorbed long ago, but not with a city or kingdom. This is similar to the appellation of the peoples living in Asia as Asians, even though a number of different countries and peoples live there. The geographical area of Canaan, what now is Israel, covered the coastline, some desert, and the hill country, but most of the population settled along the Mediterranean coast in a series of Amorite cities. (Kent, p. 17, 70-71; Wikipedia; science.org; Glueck, *River* p. 23-24)

<<< Canaanite god Baal

When Torah announces that Abraham entered the land, varieties of Canaanites and Amorites were present. Abraham is called an Aramean, not an Amorite, and also his Hebrew/Apiru culture separated him from the others. We see at that time, no group could call itself indigenous to Israel. It is possible that some of the population was known to him due to his trading activities and his stature as a leader. However, the differences that develop between cousins can be monumental. Canaanites and Amorites worshiped an array of gods and practiced child sacrifice. Hebrews did not practice child sacrifice as the Abraham – Isaac story showed. Canaanites fashioned idols and images of gods to worship while Hebrews did not. Hebrews only erected stones as commemorations of events, as Abraham did upon his entry into Canaan. Furthermore, Canaanites did not participate in the Apiru experience.

In an oblique admission of the bleak situation for the Hebrew followers, Abraham did not even control enough land to bury Sarah. He needed to purchase a gravesite from Hittites, who were themselves recent additions to the Canaanite landscape. Continuing with his attempts to secure a future for his Hebrews, Abraham "married" again. This produced another stream of Semitic clans, which retained some of the Apiru culture, but not the Hebrew religious tradition. The later progeny refer to eponymous clans and groups that included so-called half brothers of his son Isaac such as Sheba, creator of the famous Sabaen trading empire in Yemen and Dedan which included the oasis city-state Dedan in Arabia, Dedan continued in Torah history as an important economic center. In *Ezekiel* 38:13, Dedan joined with merchants of Tarshish to protest the coming Babylonian invasion. Also, *Isaiah* 21,13-17 mentions Dedan. All of these places, and more, represent actual historic locations and organized societies.

votive and mask.

Sabean plaque funeral

Torah relates how, despite the connection of Abraham to his cousins including Canaanites and Arameans, and despite all of the progeny from both Hagar and from his second wife Kiturah, the future of the Hebrew idea was maintained by a thin thread, and that thread was Isaac. Abraham sent a staff manager with an impressive array of camels and wealth to find Isaac a wife. He found Rebecca. Some would say that Rebecca held that thread together by promoting her son Jacob to become leader of the Hebrews. The other son of Abraham, Esau, also became an important leader.

"Tomb" of patriarchs and matriarchs Abraham, Sarah, Isaac, Rebecca, Jacob, and Leah over caves known Biblically as the Machpela, double cave. Due to current Arab hostilities, the caves under the structure have not been properly explored in modern times with newer technology. A clandistine search and lab tests of material from the caves show them to be containing human bones and signs of Bronze Age construction. The Early Bronze Age is the period of Abraham. The striped structures are symbolic tombs without patriarchal bones. The sealed caves are underneath a different area of the compound (Public photos).

Pictures show the stairs into the cave area, the entrance to the first cave, and the entrance to the second cave.

(https://www.israel365news.com/81859/secret-hidden-chambers-hebrons-cave-patriarchs-finally-revealed-photos/) photos by Noam Arnon

Who got the better deal, Jacob or Esau?

6 Tol'dot Genesis 25.19-28.9 תולדות generations

According to Torah, Isaac settled in Gerar, close by Beersheva in the Negev Desert, where he accumulated additional wealth (*Gen.* 26:1-26) These towns are along the very trade route favored by Abraham. Heading west, this route winds past rich copper mines like the one in Timna, near today's Eilat, then past the desert of Shur or southern Sinai, then onward to Egypt. It appears that in finding a home, Isaac by-passed the sparse and difficult central hill country of today's Israel in order to be closer to copper mines and trade. Isaac fathered two sons with his wife Rebecca. Genesis 25 had predicted that these sons would present the world with two nations. This came to be. One son, Esau, moved south to the copper mines of the Negev desert where the tribal nation of Edom was born. Torah could have referred to Edom or to another desert tribe known as Shosu. Jacob is credited with organizing the tribal alliance that founded Israel. Torah gives the names Isaac and Esau. (*Gen.* 25). The name Jacob, or Yahqub or Yahqub-El is noted in Abraham's Syrian homeland (Gelb). How his brother Esau ended up in the South is an example of how to fold back the pages of Torah to reveal history.

Esau was happy to inherit Edom, the word for "red" and the area of red copper. The Torah depiction of Esau implies that Esau fully realized the value of the copper trade when he said to Jacob, "Give me some of the red stuff to gulp down...," which is why he was named Edom (Gen 25.30). Esau recieved the riches of copper and not the problems of the hill country. As "a man of the outdoors," Esau was well prepared to join his father in fashioning a Hebrew nomad empire, which is what they did in allying with desert peoples into what Egyptians would call the YHWH-worshipping Shosu (outsiders) from Seir (Inscriptions at Amara and Soleb, more on this later and in other chapters).

Above - Shosu who worship YHWH in the land of Seir on an Egyptian inscription

History shows that copper was smelted in that same Gerar area, especially in Beersheva beginning 6,500 years ago in a process kept as a closely guarded secret. The smelting could take place only because of the high heat created from the invention of the blast furnace. The copper came from further south, Edom, controlled by Esau. By distancing the smelting from the mining, the process could remain secret (Tel Aviv U.)

<<< *Israel Antiques Authority Tel Aviv University, Wikipedia*

Meanwhile Isaac's wife Rebecca was drawn to the hill country, and so retained her favorite son Jacob to that land. Jacob settled in the hill country. Everyone was happy. Esau got copper and Jacob got wooded hills. But Rebecca was quite distressed by Esau's infatuation with other cultures, specifically Hittite, so she sent Jacob back to Abraham's homeland of Padan Aram with Amorites, represented in Torah as Laban, to insulate Jacob from similar heathen influence. Rebecca put her faith in the organizing skills of Jacob while Isaac evidently preferred the opportunities to the south in the desert areas associated with Esau. This may explain why the narrative has Isaac favoring Esau and Rebecca favoring Jacob.

The story of Isaac and Esau concentrates in the areas of Canaan and Edom. At this time in history, Canaan and Edom were land areas consisting of numerous groups or states. Canaan hosted kingdoms and ethnicities such as nascent Israel, Hazor, Megiddo, and Byblos (Lebanon), plus Syria; Edom (today's Southern Jordan) was uncharted and included tribal areas for Kenites, Shosu, and others, but no kingdoms.

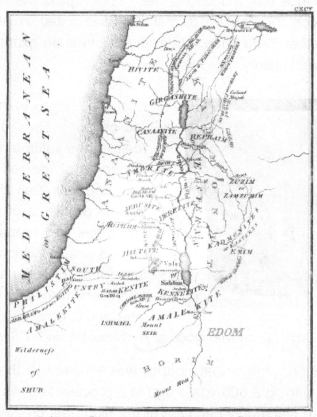

A MAP of CANAAN, adapted to the BOOK of GENESIS.

The map shows the area of today's Israel at the time of the Patriarchs. Note that peoples then were different from the ones at the later time of Joshua. The area was in flux as one warlord replaced another.

Edom was a dry area. The north got a bit of rain, but only enough to maintain a marginal agricultural livelihood. Instead, the area supported largely self-sufficient pastoral groups of nomads with some characteristics similar to the Bedouin of today. But three major differences separate the Bedouin at the time of Isaac from those of today: trade routes, copper, and tribal independence.

Consideration of trade routes focuses on the King's Highway, the road from Syria to Egypt, that passed right through Edom, the Negev, and the southern Sinai. This is an inhospitable area. More favorable than this desert road was the road that lies along the welcoming Mediterranean Coast, the Way of the Sea. However, Amorites controlled these cities and the tarrifs may have been onerous. There, coastal cities like Hazor and Meggido controlled trade. In the desert, Bedouin controlled the territory and trade routes.

The second consideration involves mining, smelting, and forging implements mainly from copper and tin. Copper is a major ingredient of bronze, and the events in Genesis transpired in the Bronze Age. Heavy trade took place between the mining areas and smelters in places including Beersheva, just a short distance from the mines. Smelters wanted secrecy to protect their intellectual and inventive processes in a time when patent laws did not exist. From the mines and smelters, caravans could fan out to far-away places. Having developed wells in Beersheva, Isaac could also grow crops to exchange in his market place (Gen 26.18-26).

The third consideration are the fierce and independent tribes who claimed control of routes and

mines. Egyptians complained about these people even before the Hebrew founders and described them as wanderers, brigands, lawless fugitives, and outcasts, just as established kingdoms to the east described the proto-Hebrew Apiru. Egypt conducted sorties against these tribes, especially ones that belonged to the Shosu or Shasu. Shosu were the eponymous progeny of Esau who worshipped YHWH and were Hebrew.

Shosu Warriors painted from Egyptian tomb by Belzoni.

Unlike Egyptian officials, biblical Abraham and Isaac were able to conduct all sorts of trade across this difficult terrain. To do this, they obtained cooperation and protection from various tribes. Key to the success of Hebrew traders Esau and Isaac were the Shosu so reviled by Egypt. Note the tassels on the Shosu warrior's kilt, which are precursors to the tassels commanded in Numbers 15.37-41 and the tallit worn by Jews today. More on this tribe later when we explore their history as Hebrews.

With access to the southern trade routes, Hebrews could avoid the tolls and dangers of the Mediterranean coast and could open markets for Sinai copper. According to Torah, the Isaac group also grew crops. With the development of this southern merchant empire, Torah explains "Isaac sowed in the land and reaped a hundredfold the same year. The Lord blessed him and the man grew richer and richer" (*Gen.* 26:12-14). Hence, we see that, while the

Hebrews of the hill country enjoyed moderate success, the group formed by Isaac and Esau grew exponentially. Torah confirms this, albeit reluctantly, "Looking up, Jacob saw Esau coming with a retinue of four hundred." At that time Jacob only had his wives, children, and household servants.

The geopolitical successes of Hebrews at that time were the result of Abraham's alignment with Egypt, which gave them a strategic ally but no land of their own, and the desert country ruled by Esau and his Shosu tribal group.

Area of ancient copper mines in Negev (author)

Torah depicts the flowering of the Hebrew movement. In the case of Esau, it is the powerful desert tribes known as Shosu that inhabited desert areas. Their power is shown by the arrival of troops accompanying Esau for his meeting with Jacob and the success of two Shosu tribes, Simeon and Levi, in securing Shechem. In the case of Jacob, it is the assemblage of tribes described as his sons and the subsequent sojourn to Egypt. In Torah, the story of Jacob is graphic and that of Esau very subtle, but each comes as a result of dramatic history.

Jacob developed as Israel; Esau developed as Shosu.

7 Va yeitzei Gen 28.10-32.3 ויצא He (Jacob) went out

Historically speaking, after a flurry of activity in the time of Abraham, not much was going on for the Hebrews immediately after 1900 BCE. The magic of Abrahamic times had passed and, although Hebrews did have communities in the hill country and further south in Beersheva, other groups at the time developed might and flexed it – Babylon, Mari, Egypt, and Assyria. Torah is correct in writing about the despair of Abraham that his legacy and inheritance might not come to fruition. However, *Genesis* gives hope because Abraham and Sarah produced a son Isaac, and Isaac produced two sons, Jacob and Esau. After this generation, the faith and ideas of Hebrews would propel them into global recognition they neither desired nor welcomed.

This portion describes how a grandson of Abraham, Jacob, found a wife - actually two wives - in the ancestral home of Paddan Aram, the Field of Aram. Paddan Aram was part of the land of the Amorite people, seed of the Semites. This was a famous grazing area. We mention this because some Amorites had already begun migration to Israel (*Gen.* 14.7, 15.16, 48.22, Barton 13-14, Clay), which is consistent with the migration of Abraham.

Plains of Syria, formerly grazing (World Atlas)   >>>

After his marriages to two of his cousins, Jacob began to raise a family. Then a bitter dispute with his relatives in Paddan Aram caused Jacob to break his ties with his Uncle Laban and bring his wives and children –the tribes of Israel – back to Israel. The departure of Jacob and his family from the land of Amorites was a significant event in the Hebrew saga. Jacob wrestled with an angel, which resulted in Jacob's being blessed with the name "Israel." His tribes subsequently became the Israelites and worshippers of God. Because this event symbolically accounts for the coalescing of tribes into a unified group, it is a watershed moment in the history of Israel. The historic background is a saga in itself. By piecing together the recorded events about the homeland of Abraham with the description in *Genesis*, it is possible to outline the relevant history. In addition, we can see that Torah presents a condensed story, resulting in a compelling work of religious literature that retained the emotional aspects of events with a narrative written in a style of poetry understood by people of the day and masterful enough to inspire the people of earth to this very day. We now take a look at the history behind Jacob.

The story referred to here is the story of tribes put together in the time of Jacob to form a tribal nation called Israel. The tribes were not yet Hebrew, but rather pagan. The homeland of some of these tribes is roughly the modern country of Syria and southern Turkey (Flemng; Pitard, pp. 207-212; Mendenhall, Hebrew; Greenberg, pp. 1-12; Bodi; Albright, From Patriarchs I, p.5; Ma'aman, Ibirta). Torah refers to the tribes as sons of Jacob, making him the father of ancient Israel, which is true in the same way that Washington is the father of the US or Ben Gurion is the father of modern Israel. The sons of Jacob were not vulnerable kids swaying in the winds, but instead influential confederations and tribes struggling and fighting for existence in a dangerous hostile environment. These groups could challenge the mighty of the day, namely the likes of Babylon, Egypt, Assyria, and Hatti. The mighty of the day based their power on idols and brute force. The mighty did not last. The sons of Jacob did not achieve the heights of the great powers, but they still exist today in their ancient nation. The only obvious thing that made them stand out from all the other nomadic tribes was the belief, slowly accepted, in One God, and, later, the laws of Moses. Fleming proposes one other unique feature, namely that the tribes also practiced rudimentary democracy, a notion supported by Albright (in *Egyptian Empire*). Torah, in its unique fashion, describes this process. Understanding that description is enhanced by extra-Biblical documentation.

In the years after 2000 BCE, the political landscape of Syria was volatile. A great nomadic tribal coalition controlled much of the area by virtue of a superior military. All nomadic tribes required some sort of military in order to protect their pasturage. This particular coalition, known as "sons of the right," (South on the Euphrates) or Banu Yamina, or more commonly, Benjamin, had concentrations in the area of Haran, where they worshipped the moon, or Sin Nanna. Their kings concluded alliances with other kings at the Haran Temple of Sin. That would be the same Haran from where Avram departed in his journey to Canaan. Benjaminites rolled over much of the area with their ferocious fighting force. Jacob alludes to this history in his final blessing of Benjamin as one who is ravenous as a wolf howling

at the moon. (Parrot, pp. 35-55; Rowton, pp. 31, 33; Fleming, pp. 24-103; Kupper, p. 56, Bodi pp. 385-7, 404-5, Parrot, pp. 50-55)

Benjamin howling at the moon, Samaritan mural (Wikipedia) ^^

Slowly, the Benjamins acclimated themselves more and more into towns and cities. Their control was far from complete as other forces migrated in Syria including Banu S'mola, sons of the left, or north on the Euphrates. Jacob is credited with assembling the Benjaminites, the Aanu S'mola, parts of Suteans, AKA Sutu or Shasu or Shosu containing Simeon (Giveon, pp. 5-6 as we will see), Apiru or Hebrews, and others into Israel, then adopted monotheism and absorbed other tribes.

Banu S'mola took dominant control in much of Syria by displacing the Benjamin dynasty. (Parrot , pp. 48-51; Gelb; Fleming, pp. 9-13, 152-161, Bodi, p. 387)   The Hebrew connection with the Banu S'mola is the possible connection to the tribe of Joseph (ch. 12 this book).

Another group is often mentioned but eludes an exact definition.   The Haneans, meaning tent people and applicable to most Amorites – certainly both Benjaminites and S'molites - and were quite numerous, but all of the Syrian tribes had "hana" – tent people. We mention them due to the Biblical association of Hebrews with a nomadic, shepherd life and also with the area known as Amurru, another word for a sub-set of Amorite, meaning Western Syria, later known as a Hebrew stronghold. Hence we see the association of Hebrews as shepherds. (Gelb, pp. 36-37; Malamat, *Mari* 16-21; Bodi, pp. 388-394; ch. 16 this book; Albright, *Egyptian Empire,* pp. 245, 251).

Hebrews developed not just as a Bedouin people, but as a unique combination of tribal and trade cultures. In earlier days, the Apiru acted as merchants and mercenaries to various kings of Syria and adjoining areas. (Kupper, p. 252, Parrot, pp. 44-45). Apiru were noted as traders and caravan operators (ch 2,3,4,7,9,10,11 this book). Despite all of the armed nomads, overland commerce was not raided or disrupted in Syria at this particular time, perhaps because of mutual needs for commerce and control of wide swaths by overarching dynasties that controlled multiple tribes (Rowton, pp. 33-36). Kings in the area derived income from taxes on caravans, a reliable source of funds (Malamat, *Mari, p.* 10).

A number of Hebrew tribes derived from desert nomads known as Suteans/Sutu/Shosu, who were a large accumulation of at least ten nomadic tribes that at various times could be found anywhere from the gates of the Nile Delta to the southern Sinai, across the Sinai to southern Israel and Jordan, clear up into Syria, and down again into Mesopotamia (Ward, pp. 50-53; Annus; Kitchen, *Egyptian Empire;* Heltzer, *Suteans*). More will be investigated concerning this group in later chapters. We refer to them here as Shosu as per Giveon. Different localities referred to them as "Seth/Sutu" in Akkadian. The Biblical line of Seth goes through Noah to Shem to Terah. This interpretation puts the Shosu tribes in the line of Abraham, Haran, and Nahor (Annus, *Gen.* 5, 10,11,). "Shasu/Shosu" is the Egyptian pronunciation of Sutean/ Seth/ Sutu (Annus, p. 9; Ward; Giveon). Shosu were related to Apiru/Hebrews (Annus,pp. 9-10;

Ward, p. 53; Armana letters 16, 122, 123, 169, 195, 297, 318; Giveon) and they interacted as allies and as enemies of other Amorite confederations.

The Shosu most likely contributed several tribes to Israel. Egypt identified <u>Simeon</u> as a Shosu tribe present at the time and place of Joseph's kidnapping (ch. 8 of this book). The Shosu King <u>Zebulon</u> – tribe of Israel - posed enough of a threat to Egypt that he appeared on pharaoh's execration figures: clay figures constructed to represent Egyptian enemies that were then broken as part of a ceremony in magic to weaken those enemies. The reference comes from the time of Jacob (Kitchen, *Egyptian Evidence;* Berlin Execration Texts; Albright, *Egyptian Empire, pp. 239, 253;* Sethe, pp. 43-58). Other connections between Shosu and Israel exist in complex patterns, such as the six tribes of Shosu written on monuments in Egypt at Soleb and elsewhere that describe Shosu as worshipping YHWH. (lists at Soleb, Aksha, and Amara West; Kitchen, *Egyptian Evidence;* Albright, *Egyptian Empire, p.* 237). A Shosu tribe mentioned as the Rabbean may or may not be the same as <u>Reuben</u>. As with other tribes, pronunciation of the name can vary over time and distance. Rabbean engaged in crafts, agriculture, and shepherding. Tribal names were pronounced in various dialects in different languages. (Heltzer, *Suteans*, pp. 11-80 esp. 54,59,80). Shosu were tribes of the desert related to Esau.

As long as we are touching on tribal ancestry, a more speculative connection can be made between the tribe of Asher, a name common in greater Syria as a god and important city, and a unreaearched specific connection to Israeli tribes. And then there is Dan. See comments on <u>Dan</u> in chapter 14.

In looking at the plains of Syria where Amorites resided, we see that at the time of Jacob, all was not well in the homeland of Abraham. There are reasons why Jacob (or whom he represents) was successful in attracting many tribes to the Israelite council, the cause of One God, and the land of Israel. The mini kingdoms of the area were under pressure. For example, one such king, Zimri-Lim, had carved out a kingdom for himself just south of the trading city of Haran, around the ancient, fortified city of Mari, Syria. The kingdom sat aside the great Euphrates River then known as the Purattu or Perat. Two great tribal confederacies formed the backbone of political power for Zimri-Lim: Banu S'mola and the defeated Benjamins. (Fleming, *Democracy, pp.* 25-103; Albright, *Yahweh, pp.* 79-80; Albright, *Patriarchs from Abraham, p.* 27; Kenyon; Keller, p. 65; Rowton; Malamat, *Mari, p.* 15).

Shosu fr Medinat Habu >>>

In addition, there is evidence that the tribe of <u>Manasseh</u> lived in the vicinity of Shechem, today's Nablus (Albright, *Egyptian Empire, p.* 235; Sethe 53).

Many of the tribes that would form the Israelite coalition crossed paths in the plains of Syria, and the Apiru, too, made their mark, not just as Abraham's trading group. Apiru could mass a couple of thousand troops, often as an ally, in order to give advantage to one side or the other. In one altercation, some 2000 Apiru troops apparently stood with a dynasty of early Assyria against the dynasty of the just mentioned Zimri Lim (Pritchard, Ancient Vol. I, p. 261; or Pritchard, Ancient 1955, p. 483). It is interesting to note that Assur/Asher was the first Assyrian capital and one of the Israelite tribes.

These tribes often united or fought each other. The S'mola displaced Benjaminites and put Zimri-Lim into Syrian power. Zimri-Lim attempted to rule with a heavy hand, but autocracy did not sit well with the independent tribes. Zimri-Lim demanded a census and conscription of soldiers, which was refused by the Benjaminites who then rebelled. Zimri-Lim maintained a large harem. He instituted rituals for a new cult and presumed to dictate religious practices. In addition, the fearsome empire ruled by Hammurabi of Babylon eventually burned down Mari, extracted slaves, and annexed Mari to Babylon. Facing subjugation, it is not surprising that several tribes followed Jacob to the safer hill country of Israel and the more compelling One God. (Fleming, pp. 45-99; Fracaroli, pp. 194-101; Wikipedia, Mari; Sasson; Hamori; Clay). Various desert Shosu tribes were pressed by Assyria, Babylon, and Egypt. They were among the first to arrive in Canaan (Heltzer, *Suteans*, pp. 52,57,81-99, Egyptian execrations texts) Two of the tribes represented in the new Hebrew movement were those "brothers," sons of the Euphrates right and left, Benjamin and Joseph (more details later).

Shasu prisoner on Ramses III's reliefs at Madinet Habu.
(Identified by tassels on clothing)

Once in Israel, the tribes had many problems, but none so great as those in Syria where aggressive empires including Babylon annexed smaller neighbors. Fortunately, the great powers had little interest in the hill country of Israel or the dry area of Beersheva.

While the Jacob contingent was gathering and moving to Israel, the Esau group managed to put together a desert confederation. We have previously described how Isaac and Esau built a trading and copper mining empire in the area of the greater Negev and how much more financially successful Esau was than Jacob at the *<<< Notice the kippah-like hats and tallit-like tassels on the kilts of Shosu shown here as prisoners. Shosu prisoners*

time of his meeting with Jacob (*Genesis* 32:1-32). As a
result, the success story at that moment would be the growing strength of Negev Hebrews or as Torah puts it very subtly, the rise of Esau and Isaac.

Torah narrates the development of Esau's heritage in a quiet manner, giving Esau's territory of Seir credit for hosting the mountain of God and accepting refugee Hebrew travelers, but not as projenitors of Israelite tribes. History, on the other hand, has more to say. The most prominent tribe, or rather confederation of tribes in that area, was the Shosu, who spanned a wide territory. With a center base in the land of Edom and Seir, the Negev and southern Jordan, they roamed clear up into Syria and down into Egypt (Redmond, p. 273). That jurisdiction of the Esau desert tribes overlaps the homeland of many Jacob tribes in the plains of Syria and the Shechem – Beersheva corridor.

The association in Egyptian and biblical references to Edom or Seir as the homeland of the Shosu occurred as early as the 20th century BCE – the era of Esau and Jacob. Edom in that era was a nomadic congregation without cities or defined boundaries, unlike the Edom of the later 7th century BCE.

Many Egyptian references to the Shosu exist, some friendly and some not (Giveon;, Nielsen, pp. 6-8; Albright, *Egyptian Empire*). The Egyptians regarded them as inferior because they lacked cities and were seen as wild raiders. Although not possessing a large army, they instilled both fear and some envy – fear because of their rough culture and ability to raid caravans, and envy from a small number of those chafing under the strict rules of Egypt. Egyptians sent troops to punish Shosu and to steal their control of certain copper mines. Nevertheless, Shosu also invoked the admiration of disaffected Egyptian youth yearning for freedom from gods, kings, complex rules, and a rigid culture. Attributes of freedom in Hebrew society must have attracted other tribes.

Egyptians unwittingly reported a connection between Hebrews and Shosu, by disclosing that Shosu worshipped YHWH (Giveon, pp. 22-26; Tebes, *Yahweh;* Avner, *Desert;* script at Soleb & Amara West; Redmond, pp. 272-273). Egyptians, however, did not realize the connection between Hebrews, YHWH, Shosu, and Apiru, although there is evidence that the Shosu may have referred to God as YHWH very early. The biblical revelation of YHWH may have been anticipated by Shosu religious practice. As Shosu are known to have frequented grazing areas clear into the pre-Syrian homeland of Abraham, it is relevant to mention that the name, if not a complete concept of YHWH, did accompany migrations such as that of Abraham, used in a fashion more universal than local gods (Bodi p. 398).

Egyptian descriptions of the Shosu mirror the descriptions of Apriru by eastern kings: wanderers, vagrants, brigands, outcasts, and outsiders, which is another connection between these two branches of Hebrews. From early in the 12th dynasty, many a child would envy the life of Shosu with freedom from authority. Not so parents of established families who viewed those nomads as dirty, unkempt, and criminal. In a later period, a parent wrote, "I provided your needs in all things…. You have lost your wits! They stole your clothes. Your groom… took the rest. He has gone over to a life of evil. He mixes with the tribes of the Shosu, having adopted the guise of an Asiatic."

It was convenient for the Egyptians to label the Shosu as undesirable at the same time that they very much wanted to steal the Shosu control of the copper trade. More than a little hypocrisy there.

Sketch of a Shosu male >>>>

The Shosu were the source of political and military power in the land of Edom or Seir, which was the province of many Shosu tribes. Esau and his successors had power and riches. Here is how to view the linguistic connection between Esau and the Shosu:

Esau in Hebrew is   עֵשָׂו

The Hebrew rendition of the Egyptian word for the Yaweh worshipping tribe Shosu is
שׁוסו
A Hebrew word for plunder, rob, loot, sack, pillage, is שׁוסות

From early in the 12th dynasty, the time of Esau, Egypt played host to Bedouin from the Sinai, allowing them to water their flocks. A letter written to an Egyptian official from a guard describes the process: "…we have finished admitting the Shosu tribes of Edom through the fortress of Merneptah to the water holes for their own subsistence and that of their flocks" (Redmond, p. 228).

When referring to the Shosu, Egyptians were referring to the tribe from greater Edom formed by Esau. This connection opens a store of Egyptian documents that connect with Torah.

The first Hebrew city: Shechem. The second Hebrew League: Shosu.

8 Va-yishlach Gen 32:4-36:43 וישלח And he sent

Genesis presents an intertwined tale involving the sons of Isaac resulting in an injection of new energy into the Hebrew effort. With the help of Rebecca and Leah, Torah gives credit to Jacob in accomplishing what Abraham could not, namely assembling a coalition of tribes into the Hebrew fold. Those tribes are identified as Jacob's children. This speaks highly of his leadership. Abraham had cried out in anguish for heirs - Hebrew associates - at the end of his life. But his ideas were awkward to say the least. The idea that there was only one God must have seemed ridiculous, even outlandish, at the time. Why would a monarch who was considered a god with unlimited powers submit his rule to a higher authority that cannot be seen? Why would priests who could determine life, death, and wealth based on their divinations of rocks, animals, or astrology give up their authority? None ever did voluntarily (and that is the case even today) – except for the Hebrew people and their Hebrew God. It was Jacob the Israelite who organized this remarkable cultural change into a polity. He somehow incorporated and folded tribes into the Israelite community. In a different manner, the southern tribes of Esau did the same. Torah acknowledges the contributions of the southern tribes from the greater Negev, descendants of the Esau group, but barely acknowledges their contribution to the Hebrew idea.

We can take a look at how two factions of Hebrews – Jacob and Esau – advanced the Hebrew cause. The experience of Jacob brought the Hebrew story back to its homeland in Haran, Nahor, and other cities in the plains area shared by modern-day Syria, Turkey, and Lebanon.

In a short span of time, around 1800 BCE, Hebrews gained new adherents, and not only the escaped slaves and stragglers that they sympathized with. We have seen how Jacob and Esau attracted a Bedouin component to join the commercial trading confederation with Apiru. Bedouin such as the Benjaminites (sons of the right or south Euphrates Benu Yamina); the Smolites (sons of the left or north Euphrates), and the Shosu (derived from Esau) pitched their tents in places between the Jordan and Euphrates up into Syria and Haran. So did the Apiru (proto-Hebrews), traders like Abraham. (Gary Thompson, pp. 31-35, Redford, pp. 153, 203, 228, 269-273). They were fellow travelers with common interests. Apiru could trade the Shosu copper in Edom and Negev, the wool products in Haran and Syria, and finished metals and glass from many places. Both shepherds and Apiru traders

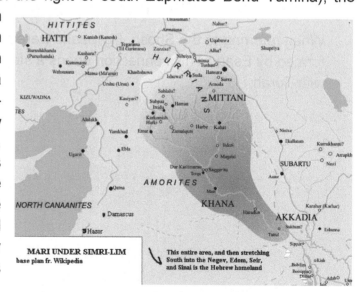

MARI UNDER SIMRI-LIM
base plan fr. Wikipedia

This entire area, and then stretching South into the Negev, Edom, Seir, and Sinai is the Hebrew homeland

faced similar problems with the constraining ambitions and religious dictates of tyrants in the Tigris Euphrates Valley. The generation of Jacob and Esau put together an historic political and religious union of freedom loving groups.

Apiru would float lumber down the Euphrates and bring goods from East and West to be redistributed from centers in Ur, Haran, Mari, and elsewhere. The Benjamites and Smolites would tend to their flocks in the same vicinity. These tribes are represented in Torah as sons of Rebecca. Around 1800 BCE, Hammurabi started a war and defeated Mari, an important kingdom in Abraham's homeland. Mari had clamped down on the Benjaminites, and new religious regulations were promulgated. By the end of the Jacob, the Apiru of Abraham and other tribes could be called Israel.
(Flemming, *Democracy, pp.* 7-8, 154, 158,97-98; jewishvirtualibrary; Wenham, pp. 1-15, p. 273,https://www.encyclopedia.com/religion/encyclopedias-almanacs-transcripts-and-maps/haran**).**

Torah relates that Jacob moved out from his father-in-law's abode into the highlands of Israel in a bitter separation. Perhaps this reflects the separation of specific tribes or clans from the Amorite fold that formed a core Hebrew group. The father and son-in-law agreed on a separate covenant. Jacob the Israelite gave the agreement a Hebrew name, while Laban his father-in-law gave the same agreement an Amorite name (Gen. 31:44-53).

Even though some additional Hebrews appeared in Israel as part of the evolving Israelite people, some remained in Lebanon or Syria. After segments of Benjaminites and Smolites moved to Israel, letters were exchanged between those who remained and the emigrants (Albright, *From Patriarchs, pp.* I, 20). Even though Hammurabi destroyed the capital of Mari shortly after 1800 BCE, other towns remained viable. Some of the events with Apiru in the area of greater Syria after the 1800 BCE era were significant. Apiru enabled the deposed King of Aleppo to regain his throne in around 1450 BCE (*jewishvirtuallibrary*, inscription on Irdimi statue). Hebrew Apiru formed a mini-state in the Lebanese part of the homeland called Amurru close to ancient Byblos sometime before the 14th century BCE (Amarna letter EA74, Mendenhall). Hebrew Shosu sparked the defeat of Ramesses II at Kadesh, Syria in 1274 BCE (inscription of Ramesses II in various temples). Until late in the modern era, Jews, like earlier Hebrews, maintained a large presence in Syria, especially in Aleppo and Damascus.

Israelite tribes appeared in Egypt and remained there for some years. In existing records, they are often lumped into the general category of "Asiatics." Separating out the Hebrews from other Asiatics is a challenge involving a bit of detective work. Occasionally, Egyptians refer to "Apiru" or record events that mirror happenings only associated with Israelites, such as the ten plagues. Then the work of discovering Israelite history is easier and more definitive.

Hill country of
<<< Israel
Shechem, the first Hebrew urban center >>>

We can also look at a sequence of events to see if they follow a logical progression that accounts for Hebrews and their successors in Israel, such as: 1. Hebrews in the hills of Israel; 2. Appearance of a person who probably was Joseph; 3. Hebrews who filled various positions in Egypt; 4. Evidence of Biblical plagues; 5. Evidence of a Moses rebellion in Egypt; 6. Records of Apiru slaves; 7. Military activity of Apiru in Israel; 8. Continuous residence of Hebrews and Jews in Israel through modern times. History reveals just such a sequence of events, and we will explore them.

Israel gained solid roots with the very early Hebrew occupation of Shechem, the first Hebrew urban center and a continuing Israelite stronghold. Torah tells a tale of the rape of Jacob's daughter Dinah as the motivation for what became an Israelite capture of the city. Maybe. A more complicated history lies within the telling of the Shechem events and how Shechem became Hebrew. Both in Torah and history, Shechem is considered Hebrew from the time of Jacob onward (*Armana Letters, Joshua*). Torah gives the tribes Simeon and Levi, "sons" of Leah, credit for assuming control of the city (*Gen.* 34). Egypt observed the tribe of Simeon in the Shechem area, specifically in Dotham – where Joseph was abducted. This comports with Simeon as conqueror of Shechem; as complicit in the plot against Joseph; and as part of the southern Shosu tribes and of Esau who is said to have been in the area with armed men. (Giveon, pp. 22-24; funeral temple of Thebes; Gen. 32, 37:15-17). Even though he was distressed over the taking of Shechem, Jacob presented Shechem to Joseph as an inheritance: אני נתתי לך שכם (*Gen*, 48:22). There is an unexplained story with Dina as her emotions or thoughts are not presented.

Egypt also may have intervened in the Hebrew acquisition of Shechem. Jacob or Israelite followers, strengthening the bonds with Egypt formed by Abraham, may have convinced Pharaoh Sesostris III that Shechem would be better in the hands of Israelite friends than under the control of one of the many unruly Canaanite mini-kings. Shechem is known to have had a non-Semitic ruler at the time due to an Egyptian execration text cursing the ruler then in power (Streit 64-65). Pharaoh Sesostris III personally led an isolated mission with his elite king's guard troops along with his commander Sebek-khu to defeat the garrison at Shechem, something the Hebrews could not accomplish. Records report this action, without making the

Hebrew connection explicit. Thereafter Hebrews controlled Shechem. *(Brested V. I, #619-639, 680-681; Wright, p. 16; Pritchard; Grimal, p. 169; Mourad, Asiatics, 34; Mourad, Rise, pp. 100-101).*

The tribes of Israel, aka sons of Jacob, represent the formation of the nation we know as Israel. He also gets is known for wrestling with an angel of God, who then blessed Jacob and proclaimed that he should be called "Israel" for he Jacob "hast striven with God and with men, and hast prevailed." After that encounter, Jacob molds his sons into the tribes of Israel. That is why some people consider this section of Torah as one of the most important. Besides Jacob, Abraham wrestled with God over the fate of Sodom; Moses did so over ramifications of the Golden Calf. With the same mentality, Israelites have deduced means of improving medicine from sacrifice to science and changing temple Judaism to Rabbinic Judaism, all while respecting God and Hebrew spirit.

In addition to the tribes of Israel, Torah also talks about the sons, or tribes, of Esau, even commenting that those tribes were organized prior to Israel. It states that early Edom, which is Esau, was organized and had kings before Israel. As we recall, when Jacob left Laban, he encountered Esau. In a demonstration of just how powerful Esau already was, Esau brought 400 troops to the meeting. But as it turned out, Esau did not mean to intimidate Jacob, but only to reestablish friendship. Esau returned to Seir, which is synonymous with Sinai, Negev, and Edom.

<<< Hill country of Edom (stock)

The Esau story is an important clue for extra-biblical research, because Seir, and specifically Mt. Seir or Mt. Sinai, was the place where God revealed the laws for Israel. It also was the home of Esau. History has equated the tribes of Esau with the Shosu Tribes. These tribes are often referred to in Egyptian records, and there are linguistic connections between the name "Esau" and "Shosu." as discussed in the last chapter. Shosu inhabited Edom, Negev, and Seir, or Sinai. The timing and actions of these tribes are compatible with Torah. History notes that the Shosu worshipped Yahweh, and records of them worshipping Yahweh precede other mention of a group worshipping Yahweh inside or outside of Torah. Hence the Shosu can be called the second Hebrew nation, although the Negev was eventually included in Israel. The two Hebrew nations exhibited only limited coordination until later. Later, there are indications that Shosu comprise some of Jacob's tribes (to be discussed).

Joseph? Potiphar? Sons Manasseh and Ephraim? Israel in Egypt?

9 <u>Va'yeishev</u> Gen 37:1 – 40:23 וישׁ'ו And he lived

A brief introduction comparing Torah and history:

(T=Torah   H=History)

(T *Gen.* 34) Simeon and Levi (previously) attacked and subdued Shechem.

(T *Gen,* 37:17) *Joseph looked for his brethren and found them in Dothan* (near Shechem) .

(H Giveon, pp. 22-24; Temple of Thebes 19th Century BCE) Simeon and Shosu were in Dothan.

(T *Gen.* 37:28) *They sold Joseph to Ishmaelites, who brought Joseph to Egypt*.

(H, Interpretation of Albright, *Patriarchs II, pp.* 26-28) Joseph (clan or person) was ejected from the Sm'ola archery tribe on the upper Euphrates

Now for some details:

We begin an epic Biblical story, the biography of Joseph, perhaps the most important vizier in Egyptian history and a man from the tribes of Israel. His story in *Genesis* aligns with Egyptian records of the 19th century BCE. Joseph was not the only Hebrew to arrive in Egypt but, unlike Joseph, most came voluntarily. Egypt was changing from a rich provincial country to a rich global country. Abraham's alliance with Pharaoh Amenemhat I (chapter 3) allowed immigration, but Egypt did not have an open-door policy. Egypt had a controlled immigration policy with a wall and armed guards. Egypt controlled the border because of threats, wars, and raids from Asia. In *The Prophesy of Neferti*, the aristocrat wrote, "Never will Asiatics be permitted to come down to Egypt." And so Amenemhat I, who relied on certain Asiatic warriors, probably Hebrews (ch.3), to gain power, built the wall –Wall of the Prince or Wall of the Ruler - to keep Asiatics out. Even a single person would have trouble passing it, as described in the Egyptian Story of Sinuhe. (Arnold, pp. 18-20, Herrman, 8)

> *I attained the Wall of the Prince, which was made to repel the Setiu and to crush the Sandfarers. I bowed me down in a thicket through fear lest the watcher on the wall for the day might see. I went on at time of night. (Tale of Sinuhe,* tr. Alan Gardiner)

Years later, groups could still only enter with permission, as reported by a guard.

> *We have just let the Shosu tribes of Edom pass the Fortress of Merneptah-hetephermaat, ... in order to revive themselves and revive their flocks . . .* British Museum Papyrus Anastasi VI 4.11-6.5) – Even though Egypt often fought Shosu. some Asiatics, like Hebrews, were escorted into Egypt.

Hebrew Abishai and entourage follow Khnumhotep II into Egypt (at Beni Hasan)

We have said that Hebrews constituted the major Asian group accepted by Egypt because of the help given Amenemhat I to gain office and the alliance with Abraham. In addition, we note that Hebrews - both the trading group and the shepherding contingent - were given to mobility, whereas "Canaanite" cities such as Hazor, Meggido, and Byblos were heavily fortified cities with captive resident serfs subject to Egyptian execration texts (curses) and conquering armies, (sampling from many among the Amarna letters to Pharaoh EA 73,74,77,81,89,148, *https://www.jewishvirtuallibrary.org/hazor,* *https://www.britannica.com/place/Byblos*).

From the time of Pharaoh Amenemhat III, who ruled in approximately 1850 BCE, and during the reigns of other pharaohs thereafter, a single person stands out as one of the most important viziers in Egyptian history. Evidence suggests that this vizier is none other than the Biblical Joseph. He went by the Egyptian name "Ankhu," meaning "He who lives." His two sons had Egyptian names also, "Resseneb" and "Lymeru I," and they succeeded him, one at a time. After that, a grandson, Iymeru II, and then possibly a great-grandson, Iymeru III, served as vizier. Proofs of his Hebrew connections include the matching of his story in both Egyptian and Hebrew writings, association with other

Amenemhat III at the Met by author

Hebrew names, irrigation works with his name, status with Hebrew and part Hebrew dynasties, his likeness in a statue in Avaris, and Hebrew artifacts in his official residence. (Beckerath, p. 263 lists nine such references for Ankhu; Ryholt, pp. 210-211; Hayes, p. 13; Grajetzki, pp. 22, 23, 25, 38, 124; Wikipedia; *Papyrus Boulaq*, 18). Joseph, his sons, and others with Hebrew names served through the 12th Dynasty into the 13th.

Studies of the Thirteenth Dynasty frequently mention names of viziers: Ankhu, Resseneb, and Lymeru (I & II). These viziers must have been the most important persons of that period, considering the number of stelae, statues, and papyri which contain their names... . The references for Vizier Ankhu show no father's name. ... The top-level official of the day was Overseer of the Fields Ankhu (Ryholt, pp. 210-211). (Beckerath on p. 263 lists nine such references for Ankhu.) Ankhu lived at the end of the Twelfth Dynasty and into the Thirteenth.(Grajetzki, p. 38).

<<< *Vizier Ankhu AKA Joseph (cover of Rohl Test of Time); Vizier Lymeru son of Joseph (Museo Egizio); Vizier Limeru grandson of Ankhu-Joseph (at the Louvre)*

Joseph supervised the entry of many new immigrant arrivals and the placement of servants. A group of 95 assigned workers shows largely Semitic people, but the names are followed by Egyptian names, new Egyptian names for new residents. Children of the servants have Egyptian names Among the Hebrew names before the change are Manahem (the tribe of Israel), Issachar (May God favor, tribe of Israel), Sakar (God has favored), Dodihu (God is loved), Shiphrah (midwife in *Exodus*, beautiful), Puah (midwife in *Exodus*, lass), Asher (a tribe of Israel), Eseb, Samson (Hebrew Biblical name), Jacob (name of the patriarch), Sadday-or (Shaddai shines), Hayyu-ur (The Living One), Ayyabum (Job – also in Torah), Hayabilu, Hayimi, Aduttu. (Brooklyn 35.1446 papyrus scroll; Albright, *Northwest Semitic Names;* Albright, *Biblical* 22; Bietak, *Hyksos Review;* The famous Shiphrah and Puah may have been incorporated in Exodus rather than Joseph in Bible or could be common names)

Another Egyptian correspondence with the biblical story concerns the government official Phatwer, whose name and position equate to the Potiphar of *Genesis*. An inscription at the Sarbut (probably Serabit) el-Khadem recites the achievements of this official, calling him, "The master of the double cabinet, chief of the treasury, Ptahwer, triumphant, born of Yata." Potiphar/Ptahwer served under Amenemhat III, corresponding to the arrival of a young Joseph on the Egyptian scene. (Brested # 728 Vol. I, Grajetzki, p. 75)

https://www.youtube.com/watch?v=lm9A TLhkujY Joseph's palace >>>>

Egypt enjoyed a period of success and prosperity under Pharaoh Amenemhat III and his father. Neither pharaoh did much militarily but rather lived in peace. Prosperity prevailed because of several factors including the development of the Egyptian Nile delta; trade from

Asiatic/Hebrew cities in the delta like Avaris; and an increase in productive farmland made possible by new canals. Avaris grew into a center of immigration, economic activity, and political power. As the major port city of Egypt, it conducted trade with other port cities on the Mediterranean such as Byblos, Lebanon, supplier of cedar. (Bietak, *From Where,* pp. 139-142; Tyldesley, *Ramesses*, p. 522). As perhaps one of the most international cities of the day, Avaris attracted many ethnicities. (Bietak, *Ethnicities*). In Avaris, the vizier held court. That vizier would be Ankhu/Joseph.

The partnership between Egypt and Hebrews proved quite beneficial in terms of prosperity, food supply, international outreach, expansion of canals, and trade. This cooperation worked for centuries, close to 1,000 years, until the time of Ramesses II. The cooperative years displayed a harmony despite differences. Hebrews ate beef, while Egyptians worshipped cows, particularly Hathor. Egyptians utilized a plethora of gods for the sun, for fertility, for the underworld, for war, for craft, for writing and wisdom - each with its own temples and bureaucracy. Hebrews, with some wavering, favored only one God. Hebrews came with a heritage of dusty, dirty donkey caravan trading and shepherding, while the Egyptian aristocracy disdained such work. Torah recognized the differences: "They served him by himself, and them by themselves; for the Egyptians who ate with him by themselves; for the Egyptians could not dine with the Hebrews, since that would be abhorrent to the Egyptians." (*Gen.* 43:23)

In Egypt, intermarriage occurred, and Hebrews like Joseph served in Egyptian administrations. Some were not cooperative. "Hebrew donkey caravanners were despised by their neighbors – Egyptians and Canaanites alike which made close relations difficult at best. Under these circumstances, Hebrew tenacity in maintaining ancient traditions is easy to understand" (Albright, *Yahweh, p.* 155).

Archeological digs at the site of Avaris uncovered the larger-than-life statue of Joseph shown in ch. 10. (Some disagree). His Egyptian name, Ankhu, was from the "ankh," a symbol of life. >>>>

Torah refers to the name Zaphenath-Paneah צפנת פענח as given to Joseph by Pharaoh (*Gen.* 41:45). Zaphenath can be Zat-en-aph or "he who is called," while Paneah can be Pa'ankh resulting in "he who lives" (Kitchen, *Reliability, pp.* 345-346). Furthermore, the Hebrew Zaphenath is close to "symbol" or "cipher" resulting in the similar name "he who lives." The title of this parshah is "and he lived."

<<< *Stele placing Ankhu and his sons in this time and place of history.*

Avaris emerged as an international trading center and agricultural hub. The most ambitious project involved the Faiym Wadi. A wadi is simply a long indentation of land that is a dry riverbed that may hold water during flooding. This particular wadi, just west of today's Cairo, proved unmanageable until the construction of a great canal. The canal channeled water from the Nile to a depression that became Lake Moeris or Birket ברכת Qarun (Hebrew for Lake). The lake became an irrigation source that spread water for agriculture. The area became a breadbasket for Egypt and even Rome. The canal has the name Bahr Yussef.

One interpretation of the name of the famous city Avaris is that the name derives from "Ish Ivri," Hebrew man. Genesis *39*:14 uses that term also, **אִישׁ עִבְרִי**, or literally, a Hebrew man.

What is the "Joseph" Canal or the "Joseph" statue?

10   Miketz   Genesis 41:1 44:17 מקץ   An End (to prison)

As in previous presentations, Joseph has been identified with the Egyptian Hebrew vizier Ankhu. Looking at the time of Potiphar/Ptahwer under Pharaoh Amenemhat III, Joseph/Ankhu's service started around the year 1820 BCE. Several years later, Ankhu is also connected with Pharaoh Khendjer around the year 1760 BCE, a life in service of some 80 years for Joseph, which may be exaggerated. During the years of service by Ankhu, a crisis arose about the line of rule. Pharaoh Amenemhat III, the mentor and supporter of Joseph, appointed a weak non-royal to succeed himself. The political situation rapidly deteriorated, ending the 12th Dynasty that had such friendly relations with Hebrews.   A 13th Dynasty with many attributes of traditional Egyptian dynasties eventually ruled Upper Egypt from a capital in Memphis while a very Semitic dynasty began rule in the delta area, forming a 14th Dynasty simultaneous with the 13th. Although dominated by Egyptians, the 13th did have probable Hebrews such as Hoteprbra who assumed a title translated as "son of the Asiatic," but could also mean son of Apiru/Habiru. (Nigro, Hotepibra: Ryholt, 69,73-76, 207-256: author's speculation of Ryholt's *htp-ib-r^c* which also appears with other probable Hebrews)

The 14th Dynasty ruled from Avaris, Ankhu continuing in service with his sons.

*Renditions of the 12 columns in the Palace of Joseph at Avaris by Rabbi   ^^^
Bar-Ron and patternsofevidence.com*

Semitic pharaohs with distinctly Hebrew names came to the throne. In the 13th Dynasty for Upper Egypt but especially in the 14th from the delta, pharaohs were typically not royal and served for only a few years.   Some observers see this as a period of instability in rulers. Perhaps. Because of lack of evidence that instability or trouble occurred with each change of a pharaoh, there may be a better explanation (Ryholt, pp. 69-117, 191-255). As evidenced in later Hebrew self-rule, Hebrews displayed disdain for absolute rulers and secession by birthright. A strong explanation to the change in pharaohs would be selection of a new ruler by methods such as rotation or election.

The capital of the Hebrew-Egyptian dynasty, Avaris, contains the remains of a large palace with twelve columns, possibly representing the Tribes of Israel, and a seal with representations of those tribes.

Next to the palace is a statue identified by some as Joseph, and also in the palace grounds stands one of the largest temples of the time, with a sacrificial altar in front that could be used in a way known to Hebrews.

<<< *Recreation of Joseph statue on cover of 'A Test of Time' by David Rohl*

Highlights of Joseph/Ankhu's and his sons' careers from non-Biblical sources include more accomplishments than many pharaohs:

- Important public works took place including the Bahr Yussef, connecting the Nile to a large system of dams, which opened an immense area to agriculture and became the most fertile region of all Egypt.

Bahr Yussef diverted water from the Nile and directed the flow to a huge depression to the west. That depression filled with water and became Lake Moeris (Birket Qarun in Hebrew). Before the canal system, the area was prone to floods. After construction of the canal, the lake area became a lush irrigation source that created a breadbasket for Egypt and, later, for Rome. The project is so

Waterway of Joseph, rsr.org/exodus

large that it can be seen from near space.

In earlier times, "all Egypt except the district of Thebes was a swamp, and none of the regions were then above water which now lie below the lake of Moeris." (Herododus *Histories*,2.7-9)

- Hebrews were well established in the delta at the time of Joseph.

- Caravan operators took up residence in Avaris, bringing trade.
- Avaris, as the major seaport of Egypt, imported and exported shiploads of all kinds of goods, olive oil, and wine (Bietak, Avaris, p. 20).
- The Hebrew donkey caravanners, traders, and craftsmen who established themselves in Egypt brought goods, jobs, and wealth to the country in a manner that did not involve military conquest and plunder.
- Joseph made Egypt into an international dynamic commercial hub.
- In addition to oversight of public works, advising kings, and being part of a process to open government to a wider group of people, Joseph supervised the six great "mansions," the name given to the Egyptian courts.
Fertile area created by Bahr Yussef >>>

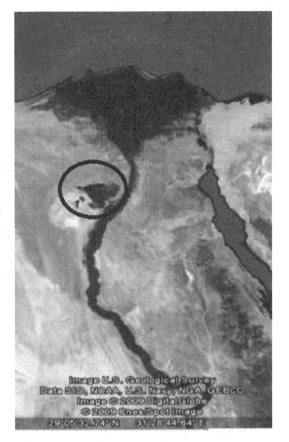

- Both the 13th and 14th dynasties lived in peace. There is no evidence of conflict (Ryholt, pp. 191-200).
- Perhaps as a result of Joseph's influence, "Asiatics" in Egypt swelled in population and became pharaohs. In another split, an entirely Asiatic dynasty, the 14th, separated from the 13th dynasty that had many pharaohs with Hebrew names. The two simultaneous dynasties, the 13th and 14th, lived with kings like Khendjer (or Hezir as in I *Chron.* 24:15; *Neh.* 10:20); Yakbin, Yaqub Har, Sheshi, Ipku son of Sheshi, Ibiaw, Aya (falcon in Hebrew, *Gen.* 36:24; II *Sam.* 3:7,21:8-11), Qareh, Ammy, Hapu, Anati, Babnum (Ryholt, pp. 220-255; Strong's; chap. 11 this book for other details).

- One of the earliest and most important papers on mathematics, the Rhind Mathematical Papyrus, was produced while Joseph served as vizier.
- A government program was continued that conscripted citizens as corvee laborers for use in public works and grain storage. This allowed for distribution of grain in times of need.
- Just after the reign of the Hebrew Pharaoh Khendjer, Ankhu was succeeded by his son Resseneb. The Hebrew Pharaoh Khendjer also used the name "Hazir," which appears in 1 *Chronicles* 24.15 and *Neh* 10.20, referring to other Hebrews. He was not of royal descent (Ryholt, pp. 209, 220). Ressoneb worked on probating the estate of Ankhu (Ryhold, p. 193, *Papyrus Boulaq* 1,8 Small).

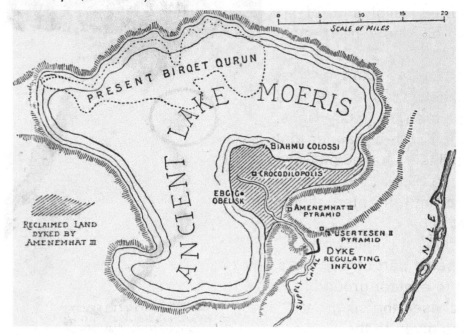

Old map of Lake Moeris (internet archive) . This is the lake created by the Bahr Yussef, part of a vast irrigation project completed by Joseph.

Two Pharaohs, one a Hebrew, rule Egypt

11 Va'yigash Gen 44:18-4:27 ויחי (Jacob) lived (in Egypt - his blessings)

Torah relates that Joseph revealed himself to his brothers who came to Egypt to seek food. It was an emotional reunion, and one of the most emotional portions in the torah, magnificently written and one of the most powerful pieces of writing in the world.   Like Joseph, Pharaoh was pleased to welcome additional Hebrews into Egypt, and as a result, many Hebrew tribes with their clans immigrated into the delta area. There is no mention of non-Hebrew groups being welcomed into the country. Egypt's border wall would have seen to that, nor is there any indication that the mini-kings of Canaan would let their subjects leave.   Egyptian records suggest that the immigration was primarily Hebrew.   Torah states that Jacob and his large family came to Egypt by way of Beersheba, which is the desert route rather that the coastal route.   Friendly tribes, descendents of the Esau southern tribes, controlled this route, as opposed to the route along the Mediterranean controlled by Amorite dictatorships.   Abraham and, later, Moses and Israelites used this route.

Why did Pharoah welcome the Hebrews as opposed to other groups? What was the benefit to Egypt ? There were several. After developing the original relationship sealed by Abraham, the need of Egypt to have a friend in the hostile land of Canaan made geopolitical sense.   Israel was not established enough to be a true buffer against acquisitive autocrats, but it could act as an outpost. That function helped Egypt when the king of Elam attempted to intrude into Egypt's trading sphere as described in the Chedorlaomer affair of Chapter 3.

Friendship and acting as an outpost was probably not enough reason to allow large numbers of immigrants into Egypt through the elaborate border wall and guard posts. As represented by Joseph, Hebrews helped to expand the economic power of Egypt by projects completed, the prime such project being the expansion of agricultural area with the Canal of Joseph described in Chapter 10.   With their trading history, Hebrews expanded commercial opportunities for the country as Avaris became a leading port in the eastern Mediterranean.   Torah echoes this aspect of the Egyptian - Hebrew chemistry:

Joseph's "brothers" continued in the trading profession when they arrived in Egypt. Albright points out that Genesis 42.34 states that Joseph will give his brothers permission to "trade" in the land. It is common to mistranslate the word for trade and instead translate to "traffic or move about" rather than to trade (Albright points out that the root SHR סחר from Gen. 42:34 is for merchant or trade and is translated as such elsewhere in Torah, *From Patriarchs I* ,pp. 12-14).

Like the typical kingdom of the era, Egypt was set up to attack, plunder, enslave, and extract tribute. Hebrews, through trade, added another strategy for the development of Egypt.

Halfway into Joseph's career, Amenemhat III died with no heirs. Two new ruling dynasties came to power, one native Egyptian, and one largely Hebrew, which retained Joseph as vizier (Ryholt).

Egypt prospered, with notable credit to Joseph. But not alone did Joseph generate so many accomplishments. Hebrew pharaohs, as can be seen from the Hebrew origins of their names, helped him. The first king of the new Hebrew 14th dynasty ruling from Avaris (Ryholt, p. 98) had the name **Yakbim** - "He will establish" in Hebrew. He was followed by other Hebrew pharaohs (Ryholt identifies the 14th dynasty as Semitic94-117, 251-256):

Ya'ammu – came from the tribe of Benjamin. His name is a contraction of the Yamammu sub-tribe of the Benjamin confederation. That tribe is referred to in various tablets of the Mari kingdom in Syria and in Egyptian texts (Rybold, p. 198).
Qareh – "by reason of chance" (name also in Deu. 23:11; Lev. 15:16).
Ammu – also derived from the Ammu or Amnanu tribe of Benjamin.
Sheshi – Hebrew for "rejoice." (Also, name of scribes in *I Kings*, 4:3, *Chron.* 18:16)   *Seal of Sheshi Walters Art Museum >>>*
Nehsy or Nehesy – son of Sheshi, probably from *nephesh* נפש, life or soul. (Name also in *Ezra* 2:5, *Nehemiah* 7:52).

The rapid turnover in pharaohs may have represented rotations of the Hebrew tribes or election by a council of elders since each king only ruled for a few years (Ryholt, pp. 94, 251-252; Fleming, pp. 45; *Strong's Hebrew; sefaria.org; abarim-publications.com/meaning*).

From about 1803 to 1650 BCE, the Egyptian and the Hebrew pharaohs lived peacefully during an era that does not receive much study. While Egypt was the center of Hebrew life at that time, Hebrews continued to live in parts of Syria, Israel, and the Sinai with seemingly cordial relationships all around. The 14th Dynasty with the Hebrew pharaohs in the delta allowed the Egyptian 13th Dynasty to travel down the Nile to the Mediterranean and onward to places like Byblos in Lebanon (Ryholt, pp. 88-89). It was the Hebrew dynasty that apparently obtained access to several traditional mines in the Sinai (Ryholt, p. 115), and the Hebrew dynasty that established closer relations with

Kush to the South. This close relationship was sealed by a royal wedding between Queen Tati of Kush and Pharaoh Sheshi (Ryholt, pp. 53,102,113,252). The ability to sail up the Nile to Kush without interference was a natural outcome of cooperation between the two regimes. It is noteworthy that some four hundred years later, Moses had exceptionally strong relations with Kush/Nubia, and in fact married a Kushite woman (Num. *12.1*).

This seal from Avaris shows the tribes of Israel: Evolving Israel tribal symbols are also presented in *Genesis* & *Deuteronomy*: Judah = a lion (Gen. 49:9); Reuben = water (*Gen.* 49:4); Levi = bird of prey (Habbani-Yemenite tradition fr. Bar-Ron); Dan = serpent *Gen.* 49:17); Simeon = gated wall of Shechem (*Gen.* 34:25); Asher = olive oil (upper left olive branches, *Gen.* 49:20; *Deut* 33:24); Naphtali = fawn (right of a ship side view of a doe, *Gen* 49:21); Zebulun & Issachar = ships (*Gen.* 49:14; *Deut.* 33:18-19.); Gad=luck upside-down mushroom (*Gen.* 30:10-11); Joseph = a bull (*Deut.* 33:17); Benjamin = symbol resting under the right shoulder of the Lord (*Gen.* 35:18; *Deut.* 33:12); the central figure might be a representation for as yet unrevealed God protecting the tribes and their holy City of Shechem between the sacred mountains Gerizim and Ebal. Hebrews in Egypt had not yet defined the AlMighty, so Abraham and Jacob traditions showed a humanoid form. (Bar Ron, *Genesis*, *Deuteronomy*, Bietak, *Avaris. pp.* 26-29 - other tribal identifications are possible. (Bietak wrote that this represents a storm god))

The depiction of the Divine as a human form in the Seal of Joseph reflects a representation of gods common at that time. Egyptian records indicate the first Hebrew mention of God as YHWH, "I am that I am," not visible or comprehensible, was written in a couple hundred years later in scripts at temples (Giveon, pp. 27,28,76,236-241,271; Redford, p. 272). Torah first reveals YHWH at the time of Moses.

*Images of gods at the time of Hebrews in Egypt: ^^^*
Syrian Ugarit war god at Los Angelos; god Amun at Abydos by Roselinni; god Ramesses ii at Abydos by Roselinni; Hittite mountain god; god Amenemhat II at Dahshur.

The Avaris seal reveals not only the presence of Hebrews in Avaris but also the presence of Hebrews in political leadership since the seal was discovered in the palace of that city. An inference that may be drawn from the twelve columns of the palace (shown in the previous chapter) is that they represent the twelve tribes. Even if all twelve tribes were not present in Egypt, Hebrews could have been corresponding with each other. There is reason to believe that a few of these tribes were pastoral, living primarily in Syria, southern Sinai and Negev. Some may have remained in Israel or even in Syria.

The giant statue of a Semitic man, found in the Avaris palace (shown in the previous chapter) in a multicolored coat should be understood to represent the most powerful person of the time, and that person was Joseph/Ankhu. While Joseph ruled in Avaris, Hebrews did not yet possess a highly organized religion. That development came later. However, they were monotheistic; there were no Hebrew idols.

12 tribe mosaic public domain
Givat Mordechai Etz Shul
Jerusalem >>>

Asher	olive tree – his bread shall be fat (Gen. 4:20)		
Dan	"shall achieve justice" (Gen. 49:16)	Simeon	gates of Shechem
Judah	crown (elsewhere as a lion)	Benjamin	utensils
Reuven	giving mandrakes to Leah	Gad	tent of Bedouin
Joseph	wheat from time in Egypt	Zeb	ship for a port
Naphtali	gazelle (Gen 49.21)	Levi	priest breastplate
Issachar	celestial (I Chron 12:32)		

After Jacob's death, Egypt succumbed to invaders.

12 <u>Va'yechi</u> Gen 47:28-50:26 ויחי (Jacob) lived (in Egypt - his blessings)

An era of history closed its doors with Torah describing the deaths of Jacob and Joseph and their farewells to the tribes of Israel. The existence of the tribes of Israel is well established in history, but the actual early history of these tribes is not so well known. Torah makes it simple: they are the children of Jacob. But Torah often uses the device of eponyms, that is, using an individual, to represent a group. We have seen this with the sons of the right or Benjamin, and sons of the left or Joseph, and progeny of Noah.

<< in Etz Yosef shul

The scene in Genesis showing the last blessing of Jacob offers insight into the history of tribes he united in order to form Israel. Jacob rails about the violence of Simeon and Levi, who captured Shechem for Israel in a manner offensive to jacob (chapter 8); he recalls that Joseph came from the upper Euphrates (see below); and he grants ownership of Sheckem to joseph.

We will go into some detail in order to examine the history of a number of tribes. This will explain how Torah reduced a tedious geneology to a work for the ages, telling the lesson of morality without getting lost in the story of history. Benjamin and Joseph, brothers and only sons of Rebecca, require a closer look. Benjamin was actually a confederation of tribes coming from the south Euphrates, which in Hebrew is Banu Yamina, sons of the right, or south Euphrates. The confederation of Benjamin contributed to the Hebrew tribe of the same name. Benjamin actually consisted of five tribes, the Yarihu (Jericho), Yahruru, Uprapu, Rabbu, and Amnanu. (Fleming, *Democracy*, p. 45; Albright, *From Patriarchs* I, p. 18; Bodi, p. 391;) Yarihu means "moon," which was worshipped by some Benjamins in the City of Haran. Interestingly, the original Hebrew name of Jericho is derived from Yarihu. The Yarihu tribe's original city of Jericho (Yeriho) is found in the Beqa Valley of Canaanite Syria. It must be remembered that "Canaan" includes parts of today's Syria and Lebanon. Canaan is not synonymous with today's Israel. (Albright, *From Patriarchs II* p. 49, Bodi, pp. 405-6) and the Israeli Jericho is situated in the land of Benjamin. Jacob blessed Benjamin as a wolf because a wolf howls at the moon, like praying and the Benjamins did worship the moon back in Abraham's City of Haran. (Fleming, *Democracy, p.* 200; *Gen* 49:27; Albright, *From Patriarchs* I, p. 18; Albright, *From Patriarchs II*, p. 49, Bodi, p. 391)

The tribe of Yahruru is shortened in Torah to Ya'r or Er or Jair – a clan of Judah - hence we see that this tribe contributed to the population of Judah (*Gen.* 38:3; *I* Chron 20:5; *Tractate Soferim* 7.4). Also, the tribe of Uprapu remained as a clan of Benjamin (Num. 13:9).

The Tribe of Joseph has been mentioned as a brother tribe to Benjamin. Joseph has a more complicated history because the name is not explicitly mentioned outside of Torah. The blessings of Jacob give more detail. Bear in mind: "The Testament of Jacob was remembered with astonishing accuracy in spite of the archaism of language and style...." (Albright, *From Patriarchs I*, p. 26). Because of the ancient nature of the words and prose, the blessing of Joseph has been mistranslated. Joseph is described as a son of Perat פרת and some have translated Perat as a vine, as fruit, or even as a wild ass. Perat is, in fact, the old name for the Euphrates. Perat is also, in fact, the modern Hebrew name for the Euphrates, **פרת** or Perat River **נהר פרת.** With that clear translation, we see that Joseph is a

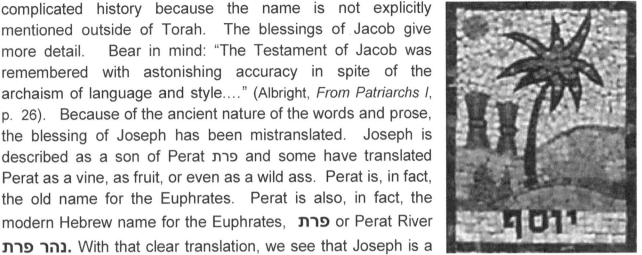

son of the Euphrates near the source, which is in Turkey, to the north. Hence for a person facing the morning sun, the tribe of Joseph would live in a direction towards the left. These tribes were sons of the left, Benu S'mola. King Zimri-Lim, as head of the Benu S'mola, gave that tribe a leading, favorite, place in the government of Mari, in Syria. It was the S'mola who defeated and replaced the Benjamins as rulers. (Fleming, pp. 24-31, 43, 49, 57) Joseph (the tribe) was involved in a bitter dispute, "Archers bitterly assailed him; they shot at him and harried him. Yet his bow stayed taut, and his arms were made firm by the hands of the Mighty One of Jacob – there, the Shepherd, the rock of Israel." i.e. Jacob assisted and strengthened Joseph in a time of need. Joseph became a favorite of Jacob. (Albright, *From Patriarch I* 18-19, 26-28; Albright, *From Patriarch II, pp.* 48-51; Gen. 49)

We note that Gad, Simeon, Levi, and Reuben are all the children of Leah or her handmaid according to Torah. Simeon and Levi stormed the fortress of Shechem, providing Israel with its first urban center. The flag of Simeon is often depicted as the walls of Shechem. Even though Jacob disapproved of this action, he included the prize city in the inheritance of Joseph. The flag of Gad often is shown with a tent. Gad, Simeon, and Reuben had large herds of animals and so were pastoral. Reuben's flag displays mandrake flowers, a sign of fertility and hope.

In discovering individual histories about the tribes of Israel, the reality and the beauty of the Torah story is more understandable. Backgrounds of more tribes will be explored in later chapters.

The Hebrew experience in Egypt continued after Joseph's death. Avaris, the city that Joseph built, prospered and many ships could dock in its harbor. They came from Carthage, Crete, Greece, Byblos, Turkey, and Spain. Merchants transferred goods south into the Egyptian settlements and cities along the Nile River, past Egypt into Kush, and along the King's Road to destinations in Syria, Israel, and Mesopotamia. Caravans came and went. Mechanisms of trade and finance continued to develop. (Ryholt, pp. 111-116)

While he was still alive, Joseph supervised the entry of many new immigrants and the placement of servants. He may have been the first one man Hebrew immigration society. Egyptian records show that a group of 95 workers were largely Semitic people, but the names are followed by Egyptian names, new Egyptian names for new residents. Among the Hebrew names before the change are Manahem (the tribe of Israel), Issachar (May God favor, tribe of Israel), Sakar (God has favored), Dodihu (God is loved), Shiphrah (beautiful), Puah (lass), Asher (a tribe of Israel), Eseb, Samson (Hebrew Biblical name), and Jacob. (Brooklyn 35.1446 *papyrus scroll*; Albright, *Northwest Semitic Names;* Albright, *Biblical, p.* 22; Bietak, *Hyksos Review*).

At this point, the Hebrew story gets complicated because all of Egypt – that ruled by Hebrews and that ruled by native Egyptians – was overrun by invaders.

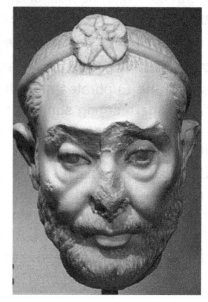

Occupation of Egypt by these invaders resulted in a dark chapter of historicity, but not a chapter in scripture. While the 13th and 14th simultaneous friendly dynasties lived in smug success, ignoring the necessity for a powerful military in an age of violence, danger lurked from fierce regimes to the north and east. Inside the Delta – Goshen in the Bible - prosperity favored the population which swelled to over three million, propelled by improvements such as irrigation installed by Ankhu/Joseph. (Butzer – also with reference to Hassan and Baer, pp. 76-77). Egypt was a wealthy fat prize waiting to be conquered. A strong army consisting of various Canaanite city states and other forces planned to do just that. They were called Hyksos. A later Egyptian priest Manetho, sympathetic to Egypt and not to Hebrews, described the invasion:

> There came, after a surprising manner, men of ignoble birth out of the eastern parts, and had boldness enough to make an expedition into our country, and with ease subdued it by force, yet without our hazarding a battle with them. So when they had gotten those that governed us [that would be Hebrews] under their power, they afterward burnt down our cities, and demolished the temples of the gods, and used all the inhabitants after a most barbarous manner; nay, some they slew and led their children and their wives into slavery. Manetho @Altes Berlin>>>

These Hyksos invaders rapidly overran Egypt in the 17th century BCE – all of the Delta and much of upper Egypt – and took control of the whole country with the exception of a small outcrop dynasty around the old capital of Thebes. The Hebrew dynasty folded. The exact nature of the Hyksos control over Hebrews lacks research. Much evidence was destroyed by the subsequent ten plagues (Redford 101-106, ch 14).

The new rulers made their capital in Joseph's city of Avaris. They took over the trade in gold with Nubia and Sudan (DeMagistris, pp. 3- 4). Hyksos unified most of Egypt under their rule and introduced a tighter system of social stratification, more along the lines of the Mitanni and Amorite autocracies. A feudal hierarchy emerged with aristocrats, noble charioteers, and an underclass of serfs, canceling any class of free citizens or councils of elders. Freedoms instituted by Hebrews vanished. A Hyksos 15th dynasty began. (Gottwald, pp. 389-401; Grimal, pp. 185-195; Gottwald, pp. 391-398). Eventually, when Egyptians once again controlled Egypt, pharaoh unleashed violent attacks against the entire Canaanite coastline up into Lebanon and Syria but exempted Hebrews.

The Hyksos had allies. Their allies were not the native Egyptians, for they were suppressed, and not the Hebrews, for their cities lapsed out of Hebrew control and their trading patterns were cut off. The Hebrew city of Shechem was threatened. However, Canaanite cities principally along the coast received favored trade, new proprietary military equipment, training in the tactics of the Hyksos, and a period of peace and cooperation with the new rulers of Egypt. Canaanites appeared complicit in aiding the rapid advance of their Hyksos allies, as did other aggressive groups (Albright, *Yahweh, pp.* 114-115). Hyksos conducted a lively trade in stolen goods. They looted Egyptian art, statues, and treasure, then sold it to various Canaanite cities. (Ryholt, pp. 132-139, 143, 147-148; DeMagistris, pp. 3- 4). According to Manetho, the Hyksos "made both the upper (Egyptians from Thebes) and lower (Delta Hebrews) regions pay tribute and left garrisons in places that were the most proper for them."

Pharaoh Seqenenre Ta'a II the Brave ruled a small portion of central Egypt from the City of Thebes. When Ta'a started to build a military, he received a warning from the overlord Hyksos king in Avaris to cease. But Ta'a intended to free Egypt. Probable Hebrews served under Ta'a in some responsible positions, such as Ineni, architect and designer; Nakht, granary overseer; Tetiky, mayor of Thebes, and Qen, priest of Mut. (Petrie Museum). That would explain the presence of Hebrew glass in the tombs of the Theban rulers. (Jensen, pp. 45-50, 120). Ta'a launched an attack against the outskirts of the Hyksos empire. His efforts proved premature as his forces could not stand up to the Hyksos. A Hyksos ax to the left side of his head severed his cheek, fractured his jaw, and flattened him. An ax to the head crushed his skull and inflicted other wounds. Decomposition set in before the body was recovered and hastily embalmed. (Maspero; Redford pp. 125-127). His brother Kamose took the throne. Pharaoh Kamose did not flinch but continued the attacks against the Hyksos. The Hebrew Emhab of Edfu near Aswan "beat a drum every day" for the king.

<<Pharaoh who rebelled and was killed.
Pledge of Emhab the Hebrew >>

Hyksos troops put an end to Kamose. A child named Ahmose, son of Ta'a, ascended to the throne with his mother as regent.

The saga of how the invading Hyksos armies were expelled has to do with the Ten Plagues, hundreds of years prior to the Moses Exodus. In Torah, recitation of the Plagues is combined with recitation of the Moses Exodus. This literary technique should be construed as a simplification that added to the power of the Hebrew saga. In order to closely follow the sequence as presented in the *Five Books of Moses,* the next chapter will concern Moses and then we shall return to the expulsion of Hyksos.

Hebrews slaves, Ramesses II, Moses, YHWH

13 Shmot   Exodus 1:1 – 6:1 שמות Names (who came into Egypt)

Torah begins its second book with a sudden change of Egypt's relations with Hebrews. Here begins the story of Hebrew affliction and enslavement and the introduction of Moses begining with a narration of his adoption by a member of the Egyptian Royal Family.   There is evidence of Pharaoh Ramesses II turning against the Hebrews, evidence of Moses as a reluctant leader; evidence of ten plagues, and evidence of a desert journey to Israel. All of the evidence, however, points to *two* events of exodus, one associated with the ten plagues in the 16th Century BCE, and one associated with Moses in the 11th or 12th century BCE. We now jump a few hundred years in order to give a historical version of Moses and will return to the Plagues later.

We know that *Shmot* is a powerful parashah, with the suffering Israelites first in bondage, then suddenly hopeful of gaining freedom. Let's have a conversation between Torah and History.

Torah: A new king arose over Egypt who knew not Joseph (*Ex.* 1:7)
History: Following the death of the Pharaoh Akhenaten, the rebel who abolished all Egyptian gods except for the sun, a muddled succession process took place. A new dynasty of warrior pharaohs came to power who crushed all those with sympathies or associations with Akkenaten.   Hebrews were among those crushed.

Torah: So they set taskmasters over them to oppress them with forced labor; and they built garrison cities for pharaoh: Pithom and Ramesses. (*Ex.* 1:11)
History: Ramesses' manager reported on "the Apiru (Hebrews) who drag stones for the great pylon of the building Ramses II Beloved of Truth" was constructing. He continues by instructing his servants to "distribute grain rations to the soldiers and to the Apiru who transport stones to the great pylon of Ramesses." In addition they are also mentioned as brick-makers, as residing in the neighborhood of the royal harem, and as having a country in Israel (*Papyrus Leiden 348*; Ben-Sasson, p. 42; *Exodus* 1:8-14; Grimal, pp. 258-259, Hoffmeier, Israel in Egypt, pp. 114-116).

Prince Amenmesse/Moses – handsome or beautiful? Photo by author

Torah: The king of Egypt spoke to the Hebrew midwives, Shiphrah and Puah, "When you deliver Hebrew women, if it is a boy, kill him. (*Ex.* 1:15)

History: Shiphrah and Puah were names for Hebrew women at the time. Joseph earlier supervised immigrants named Shiphrah (meaning "beautiful") and Puah (meaning "lass"). All we can say is that Hebrew women with these names existed (*Brooklyn 35.1446 papyrus scroll*; Hayes; Albright, *Northwest Semitic Names;* Albright, *Biblical, p.* 22; Bietak, *Hyksos Review*)

Torah: A Hebrew woman conceived and bore a son, and when she saw how beautiful he was she hid him for three months. The king of the oppression died (*Ex.* 2:2-23).

History: After the death of Ramesses II, his son Merenptah ruled for a short time. He got into serious political disputes with Prince Amenmesse, known as Moses born of Amun, or Moses for short. His parentage is uncertain, which is very unusual for a person of such elevated status at that time. He was handsome. Like other Egyptian aristocracy, he owned a tomb but it never received his body (Schneider; Dodson all 3 references; Yurko; Callender; Tyldesley, *Ramesses*).

Torah: Moses saw an Egyptian beating a Hebrew…. He struck him down and buried him (*Ex* 2:11-12).

History: At this time, pharaoh did not provide money for workers and the starving men often robbed tombs. Tomb worker Paneb was accused of such robbery and disciplined. A nasty altercation followed, and the supervisor who meted out the punishment was killed. Viceroy Amenmesse was accused of the murder and thereafter declared "enemy of the people" (Tyldesley, *Ramesses, pp.* 191-192; Callender, p. 28; *Salt Papyrus,* 124 tr. in Cerny; Dodson, pp. 37, 57-64; Kohl).

Torah: When Pharaoh learned of the matter, he sought to kill Moses, but Moses fled to Midian (*Ex.* 2:14-15).

History: The pharaoh dismissed Amenmesse and a bevy of officials for undisclosed reasons, whereupon the activities of the prince are vague for a number of years. (Schneider; Dodson, all 3 references; Yurko; Callender)

Torah: Moses made his way to the mountain of God and came to a flame from the ground that did not consume a bush. Moses was commanded to return to Egypt, the land from which he fled, and demand that Israelites be freed. God revealed the name by which God may be referred to: I am that I am, or YHWH (*Ex.* 3:2-14).

History: YHWH had been recorded as the God of the Shosu tribes, which included Simeon, 300 or 400 years earlier. It is not clear when other Israelites adopted YHWH, but the Jacob Israelite and Esau Shosu cultures (more on Shosu and Simeon to come) seemed to coordinate closely at that time. The two who separated as Jacob and Esau once again united. Shosu lived by the mountain of God. Midian Kenites, known in history as a budding nation and in Torah as the clan of Moses' father-in-law, lived near the mountain in the mining district of Timna. Hebrews from Israel or those previously escaping from Egypt could easily gather near God's mountain. With regard to the burning bush, a spontaneous phenomenon of sub-surface buried turf or peat burning occurs in some deserts that resembles a bush afire, although other phenomenon are possible as Divine manifestations. Certain amazing Biblical occurrences are well known to local Bedouin. (Rothenberg; *Biography of Ahmose Pen-Nekhbet* ~ 1490 BCE; Amenenhat III at Soleb ~ 1380 BCE)

Torah: God commanded Moses to cast his staff upon the ground. Moses obeyed and the staff turned into a serpent.

Copper Snake found in naos / Holiest Place of Midianite Shrine at Timna, with a close-up of the head gilded with gold.

History: In the middle of Seir, home of YHWH-worshipping Shosu and home of the Kenites who purportedly provided refuge for Moses, sits the Timna mining area, a center of rebellion against Egypt. Here, archeologists have uncovered a variety of objects compatible with the Biblical Exodus such as a serpent with a body of copper and a golden head.

Torah: With a strong hand pharaoh will drive Israel out of Egypt. (*Ex.* 6:1)

History: The forces of Amenmesse lost a civil war and were driven out of Egypt (Seti II, Schneider, Dodson, pp. 46-47, 51-57, 64-67; Tyldesley, *Ramesses, pp.* 189-192; Kitchen, *Pharaoh, p.* 216; *Admonitions of Ipuwer).*

Beginning of the *Admonitions of Ipuwer:*
Papyrus Leiden 344 in Leiden, Netherlands below

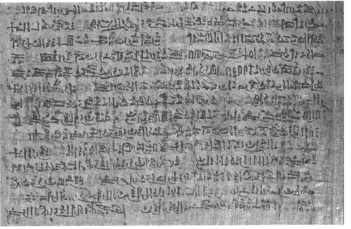

The face is pale. The bowman is ready. The wrongdoer is everywhere. There is no man of yesterday as all is full of confederates. A man goes out to plough with his shield. The doorkeepers say let us go and plunder. The confectioners.... the bird catchers draw up in line of battle. People of the Marshlands carry shields.... A man looks upon his son as his enemy. A man smites his brother, the son of his mother. What is to be done? A man is slain by the side of his brother. He tries to save his own limbs. He who has a noble lady as wife, her father protects him. He who has not they slay him. Men's hearts are violent. The plague is throughout the land. Blood is everywhere. Death is

not lacking. The mummy cloth speaks before ever one draws near to it. The river is blood. Men drink of it and shrink from the taste of people. Men thirst after water.

The fire has mounted up on high, its burning goeth forth against the enemies of the land. No craftsmen work, the enemies of the land have spoilt its crafts. ["Enemies" here means those the scribe calls "rebels."] Men have ventured to rebel against the Uraetis, [cobra symbol of pharaoh on his crown] the son of Re. A few lawless men have ventured to despoil the land of the kingship. The Desert is throughout the Land. The nomes [political areas of Egypt] are laid waste. A foreign tribe from abroad has come to Egypt. The Delta is overrun by Asiatics. [Allies of the Delta rebels entered the fight.] The Marshland in its entirety is not hidden. The North land can boast of trodden ways. What shall one do? Behold it is in the hands of those who knew it not like those who knew it. The Asiatics are skilled in the arts of the Marshlands. So deep a root have these barbarians taken in the land that they are no longer distinguishable from true Egyptians. The tribes of the desert have become Egyptians everywhere. There are no Egyptians anywhere.. Tents are what the Egyptians have made like the desert tribes. (It clearly seems like Ipuwer is sympathetic to the Theban side.)

Torah: Moses spoke directly with YHWH. Torah starts with God speaking the world into being and the divine voice is heard in pivotal moments of the narrative - while in Egypt, at Mount Sinai, and when Hebrews are ready to cross into Canaan. God's voice is heard in thunder on Sinai. Torah suggests several ways to understand such a voice: perhaps not the manner of what is called conversation. We will explore this concept in future discussion.

History: History does not record private conversations. It may refer to the history of theology but does not engage directly with theology or religion. In future sessions we will explore what the term "Speaking with God" might mean in the context of history, realizing that there are many theological and secular interpretations.

The Exodus Before the Moses Exodus

14 Va'eirah Exodus 6:2 – 9:35 וארא See (What I will do to Pharaoh)

During the 16th century BCE, the Hyksos, a foreign power that also called their leader "pharoah," ruled most of Egypt. Native Egyptian pharaohs, with support from Hebrews, rebelled against the Hyksos but failed miserably. Hyksos established their Egyptian home base in the Hebrew city of Avaris. Descriptions of how Hebrews, in particular, were treated are lacking, except for the general statement of the Egyptian priest Manetho, already given: Hyksos burnt cities, demolished temples, used inhabitants barbarously, slew or sold children and wives into slavery, and exacted tribute. One indication of the difficulties pressed on Egyptians by Hyksos is the record of the Dan Tribe exiting probably prior to plagues.

Some Hebrews are shown to have escaped, such as members of the Dan Tribe. Here are some references:

Parian Chronicle Since a ship with fifty oars sailed from Egypt to Greece, and was called Pentecontorus, and the daughters of Danaus   1511 BCE (Greek chronology covering 1582 – 299 BCE)

Hecataeus of Abdera In ancient times a great plague occurred in Egypt, and many ascribed the cause of it to the gods. All the foreigners were forthwith expelled, and the most valiant and noble among them, under some notable leaders, were brought to Greece and other places, as some relate; the most famous of their leaders were Danaus and Cadmus.   (Cadmus is credited with founding the Greek city of Thebes – with the same name as a capital of Egypt (Bury p. 34). But the majority of the people descended into a country not far from Egypt, which is now called Judea (written 4th C. BCE)

The Aeschylus play *The Suppliants*, Fifth century BCE: Danaus and his daughters, exiles from Egypt, fleeing from the brother Egyptus, since they feared an unholy alliance.

Wall *Mural in Santorini* 16th *C BCE* showing escape from fortified Avaris in Egypt and sailing to Santorini. Graves and gold art found in Mycenae suggest they moved on to Greece as the volcano in Santorini showed signs of eruption

Diodorus of Sicily Danaus together with his daughters fled from Egypt …. Sailed on to Argos together with their father Danaus. (Histories 5.58.1) Argos goes to the heart of

Greek formation mythology Danaus was a king there, shortly followed by Acrisius whose daughter Danae produced a son, the hero Perseus, with Zeus as the father.

Another historical trend of Dan in Egypt is a construct of proto-Greek Nile trading settlements who adopted Egyptian gods to Greek sensibilities. Perseus, descendent of Danaus, was celebrated, seemingly as a Greek version of Horus and his parents along with adventures similar to Egyptian and Syrian lore (Loyd; Herodotus Histories 2.91, 6.53; Harper Dictionary) .

Thus tribe of "Dan, Danoi, Denyen, Danaus, is referenced by Greek, Egyptian, and Hebrew sources in a manner that links them all. We will meet up with Dan again in chapters 36 and 42.

From a 16th century BCE mural in Akrotiri, Santorini, Greece showing Hebrews from fortified Avaris and the Nile River in Egypt sailing to Santorini. Graves and gold art found in Mycenae suggest they moved on to mainland Greece when a volcano in Santorini showed signs of erupting. (Jacobovichi, Wikipedia – there are other interpretations)

At the apex of their power, the Hyksos defeated two attempted Egyptian uprisings and killed two pharaohs from the weak Theban state. Ahmose, a child of the first rebel pharaoh, was installed with his mother as regent.

At that moment in history, Torah tells us that God delivered a message to the Israelites through Moses that "I will bring you out from under the burdens of the Egyptians, and I will deliver you from their bondage . . . "

Then suddenly, in the middle of the Sixteenth century BCE, a force more powerful than any dynasty or army wreaked havoc. A gigantic volcano under the Mediterranean island of Santorini erupted over a period of several months, causing one of the largest explosions in history, one that destroyed Minoan civilization. For comparison's sake, Hurricane Katrina that destroyed New Orleans and caused total evacuation was a mere spring shower compared to the events at Santorini. Even Cyprus was covered in 12-15 feet of pumice and then hit with a tsunami .The initial earthquake blast was heard as far up the Nile River as Thebes. Shifting fault lines sent tsunami waves that demolished Crete, and an hour later, hit Goshen and Avaris. (Bury pp. 17-18)

At that time, the child pharaoh of Thebes, Ahmose, came of age. His government accepted its vassalage under the Hyksos pharaoh who resided in the Delta City of Avaris. Hyksos seemed invincible. They had established relations with areas of the Mediterranean world including Greece, Turkey, Syria, and even Spain.

In Thebes, located in the Upper Nile, Pharaoh Ahmose attended an event to honor the Egyptian god Amun, and possibly to celebrate his coronation, having reached the age of maturity and no longer requiring the regency of his mother. The third pylon at Karnak gives the Egyptian description of the events known to Hebrews as the ten plagues. Egyptians finally recognized the work of the "Great God," who ruled over any Egyptian god. Thousands of years of Egyptian dedication to idolatry made it hard for Ahmose to fully comprehend the insignificance of his idols. He offered gold and silver to his gods to set things straight. Ahmose recorded his experience:

<<<Pharaoh Ahmose of Theban Egypt, one of two pharaohs at the time of the 10 plagues (Met). The other was Pharaoh Apopi, Hyksos pharaoh of Egypt, based in the Delta City of Avaris. Dagger with name of Apopi.   >>>

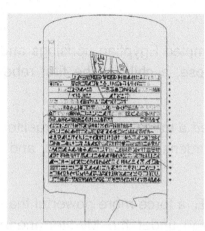

<<< Sketch is the Tempest Stele 16th C. BCE describing destruction of Thebes by rain, darkness, storm, explosion, floating corpses, and ruined temples. (Wiener & Allen)

An inscription from Ahmose official at Karmak: The gods complained of their discontent. The gods caused that the sky to come in a tempest of rain, with darkness in the condition of the West (i.e. underworld), and the sky being in storm without (cessation, louder than) the cries of the masses, more powerful than on the mountains louder than the sound of the underground source of the Nile that is in Elephantine. Then every house, every quarter that they reached (and bodies) floated on the water like skiffs of papyrus outside the palace audience chamber for days while no torch could be lit in the Two Lands. Then His Majesty said, 'How much greater is the wrath of the Great God than the plans of the gods!' His Majesty then descended to his boat, with his council following him, while the crowds on the East and West had hidden faces, having no clothing on them after the manifestation of the wrath of the God. His Majesty then reached the interior of Thebes, with gold confronting gold of this cult image, so that he received what he desired. Then His Majesty began to reestablish the Two Lands, to give guidance for the flooded territories. He did not fail in providing them with silver, with gold, with copper, with oil and cloth comprising every bolt that could be desired. … Then His Majesty was informed that the mortuary concessions had been entered, the tomb chambers collapsed, the funeral mansions undermined, and the pyramids fell. Then His Majesty commanded to restore the temples…. (Ritner; Tempest Stela of Karnak)

The events that occurred can be described as thus:

1. Immense quantities of ash and iron ore covered the entire area. They blotted out the sun. The oxidized iron, along with unusual algae blooms, turned the Nile the color of deep red, as described in Exodus *7:15-21, "The water of the Nile turned to blood."*

2. The contamination of the waters chased amphibious animals out to look for shelter, as described in Exodus *8:7-10, "Frogs covered the land."*

3. The lack of clean water caused diseases and an infestation of gnats and lice, as described in Exodus *8:12-14, "The dust of the earth turned to lice."*

4. With the depletion of oxygen, fish died and littered the landscape, decomposing and attracting insects, often a distance from their watery home, as described in Exodus *8:18-27, "Swarms of flies covered the land."*

5. The volcano continued to belch ash, rock particles, iron specks, water vapor, and sulfur dioxide in a most violent series of convulsions. The sulfur dioxide mixed with the water vapor to create sulfuric acid in the air. The sky rained acid on grasses. Wheat, barley, and other plants wilted. Grass-eating animals like sheep, cows, and deer ingested this acid and died, as described in Exodus *9:3-11, "The hand of the Lord will strike your livestock with a severe pestilence."*

6. The acid also rained on humans and animals, burning exposed skin, as described in Exodus *8:8-11, "It caused an inflammation, breaking out in boils on man and beast."*

7. The sky swirled with toxic mixtures. Ash of fire poured down from the lower atmosphere. Water vapor collected in the upper atmosphere. Hail and fire pounded the land at the same time, as described in Exodus *9:22-35 - The hail was very heavy, fire flashing in the midst of the hail."*

8. The extreme weather changes included cold temperatures, caused by the blocking of the sun, signaling other insects like locusts to swarm, as described in Exodus *10:4-19, Locusts invaded all the land of Egypt."*

^^^ *Santorinin Bay, a body of water created by the volcanic eruption at Santorini (Wikipedia)*

9. Clouds of pumice, ash, water vapor, rock fragments, sulfur, and iron specks blotted out the sun for prolonged periods. Thus, it seemed that the Egyptian sun god Re had retreated and failed his worshipers. Darkness fell on the land, as described in Exodus *10.21-23, "Thick darkness descended upon all the land of Egypt for three days."*
(Re: Ahmose and plagues – Ritner & Moeller; Foster, *Ahmose;* Foster, *Texts;* Goedicke; 252-262; Bietak *Avaris, p.* 78, MacGillivray, 160).

10. Many, including children, were killed by infected boils, typhoid, mucus membranes corroded from inhaling sulphuric acid, and disease. Mass graves for youths were quickly dug. The fate of the son of Hyksos Pharaoh Apophis is not known. The son of Ahmose did die, as described in Exodus *11:4-12:32, "Death of the first born."*

With a population of about 3 million in the lower Egypt, including the area irrigated by Joseph, it is not unreasonable to estimate that a mixed multitude of at least 600.000 fled the land, as described in *Exodus* 12:37. (Butzer – also with ref. to Hassan and Baer, pp. 76-77). It is easy to see a Divine arrangement in Exodus and why millions of people believe Exodus was part of God's plan.

(In addition to the above references, see Bury & Meiggs, p.18, Ritner & Moeller, Luce & Bolton, McCoy and Haiken, Whipps, Silvertsen)

The events know as the Ten Plagues are merged with the exit of Moses from Egypt to form the *Book of Exodus*. We will return to the years between the 16th Century BCE exit and the 12th Century BCE of Moses several times while completing the history of Moses.

The last plagues and the first Passover

15 Bo Exodus 10:1-13:16 בא Go (Unto Pharaoh) by Ellen Poster

Parsha Bo begins with Moses warning Pharaoh of the eighth plague of locusts, then tells of the ninth plague of darkness, and finally ends with the Hebrews leaving Egypt after the tenth plague, the killing of the Egyptian first-born.   The Pharaoh of the oppression in the Exodus story may have been Ramses II, as has been previously discussed.   Moses as written in the Torah is "Moshe," from the Hebrew verb "to draw out".   The name "Moses" in Egyptian means "is born" or "son of" and was a common Egyptian name at the time of Ramses II (1279- 1213 B.C.E), thus providing an Egyptian connection for the Moses of the Torah.

But what of the plagues? Science raises tantalizing possibilities. The eighth plague of locusts may have resulted from the volcanic eruption on Santorini as previously discussed. The ash could have caused unusually higher precipitation and humidity, conditions favorable for locusts. (*Below – Swarm of Locusts BBC*)

The ninth plague of darkness may have resulted from a solar eclipse or ash from the Santorini eruption. We note that neither of these explanations are a perfect fit for our Torah narrative. A solar eclipse does not account for the light in the Hebrew homes as recounted in the Torah.

The Santorini eruption was 500 miles from Egypt and predated the time of Ramses II by 300 years. For this reason, some propose that the Exodus in Torah was actually two events, combined for more effective reading.

The last plague, the death of the first born, could have been the result of toxins released by red algae blooms in the Nile. The toxins released by such densely concentrated algae can disburse in the air causing breathing problems for humans.

Finally, as to Pharaoh's hardened heart, according to Rabbi Ed Gelb, it could be that Pharaoh's hate "physiologically changed his internal organs and corrupted them. As he committed evil acts, his heart became like stone." While a hardened physical heart is not the same as a hardened will, we can perhaps agree that our thoughts can positively or negatively affect our biological functioning.

The history of the Jewish people begins

In Exodus 12:2, God presents the Hebrews with their first Mitzvah (good deed): "This month shall mark for you the beginning of the months; it shall be the first of the months of the year for you." This is understood to mean the new moon is the beginning of the Hebrew month. It also means that the month of Nisan, the month of the liberation from Egypt, is the beginning of the Jewish calendar, "the first month of the year." (Until the Babylonian exile, there were no names for the months, only numbers, and Jewish month number one is Nisan. Rosh Hashanah is referred to in the Torah as "the first day of the seventh month.") We celebrate Pesach on the fifteenth of Nisan - the anniversary of the exodus from Egypt. According to Rabbi Dr. Warren Goldstein, Chief Rabbi of the Union of Orthodox Synagogues of South Africa, "God established the Jewish calendar at this point in our history, which framed events for all time."

History as a call to divine partnership

The Torah presupposes a God that speaks, starting in the first parshah of Genesis, Bereshit, when God speaks the world into being: "God said 'Let there be light', and there was light." *Genesis* 1:3. *Parshah Bo*, also begins with God's speech, "Then God said to Moses, 'Go to Pharaoh. For I have hardened his heart and the hearts of his courtiers, in order that I may display these My signs among them.'" Exodus 10:1. What does it mean that God speaks? In *Parshot Bereshit* and *Bo*, the Hebrew "*vayomer*" is translated as "said." But in Genesis 1:5, translated as "God called the light Day," the Hebrew word for "called" is "*Vayikra.*" Rabbi Sacks argues that this word "*vayikra*" is important to understanding how the God of *Torah* is the God of history and of relationship between God and the Jewish people.

80

A call vs. happenstance

In his article *Vayikra (5773) - Between Destiny and Chance*, Rabbi Sacks makes a distinction between *vayikar,* a chance encounter, *and vayikra,* a call from God. The only difference between the two words is the letter *alef.* If you look at v*ayikra,* the first word of *Leviticus,* in the phrase "God called to Moses," you will note that the final letter of *vayikra,* the *alef,* is tiny compared to the other letters. There is a midrash that Moses wanted to write *vayikar,* suggesting God was communicating with him as if in a dream, but God told him to write *vayikra* with the *alef,* signifying that he was hearing God's call. Moses obeyed, but with his extreme humility, wrote the *alef* much smaller than the other letters. According to Rabbi Sacks: "The letter *aleph* is almost inaudible. Its appearance in a *Sefer Torah* at the beginning of *Vayikra* [*Leviticus*] (the "small aleph") is almost invisible. Do not expect - the *Torah* is intimating - that the presence of God in history will always be as clear and unambiguous as it was during the exodus from Egypt and the dividing of the Red Sea. For much of the time it will depend on your own sensitivity. For those who look, it will be visible. For those who listen, it can be heard...If you choose not to see or hear, the *vayikra* will become *viyikar.* The call will be inaudible. History will seem mere chance."

Measure for Measure

Rabbi Sacks is talking about the relationship between God and the Jewish people. *Middah kenegged middah,* measure for measure.
We are in relationship with God, according to Rabbi Sacks, to the extent we choose it. "If you believe that history is chance, then it will become so." It is not enough to "say that it is the way of the world for such a thing to happen to them, and that their trouble is a matter of pure chance." According to Rabbi Sacks, we must respond to God's call, to "sound an alarm" in times of trouble, "to testify to the presence of God in our midst," for our history as a Jewish people to continue.

Bat Kol

Is it possible for us today to hear God's call and participate in our own history? Yes, according to the Sages of the rabbinic era. The Sages were the teachers and masters of Jewish law and the contributors to the Talmud, including Hillel and Shammai. The Sages saw themselves as heirs to the Prophets, indeed greater than the Prophets. While in the Tanakh, Moses and the prophets heard the voice of God directly, the *vayikra,* our Rabbis of blessed memory understood that prophecy had come to an end five centuries before the destruction of the Second Temple. They believed that the most one could hear from heaven was a *bat kol, a distant echo,* literally the "daughter of voice." And this echo can be heard by everyone, and everyone, hearing it, has the responsibility to act for the good of the community.

The *bat kol* co-existed with the *vayikra* in the Tanakh [although the term *bat kol* itself does not appear]. So Elijah recognized God by a "still, small, voice". (*1 Kings* 19:1-13). Rabbi Lawrence Kushner in *The Book of Letters* writes that the *alef,* which has no sound, is the first letter of the first name of God in Torah, *elohim,* the first letter of *echad,* One, and the first letter of the first word of the Ten Commandments, *Anochi,* I. "It is no accident that all these words begin the Alef. The most basic words there are begin with the most primal sound there is. The almost sound you make before you can make any sound." As it says in *Deuteronomy* 30:11-14: Surely, this Instruction which I enjoin you this day is not too baffling for you, nor is it beyond reach. It is not in the heavens, that you should say, 'Who among us can go up to the heavens and get it for us and impart it to us, that we may observe it?" Neither is it beyond the sea, that you should say, "Who among us can cross to the other side of the sea and get it for us and impart it to us, that we may observe it?" No, the thing is very close to you, in your mouth and in your heart, to observe it."

"Army of the Egyptians and army of the Israelites:" What is that?

16 Beshalach   Exodus 13:17 – 17:16   בשלח   (pharaoh) let go (Israelites)

Historic evidence strongly indicates two separate incidents of Hebrew exodus from Egypt to Israel. Torah describes one single exodus. We make no assertion as to the reason for this difference. Characteristics from each are combined into one narrative. Throughout this book, each exodus and events between the two are explained from a strictly historic viewpoint. We do hazard an observation that the combination makes a more compelling retelling and that Torah makes no claims to historicity or timeline. That said, Exodus 13.7 begins with the second exodus. The first exodus involved the ten plagues and the eruption of Santorini. Before delving into the second exodus, we look at the time between the first exodus, which occurred in the sixteenth century BCE, and the exodus of Moses in the 12th century BCE. Then we consider the second exodus. So much happened in history between the two exodus occurrences that here in our examination of *Beshalach* only a few events will be mentioned, with more details to follow in later chapters. In the first exodus, a mixed multitude of Hebrews and their masters, the Hyksos who controlled Egypt, fled the devastation of plagues in Egypt. The Hyksos spread out along the Mediterranean coast from the Nile Delta to Syria. The Hebrews, on the other hand, headed for the hill country of Israel. Egyptians conducted a several hundred-year war of vengeance against the Hyksos and their Canaanite friends along the coast. This left the Hebrews, still called by the Egyptians Apiru or alternatively Shosu tribes, to freely establish themselves in Israel, inland from the Mediterranean.

The Hebrews who remained in Egypt enjoyed a great degree of freedom. The new Eighteenth Dynasty formed after the plagues included a series of powerful pharaohs

such as the female Hatshepsut, who took it upon herself to rebuild: "I have restored that which was ruins. I have raised that which was unfinished since the Asiatics (Hyksos) were in the midst of Avaris of the Northland, and the vagrants (Apiru/Hebrews) were in the midst of them… (Breasted Vol. II #303, p.125; Ryholt; *Speos Artimedos Papyrus* 148, trans.. part by Hans Goedicke and part by James Allen (contested translation).

Temple of female Pharaoh Hatshepsut >>>>

The female pharaoh continued, "This was the directive of the Primeval Father (literally the father of fathers, Nun the primeval water) who came one day unexpectedly." Hatshepsut appears to refer to the deluge. (Ryholt   Speos Artimedos papyrus 148 tr. part by Hans Goedicke and part by James Allen – contested translation)

In her statement, Hatshepsut recognized the difference between Hyksos/Canaanites and Apiru/Hebrews (*Breasted V II #303*, p.125 note d). Hence, Hatshepsut continued the Egyptian-Hebrew friendship, and a number of probable Hebrews worked with her and her successors. This included advisors and ministers who retained Hebrew names in the face of a general practice of giving immigrants Egyptian names such as later day **Phineas, or Pinchas** who accompanied Moses (*Brooklyn 35:1446 papyrus scroll*: Albright, *Northwest Semitic Names From Patriarchs II, p. 55;* Morris, *pp. 374-9;* Trigger, pp. 155-159; Morris; Snoden). **Ineni** (Here I am – *Gen.* 22.1, 27.1; *Ex.* 3.4, 19.9) was chief architect under four pharaohs. The high advisor **Yuya** (ya is God, *Ex.* 15.2) had a daughter Tiye who married Pharaoh Amenhotep III and had son Pharaoh Akhenaton. Tiye's brother Ay became pharaoh later on. This genealogy makes the famous Tutankhamen Yuya's great-grandson. **Yanhamu**, an Egyptian commissioner in Canaan must have been Hebrew (Albright, *Biblical, p.* 14). There are other examples.

Some Hebrew words that made their way into Egyptian included sus = horse; kamal = camel; abir = type of ox; rosh = head; sar = king; beit = house; bir = spring; birkat = lake; ketem = gold; shalom = hello or goodbye or peace; barak = to bless (Brugsch, pp. 76-77).

Even though Hatshepsut brought about a rejuvenation of Egypt's monuments and a renewal of its spirit, she did not eliminate the danger from Canaanites and Hyskos, who regrouped just east of Egypt and planned rebellion to recoup their power. (Ben-Sasson, p. 13; Albright, *Biblical* , p.31)

Egypt could not tolerate an adversarial Hyksos entity next to its borders. The successor to female Pharaoh Hatshepsut, Thutmose III, the "Napoleon of Egypt," reformed the Egyptian army and stormed up the coast. According to his annals, Thutmose captured over 300 cities clear all the way to the Euphrates, including Megiddo, Hazor, and Aleppo, making Egypt into an empire.   One of the first battles took place at the city of Megiddo, a conflict so horrible and bloody that it spawned the word "Armageddon." Two areas were spared destruction and defeat seemingly because they had no dispute with Egypt. These were Hebrew areas, one in the hill country of today's Israel and the other north of Byblos along the Lebanon-Syria border called Amurru.   Hebrews aided Thutmose in some capacities such as stationing Israelites in the Egyptian fort at the strategic Beth Shean city at the intersection of the Jordan and Jezreel Valleys. Thutmose listed countries which he conquered or over which he exercised domain. The lack of recorded violence and cooperation with Hebrews puts Joseph-El, Levi-El, and

Jacob-El in the category of voluntary – probably grateful – acceptance of submission. (Mazar, Garrison, p.152; Mazar, *Tel Beth*, *Armana* 289, Gabriel, pp. 41-175; Cline and O'Connor, pp. 370-391; Anals & Poetic Stele of Thutmose III in Lichtheim v II; Pritchard pp. 242-243).

Thutmose installed topographical lists with peoples of his ancient world that included the Tribe of Joseph El in the northern Galilee; Ard, a clan of Benjamin in Upper Galilee; and Shela, a clan of Judah's third son (Klenk, p. 19; Num. 20,26,40). We note again that these events took place between Exodus I and Exodus II.

Even though two Hebrew areas were spared the sword of Thutmose, over a period of several pharaohs the hill country of Israel and Amurru experienced a rebellion of Hebrews against autocrats because Israelites sided with serfs and sympathetic rulers against establishment warlords, mini-dictators, and remnants of Canaanite kings. Parts of this rebellion were thoroughly documented in letters between pharaoh and mayors or rulers. The letters are known as the *Amarna Letters* and will be reviewed in a later chapter. The friendly relations between Egypt and Hebrews continued for the long line of pharaohs that

Slaves of Ramesses II shown at his Abu Simbel Temple

began at the time of Abraham and continued with Pharaoh Ahmose of the ten plagues, who started the 18th Dynasty. Warm relations ended with the next dynasty, the 19th of Ramesses II, the pharaoh of the oppression. In conformance with developments covered in Exodus 13:17 – 17:6, this chapter will examine aspects of the Moses retreat

from Egypt leading to Sinai after Exodus I. We will return to details of the period between the two events of exodus in later chapters.

The 19th Egyptian Dynasty wrested power from a weakened 18th Dynasty with a move by military generals that excluded royals. Friends of the 18th Dynasty found themselves in trouble and subject to retribution by the new rulers, which led to the second Exodus led by Moses and his Israelite followers some four hundred years after the first exit.

When Pharaoh let the people go, God led them not by the way of the Philistines, …. God led the people about, by the way of the wilderness by the Sea of Reeds, and the children of Israel went up armed out of the land of Egypt (Ex. 13:17-18).

According to Torah, the route taken was more or less the King's Highway through the desert, known to Hebrew caravans since at least the time of Abraham. Due to the collapse of Egypt resulting from various wars, Hebrew civil war, profligate spending, and general oppression, Egypt's soldiers could no longer patrol this route.

Torah emphasizes the **military nature** of the second Hebrew Exodus. Before the act of Exodus, God proclaimed that army will be saved. Moses is told, "And ye shall observe the feast of unleavened bread, for in this selfsame day have I brought your **army צבאות** out of the land of Egypt." (Ex. 12:17) Translators often do not see the "army" in **צבאות.** "Israelites went up **armed** out of the land of Egypt. (Ex. 13:18). "the angel of God … had been going ahead of the **Israelite army**," "a cloud … came between the **army of the Egyptians and the army of Israel**." (Ex. 14:19-20).

Note that Hebrew weapons could have come from insurgent slaves; rebellious Nubians where Moses was viceroy; Syria; Hebrew Shosu, or Israel. Israelites quickly encamped at Etham, where they could cross a sliver of land between lakes and access the Sinai route to Israel. However, crossing into Sinai at that point would put them into flat, open territory with not even a hill for defense, and thereby subject to attack by chariots. On Divine instruction, the entire Hebrew community suddenly doubled back into Egypt close to the Via Maris, the highway through Philistine territory along the Mediterranean, amounting to a huge detour that put them next to a route also easily traversed by chariots. This detour at first glance appears to be folly. With backs to a Sea of Reeds, facing the main highway out from Egypt, they camped. The Lord said, "Pharaoh will say of the Israelites, 'They are astray in the land; the wilderness has closed in on them.'" (Ex. 13:20 – 14:20). Indeed, that appeared to be the case.

Lake Ballah, from Egypt.com >>>

But there is another interpretation of this course of action. Israelites had been travelling both the Via Maris along the coast and the Kings Highway through Sinai for at least a thousand years. They knew the necessity to avoid the coastal Philistines, and they knew that Egypt no longer controlled the King's Highway through the desert. Previously, Moses must have used the King's Highway when he escaped from Egypt and met Jethro. Hebrews also knew about the shallow Sea of Reeds. They knew that under certain tidal and wind conditions, the shallow waters would recede for a short while. That could be why Moses and God brought them to a seemingly hopeless encampment, namely to entice the army of pharaoh into a deceptive chase.

This amounted to a brilliant and risky military trap. "Then I will stiffen Pharaoh's heart and he will pursue them, that I may gain glory through Pharaoh and all his host; and the Egyptians shall know that I am God. And they did so." (Ex. 14:4)

As a side note, the literary craftsmanship and poetry in explaining the Israelite escape and the entrapment of the enemy army makes for what is assuredly one of the world's most dramatic narratives.

Torah reports that this plan worked perfectly with the guiding hand of God. The Israelites crossed during a night of high wind and tidal favor. As morning weather changed, Egyptian charioteers charged retreating Israelites only to find themselves vanquished as waters flooded back. In addition to meteorological and military explanations of the escape, the songs of Moses and his sister Miriam in *Exodus* 15 appear to be in very ancient Hebrew, possibly contemporaneous with the event. Also, thereafter, the Sea of Reeds was known as Lake El Ballah, the "Lake where God Devoured."

Miriam: "Sing ye to the Lord, for He is highly exalted;
     The horse and his rider hath He thrown into the sea."

Song of Miriam by William Blake 1840 – 1921

Not only did the Song of Miriam, but also those of Moses, and later Deborah, exhibit ancient Bronze Age poetic construction, and were so important to the history of Israel that it makes sense that they are essentially intact. (Ex. 15; re: ancient timing: Albright, *From Patriarchs* II, pp. 59-61; Cross and Freedman). In another indication of the ancient nature of the text, Torah is insistent on the military nature of the Israelite retreat. Concerning the effects of wind, British Major-General Tulloch witnessed the shallow waters of the adjacent Lake Menzaleh driven back by the wind for seven miles, leaving the bottom of the lake dry. (Drew, Kent, pp. 113-114,) The water of the Yam Suph or Lake Ballah, The Lake where God Devoured, can be seen driven back when there is a strong east wind, retreating so rapidly that shoals of fish are left dead on the exposed lake bottom, the sea is changed into dry land, the waves flow backward, and a way is opened through the midst of the sea, a practicable roadway for a host. (Weld, p. 295; Humphreys, pp. 244-260, who explains wind action but concludes it was at Gulf of Aqaba; Bonar, p.76 confirms shallow depth of lake systems; Chesney; Robinson; *http://www.bibleorigins.net/RedSeaCrossingExodusIsraelBallahLakes.html*)

The treacherous nature of the shallow lakes in and surrounding the Nile Delta have claimed many lives and pharaoh was not the only one to loose an army there. Lake Sirbonis, now called Sabkhet el-Bardawil, is a huge marsh lagoon on the northeastern border of Egypt, separated from the Mediterranean by only a narrow strip of land. Sand blows over the surface and make the water appear as solid land. This trap swallowed a Persian army, and an army of Ptolemy XII (Fadl).

Torah then explains problems incurred by Israelites in the desert route along the King's Highway which passed non-potable saltwater bodies known as the Bitter Lakes and the Red Sea. What to drink? (Ex. 15:22-24) History tells us not to worry. Small springs and oases sprinkle the landscape, many only known by Bedouin. Remember that Moses spent time with Bedouin and Shosu Bedouin allies who may have accompanied the Israelites.

Then there is the matter of no bread or meat and the resultant Israelite grumbling and questioning to Moses and Aaron. God provided a solution of manna from the sky, akin to a honey dew. (Ex.16:1-36). That honey dew is common in the Sinai, coming from a tree known as the manna tree, or tamarisk. Torah reported that Abraham planted a tamarisk tree in Beersheba almost a thousand years before the Moses Exodus (Gen. 21:33-34). A parasitic scale on the tree produces an edible honey dew. (Cannon; Kekker, pp.129-130; Albright, *from Patriarchs II* , p.63). But, then, there can be debate as to whether manna grew in the desert as an advance plan by God, or even if the Torah manna was a different sort, as there are multiple varieties.

Tamarisk or Manna Tree >>>

Torah relates other difficulties of the trip in the desert for Israelites that history cannot comment on due to lack of evidence one way or the other.

Speaking with God II

17 Yitro Exodus 18:1 – 20:23 יתרו Jethro

Torah tells us that Moses led the people of Israel into the Sinai, reuniting with his father-in-law, the Midian Kenite priest Jethro, his wife Zipporah, and his children. With advice from Jethro, Moses organized the Israelites into political groupings, based neither on primogeniture nor god-kings with absolute power but rather on meritocracy and piety. The Israelites continued their journey, stopping at Mount Sinai and remaining there until the push into Israel.   It was there that an intense religious experience occurred, including the introduction of the Covenant Code with the Ten Commandments from God.   Many reasonable people might think that after 3,000 years, ideas like "Do not Murder. Do not steal. Do not worship false gods" would be universally accepted. These commandments receive universal lip service.   However, quite a number of dictators today regularly murder journalists, political opponents, and inconvenient groups. These dictators, more often than not, have the powers of ancient kings, despise and oppress religions, and crush individual freedoms. However, in an early act of proto-democracy, Hebrews voluntarily agreed to accept God and God's commandments rather than have a system imposed on them by a ruler.   The Ten Commandments served as an introduction to an extensive set of laws:

Have no other gods before Me.
Make no idols.
Do not take the name of the Lord your God in vain.
Keep the Sabbath day holy.
Honor your father and your mother.
Do not murder.
Do not commit adultery.
Do not steal.
Do not bear false witness against your neighbor.
Do not covet.

History can verify key aspects of this moving Torah portion. Hebrews did:
- Escape Egypt, probably through the Sinai on the way to Israel.
- Create a religious creed that changed much world-wide religion, morality, and law.
- Leave evidence of a convocation near Eilat, in the area Torah calls Se'ir or Sinai.
- The religious and legal traditions of two Hebrew nations, Jacob's Israelites and Esau's Shosu, appeared to have merged at that time. (More later)
- Israelites and Shosu both appear literate and could have written down Sinai activity.
(More later)

In Torah, Hebrews attribute much of their inspiration and action to Divine instruction. We previously mentioned that there are several ways to view Divine communication. As a result of Hebrew Divine communication, history has been changed and idols, humans, and animal gods are no longer regarded as divine.

<<< Sinai desert scene   (Public domain)

History does review different interpretations on the nature of speaking with God. For instance, there is the observation that primitive roots for words like dâbar דבר or âmar אמר have many translations in addition to the traditional "say" or "speak." However, simple translations will not suffice for *Torah*. Other meanings include "commune," "think," "consider," and "determine." "Dabar" is also the root for the word "thing," as in "anything" or "everything." Amorite uses the same root as "amar." This opens the door to many secular and religious ideas in addition to "the voice from the sky" promoted by many film and popular presentations. "Dabar" tends to be a more stringent voice.

The Hebrew word "amar" is used in *Genesis* 1 when God created light, separated land from water, and created living creatures. Many of God's commands to Avram (*Gen.* 12, 13, 17) came using "amar," except in the Gen. 1501 vision where both verbs are used. Then with the giving of direct instructions to Moses in *Ex.* 25 and 30, "dabar" is used. In general, either verb can mean the whole gamut of translations. In stringent situations such as detailed instructions to Moses, "dabar" is more likely the choice of words.

In analyzing the significance of words associated with God, a deeper interpretation is offered by Rabbi Jonathan Sacks, whom we introduced a couple of chapters ago. He often advocated for a moral society based upon instructions from the Divine (Sacks, *Morality* and other Sacks books). He offered a very penetrating example of speaking with God, and at the same time, the companion question of whether the Hebrew experience is Divine destiny or chance and human genius (Sacks, *Vayikra*). Torah is packed with the plain meaning of the words that teach us morality, law, and responsibility. For those so inclined, deeper meaning is available with study.

And so, the first word in Hebrew of the *Book of Leviticus*, with instructions to priests, seems happenstance. However, the last letter of the first word is always written in a very small font, so can be ignored. It is the Hebrew aleph א. The word including the last letter is "Vayikra ויקרא". Sacks argues that this is deliberate. Ignoring that last small letter would yield the translation, "Moses dreamed of or chanced upon a Divine command." With that last aleph included, the translation reads, "The Lord called upon

Moses." To the casual reader who ignores the last letter, God's message is as in a dream and somewhat dependent upon human genius, so can be debated. The interpretation of "The Lord called…" concludes that God's message is strictly revelation, and should be studied. Note the major difference. The choice is up to the individual, the clergy, and the religion.

Of course, there is another way to look at the subject. One could conclude that the Bible is Divinely inspired but put into words by humans. A partnership of divine and human writing would allow for both study and debate. This is a question for the individual and clergy. Such an interpretation – putting Divine inspiration into words of humans with the possibility of limited debate – remembers the Hebrew idea of wrestling with God.

No matter the viewpoint, the resulting document, known as *Torah*, Pentateuch, or the Five Books of Moses, is believed by many to be the most influential and popular book ever presented to humanity, probably the most dramatic, and, if studied properly, the most morally instructive.

Although many thoughts on the matter have been offered, one other will be presented here. This is the idea of the Bat-kol, the literal meaning being, "daughter of a voice." *The Forward*, a periodical, offers an explanation:

> *Bat-kol is a unique Hebrew expression that has no real equivalent in other languages that I know of. Literally the "daughter of a voice," it goes back to early rabbinic literature, with two meanings. One is that of an echo . . .*

> *The second meaning of bat-kol is unusual. It is of a voice that may resemble an echo in its mysteriousness, elusiveness, or eeriness, but that is not an echo at all. Rather, as the Hebrew Eliezer Ben-Yehuda defined it in his 16-volume dictionary, it is "A voice that is heard as though out of nowhere, so that it is impossible to know whence or from whom it comes…especially as a supernatural voice that may reveal God's will."* (Philogos)

Some of the most transformational scenes in Torah history occur with dramatic backdrops and Divine conversations including the murderer Cain (Am I my brother's keeper?), Jacob wrestling with angels (Thereafter tribes are united as Israel), and Moses confronting the burning bush (Hebrews shall be freed to worship God and follow the commandments that changed the world). Remembering the use of poetry in Torah, another interpretation compatible with Rabbi Sacks is that these types of events were so overwhelming that only poetry can begin to describe an ineffable scene, so the poetic impact is more important than the descriptive version.

Hebrew Law Compared with Other Ancient Law

18 Mishpatim   Exodus 21:1 – 24:18   מִשְׁפָּטִים   Judgments

God begins an introduction of laws for Hebrews in this portion, presenting 53 of the 613 laws referenced in Torah. (The) *Mishpatim* הַמִּשְׁפָּטִים are judgments. Many are laws and moral statements that are quite relevant today, such as prohibiting enslavement of Hebrews (but permitting a six year indentured servitude); allowing the death penalty for human trafficking, "he that stealeth a man, and selleth him;" and freedom for an abused slave. For some time, Hebrews so revered their laws that they appointed judges to lead the nation rather than a king.

This portion on judgments and the previous portion containing the Ten Commandments contain a distilled essence of Hebrew instruction that so changed the course of human morality, law, and religion. Some are so basic that it is hard to realize their boldness 3000 years ago or that they are still not universal today - such as do not murder, steal, or worship idols. Some require study in order to realize the advances they represented in antiquity – such as restitution rather than revenge, equal rights, and protections for personal property. Hebrews lifted their laws above the purview of kings by accepting them as divine and then, in one of the most audacious actions in ancient or modern times, put them up for vote twice before all Hebrews, presumably rich, poor, slave, free person, warrior, and laborer. Other votes came later. Although not explicit on the subject, the vote does not claim to be for males only. Also, by inference, all eligible and willing voters were present, so voting fraud was avoided. (Ex. 19:5-9, 24:3-8)

The law chart below compares a small portion of Hebrew law with those of Hammurabi, Hatti, and Ramesses II. Because the Hebrew law is more comprehensive, only a portion of that law is shown. Notable is that Hebrew law requires kings to obey, while other law came from kings who were exempt and could easily reverse what was legal.

| Hebrew Commandments | Hammurabi the god king | Hattusili I | Ramesses II |
| All subject to same law | makes law | God-king makes law | God-king makes law |

LEGAL CONCEPT	LAWS OF MOSES IN MISHPATIM	CODE OF HAMMURABI	HITTITE LAWS HATTUSILI I	RAMESSES II EGYPT (no code)
Slaves/servants	7 yr limit	Debtors can be enslaved. The state has slaves.	Owner can buy and sell	Owner can buy and sell
Marry a slave girl	She gets full rights	No guidelines	Children are free, she gets full rights	Wife has rights
Murder	Death	Compensation	Heirs decide death or compensation	Death
Kidnapping	Death	Death	unknown	No guidelines
Involuntary manslaughter	Pay doctors and restitution	Restitution	Restitution	Flogging, forced labor
Killing a slave	restitution	Restitution	Fine	Permitted
Abuse of a slave	Free the slave	Fine	Fine	Permitted
Causing miscarriage	Compensation	10 shekels	5 – 10 shekels	No guidelines
Your animal kills	Kill animal	Fine owner	Fine incl animal that does damage	No guidelines
Your dangerous animal kills or destroys	Compensation	Fine owner	Compensation	No guidelines
Attractive nuisance	Compensation	No rule	No guidelines	No guidelines
Theft – stealing	Restitution + more	Death or fine	Compensation	Pay 3X, 100X, or death
Accidental fire	Restitution	No guidelines	Compensation also for setting fire	No guidelines
Embezzlement	Double restitution	5 X restitution	No guidelines	2X return
Damage while borrowed	Restitution	Restitution	No guidelines	No guidelines
Seduction of virgin	Marriage and pay bride price	Not clear - Payment or death	No guidelines	Death
Sorcery	Not permitted		Not permitted	Permitted
Bestiality	Not permitted possible death	No guidelines	Death	No guidelines
Abuse of widow or orphan	Possible death/ brother takes brother's widow	Payment for divorce	Brother takes brother's widow	No guidelines
Equal justice	Embedded in law	Hierarchy of class	Hierarchy of class	Hierarchy of class
Found goods	Must return	Must return	Must return	No guidelines
Bribes	Not permitted	penalty	No guidelines	Dismissal or degrade rank
False witness	Not permitted	From fine to death	No guidelines	No guidelines
hold escaped slave	Permitted	Death	Fine	No guidelines
Injury to person	Eye or payment	Eye for eye	Fine	Flogging

The imprint of the Hebrew patriarchs lies not merely on stones or parchments but rather on a far greater canvas, the conscience of humanity. Those who built temples, tombs, and towers also commanded armies of soldiers and slaves. In contrast, Abraham, Isaac, and Jacob built a foundation of faith based on human dignity, compassion, and opportunity. Hebrew or proto-Hebrew traders and craftsmen came to disdain the vicissitudes of warlords or king and therefore adopted the fairness and certitude of Hebrew statutes.

As the famous Rabbi Jonathan Sacks remarked, "The religion of Abraham is a protest against the will to power (Sacks 6)."

An agenda emphasizing freedom with responsibility opposed slavery from the beginning. The record on this issue is often misunderstood. From the most ancient times and into modern times, Hebrew and Jewish efforts have been in the forefront of anti-slavery sentiment. Torah and Hebrews have been the earliest and most consistent agitators for freedom from slavery.

4500 years ago: A group of outcasts accepted into their midst runaway slaves, ignoring laws mandating the return of slaves to their master. These outcasts were called "Apiru" or "Habiru," cognates of "Hebrew." (Ch.2; G. Thompson, pp. xi-xii; Wolfe, p. 17)

4000 years ago: Proto Hebrews, or "Apiru" continued to live on the outskirts of established monarchies, but had gained skills and a vast network for trading by donkey caravans as well as military experience to protect those caravans. As King Shulgi of Ur heard from his adviser, "Their encampments are wherever they pitch them, the decrees of Shulgi, my king, they do not obey." Proto-Hebrews continued to expand their ranks with runaway slaves, among others. (Wolfe, p. 2; ch. 2; William Albright, Patriarch to Moses I, pp. 5-33)

3900 years ago: Abraham, founder of monotheism, arrived in Israel with his entourage of souls, and later, with Sarah's "handmaiden" Hagar, sometimes misinterpreted as "slave." In Torah, the word עבד is freely used for situations denoting everything from chattel slavery to household employee. This is a pity, for the then new Hebrew language, recently introduced to the world, needed more precision. The admonishment against outright slavery is clear. It is also clear that Abraham's household manager, purported to be Eliezer, was an employee and not a slave עבד. The singular word עבד **appears** in Torah to describe situations that have multiple words in English:

Slavery: Know well that your offspring shall be strangers in a land not theirs, and they shall be enslaved and oppressed. Genesis 15:13

Employee, worker: So the servant put his hand under the thigh of his master Abraham and swore to him as bidden. Then the servant took ten of his master's camels and set out, taking with him all the bounty of his master. Genesis 24:9-10

Contract: I will serve you seven years for ... Rachel. Did not I serve with thee for Rachel? Genesis 29:18,25

Subjects to a ruler: And they said unto pharaoh: Thy servants are shepherds... come... to sojourn... Genesis 47.

Ruthless imposition, murder, genocide: Egyptians ruthlessly imposed upon the Israelites. When you deliver the Hebrew women, look at the birthstool: if it is a boy, kill him. Exodus 1.13-16.

Service: When thou hast brought forth the people out of Egypt, ye shall serve God upon this mountain. Exodus 3.12

Follower: Thou hast spoken unto Thy servant (God speaking to Moses) Exodus 4:10

Courtier: For I have hardened his heart and the hearts of his courtiers. Exodus 10:1

Indentured servant: These are the rules that you shall set before them: When you acquire a Hebrew slave, that person shall serve six years – and shall go free in the seventh year. Exodus 21:1-6

Bondage: Egypt, the house of bondage. Exodus 20.2

"Slaves" have rights: When a slave-owning party strikes the eye of a slave, that ... slave shall go free. Exodus 21:26-27

Worshiper: For it is to Me that the Israelites are servants; Leviticus 25:55

Work, worker: You shall observe a sacred occasion; you shall not work at your occupations.

Give refuge to slaves: You shall not turn over to the master a slave who seeks refuge with you. Deuteronomy 23:16-17.

3800 years ago: Escaped slaves were accustomed to find asylum with the Proto-Hebrew "Apiru," often on the other side of the border between the Hittite empire and the vassal sate of Ugarit, a practice forbidden as the runaways were, by law, supposed to be extradited. (Wolfe, p. 3; William Albright, Yahweh and the Gods, p. 86).

3400 years ago: In perhaps the first recorded revolt of slaves and serfs, Hebrews invite the people oppressed by Canaanite overloads to join in a freedom rebellion (Chapters 36, 42).

--My lord, Aziru (Hebrew leader) *took men of Qatna, my servants, and has led them away out of the country* (Freed slaves in Qatna and taken them to freedom with the Hebrew Amurru, EA 55 from Qatna near Damascus)

--All lands will be joined to the Apiru (Hebrews).... I am afraid the peasantry will strike me down. (EA 77 from Byblos)

--My peasantry long to desert me. (EA 114 from Jerusalem)

3100 years ago: Moses leads a revolt of slaves with allies such as the oppressed Nubians (Chapters 18, 25, 29, 36, 47, 50, 54, and others).

Egyptian slaves making bricks from tomb of Rekhmire, Wikimedia >>>

Though often misunderstood for thousands of years, they [the Five Books of Moses] bear the imprint of their basic authenticity in the events and situations which they describe. The Israelites preserved an unusually clear picture of simple beginnings, of complex migrations, and of extreme vicissitudes. – William Albright [founder of modern Biblical archeology].

Tent of Meeting Reflects Previous and Subsequent Designs

19 Terumah Exodus 25:1 – 27:19 תרומה Offering

"Speak unto the children of Israel, that they take for me an offering" (Ex 25.1). The Israelites prepared an altar and a tent of meeting in order to worship God and make offerings. Even though they were in the desert, the tent, or Mishkan, would need to be of the best material that could be collected. In this Torah reading, the design for the tent is presented.

Israelites gathered in Sinai/Seir, after a defeat in Egypt and a difficult journey through the desert. The most likely sites stretch along the historic King's Highway from Saint Catherine's Monastery in the middle of the south Sinai to the Timna copper mines just north of Eilat in Israel, a distance of about 120 miles.   The precise location of the Hebrew gathering at Mount Sinai continues to present a challenge to researchers. There is evidence of an ancient gathering and a tent of meeting at the Timna mining site in the Israel Negev. Particular details of events at Mt. Sinai are just as uncertain.   The Saint Catherine Monastery's leaders believe that Mt. Sinai sits next to their property. On the other hand, architectural findings give evidence that Timna sits next to Mt. Sinai. This evidence includes a temple to calf worship, remnants of a tent similar to the Hebrew mishkan, or tent of meeting, arrangements, and implements like a copper and gold snake such as the one held by Moses.

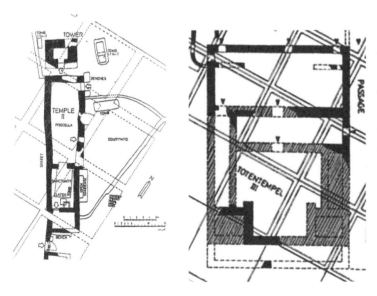

A plan for a worship temple evolved in the time of Joseph at his capital city of Avaris, before Moses,. The smaller one was probably at the time of Joseph and the larger, one of the largest in Egypt, was built when a son or grandson was vizier. Note the three sections of both, similar to the Moses tabernacle: a convening area, a sanctuary, and a holy center area.

Fr. Bietak, Avaris

Both the Timna and the monastery locations stand within the homeland of the Hebrew Shosu, but Timna is at the epicenter. A large gathering, particularly of an armed group, was not possible without the consent of the Shosu. Furthermore, Shosu may have assisted Hebrews in their revolution in Egypt. Either location, particularly the one at Timna, meant that the Hebrews then living in Israel could have sent representatives to the Sinai convocation. *Torah* attributes the formation of laws that would serve as a constitution for Israel as revealed by God at Sinai and that all tribes were present. For instance, *Torah* makes note that the clan of Shechemites from Shechem were present (*Num.* 26:31). To summarize, Shechem was acquired by the tribes of Simeon and Levi; was presented to Joseph as an inheritance from Jacob; had a third generation ruler by the name of Labayu who expanded the territory of Shechem during the 14th century BCE; and came under the governance of the Joseph tribes Ephraim and Manasseh. In certain aspects, the recitation of Torah and the evidence of history correlate so closely that Torah and history do not need separate explanations.

Torah speaks of Jethro, father-in-law of Moses. History has located a certain local tribe of Kenites inside the larger domain of the Simeon Tribe who were inside the Shosu who were then inside Esau's domain. All of these were in the greater area of the Timna mines where a relatively short period of Egyptian control had ended. Torah describes this area as Sinai or Se'ir, the Hebrew word for hair, namely the hair of Esau. Egyptian documents identify this as the homeland of the YHWH worshipping Shosu. Both Torah and history put Kenite priests and copper smelting operations there (Giveon, pp. 22-27, 74-77, 157; *Toponyms at Soleb*).

With all the tribes at one place, there had to be meetings. Torah confirms this, and architectural findings imply this. The Timna mines are close to Shechem, Jerusalem, and the Hebrew caravan routes so that it is easy to imagine representatives from the formative Israel. Of course, the Moses contingent also arrived. It was an important group. They brought the charismatic Moses, but he did not seek a dynasty. An entire army could have been present, and certainly leaders with the capability of assembling a military force were present. No wonder that, as Torah states, neighbors like the

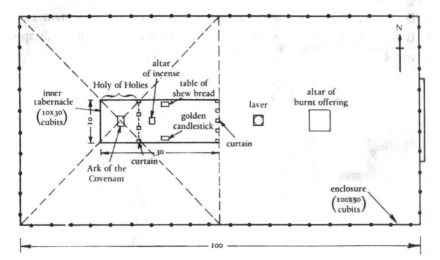

Shown is the design of the Tabernacle as described in Exodus 25-27. It follows previous designs made in the time of Joseph and later designs under Solomon and then the Second Temple (Plaut)

pastoral Edomite confederation felt threatened and so refused permission for the group to traverse their territory. Shosu, Shechem Israelites, and relatives of the Moses Hebrews all had roots in Israel. Unlike other groups with national aspirations, this one did not meet for the purpose of plunder, kingship, captives, or tribute. They wanted to worship YHWH, cast out idols, move to their indigenous land, and formalize their religion. They wanted to make a worship structure. Torah says that Hebrews engaged God as their architect. God drew plans for the dwelling, or tent of meeting. The plans called for a courtyard for sacrifices surrounding a tabernacle made of tent materials. It was definitely made of nomadic materials reflecting more the Hebrew Shosu tribe than the settled structures of the Hebrews from Egypt or from Israel proper. The layout can be traced back to Joseph. The tabernacle included an outer holy space with menorah and incense altar, and then an inner Holy of Holies room behind a curtain where the arc of the covenant resided. The architectural design of the Mishkan came with specifications including items described in *Torah* and found at the Timna site. Old habits stay with us. For example 20th century historic Rodeph Shalom synagogue in Philadelphia has outer community rooms, an inner sanctuary, and inner-inner holy space (today called the ark).

Recreations First Temple & interior in Le Temple de Jerusalem et la Maison de Bois-Liban by Chipiez & Perrot, then Second by Jerusalem.org

More recent but still historical Synagogue Rodeph Shalom in Philadelphia showing one of the community rooms, the sanctuary, the arc – no longer portable as in ancient times – and the arc opened with Torahs (author & RS site)

Priestly service in the *Mishkan – Tent of the Meeting*

20 Exodus 27:20-30:10 *Tetzaveh* תצוה You shall command   By Ellen Poster

Tetzaveh is Hebrew for "you shall command." At the very beginning of the portion, G-d, speaking to Moses, uses *v'atah*, meaning "and you," but the name Moshe does not appear anywhere in *Tetzaveh*. According to Rabbi Ephraim Mirvis, who succeeded Lord Jonathan Sacks as Chief Rabbi of the British Commonwealth, there is much to learn in the absence of Moses' name. He teaches, "Legacy has nothing to do with names. It has everything to do with impact...The name of Moshe may be absent but the Torah that he taught, the values that he imparted, they are with us to this day and that is the essence of legacy."

The *Ner Tamid* of *Tetzaveh*

The first act which Aaron and his sons were instructed to perform in the *mishkan* was to light the *ner tamid*. "You shall further instruct the Israelites to bring you clear oil of beaten olives for lighting, for kindling lamps regularly." (Exodus 27:20)   An article published by Temple DeHirsch Sinai, *Two Minutes of Torah, Tetzaveh* suggests that the *ner tamid* as described in our *parsha* isn't eternal at all. Rather, it lights the place where G-d and the Israelites would be in relationship "from evening to morning." The *ner tamid* was a "regularly" kindled light, "a glowing nightlight," rather than the eternal flame we now associate with the eternal light. According to Rabbi Berel Wein, the commandment to have a flame constantly burning on the altar of the *mishkan* actually appears in *Parsha Tzav* (*Lev.* 6:1-8:36).

The emerging religion of the Israelites perhaps influenced and was influenced by other great cultures and religions, or to look at it another way, how divine sparks were spread among many peoples. (See *Urim and Thummim, A Suggestion as to Their Original Nature and Significance,* by William Muss-Arnolt, *The American Journal of Semitic Languages and Literatures,* July, 1900.). For example, the *Book of the Dead* (circa 1550 BCE), whose title can be translated from the Egyptian as the *Book of Going Forth by Day,* is an Egyptian text to aid a person in the afterlife. A lamp lit from night to morning lights the way of the deceased. The tomb of Paheri, an Eighteenth Dynasty [1550/1549-1292 BCE) monarch of Kekhen, had a poetic description of this existence:

Your life happening again, without your ba [personality] *being kept away from your divine corpse, with your ba being together with the akh* [the deceased] *. . . . You shall emerge each day and return each evening. A lamp will be lit for you in the night until the sunlight shines forth on your breast. You shall be told, "Welcome, welcome into this, your house of the living."* (James W. Allen, [2000] Middle Egyptian: *An Introduction to the Language and Culture of Hieroglyphs*, Cambridge, UK: Cambridge University Press)

Both our *parsha* and the Book of Going Forth by Day refer to a lamp lit in the night that burns until morning. In *Tetzaveh*, the *ner tamid* has been compared with the creation of the world: "And YHWH said, 'Let there be light!' And there was light!" (*The Ner Tamid, What is this Light? Tetzaveh* by Rabbi James Greene). The *ner tamid* placed as it is in the *mishkan* has an aspect of the sacred. The Egyptian description of a lamp to aid in the afterlife seems to refer to the divine as well.

Fire is also sacred in the Zoroastrian religion, an ancient religion of Persia which may have originated as early as 4,000 years ago and still has adherents today. Its places of worship are sometimes called fire temples. Each fire temple contains an altar with an eternal flame that burns continuously and is never extinguished. This description of the eternal flame must remind us of the *ner tamid* described in *Parsha Tzav* and in use in our synagogues today.

The *Choshen* (breastplate), *urim* and *tumim*

Parsha Tetzaveh also deals with G-d's command concerning the garments to be worn by the priests of the *mishkan*. The breastplate (*choshen*) was one of the eight priestly garments worn by the high priest (*kohen gadol*) when serving the *mishkan*. It featured twelve precious stones corresponding to the twelve tribes of Israel. As described by Rabbi Yehuda Altein, the breastplate consisted of a rectangular piece of fabric (two zeres long and one zeres wide (a zeres is about 9 ½ inches) folded over to create a square. The fabric was woven from five yarns: gold cut into thread-like strands; wool dyed blue (*techelet*); wool dyed purple (*argaman*); wool dyed scarlet, and linen. The twelve gems set in gold were embedded into the breastplate, each inscribed with the name of one of the twelve tribes of Israel. The gems were arranged in four rows and three columns, or in three rows of four columns (*Minchat Chinuch, mitzvah* 99). Additionally, the breastplate contained the names of Abraham, Isaac, and Jacob, and the words *Shivtei Yeshurun* ("tribes of Jeshurun") thereby including all twenty-two letters of the Hebrew alphabet. (Alternatively, *Shivtei Yisrael,* "tribes of Israel." (*Jerusalem Talmud,* Yoma 7:3)

A piece of parchment upon which was written one of G'd's sacred names, (or a pouch with a small flat object or objects) known as the *urim* and *tumim,* was inserted within the folds of the breastplate. The purpose of the breastplate was to seek direction from G-d when there was a question affecting the Jewish community. The high priest would stand facing the ark, and a representative of the community would stand behind and ask the question. The high priest would reflect on the name of G-d, light would shine out from the engraved letters which would rearrange to form the answer [Altein]. It has been suggested that the *urim* and *tumim* could be used to determine guilt or innocence. The *tumim* is from the root *taf, mem, mem* ("innocent") and *urim* from the Hebrew word *arrim* ("curses.")

Assyriologist Muss-Arnolt refers to texts suggesting that the *urim* and *tumim* were a way of casting lots, perhaps two stones of different colors, one of which gave the affirmative and the other the negative answer to a question. He states that they have been compared with the little images of "truth" and "justice" found hung on the neck of the mummy of an Egyptian priest. Muss-Arnolt suggests that the singular forms, *ur(im)* and *tum(im)* can be compared with the Babylonian terms *urtu* (oracle) and *tamitu* (command). He also finds similarities between the *urim* and *tumim* and the Tablets of Destiny described in the Babylonian version of the creation of the world. The Tablets of Destiny were worn by the god Marduk on his breast when he presided at the assembly of gods when fate was determined and lots cast. Muss-Arnolt concludes his analysis by asking if it is not probable that the concepts of the Tablets of Destiny and the *urim* and *tumim* had common roots. He states his own belief that divine inspiration could be a gift given to more than one people.

The complete Hebrew name for the breastplate is *choshen mishpat, mishpat* meaning "judgment." In *Exodus* 27:30 we see that "judgment" is related to the *urim* and *tumim* that are part of the breastplate. Inside the breastpiece of decision you shall place the *urim* and *tumim*, so that they are over Aaron's heart when he comes before Adonai. Thus Aaron shall carry the instrument of decision for the Israelites over his heart before Adonai at all times." (See *The Choshen* by Rabbanit Sharon Rimon.)

Rabbanit Rimon suggests that the *urim* and *tumim* were fashioned by Moses at G-d's command, or perhaps the work of G-d, and were the Tetragrammaton - G-d's name, since there is no mention of how they were fashioned and the concept of "before G-d" is repeated twice in Verse 30. She concludes that the breastplate and the *urim* and *tumim* are reminders of the relationship between G-d and the Jewish people. There are references to the *urim* and *tumim* in *Leviticus, Deuteronomy, Numbers,* and *I Samuel* 14:41.

What were the identities of the stones and which tribe was inscribed on which gem? There are over 30 opinions. According to Rashi, the banner held by each tribe as it marched through the desert matched the color of the stone on the breastplate.

Here is a version ascribed to Rabbi Bachya ben Asher by Rabbi Altein. (The Sefaria translation identifies some other stones than those listed here.) We will explore later possible reasons why Reuben, Simeon, and Dan are so disrespected in the descriptions of the gem stone explanations when the gathering was supposed to be for unity.

Ruby and Reuben - Reuben slept with his father's concubine Bilhah. The ruby's red color represents Reuben's shame. (*Genesis* 35:22)

Prase and Simeon - The tribe of Simeon sinned with the daughters of Moab and Midian, causing their faces to turn pale, resembling the greenish color of prase. (*Num.* 25)

Carbunkle and Levi - The tribe of Levi transmitted the teachings of G-d as the Carbunkle's sparkle symbolizes the Torah's radiance. (*Deut.* 33:10).

Emerald and Judah - The green is reminiscent of Judah's pale visage when his father suspected him of murdering Joseph. The gem's radiance represents Judah's shining face when his father later praised him for saving Joseph from death. (Rashi on *Genesis* 49:9)

Sapphire and Issachar - The tribe of Issachar was renowned for its greatness in Torah study. The two tablets were formed from sapphire.

Pearl and Zebulun - The tribe of Zebulun engaged in commerce, amassing great wealth. The white pearl resembles the color of silver coins.

Leshem and Dan - The streaks within the leshem appear similar to a backward human face. This alludes to the tribe of Dan's "backward" conduct in fashioning an idolatrous image. (*Judges* 18).

Turquoise and Naphtali - Turquoise was carried by members of the cavalry. The closeness between rider and horse is associated with the name Naphtali, Hebrew for connection.

Crystal and Gad - crystals are widespread and the tribe of Gad was numerous.

Chrysolite and Asher - Chrysolite takes on the color of olive oil, a substance found in abundance in the land of the tribe of Asher.

Onyx and Joseph (Joseph's sons Manasseh and Ephraim) - The letters of the Hebrew name for onyx, *shoham* can be rearranged to spell *Hashem,* a way to refer to G-d, alluding to G-d's intervention when Joseph was in the home of Potiphar. (*Genesis* 39:2)

Jasper and Benjamin - Jasper has many colors. Benjamin had various thoughts about whether he should reveal what happened to Joseph to Jacob. (*Bereishit Rabbah* 71:6).

Conclusion - There was "an aesthetic dimension of the service of the Sanctuary. It had beauty, gravitas, and majesty...Beauty speaks to emotion and emotion speaks to the soul, lifting us in ways reason cannot do to heights of love and awe, taking us above the narrow confines of the self into the circle at whose centre is God." (*The Ethics of Holiness, Tetzaveh,* Rabbi Jonathan Sacks.) According to our sages and contemporary commentators, this centrality of G-d is the Tetzaveh message of the *ner tamid* and the *choshen, urim, and tumim.*

We don't worship the golden calf; what do we worship?

21   Exodus 30:11 – 34:35   כי תשא   Ki Tisa   When you count

Torah describes an unsavory incident that occurred when Moses was up on Mount Sinai obtaining tablets of holy law. Some of the Israelites crafted an idol, a golden calf, anathema to Hebrews, and began to worship it. The calf was one of many Egyptian idols – this one called Hathor. Moses destroyed the golden calf and a pitched battle took place between the forces of Moses and the adherents of the calf. The forces loyal to Moses won the day with many casualties to the opposing crowd.

The forces of Moses also won the heart of the new Hebrew religion. Hebrews would worship the only God and would do this by veneration of God's revelation of sacred testimony and instruction. The written covenant would be placed in the Arc of the Covenant (Ex. 25; 37:1-9; 40:1-7). Synagogues today have a Holy Arc into which they place one or more scrolls of the Holy Word. A scroll is taken out for services, read, and studied.

Torah follows the path of Moses and the Hebrew people. That path is consistent with archeological finds and ancient scripture. Evidence reveals the presence of Hebrews in the vicinity of the Timna mines just north of Eilat, within the modern border of Israel. The Moses group of Hebrews could have included freed slaves from various mines in addition to freed slaves from Egypt itself. Bedouin Hebrews of the previously described Shosu tribe controlled that area with the exception of one extended Egyptian incursion, and could host the Moses refugees. Moses enjoyed some safety within the desert because Egypt's power had collapsed, and, as a result, Egypt abandoned the entire area, including a number of mines and temples in Sinai. Most notable among the temples was the one dedicated to Hathor, the god calf/cow at Timna, specifically the Timna National Park of Israel (Rothenburg, chapter 22).

TIMNA HATHOR TEMPLE RECONSTRUCTION FROM TIME-LIFE BOOKS

Hathor the Egyptian god (Met)

With Egypt gone from Timna, the Hebrews moved in. It is quite possible that a convocation took place outlining rules of the new religion, rules compatible with existing Hebrew culture. Hebrews came with a mixed multitude. Some could have been deserters from the Egyptian army previously controlling the area, so it's not surprising that not all of the group were committed to the invisible God. Many doubting followers and nonbelievers could have continued to be attracted to the Hathor temple and its cult of calf worshipping. Evidence shows destruction of the Hathor Temple and an end to calf worship (Rothenburg).

Whatever actual event resembling the golden calf incident of *Exodus* 32 took place, it did not impede the Hebrew movement. But just after that incident, Torah raises one of its most profound questions, namely, what is the nature of the Hebrew God? And why does this God surpass idols? History, too, asks this question because the new Hebrew religion, propounding one God only and laws giving moral guidance was part of a world-changing revolution. To compete with and surpass established approaches to religion, namely idol-worship and no constitutional limit on kings, it was imperative that Moses and the Hebrews reveal something about this inscrutable, elusive, ineffable God. In a crucial small segment of Torah, scripture explained that the creations of God are visible and understandable, but the Hebrew God is not visible and not entirely understandable. Consider *Exodus* 33.12-23.

Question: What of God can Moses/Hebrews see? Moses appeals to God, "Oh, let me behold Your Presence!"
But the answer is, "You cannot see My face, for man may not see Me and live . . . you will see my back."

The back of God, i.e. creation: Galaxy (NASA) Field (Pinterest) Mountains (wallpaper)

These answers describe how this new religion will define itself.
Not to actually see a god introduced a difficult concept for that time. What could the back represent? It could represent the creations of God. Rabbi Abraham Joshua Heschel wrote of experiencing God through the awe felt in contemplating nature and the universe. However, not to see the face introduces the idea of something beyond human understanding: YHWH or

Hashem, the unknown and unknowable. "I am that I am." Or, "I will be what I will be." Human comprehension is limited, but God is not. Such ideas defined a new dimension for theology.

Question: What does Torah say that God will do for Moses and the Hebrews? Torah says of God, "I will make all My goodness pass before thee, and will proclaim the name of the Lord before thee; and I will be gracious."

As to the question of what God will do for the Hebrews? Jewish commentators offer differing opinions.

1. ***Not to change laws of nature but perhaps use or align them to help*** i.e. Manna is from the tamarisk tree. In providing manna in the desert, did God suspend the laws of nature of perhaps aligns them to provide a food supply for Israelite refugees? The same question applies to the Ten Plagues.

1a Guide for the Perplexed: It is impossible that there should be a change in the laws of Nature, or . . . a change in the will of God (as regards the properties of things) after they have once been established.

1b. *Zevach Pesach on Pesach Haggadah, Magid, First Fruits Declaration 18:1* Angels carry out laws of nature. Divine providence takes place when God uses the natural forces of the world to carry out His will.

 2. *God will suspend the laws of nature to help*

2a. *Avot D'Rabbi Natan 32:1* perchance they would notice it, be awestruck and repent; but they did not do so, therefore it is stated, "And it came to pass ... and suggest that God interfered with the order of nature, as laid down at the creation, in the hope that mankind would be awestruck at the phenomenon and repent."

2b *Legends of the Jews 3:2:52* In order to convince Israel of the unity and uniqueness of *God, He bade all nature stand still, that all might see that there is nothing beside Him.*

This discussion has parallels with previous presentations about speaking with God. History does not draw a theological conclusion. It notes the issues, the conversations, and the considerable results.

Hebrew ideas slowly permeated other religions, giving outsized attention to an undersized population, and a general process can be observed:

First, idol worshippers designated one idol as the sole god. The Egyptian Pharaoh Akhenaten, whose mother Tiye and grandparents Yuya and Thula were probably Hebrew, imposed the worship of the sun Re on his country in a religious revolution that was reversed by a counter-revolution of military forces.

Second, the concept of a superior god who ruled over subordinate gods gained traction, perfectly represented by the Greek king of gods Zeus who directed the Trojan war but lacks a humanistic set of laws, infinite wisdom, and unknowable origin. Several Mesopotamian gods also rule a roost of lesser deities.

Third, Greek thinkers proposed that, while gods still ruled, there was an intelligent design behind creation.

Forth, The attributions to a great divine were expanded, but the paraphernalia of multiple gods could not be shaken. The god Apollo spoke through an oracle written in stone located in the town of Oenoanda, then in Lycia, Greece, now in Turkey, "Born of itself, untaught, without a mother, unshakeable, not contained in a name, known by many names, dwelling in fire, this is god. We, his angels, are a small part of god."

Other attempts were made, like from the Stoic Cleanthes addressing Zeus, "God, being one, has many names."

Or apologist Apuleius, "It makes no difference whether we call Zeus the Most High or Zeus or Adonai or Sabaoth or Amounn like the Egyptians, or Papaeus like the Scythians."

(Athanassiadi & Frede, pp. 1-49, 81-92)

Zeus for Greeks or Jupiter for Romans – a monotheistic idol >>

But it does make a difference. Hebrews were very clear from the time of Sinai, "Hear, O Israel: The Lord our God, The Lord is one." (Deu. 6:4)

God is unknown and unknowable:" I am that I am," or "I will be what I shall be." (Ex. 3:14)

God has given laws to Hebrews and Christians also accepted them: "It is your God Adonai alone whom you should follow, whom you should revere, whose commandments you should observe, whose orders you should heed, whom you should worship, and to whom you should hold fast. (Deu. 13:5) This was qualified by Maimonides to mean that the laws of a land are respected.

Tent of Meeting rebuilt from discovery at Timna National Park

22 Va'yakhel   Exodus 35:1 – 38:20   ויקהל   And he assembled.

Torah explains that Moses was commanded to build a religious structure in the desert and not wait until their travels were over.

The southern Sinai and Negev Deserts are littered with ancient history pertinent to both Israel and Egypt. That south desert area can sustain a small population, unlike the central Sinai which is unbearably hot. Spotted oases and scattered scrub brush allow for a largely Bedouin residence. Beginning more than 5000 years ago, the area attracted traders like Abraham who preferred the Sinai route (between the Mideast and Egypt) to the route along the Mediterranean. One reason that traders favored the Sinai route known as the King's Highway was the vast quantities of minerals there, especially turquoise and copper. Copper fueled the Bronze Age. For centuries, Egypt controlled the western mines and the Hebrew Shosu tribal confederation controlled the eastern mines. The Shosu come from Biblical Esau. Egypt captured many Shosu mines, especially in the area of Timna and held them for perhaps a century. During the Egyptian occupation, a temple for the Egyptian cow or calf god Hathor was built. Turbulent times then triggered the end of Egyptian hegemony, the retreat of Egypt from both the southern and the Mediterranean trade routes, and the Hebrew revolt against pharaoh that led to the journey of Moses to Israel more or less along the King's Highway (Rothenburg).

The King's highway passes by the Timna mining area in the Negev within the Shosu homeland. Torah refers to the area as Sinai or Seir, home of Jethro, as well as the home of YHWH, as spoken by Moses.
YHWH, when you went forth from Se'ir (Judg. 5:4).
YHWH came from Sinai, and rose from Se'ir to them (Deu. 33:2).
"A Land where you can dig copper out of the hills" (Deu. 8:9)
 Artifacts found at Timna mirror the description in Exodus 35:1 to 38:20, known as Va'yakhel. Various persons, probably Hebrews, violently destroyed a small temple dedicated to the Egyptian cow god Hathor.

Hathor statue at Egyptian Museum and Artist depictions of the Tent of meeting (Time- life and Holman Bible 1890)

A more modest structure, actually a tent of meeting assemblage, took the place of the destroyed Hathor temle. (Rothenberg).

The Torah account of activities is supported with archeological artifacts at Timna. The timing of events is not precise. The Moses exodus could have included a number of separate groups, and events might have taken place in more than one location, but events and locations seem to have been combined into one recitation. This would be natural for the sake of compressing the story and focusing on the written document. Likewise, Torah goes into some detail about the ornate components of the Tabernacle and priestly garb. This description cannot be verified in part because of the artifacts. However, without doubt, Timna was a center of vast wealth due to copper mining. It imported many precious items.

As the saying goes, a picture is worth thousand words, and so here are some pictures of findings at Timna:

The copper mines at Timna produced plentiful copper, and Moses used it often. Ex. 35:5, 16, 24, 32, 36.18, 36:38, 38:2, 6, 8, 10, 11, 17, 19, >>>>>>>>>>>
Timna Park

==

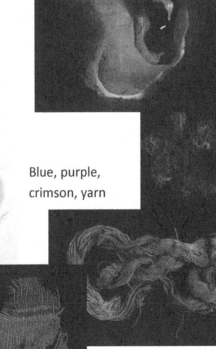

Blue, purple, crimson, yarn

and curtains *Ex. 35:6, 12, 23, 25, 36, 36.8, 11, 12, 15, 16,17, 36.35, 37, 38:9, 18,* *(Tel Aviv U & Is. antique Auth)*

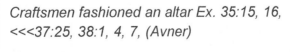

Craftsmen fashioned an altar Ex. 35:15, 16, <<<37:25, 38:1, 4, 7, (Avner)

Stones were carved and arranged Ex. 35:33 (Rothenburg) >>>

*Acacia tree Ex. 36:20, 31, 36, 7:1, 4,10,15, 25, 28, 38:1,6
pics below by author exc. Snake by jimdofree.com*
>>>>

Copper Snake found in naos / Holiest Place
of Midianite Shrine at Timna, with a
close-up of the head gilded with gold.

^^^^

*The Timna area showing the
rearranged stones probably of
Israelites, the geology, and a
simple Timna Park version of the
Tabernacle showing size but not
the ornamentation   vvvv   >>>>*

How the alphabet was discovered in time to record events

23 *Pekudi* Exodus 38;21 – 40;38 פקודי *accountings*

In this last section of Exodus, Moses has just dealt with the uprising over the golden calf, and then proceeded to construct the Tabernacle, or Tent of Meeting, according to the design of God discussed in the *Terumah* portion. In the present portion, an accounting of craftsmanship and materials used for the tent of meeting is performed. With their temple made of cloth finished, the Israelites were ready to offer sacrifices, have prayer meetings, and recite commandments.   Could they have written down the instructions from God? Did they need to memorize them? According to Exodus *17:14 and 24:4*, Moses was specifically instructed by God to write down God's commandments. We will seek evidence as to whether Israelites had possession of language and scribes to write down commandments of their religion.

What was the status of written language at the time? Before the time of Abraham, Sumerians were writing a type of cuneiform and Egyptians *<<< hieroglyphic wall covering*

used hieroglyphs. Evidence shows that Hebrew existed at that time, but not with its own script and was part of the Western Semitic languages spoken in the area of Syria.   The early Hebrew used cuneiform as a vehicle for writing and cuneiform tablets show discussion of mundane activities like baking and religious activities to "make a sacrifice to my God." (Aderet).   Researchers often refer to "Asiatics" or "Canaanites" when discussing events related to Egypt or Mideast history, and the speaking of Hebrew adds to the tools mentioned herein that separate Hebrews from other Canaanites. At the same time as the cuneiform tablets were written, Hebrews began to adopt their own script, and in so doing, invented the alphabet.   The invention started by selecting common hieroglyphic words and reducing the sounds of those words to letters.   For instance the hieroglyph for a house is a picture of a house plan. A house plan was used as a sound like the Hebrew " ב" or the modern "b."   The hieroglyph for a bend looked like an angle shape and

Hebrew Block-Letter	Projected Proto-Hebrew Original Letter	Middle-Egyptian Hieroglyphic Exemplar (Sign-List Number)	Original Hebrew Alphabetic Name (NIVEC Number)	Hebrew Consonantals of Middle Kingdom (*ca.* 1842–1760 BC)	Hebrew Consonantals of New Kingdom (*ca.* 1560–1307 BC)	Hebrew Consonantals of Iron Age - Canaan (*ca.* 1150–587 BC)
א		(F1)	*'elef* אלף cattle (477)			
ב	Sinai 92, 405	(O1) (O4)	*bayit,* בית house (1074)			
ג	Sinai 112	(O38)	*gāhar,* גהר bend (1566)			
ד		(O31)	*delet,* דלת door (1946)			
ה	Sinai 92	(A28)	*hālal,* הלל praise (2146)			

sounded like a "g," and so the modern Hebrew "ג," sounds like a "g."

The process of alphabet that led to most modern writing from English to Greek started in the Egyptian western desert on a supply and military route station called Wadi el-Hol. The favored date would be the reign of Amenemhat III, which began in the 19th C. BCE.   An earlier date could be possible because the presence of "Asiatics" in the area is attested before 1990 BCE when "Asiatics" helped place Amenemhat I on the throne.   The era covers the time between Abraham and the beginning of the Joseph era. (See ch. 3)

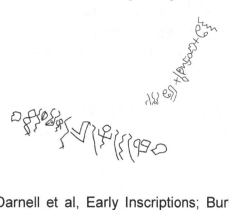

<<< Paleo Hebrew with interpretation in dispute, but the vertical refers to God possibly surrounding "the crooked one" and the other refers to wine and bread. An adjacent script refers to General Bebi, General of the Asiatics. Considering the location, he is probably a Hebrew. The name could be like

Bebai in Ezra 8.11 or Khebeded the Hebrew supervisor for mines in Sinai in ch. 24 herein, or Bedad of Gen:36:35.

(Darnell et al, Early Inscriptions; Burke, Amorites, 217-222;   Petrovich, World's Oldest, pp. 36-51; Rollston, Emergence, pp. 65-70, 75-76)

With a mere 22 letters, tens of thousands of words could be easily written by applying the principle of phonetics rather than the principle of rote memory used with hieroglyphics or cuneiform.   The Wadi el Hol roadway was used by troops, commercial interests, and travelers. At the time of Abraham a heavy use by armies was taking place as the new 12th dynasty under Amenemhat I was establishing itself by military force.   A large body of evidence attests to a significant Asiatic presence, one which we identify as proto-Hebrew. It is not surprising that the first alphabet, which is in Hebrew, mentions names that are Hebrew names, so we conclude that proto-Hebrew troops were in the Egyptian desert in the early 12th Egyptian dynasty. The Hebrew name (General) Bebi or Bebai can also mean fatherly, also a town in Judith 15:4. It is not hard to draw the conclusion it that was proto- Hebrews or Apiru among "Asiatics," who established a warm relationship with the Egyptian dynasty.   (Koller; Darnell et.al, *Early Alphabet*; author's conclusions).

NOTE: We discuss here the ethnicity of General Bedi/BebaiBedei and suggest that he and Khebeded in the next chapter are Hebrew, and, indeed, it is the Hebrew/Apiru language developed in the Sinai and the Hebrew/Apiru people who sojourned in Egypt before Exodus. Others have tactfully referred to "Asiatics," or "Cannanites," and we invite an inspection of evidence to determine relevant ethnicities. The following presentation of the Hebrew name "Beded, or בדד or בד or לבד   " comes from Abarim Biblical Dictionary. Petrovich agrees regarding Hebrew.

" The root בדד (*badad*) occurs all over the <u>Semitic</u> language area and signifies separation, isolation and more specifically the formation of a singular identity from a pinched off subset of a larger continuum. As a verb it may mean to disunite or divide into parts, or to go alone or act independently. It's used in the Bible a mere three times: and Psalm 102:7 speaks of a bird perched lonely on a house top, Isaiah 14:31 of a straggling soldier, and Hosea 8:9 of a wandering solitary donkey.

The derived masculine noun בדד (*badad*) means isolation, separation or exclusivity. It occurs more often than the verb and may speak of dwelling in isolation because of quarantine (Leviticus 13:46), mourning (Lamentations 1:1) or a quest for safety from violation (Numbers 23:9, Deuteronomy 33:28, Jeremiah 49:31). This noun may speak of a place or condition of untouchability where God places his people (Micah 7:4), or it speaks of the exclusivity of God to lead his people to safety (Psalm 4:8). Deuteronomy 21:12 reads: "The Lord *alone* led him; no foreign god was with him." Likewise Jeremiah 15:17 reads, "Because of Your hand upon me I sat *alone*, for You filled me with indignation."

The much more common masculine noun בד (*bad*), likewise, describes separation. It very often occurs in conjunction with the prefix ל (*le*), to or onto, to form לבד (*lebad*), meaning by itself, by himself or by themselves (Exodus 26:9, Judges 7:5, Isaiah 5:8). The famous statement of Genesis 2:18, "It is not good for the man to be *by himself*" uses לבד (*lebad*). Significantly, however, this noun does not so much describe a complete severance from its maternal medium but rather the formation of an identifiable entity within it. Our noun בד (*bad*) often occurs to mean part or part of, suggesting that there are more parts and that all these distinct parts together make up an integrated whole (Exodus 30:34, Job 18:13, Ezekiel 17:6).

Some scholars identify a second but identical noun בד II (*bad II*), which others (including us here at <u>Abarim</u> Publications) surmise is rather a specialized usage of בד I (*bad I*). It denotes the signature white linen ephod of the priestly class of <u>Israel</u> (Exodus 28:42, Leviticus 16:4): <u>Samuel</u> wore one (1 Samuel 2:18), <u>David</u> wore one (2 Samuel 6:14) and angels show up in them too (Ezekiel 9:2-3, 10:2, 10:6).

A third identical noun בד III (*bad III*), which may in fact again be the same one used specifically, describes speech that is notably separate from common human discourse: idle talk (Job 11:3, Isaiah 16:6) or empty talkers (Isaiah 44:25, Jeremiah 50:36). Note that the familiar <u>Greek</u> word ιδιωτης (*idiotes*) expresses a similar idea and literally means "in a category of their own".

The verb בדא (*bada'*) may have nothing to do with the previous (as scholars assume) but it may also be a continuation of the concept expressed in בד III (*bad III*). It means to connive (Nehemiah 6:8) or vainly invent (1 Kings 12:33), and is used these mere two times."

Paleo Hebrew to modern Hebrew:

is a house is Hebrew letter beit ב

is water is Hebrew letter mem מ

Agricultural calendar from Gezer in Istanbul Museum just after Moses

IT Is DECREED:

To his month of harvest;

to his month of sowing

To his month of last fruit gathering

To the month of hemp thrashing

To the month of barley harvest

To the month of (wheat) harvest and storing in barns

To his month of pressing (olives, grapes, etc.)

To the month of summer fruits

OF THE PRINCE OF GEZER (Gobiet)

By the time Moses arrived at Mount Sinai, the Hebrew language had already undergone a transition from pictograph to alphabet, indeed long before any other alphabetic language that is known, thus enabling an ease of literature new to the world and ready for an extended complex document such as Torah.   The system of deriving an alphabet from symbols probably contributed to the root system embedded in Hebrew in which one root is expanded into a number of related concepts and descriptions.   The root for "strong" can develop into words for "leader" and correlated ideas.   Hebrews and Hebrew writing skills were ready for the events in the desert that depended on writing in order to preserve them.   Roots could easily expand to encompass a multitude of expressions and common people could easily write.

Paleo Hebrew 1500 BCE from Sinai mine At Serabit el-Khadim meaning "Death to Baalt," feminine form of Baal. From Ancient Hebrew Research Center (Harris & Hone)

Let the writing begin for the Priestly Code

24 Va'yikrah Leviticus 1:1- 5:26   ויקרא   and He called (with instructions)

This chapter begins the *Book of Leviticus*, consisting of priestly instructions. The previous two books covered the early story of Hebrew patriarchs and their introduction of an entirely new plan for human relations. Their story, thousands of years old, has captured the attention of humanity like no other written work, especially considering that Hebrews had to create the alphabet in order to tell their story. After the narration of struggle, conflict, and a modicum of success, comes the moral of the sorry. Well, one could say, something over 600 morals when all the laws of Moses are counted.   Animal sacrifice played an important role for Hebrews at that time and instructions for such sacrifice begin the new book. The procedures for sacrifices were made generally available outside of the priest's quarters.   That was revolutionary 3000 years ago because Hebrews displayed priestly instructions to all who wished to view just what priests did, as opposed to secreting those activities in temples.   After the era of Torah, Judaism moved away from animal sacrifice and continued to modify ritual as it changed to a rabbinic religion. However, fundamental ethical concepts stated in Torah remain, such as obeying commandments, caring for the needy, and administering laws impartially.   This evolution is an example of exegesis, or ongoing development, preserving Torah essentials, but adjusting to contemporary realities.   A new alphabet with the potential for thousands of phonetic words is perhaps the greatest unsung miracle in Torah.

With a ground-breaking alphabet, the Hebrew language was able to create written manuscripts that could have let Israelites record happenings at Mount Sinai at the time of Exodus. Religious instructions were written and available for the newly literate people, as can be seen in the Ostracon from khirbet Qeiyafa below.   The activities of Abraham and his Apiru predecessors required literacy and math skills to conduct trade, investment banking, and legal activities. Joseph had a more developed rendition of Hebrew with which to conduct affairs of government, in addition to the use of hieroglyphs. With an alphabet used by the masses rather than only scribes, at the time of Moses, Hebrews had become somewhat literate and deserved the title "People of the Book."

At the time of Joseph and his mentor Pharaoh Amenemhat III ancient mines in southwest Sinai were the focus of intense operations to produce turquoise for luxury items and copper for the making of bronze. The most important of these mine locations was called Serabit el Khadim, a site that displays hundreds of written carvings on cave walls and stelae in proto-Hebrew, Hieroglyphics, and a mixture of the two. The authors of the writings at the mines and also, later, in Israel record everything from a simple cry to God, possibly from a slave, to more complex statements.

*Script at Sinai mine reads **From God**:
in Hebrew מאל , pronounced
"Me'el." The wave line symbol for water is
an "m" Sound. Ox head is an "e" sound in
this case, while the shape of a staff
represents an "L" sound: hence me'el.
 (Benner)   >>>*

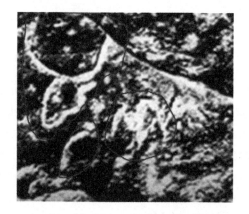

An important official had multiple visits to the mines scripted. The dignitary Khebeded, is featured in many places, and thus has gained a bit of celebrity in modern times. Khebeded is often referred to as "brother of the ruler of Retjenu (could mean Asiatics, Amorites, Apiru, Syria, Lebanon, or Israel)." His name comes from כבוד יוכבד, will be honored, as in Yokebed, mother of Moses, daughter of Levi. Khebeded's assistants seem have roots in Shechem and Damascus (Saretta, pp. 183-186, Strong's).

*Khebeded walking
with another official
(Goldwasser, Mists)
and riding on a
donkey (Petrovich)*

Petrovich sees the mixed hieroglyph as identifying Khebeded as an Apriru (Hebrew). Goldwasser remarks on Khebeded's duckbill axe, scimitar, donkey, hairstyle of Avaris leader previously identified as Joseph (ch.10) – things also in the immigrant parade from Beni Hassan mural (ch. 3). Goldwasser (Out of the Mists..) posits a close relationship between development of the Hebrew alphabet and Khebeded, although she and others diplomatically refer to "Sinai" script rather than the obvious "Hebrew" script. Multiple stele record visits of Khebeded over a decade. The Khebeded scripts are examples of positive representations of Amu, usually only done when those Amu are Hebrew.

The identification of Khebeded as an Apiru Hebrew is further enhanced by tracing his brother, the "Ruler of Retjenu." As it happens, the tomb of the brother, ruler of Retenu, Overseer of the foreign countries, and caravan leader, sits in the Hebrew city of Avaris as the largest in a small graveyard of nobles. Unlike Egyptian tombs, mud bricks form the walls, and, like apiru caravan traders, a number of donkeys were interned along graves. The Egyptianized name of the brother was Sebekemhat. He lived in the era of Joseph, about the time of Pharaoh Amenemhat III. (Groffrey Martin; Saretta, pp. 183-187; Lange-Athinodorou, Palace Cemeteries; Mourad, Rise, pp. 28-29; Petrovich, Origins, pp. 45-86,

Burke, the Amorites, pp. 207-216; Bietak, From Where Came, 147-150; Rollston, Emergence, pp. 65-70, 75-76)

That the early alphabet in the Sinai represents Hebrew has broad agreement. Due to the age and deterioration of the carvings, translations are usually in dispute. For instance, we look at the Hebrew on

the script known as Sinai 349 written in the time of Joseph, 19th C. BCE. The first rendition by (Goldwasser, Miners) depicts a difficult carving about a "chief miner.' In the second script, an amalgam of distinguished translators suggests that it says, "This is the equipment of the chief of the prefects. The apparatus for the work...brothers... ten captives, men of Arwad... " (Corlless). Then we have a creditable translation by (Wilson-Wright, Mat) that sees a witnessing of a promotion to a miner on behalf of Khebeded, ruler of Retinue, "O you who have returned, Mat has become chief of miners. He prepared for the Lady on behalf of the Brother of the ruler of ... an offering of a dove... an offering of... and offering of..."

<<<< *Other scripts from the same era. (Corlless):*

By the era of Moses, use of Hebrew had advanced. Calendars were written as shown in the previous chapter.

The shard to the right was found near Beit Shemesh at the Khirbet Qeiyafa antiquity site in Israel from the approximate era of Moses. Do we see there a practice writing practice exercise or a Biblical quote? Either way it shows the wide-spread use of Hebrew is Israel at the time. Demsky (Demsky, Writing Exercise) takes the minimalist approach using words like "goddess, slave, gods, ruler, alien, men, and judge." (Tsur) agrees and places the date of the writing possible before Moses. (Galil) takes a maximum approach with the following:

1' you shall not do [it], but worship the [Lord].
2' Judge the sla[ve] and the wid[ow] / Judge the orph[an]
3' [and] the stranger. [Pl]ead for the infant / plead for the po[or and]

4' the widow. Rehabilitate [the poor] at the hands of the king.
5' Protect the po[or and] the slave / [supp]ort the stranger.

Torah itself gives evidence of literacy: *And the LORD said unto Moses: 'Write this for a memorial in a book* (Ex. 17:14). *Moses wrote down commandments (Ex.24:4). The Lord said to Moses, "Write down these commandments." (Ex. 34:27) "Moses recorded the stages of their journey" (Num. 33:2; Colles).*

The background of the Hebrews demanded multi-lingual literacy. By reading and writing in various languages, they conducted international business in trade, in contracts, in investment banking, and in manufacturing. Joseph and his associates needed literacy to run government, design canals, and perform accounting. In addition, even though there were Hebrew scribes, the Hebrew alphabet democratized literacy. Rather than memorize thousands of symbols for a language, a person could write phonetically, so, as seen, even slaves could do some writing. With such tools of literacy, more complicated ideas could be put to paper or to stone, including ideas like the Hebrew religion with its laws.

Moses, as an Egyptian prince, could surely write. Egyptian inscriptions identify the Samath clan, a family of Kenite scribes. These were Shimeathites from tribe of Simeon, referred to as Kenite scribes and sons of Jethro (*I Chron.* 2:55, *Sanhedrin*, 104a:2; *Jerusalem Talmud Shkaliim*, 5:1:4 and elsewhere). Egyptian inscriptions in the Sinai desert also include references to the Hebrew scribes Lua (Levi), the Asiatic Werkherephemut, Rafi, Dedia, Hori, Oz-Romem, Hophni, Pinhas, Pashhur, Ben-Azan/Adon, Ye'uel (Avner, *Desert*). However, records of any words written at Mount Sinai did not survive the ages. Research using linguistic techniques concludes that Torah may have received revisions at the time of Josiah and Ezra, but this is not known. Research also confirms that some of the Torah teaching was present in Hebrew inscriptions and culture at the time of Sinai and before. It is not known how much writing was on papyrus (Avner).

Identification of the above scribes as Hebrew and similar identification of others as Hebrews follows procedures. There is no agreement with the outcome. Too often, researchers will refer to "Asiatics," "Canaanites," or West Semites without attempting to further define just what group is referred to. Because so much of the history covered relates to the Hebrew experience, a greater effort should be made, and here we have made that attempt. There are several methods used in determining the ethnic background of a person, and none of them is perfect. A combination of a name known as belonging to a particular group, pictured clothing of a person, activities of a person, self-identification, and identification in documents are all ideal methods. The scribes above were investigated (Avner), and that helps clarify the relevant history.

Avner along with others observed names that were written on stelae in "proto-Sinaitic script," which is another word for proto-Hebrew. Avner described the names as "Asiatic" and wrote several of them using modern Hebrew, which is to say they were most likely Hebrew persons. Other indications point to Hebrew identities such as pictures on stelae. Still more indications would be the use of a person's name in other Hebrew documents such as Torah, other parts of the Hebrew Bible (aka *Tanakh*), extra Biblical documents using a name together with a Hebrew identification, and references such as *Strong's Hebrew Dictionary* or *sefaria.org*. For instance, with regard to the scribes above, Ye'uel **אואל ,** which means will of God, was a son of Bani (*Ezra* 10:34), and forms part of the names Samuel, Shmuel, and Ruel. Another is the scribe Hori (tribe of Simeon, father of Shaphat *Num.* 13:5, related to Ben-hur, Hiram, Nahor, Haran), whose name appears on other stelae in the Sinai mining area of Serabit al-Khadem. He lived in the time of Moses and wrote a satirical letter criticizing another scribe.

This approach has great limitations in that many immigrants to Egypt obtained Egyptian names, pursued Egyptian careers, and lacked the status for lasting documentation. This story is oft repeated with immigrants throughout the ages.

Treasure trove of proto-Hebrew stelae at the Serabit al-Khadem mining area (Trip Advisor) >>>>
Below from Benner:

119

What did the Original Torah Contain ?

25 Tzav Leviticus 6:1 – 8:36 צו command

The Hebrew people who gathered at Sinai and who otherwise made their way to Israel were already, to a degree, observant of the laws of God. They were definitely not a pagan illiterate group who were suddenly exposed to the notion of a Single God and all the commandments of that deity. Hebrews already were accustomed to obeying many laws that were accepted at Sinai. New laws were revealed at Sinai, and organization of known laws and practices could have taken place. However, in addition to revelation, the monumental achievement at Sinai was the acceptance of Torah by vote (Ex. 24:3) and the codification of laws. Torah makes this point in the first of many votes. The idea that a people could vote on laws was indeed historic. Torah at Sinai contains history, poetry, and various other forms of literary technique that were at Sinai or elsewhere such as the song of Miriam, the blessings of Jacob, and stories of Abraham. Also, before Sinai, the Hebrew history of Abraham, Isaac, Jacob, Joseph, was certainly already known.

We therefore propose that the importance of Sinai rests on several pillars, which include:
a code of behavior extensive and unique enough to influence the development of a modern civil society, revelation, acceptance by democratic vote, codification of law, acknowledgement of One God, and coalescing of the tribes. As wide-reaching as the Torah is, everything might not have been first revealed at Sinai. However, the extent that Israelites already practiced many of the laws made them ready to accept the Laws of Moses.

Here are some Hebrew practices prior to Sinai:

Belief in One God had been fundamental to Hebrew instruction since Abraham as stated in Torah; also as stated in Egyptian lists at Soleb, Medinet Habu, Amara, and Manetho; and also in Greek texts referring to the Hebrew belief in One God, often in disparaging remarks, from the likes of Strabo, Diodorus, Eusebius, Tacitus, and others.

Existing commandments include, as a sample:

- Oral laws known before written laws were observed –Gen 26.5
- Only One God – Ex. 10:18, 8:6
- No murder – Gen. 4:8-12, 15, 9:5,6; Ex. 20:13
- Dowry – Gen. 34:12; Ex. 22:16
- No stealing – Gen. 30-33.; 44.1-17.
- No idolartry – Gen. 1.26; 21:37; 31:32,35; 35:1-4
- No adultery – Gen. 12:18, 20:3, 9; 26:10, 11:38, 39:4-9.
- Covenants – With God, Gen. 6:18, 15:1-3, 15:18   Between people, Gen. 21:22-33; Gen. 29:15-29.21 (Laban's broken covenant led to problems);   Gen. 38:17-26.

- Sabbath – Gen. 2:3; Ex. 16:23; Gen. 16.
- Respect of parents – Gen 28.6-7.
- No false witness – Gen. 4
- No eating of blood or of a live animal – Gen. 9:4-5
- Work for a living – Gen. 3:17-19.
- No rape – Gen. 19:6-8, 34
- Passover instructions – Ex. 12.
- No incest – Gen 2:24, 21:25
- Set up courts – Ex. 18:21-24
- Impartial judges – Ex. 18:21-24
- Personal liability Ex. 22
- Treat Strangers fairly - Gen:18
- Protection of widows & orphans – Gen. 38:8
- Honesty in business – Ex. 15:26
- Humans must work for a living – Gen. 3:19
- Slaves have rights and chance for freedom – Gen. 17:10-15; Ex. 1- 10.

Also the Hebrew experience with business caused them to set up courts, and deal fairly. Courts are clear evidence of the power of law. Early Hebrews, Apiru, set up trading cities, or port authorities that were each administered by a college of Judges headed by a overseer of merchants (Albright , From Patriarchs I, p. 7). Laws and contracts were not only known by Hebrews, but also the existing city states. Records show contracts to rent or sell land; and to create commercial loans with interest. Rulers enacted laws dealing with both commercial and criminal issues that appeared in Torah, albeit in a more simple form. An example is the Hammurabi code, which deals with theft, murder, debt, slander, marriage, and construction. (Renger; especially p, 190; Mark, *Trade*)

The assemblage of Hebrew law into Torah gave access to it's contents to common people as well as priests. In *Parashah Tzav*, the Lord continues to instruct priests. Today, the elaborate sacrifices of animals have largely been replaced by prayer due to the transition to rabbinic Judaism. With this in mind, history asks just what written Torah looked like at Sinai and what, if anything, happened with the content since then. As shown, history and archeology have evidence showing that Hebrews did assemble in the desert, that they did have the language skills to write a document such as Torah in proto-Hebrew. *Az-romem (who the Mighty One elevates) the expert in writing (scribe, fr. Wimmer, about the time of Moses)* >>

The emergence of the Hebrew language and the Hebrew God were connected. God forbade graven images, and an alphabet was needed to accomplish this. The abstract concept of a largely invisible God required a language based on abstract symbols and a people capable of understanding abstraction. By the time of Moses, any number of scribes, or even Moses himself, could have done the recording. By then Hebrew had spread to Biblos, also a Hebrew stronghold (Ouaknin, pp. 44-47, 103, 318-352). Az-romen, whose proto Hebrew signature is shown, represents an example of a Hebrew scribe.

Today, there are many variations of Torah and Bible, both in the Jewish and Christian religions. Was there an original version at or about the time of the Moses exodus to Israel ? Quite possibly.

Timna, with its copper mines and Biblical friendly artifacts, is one nomination for an Israelite convocation. A large number of individual mine shafts dot the area. (Reinhart, Pinterest)

After apparently suffering a disappearance, Torah reports its own reclamation. Whether this represents a symbolic loss or an actual loss is not known. Before 600 BCE, "Hilkiah the high priest said to Shaphan the scribe, "I have found the Book of the Law in the Temple of the LORD." (*2 Kings* 22:8; *2 Chronicles* 34:15) He read in their ears all the words of the book of the covenant which was found. (2 Kings 23.2,) And the inhabitants of Jerusalem did according to the covenant of God" (*2 Chronicles* 34:32).

"Book of the Covenant," "or "Covenant of God" generally refers to *Exodus* 20.:19 – 23:33, the Covenant Code, as distinguished from *Leviticus* and its *Priestly Code*, or *Deuteronomy* and its code which is more a national code. Intense scrutiny of Biblical writing has suggested different styles and possibly different authors. *Genesis* contains structure allocated to an "E" scribe who referred to God as Elohim while displaying bias to Aaron and Israel. A "J" scribe refers to God as YHWH while indicating more sympathy to Moses and Judah. The renditions are very similar within *Genesis* and *Exodus*. Since both versions are shown together and alike, rather than redacted, the result can be taken as an indication of their antiquity. As students of history, we conclude that one or more persons could have recorded events at Sinai. At that time or shortly thereafter the northern tribes and southern tribes disagreed on minor details. (Gabel & Wheeler, Metzger & Coogan, Friedman) Later, the two version would have been combined.

Leviticus, a document of priestly instructions, and *Deuteronomy*, a national codification for Torah, display different writing styles and content. However, they both continue the culture of *Genesis* and *Exodus* such as:

Ye shall keep My Sabbaths...Turn ye not unto the idols, nor make to yourselves molten gods.... Ye shall not steal; neither shall ye deal falsely, nor lie one to another...Thou shalt not oppress thy neighbor. (Lev. 19)

Hear, O Israel, The Lord our God, the Lord is One.... These words...shall be upon thy hearts...thou shalt teach them,... thou shalt bind them for a sign upon thy hand (Deu. 6:4-9) A repetition of the Ten Commandments (Deu. 5)

Early examples of Hebrew script come with controversy. Here is the writing on the carving known as Sinai 353 showing complete thoughts in 1500 BCE as rendered by Colless >>>

Provided here are a few interpretations. In general, some translations of Hebrew are quite secular, and while sometimes appropriate, such a literate and God loving people would naturally have religious quotes from the beginning of writing.

1. *Clear away this [false goddess], O travelers. This is shameful! Remove yourselves from Ba'alat [Hathor]! (Bar-Ron, Exodus)*
2. *It is a time to be hopeless. The lady (Baalath) ha organized for battle. We banded together to remain with heads held high. We celebrated a festival of the sun, which came out in order to hold us back. – (Petrovich, World's Oldest p. 129)*
3. *This is the metal-melting furnace beloved of Baalath. This is the garden of Shamash, an irrigation field, for gathering (provisions) In this garden gather provisions.(Colless)*

The last two books of Torah have their own areas of concentration. In particular are the minute priestly instructions for dress, sickness, and sacrifice in *Leviticus*. *Deuteronomy* includes details of the Israelite experience including information about the death of Moses and identification of the Arabah as one area of gathering. Timna is in the Arabah. *Deuteronomy* does form a natural extension of earlier instruction in the first two books. Many commentators say that *Leviticus* and *Deuteronomy* were written or rewritten by later officials. Ezra, coming back to Israel after a destructive war and exile to Babylon is a candidate for rewriting.

If extant versions of Hebrew are the pinnacle of literary expertise at the time of Moses, it would seem that original Torah was either in compact poetic form such as the songs of Moses, Miriam, and Deborah or the Ten Commandments; or that detail was oral for some time; or that detail was filled in later; that a multi-lingual approach was taken, or, of course, a gift from God.

Which Instructions were actually followed 3000 years ago?

26 Shemini *Leviticus* 9.1 – 11.47 שמיני Eight Days

After a number of sacrifices and seven days of consecration, Aaron and his sons emerged from the Tent of Meeting. They made preparations for a sin offering of a bull calf and a ram.

The laws promulgated in the Torah attributable to Sinai and God represent the most extensive set of written laws in existence in the 12th century BCE that this research can locate. This brings up a number of questions, but first note that the dietary laws represented in Shemini, Leviticus 9.1 – 11.47 give a glimpse into how laws were presented and their detail.

Moses said that the Lord commanded:

To Aaron: Take a bull-calf for a sin-offering and a ram for a burnt-offering. 9.2

To Israelites: Take a he-goat for a sin-offering and a calf and a lamb for a burnt offering 9.3,8

> An ox was for a peace offering and an offering of meal and oil. (Israelites eat calf, while Egyptians worshipped a calf.

Further instructions pertained to the kidneys, the liver, the flesh, the skin, the head, how to wash, and burning of fat.

Fire consuming the burnt offerings signified consumption by the Lord.

Israelites could eat: beasts that both had cloven hooves and chewed their cud; only fish with fins and scales; a limited number of birds; and certain insects.

There are a number of rules for other animals and for pots that have touched unclean animals.

The level of detail in the dietary rules also applies to considerations of cleanliness or quarantine. The Talmud doubles up on many of these rules. All the laws amount to quite an extensive array and require a number of consultants or priests and tremendous education. There is also the question of whether a poor rural farmer or indigent laborer was expected to follow all the laws.

An old tale relates how the Israelites, after Sinai, hastily departed so that they would not be given any more laws (Ginzberg, *Legends*, 3:242).

In order to understand the historic ramifications, the first step is to identify the three separate codes in the Torah. The Covenant Code comes from *Exodus* 20-23 and includes the most basic of laws like the Ten Commandments. Then in the next book, the Holiness Code of *Leviticus* 19-25 is dedicated to priestly instructions. Finally, in the last Book of Moses, the Deuteronomy Code sets up laws for a nation. Each accents different aspects of social behavior and has a different writing style. The Torah states that all three codes emanated from God via Moses during Exodus. We will discuss this in another presentation. Torah, however, separates these codes into the three mentioned books (Walzer, *Code*).

So Torah presents us with three codes addressing three different ideas for Israelites, and this brings the discussion back to question whether a poor rural farmer or indigent laborer followed the laws. At the time, Israel was a developing nation, fighting wars, facing poverty, recovering from a lost revolution, bringing various parts of the Hebrew alliance together, and still establishing itself.

Our conclusion is that only the Covenant Code enjoyed a large degree of adherence in the period following Moses, and even that code required extra-ordinary enforcement.

Evidence for this conclusion comes right from Torah. Joshua and Kings, make virtually no mention of the codes from Leviticus or Deuteronomy. Besides fighting off enemies intent on destroying the nascent nation, both the leadership and the Lord faced a major task in eliminating both idol worship (i.e. Judges 2:11-23, 3:7) and theft (*Josh.* 7.1). Better success occurred in making sacrifices on altars, since God had proclaimed that even an earthen altar was acceptable (*Josh* 8:30), and in observing Passover (Josh 5.10-12). Joshua read aloud "all the words of the law, the blessing and the curse, according to all that is written in the book of the law (Josh. 8.34 We take "book of the law" to mean the *Covenant*.). Even though the worship of God exclusively was uneven, it seemed prevalent (Josh. 24:21-24). Finally, in Samuel, priests began perform religious duties, which opened the door to the *Leviticus Code*..

In a plain manner, the Exodus Covenant Code presents the most straight-forward of the codes. It includes the Ten Commandments; forbids kidnapping; gives laws of personal injury; places limitations on slavery; mandates control of animals; demands equal justice; provides directions for festivals, and provides a prohibition against rape – usury – bribes – or oppressing the weak.

THE TEN COMMANDMENTS

I
I AM THE LORD YOUR GOD. YOU SHALL HAVE NO OTHER GODS BEFORE ME

II
YOU SHALL NOT MAKE FOR YOURSELVES AN IDOL

III
YOU SHALL NOT TAKE THE NAME OF THE LORD YOUR GOD IN VAIN

IV
REMEMBER THE SABBATH DAY, TO KEEP IT HOLY

V
HONOR YOUR FATHER AND YOUR MOTHER

VI
YOU SHALL NOT MURDER

VII
YOU SHALL NOT COMMIT ADULTERY

VIII
YOU SHALL NOT STEAL

IX
YOU SHALL NOT GIVE FALSE TESTIMONY AGAINST YOUR NEIGHBOR

X
YOU SHALT NOT COVET

Exodus 24:7 explicitly underscores the Covenant Code when Moses, before ascending the mountain, "took the *Book of the Covenant* and read it to the people. They responded, 'We will do everything the Lord has said; we will obey.'" Moses read from the *Book of the Covenant*, and not from the Leviticus Priestly Code or the Deuteronomy National Code. In perhaps the first time in known history, a people voted for the laws of governance. Democracy was born.

So it is plain that for some time the Israelites concentrated on the Covenant and not the other codes. How is it that the codes are separated neatly into three parts, with some duplication, and very little coordination? Walzer proffers an explanation that Israelites were not allowed to change God's law, unlike the law of kings or assemblages or constitutional conventions. The Covenant could not be changed, only added to, and likewise, the Leviticus Priestly Code could not be changed, only added to. This very neatly preserves the historic evolution of Torah. Walzer refers to Deuteronomy 4:2 to explain his theory: "You shall not add anything to what I command you or take anything away from it, but keep the commandments of the Lord." This does not contradict the contention that all laws were presented at Sinai, even if in separate batches.

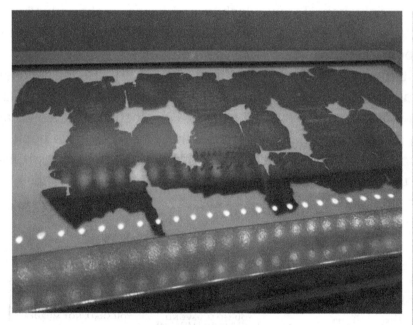 

Dead Sea scrolls Torah at Israel Museum (Author)   *Rothschild Torah at Getty 700 years old*

Hebrew Medicine – A slow start but eventually becomes a leader

27 Tazriah Leviticus 12:1 – 13:59 תזריע Delivering (a child)

Parsha Tazria introduces the concepts of *tumah* and *tahara*. Some translate them as "cleanliness" and "uncleanliness," some say "ritual purity" and "impurity," so there is a range of interpretations. The words are best understood in the context of the Hebrew language and are unique. In general, *tahara* is associated with "enduring forever," "everlasting," and "never deteriorating." *Tumah* is the opposite; it stands for mortality, ephemeral, or finitude. *Tumah* represents decay in the sense of a corpse or something wasting (A. Weiss). These concepts are introduced in the context of the medical aspects of childbirth, which has aspects of the continuity of life, and, sometimes the end to an individual life. They are concepts inherent in Hebrew culture, but exact translations elude us.

Tahara and *tumah* relate to two major medical concerns of the day, namely leprosy and childbirth. Some of the treatments, like quarantine and cleanliness, seem positive. Some treatments, like sacrifice (Lev. 14:10-20) and cleaning with bird blood (Lev. 1:.3-7) were not only without merit but prevented constructive medical research.

The propensity in those early days of the Israelites regarding medicine was 1) to regard the Divine as the ultimate healer as in "I am Adonai, your healer;" (*Ex.* 15:26); 2) sacrifice as a legitimate cure (Lev. 12:6-8, 14:10-20), and 3) wickedness as a cause of disease as in "if ye will not hearken unto Me, and will not do all these commandments, and if ye shall reject My statutes…. I will appoint terror over you, even consumption and fever, that shall make the eyes to fail…" (Lev.26:14-16).

Hence, the emergence of medicine took some time for the Israelites. King Asa of Judah (~ 900 BCE) was chastised because "in his illness he sought not God but rather

physicians." But, by implication, the art of medicine had begun for Israel. It took the physician/philosopher/ scholar Maimonides to solidify the place of rational thinking within medicine. He wrote on medical aphorisms, poisons, coitus, causes, symptoms, treatments, hemorrhoids, & asthma (Bos)

Ipwy Tomb

127

Egyptians developed early medical treatments, although they did not have a distinction between rational science and magic. Very early records of medical care coming from Egypt, utilize both prayer and herbs. The process of mummification enabled them to learn about the human body and this knowledge transferred to medical techniques. These techniques were included in the Ebers papyrus, which also includes some 700 remedies, magic formulas, and incantations. In this work, recognition of the heart as the center of blood supply is revealed, although the heart was also given credit for forming tears, urine, and semen. Advice abounds in matters of skin ailments, dentistry, parasites, and surgery (Brazier)

In Babylon, healing was within the purview of powerful priests. Illness came from gods,

Medical seal Mesopotamia

demons, and other evil spirits. Therefore, treatment included divination, offerings, exorcism, and, later, herbs or empiric therapy. Medical fees were included in the Code of Hammurabi.

<<<< *Two kinds of doctors: the Asu, skilled with herbs and minerals, and the Asipu, who determined which god or demon was causing illness.*

Israelites and then Jews caught up to the rest of the world in medical knowledge, then became frontrunners. By 180 BCE, influenced by Greek medicine, Israelites came to believe that the wisdom of the physician comes from God, thus giving doctors authority to administer health remedies without risking conflicts with priests. Doctors gained respect; for example, in certain parts of Torah, like *Exodus* 21:19, "one who smites the other… shall cause him to be thoroughly healed" could be interpreted as meaning to engage the services of a doctor. Philo of Alexandria and Josephus both mention physicians in a positive light (Allan). By the time of Maimonides, medicine had become an exalted Jewish profession.

Maimonides with his signature >>>>>>>

Thinking Out of the Box to Solve Problems

28 Metzorah Leviticus 14.1 – 15.33   מצרע   leprosy

Priests, not doctors, administered health remedies. They often saw illness as the result of wickedness and healing the result of a merciful God. Other cultures of the time associated illness with demons and gods. Egyptians sought the help of gods through incantations as part of the healing arts, but also learned practical applications that included herbs, primitive surgery, and some medicines. Many remedies described in Torah this chapter and the chapter before are plainly without merit. Miriam is said to have contracted leprosy because she criticized Moses (*Num.* 12). In prayer used even today, Moses asked, "נא רפא נא להאל Please heal her." However, some of the Hebrew approach was sophisticated for the time, like quarantine and cleanliness. The detailed description written in Torah to diagnose leprosy is still used in this modern era to aid in

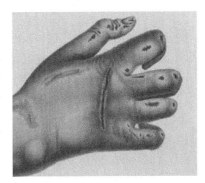

identification.. Also, the technique of quarantine is used for modern afflictions like Covid. It took many years, but eventually civilizations world-wide comprehended that gods, demons, and evil spirits do not control medicine and health. With this realization, medicine became a more understandable and reliable asset for humans. Humans could explore avenues in health and illness that benefit people and did not need sacrifices and incantations. Without realizing it, they had discovered that medicine is part of a system involving the body, external organisms, accidents, and human behavior.

Leprosy – scourge of antiquity (in Wellcome Library)

<<<< *Priests practiced medicine (public domain)*

The idea of medicine as a system could also be applied to agriculture, engineering, metallurgy, finance, transportation, and a host of other endeavors. So in order to better living conditions, study and invention replaced idols, sacrifice, and god kings. Primitive religion came to an end.

Unlike idol-worshipping religions, Torah was found to be consistent with a more modern world, that is, with the study of biological, chemical, and geological systems. These systems came to be called "science." Torah supports the idea that science, philosophy, and nature are all part of Creation, and Creation is the gift of God. Thus, Israelites came to understand that physicians did not compete with God, but served the important purpose of working within the system, or science, of God-given given human bodies.

When reading Torah, we see that after Sinai and Joshua, Israelites could not rely so heavily on God for their safety and well-being. More self initiation was required. Their gradual acceptance of science and scientific systems enabled them to excel not just in medicine but in other areas as well.

Through the historical lens, it is possible to look at the emergence of Hebrews in many ways other than those described in Torah. By looking at human development as a system, other explanations are possible.

Torah suggests that the new monotheistic religion came about from multiple commands of God to Abraham, who willingly obeyed; from Jacob's wrestling; and from Moses. So, it is easy to view Torah as presenting the development of the Hebrew religion as coming from the hands of YHWH to a willing but not initiating population. Monotheism matured in spite of contemporary regional rulers who did not want to give up their idols and forcefully rejected the Hebrew idea. There are other explanations of how Hebrew culture was inevitable as well. Studies in system theory and game theory could offer suggestions.

Nature operates in accordance with "rules." Systems theory explores how this might work (Bertalanfly; Ruben). Systems theory is compatible with theories of Creation. We observe that the components of Creation interact in what seems like a grand plan. Scientists like Humbolt, who influenced Darwin and Thoreau (Wulf), have observed that the earth is really a total living organism. Systems theory and game theory go further in clarifying how groups of people, ideas, and machines work. A system of humans suggests that when a group is defined, there will be some leaders, some successful, some not, and a few outcasts. Those outcasts can often provide harsh criticism of the large group and might form a small group of their

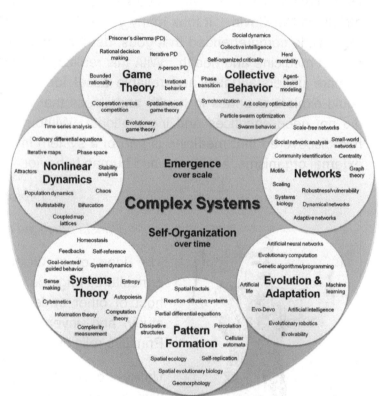

own. This smaller group might be called rebels, criminals, disrupters, or undesirables. However, time may prove the smaller group correct. The idea of how systems work can be called a hidden face of God.

Chart by Hiroki Sayama

In more than a few incidents, disrupters can introduce new or revolutionary ideas to business, politics, communication, and religion. We can think of the introduction of chariot warfare, Galileo, and computers. However, outcasts and weaker members of a wider group need to beware of another sub-group. That would be the predators. Predators always manage to have their say in the path of history. As an example, consider world geopolitics today. From the perspective of ancient rulers and their subjects, Apiru/Hebrews, were disrupters of the god-king political hierarchy. Here is how it unfolded in conformance with human systems:

In the days of god-kings, slaves, and wide open spaces, a number of outcasts roamed areas outside of royal jurisdiction. These included Apiru. Their ranks grew by accepting runaway slaves and disaffected people. In their wanderings, they offered services to established groups, services like temporary labor, armed protection, or delivery of goods from distant places. The delivery of goods led to a vast network of trade so successful that Apiru were able to establish their independence from ruling despots while still making a comfortable living. They had to convince kings and warlords to accept trade rather than plunder when it came to trading with Apiru. Then Apiru developed banking, institutions like dispute courts, and an alphabet that enabled easy portable writing. Apiru also developed a tradition of craft, a limited expertise in military service, and, most important, a religion different and more expansive, ethical, and abstract than petty idols and human gods. Apiru, as Hebrews, and, to this day, as Jews, still maintain a component of the outsider. Jews are very clearly not unified in opinions, but certain common traits are often found: religion both abstract and pragmatic based on Torah, sympathy for outcasts and underdogs, reliance on trade and contracts, and robust innovation.

Innovation continues in the world, but it requires work and thought. As is discussed in chapter 30, when Eve and Adam dined on the tree of knowledge, they chose to work rather than to wait to be served.

Atonement and an Israelite declaration of independence

29 Acharei Mot Leviticus 16:1 – 18:30 אחרי מות After death

The Torah relates the giving of succinct instructions to the children of Israel by YHWH embodying earthshaking principles that changed the world (Meyers, 9; Walzer; Sivan; Nelson; Berman; etc.) The giving of instructions was interrupted by two sorrowful deaths, namely the deaths of Nadav and Avihu, sons of the High Priest Aaron and nephews of Moses himself. They had accompanied elders in a prayerful ascent up Mount Sinai (Ex. 24:9) before committing a crime related to a "strange fire" judged so objectionable that death immediately ensued (Lev. 10:1-7).

The sudden and unexpected loss caused near panic among Israelites. We have no idea as to the nature of the crime. A flurry of sacrifice began: for Aaron to atone on behalf of himself and his house and for the sins of Israel. Aaron symbolized the actions by confessing them upon a goat, which was then cast out and became known as a scapegoat. (*Lev.* 16)   All Israel was commanded to confess and make atonement on an annual basis on the tenth day of the seventh month, a day known as the Day of Atonement or Yom Kippur. In addition, it was declared that Israel must follow a list of laws, laws that define a modern civil society, one that the world has to a large extent endorsed.

The "strange fire" of Aaron's sons in some sense mirrored another problem. The budding Israelite nation lit another strange fire, but this one pleasing to YHWH. By embracing the dictates of YHWH, the humanitarian and egalitarian ideology of Torah distinctly separated Israel from the dominant sociopolitical systems of the world found in Egypt, Babylon, and Canaan (Meyers, 9; *Lev.* 18:4). In following centuries Hebrews held true to Torah against the likes of Egypt, Babylon, Greece, Rome, Spain, Ottomans, and others. These vestiges of the old order resented the Hebrew affection for God over tyrants.

The old order's child sacrifice (Moloch), self- aggrandizement (Abu Simbel), and plunder (Beit el-Wali). Dictators and warlords still engage in these practices today.

Hebrews never planned a sojourn in the desert and a large migration back to Israel. They were accustomed to serving other regimes and not to have their own. It is possible to say that their independent nature and criticism of the existing order made a separation inevitable. It is also possible to say that YHWH planned for the return all along. In any case, events in the desert climaxed a number of Hebrew events that lined up over the course of some 1000 years: (1)

The innovations of Abraham, Sarah, Isaac, Rebecca, Jacob, and Joseph. (2)The ten plagues resulted in the escape of Hebrews to Israel from the Hyksos pharaohs who once ruled; (3) Some Hebrews remained in Egypt living peacefully with a new Egyptian dynasty; (4) Battles commenced in Israel against Canaanite overlords by Apiru/Hebrew rebels especially around Shechem that were tolerated by the sun-worshiping Pharaoh Akhenaten and his father; (5) Ramesside generals overthrew the Hebrew friendly 18th Egyptian Dynasty, then sought revenge against the former hierarchy. Hebrews were enslaved by the likes of Ramesses II; (6) A Hebrew revolt and civil war led by Moses did not succeed and resulted in Moses bringing his people armed out of Egypt. (7) At Mt. Sinai, in the Sinai and/or Negev Desert, Hebrews – despite dissenters like golden calf worshippers – accepted from their God YHWH a new unique set of laws befitting literate ex-slaves. They pledged allegiance to YHWH rather than to a god king or idols, and prepared to enter Israel. The institution of a Day of Atonement sanctified the process.

Hebrews declared independence from the ancient world and introduced the modern world with the Institution of atonement as first mentioned in *Exodus* (28.38 & 30.15), marked by the holiest day in the calendar for Hebrews (*Lev.* 16-19). The formalization of these procedures further codified the new monotheistic religion, which was the goal of Leviticus. The introduction of atonement provided another separation between the laws of kings and the laws of God. This separation was later defined more specifically by the sage Maimonides who emphasized that Hebrews are subject to the laws of a resident country. Hebrews proposed – for themselves – to live by a moral code sanctified by their God:

1. Not living after the doings in (ancient) Egypt and Canaan (Lev. 18.3-4).
2. Keeping the Divine Statutes such as the Decalogue.
3. Proscribing laws against practices of the times including incest, bestiality, sacrifice of children (to Moloch).
4. In general, replacing idols and worship of humans with worship of YHWH, and replacing the culture of plunder and slavery with trade and craft.

All the while reserving the right to defense and self-preservation.

A different view of life with trade, craft, divine morality, and monotheism. (Israel museum, Chaves 1674, NASA)

Within the backdrop of the violent world about them, Hebrews could be described as innocents, almost "flower children."

At the time and over the centuries the Hebrew declaration of independence riled existing rulers and promised to deprive them of slaves. The colonial powers of the ancient world were not amused at losing property. Colonial Egypt lost slaves and the Canaanite warlords were served notice that subservient Hebrews and other serfs would obey no more. In Israel, a degree of independence had already been achieved by Hebrews residing there (See chap. 32 with *Amarna Letters*). This Hebrew revolution, however, was much more dramatic than the loss of slaves and serf property. Such a loss would have been fair game if the former slaves could defend themselves militarily. But Hebrews struck a much more serious blow. Their independence from the system of idols, plunder, aristocratic privilege, and arbitrary laws could endanger the powers that were. This Hebrew revelation, meant only for themselves, is still reverberating throughout the world.

The eventual acceptance by the world's population of many Hebrew principles such as the elimination of idols, made it easy for Hebrews to easily connect with the cultures of the globe. However, some three thousand years ago, Hebrews needed to further define their religion, form a constitution, and gird for war. They had spent the previous one thousand years shuttling between different localities with trade and supplied many of those localities with services while their homeland remained a backwater. The time had arrived to go home. Meanwhile, their little haven in the desert was surrounded by enemies.

The Scapegoat by William Holman Hunt, 1854

Women Who Pierced the Glass Ceiling

30 Kedoshim Leviticus 19:1 – 20:27 קדשים Holy Ones

Leviticus relates how Moses instructed the Israelites that they are to be holy. He informed them of the duties that holiness brings including making sacrifice offerings to the Lord, leaving a corner of harvest fields for charity, and refraining from stealing or dealing falsely or lying. Other instructions were to treat neighbors well, to pay laborers immediately, and not to take advantage of the infirm. These rules are the basis for a humanistic civil society. They further tell us to love our neighbor, to be righteous, and to deal honestly with women. That brings up the situation for women at that time in history.

In drawing conclusions about the status of women three to four thousand years ago, we must first consider the status of people in general. As city-states and nations developed, so did the authority of a military leader who could defend a given territory. Inevitably, this leader became a king, and the king or successor set out to acquire additional territory, plunder, slaves, and tribute. An aristocratic society existed with many serfs or slaves, and a few political or military positions in-between. Women who were not slaves, however, contributed to family well-being and businesses. They often could inherit.

In early societies women could infrequently become heads of state. One of the earliest of female rulers was Lubaba of Sumer (*On the right, a relief in the Anatolia Museum*), who owned a brewery [beer was a gift of the gods] before her elevation to queen, proving also that women ran businesses in the oldest civilization. Egypt, too, had several female pharaohs, but there was a catch: they first performed duties as regent for a stepping-stone. Hatshepsut (*On the left, a statue at Metropolitan Art Museum by author and her temple in Egypt*) stands out as the most famous ancient female head-of-state. Her's was a long tenure featuring her temple, and reconstruction of Egypt that had been compromised by the ten plagues. Early Israel was ruled by judges and Deborah gained prominence as both the fourth judge and a prophet. Military leaders were almost all men. Deborah was an exception. Together with her successor, Barak, and another woman, Jael, her forces routed the army of Hazor, whose king had oppressed Israel. The Hazor general was killed. The *Song of Deborah*, generally regarded as contemporaneous to the battle era, represents the use of poetry in Torah (Judges *4-5; picture from Dore Bible, lower right)*. Aristocratic women had limitations. A king's daughter could be "given" to another king as a sign of friendship to become a third or fourth wife. Later civilizations in Greece, Rome, and China, diminished the status of women further.

Eve by Lucas Cranach the Younger in Alte Meister Dresden

Carol Meyers, author of *Discovering Eve,* presents a feminist interpretation of the metaphoric Eve as perhaps the most influential woman over the ages. Repudiating the frequent depiction of Eve as a sinner, Meyers' construct prepares Hebrew women to take on important, affirmative roles. She uses a closed reading of *Genesis.* First, the origin of Eve: the translation, "Let us make humans in our image," makes more sense than "make man in our image." Next, the "help" Eve brought to Adam was not subservient but equal. The interpretation that Eve brought wisdom to humankind makes her story part of wisdom literature. Consider the Torah description of Eden. The Tigris and Euphrates Rivers in Mesopotamia flowing from Eden, as well as other rivers feeding the Nile, were two locations of easy and plentiful plants.   Eve realized that wisdom and knowledge, represented by the apple, could not be gained in Eden because this setting of ease lacked challenge. Wisdom and knowledge needed to be sought, rather than avoided. After the eating of the apple, God cursed no person but rather the ground, which provided food without effort.   The progeny of Eve gained wisdom by experiencing hardship, and by scratching out a living from the rocky soil of the Israel hills.

Eve departed Eden for knowledge.   Abraham departed Haran in order to worship God. Israelite trips followed so they could form a new society.   Moses exited Egypt to establish a land with freedom and more laws.   The theme of moving to a better place is repeated.   Other works associate wisdom as female, including *Proverbs* 8: "Does not wisdom cry out, And understanding lift up her voice? She takes her stand on the top of the high hill, beside the way, where the paths meet. She cries out by the gates of the city…" (Meyers, pp. vii, 11, 72-94)

Turning to the ancient peoples of the mid-East, we see that they lived in poverty, servitude, and subsistence living. For those living on the edge, both men and women, life was short and prospects dim.   Women did not enjoy the same status as men. Nevertheless, for families able to sustain a household, a woman gained status as domestic captain.   Their domain included the raising of children, preparation of food, management of home finances, and work with textiles. Cash and power pursuits such as politics, military, business, priesthood, and scribes were endeavors off-limits. However, Egyptian women of class and ordinary Israelite women were literate. This literacy contrasts with widespread illiteracy in, for instance, Assyria, where a poor girl often ended up threshing grain or prostituting herself.

There were certain pursuits in which women could go beyond the home. When Hebrews settled in Israel, the citizens took on the life of pioneers. That "land of milk and honey" was the same land many Hebrews had earlier abandoned due to drought. It remained hilly, dry, full of rocks, and largely empty of population. Survival required careful allocation of duties between a wife and husband in order to tame the land. Hard manual work was the order of the day (Robins, pp. 142-155; Meyers, pp. 154-180).

<<< Egyptian Queen Nefertiti, one of the most famous of women. (Berlin Mus.)

One promising area was business. An able woman could produce extra textiles from her loom or spinning wheel and surplus vegetables from her garden. Opportunity in Egypt was slim because trading and business were usually conducted by foreigners. Assyrian women in small businesses and the wives of merchants or land owners held an unknown amount of influence and limited legal rights. Business was a bright spot for a few Assyrian women, who could participate in a husband's business, make decisions, retain profits. (Robins, pp. 104-5, 129)

An Egyptian woman could inherit and own land, household objects, various possessions, and slaves, which gave her possibilities of some security. These options were more limited in Assyria, where a financially distressed husband could present wife, daughters, wife's property, and slaves to a creditor. The right of Hebrew women to inherit is emphasized in *Judges* 11:30-35. Metaphoric representations attributing power to women appear in the *Song of Songs* where women are compared to military objects: "an army with banners" or a wall with "battlements" (*Solomon Song of Songs*, 1:9, 4:4, 8, 6:4,10, 8:9,10). It also links women to powerful animals like the lion or leopard (408) (Robins, 127-136; Meyers, 170- 179).

Assyrian law – A woman who steals from her deceased husband's house shall be killed. (Vorderasiatisches Mus. Berlin) (Robins, pp. 114-126; Stol, *Ancient, pp.* 663-665)   >>>>>

Marriage and raising children could determine a woman's future, and she had very little, if any, say in the matter. An Egyptian man could give his daughter to whom he pleased. Only one wife was common, but more were permitted. Pharaoh, however, acquired multiple wives, many as gifts. Children of slaves sometimes were welcomed into the family and sometimes were accepted as spouses. Divorce was the prerogative of the husband. Although women had some rights under Hammurabi in Mesopotamia, the ascent of Assyria circumscribed their options. Marriage was, quite simply, a purchase, with the husband retaining rights to degrade the wife under new spouses. Although slave girls had no rights, a poor girl could be ceded to a well-off family who worked her and eventually sold her into marriage. Child brides are still seen in the area today. To a surprising extent, notwithstanding male leadership, life on the Israeli settlement farm was necessarily egalitarian. The Hebrew woman was generally not exploited, not reduced to prostitution, but an equal partner on the farm. This status was eroded somewhat after the formation of kingship (Robins, pp. 56-75; Meyers, pp. 169, 189-196).

Although not usually accepted into the regular bureaucracy, an Egyptian woman could become a low-level overseer of ornaments, maker of cloth, a singer or dancer, butler, or keeper of the chamber. Female servants could earn a bare living by milling, baking, spinning, weaving, small crafts, or being a nanny. If the position involved working for a wealthy family, the remuneration could be generous. Exceptions did abound such as female "keepers of the seal," an important security job. By contrast, Assyrian women were largely invisible. Israeli women were involved in education, small crafts, singing, and dancing. They also contributed to defense, including command roles like Deborah. Pre-state Israel lacked public institutions. Women managing households put them in important positions. (Judg.4-5; Meyers, pp. 148-151, 164, 176)

In some circumstances, women could participate in religious orders. The Egyptian god Hathor, known for fertility, employed a Priestess of Hathor. Similar options existed for Assyrian women. Israelite religion lacked the immense system of temples, priests, lands, and slaves as elsewhere. Women did serve as attendants at the Tent of Meeting (*Ex.* 38:8, *1* Sam 2:22), but more important was religion in the home, and, there, women played a strong role (Meyers, pp. 160-163).

We conclude with the question of what were the domains of men and women in a patriarchal society such as those in the ancient Mideast? Male dominance in a violent world required physical strength including for military service, control of slaves, mining, stonework, and shaping land into canals or farms. Males leveraged these areas into political and scribal power. Women had clear control of the household, an area that should not be underestimated because of its necessity in child rearing, sustenance for the family, and economic decision-making. Women staked out their primacy in the home in Egypt, Assyria, and Israel. Women in these locations also made inroads in business, usually as small practitioners or silent partners of their husbands. In these roles, they could make important decisions.

Across the cultures, women could enter respective religious hierarchies, but not as prime movers. Israelite women achieved notable success here. The Hebrew Bible, the *Tanach*, specifically lists five women prophets: Miriam, who had the stature to challenge Moses; the unnamed partner of Isaiah (*Isa.* 8:3); No'adiah, who defeated the attempt of prophet Nehemiah to establish rules of ethnic purity (*Neh.* 6:14, Gafney, p, 5); Huldah, who was called upon by Josiah to validate the found Torah scroll, and Deborah, who was also a judge. Music, funeral, scribal, and even prophet guilds were often headed by Israelite women, giving women a chance at education and advancement (Gafney, pp. 119-130). The *Megillah* 14a-b names Abigail as a prophetess. Other women, unnamed, are recognized as prophets (*Ezek.* 13:17). There is a strong suspicion that a number of women prophets were not given written credits or had their names written in masculine form, but they existed nevertheless (Gafney, pp. 17,108-109, 114-117, 160-165). Prophets usually advised kings, sometimes made kings, and exerted a powerful influence over the population at large.

Holiness Code – more than moralizing

31 Emor Leviticus 21:1 – 24:23   אמר   (The Lord) said ....

The Lord spoke to Moses, giving instructions. Students of Torah view *Leviticus* 17 – 27 as the Holiness code, and rightly so. This code can also be viewed as a forward to the codification of commandments into a constitution of early Israel more fully outlined in *Deuteronomy*.   A look at this code will reveal how some parts are embedded in modern civil society's laws and sensibility and some parts are used as personal moral guidance. Highlights:

EMBEDDED IN MODERN CIVIL SOCIETY CODES	NOT RELEVANT TODAY
No child sacrifice, even a for a stranger (to Molech) 18:21, 20:2-7	Animal sacrifice only to the Lord, not to others 17:3-9, 21:17-32, 23:9-21
Leave something for the poor 19:9-10, 23-22 (social safety nets)	Rain & peace for obedience, plague for disobeying 23
Do not steal 19:11	Land redemption 25:8-22
Do not deal falsely 19:11 (False ads, representations)	Return of land to debtors 25:23, 35
Do not oppress neighbor 19:12 (trespass, harassment)	Don't mix cattle or seed stock or textiles 19:19
Do not rob neighbor 19:12	No divination or soothsaying 19:26
Do not lie to one another 19:11 (in court)	Those with blemish shall not approach altar 21:16-19
Pay laborer immediately 19:12 (labor laws)	
Eye for eye beast for beast 24:17-21 (monetary substitution)	**GENERALLY RELEVANT TODAY**
Stranger will obey laws of Israel 24:22	Avoid the doings of Canaan and Egypt their statutes 18:1
Limits of servitude 25:35-55	Keep my ordinances and statutes 18:4-5, 26, 19:19 19:35-36, 20:8, 22
Do not curse deaf, make blind stumble 19:14	No incest or adultery 18:6-29, 20:10-14, 17-20
No unrighteous in judgment 19:15 (impartial laws)	No idols 19:4, 26:1
Do not favor the mighty 19:15 (equality under law)	No bestiality 18;23, 20:14-16
No tale-bearing gossip 19:16 (libel)	Keep the Sabbath 18.24, 19.30, 23.1-3, 26.2
No idling when neighbor bleeds 19:16 (don't leave accident scene)	Do not profane name of God 19:12
No rape 19:20	Do not lie to one another 19:11
Do not prostitute a daughter 19:29	Leave land fallow 24:1-7
Do not do stranger wrong 19:33-34 (re: law)	Don't hate brother 19:17
Keep meters, weights, measures true 19:35-36	Love neighbor as thyself 19:18
Value of a person in shekels 27:1-8 (compensation)	Honor parents 20:9
Beast for beast 27:9-15 (compensation for damage)	No ghosts, spirits 19:31, 20:27
Value of a field of barley etc 27:16-25 (compensaton)	
Do not follow laws of other nations while in Israel 20:23 (Each nation sets its laws)	**RELEVANT MAINLY TO JEWS**
No prostitution 21:1-9 (especially human trafficking)	Do not eat blood of beast or fowl 17:10-16, 19:26
	Day of Atonement 23:24
	Sukkot 23-43
	Keep Passover 23:4-8
	Don't round corners of head or beard 19:26

The ancient *Holiness* Code continues to be an inspiration to modern civil society and a reference by which to judge unsavory, illegal, or outright oppressive behavior. What comes later in *Deuteronomy* will provide further guidance for how to create a civil society.

The Holiness Code by the numbers with 52 items in this list:
26 items embedded in modern civil society codes;   7 items not relevant today;
13 items still relevant today but not in codes;   5 items still only relevant to Jews;

87% of the items in the *Holiness Code* are still guiding people today. Half of it has been adopted within formal legal codes in one form or another. Of course, the *Holiness Code* of *Leviticus* is an addition to the *Covenant Code*, which included the *Decalogue*, of *Exodus* 20:22-23:33. The two are generally compatible and are joined by the *Deuteronomy Code*, all three attributed in some way to Sinai. They worked together; could be interpreted; but not replaced as per *Deut.* 4:2, "You shall not add... or take anything away..."

The kings of Israel could neither make laws nor ignore them. Torah relates that David broke a number of laws including coveting, committing adultery, and accessory to murder. The prophet Nathan denounced him (*2 Samuel 11-12*). Solomon and his son Rehoboam acquired excessive wealth, allowed idols, and over-taxed the people. Their excesses split Israel into two kingdoms and brought condemnation from the prophet Shemaiah.   (*1 Kings* 11-12; *Deu.* 17.16; *2 Chron* 1.16, 9:25). Ahab was involved in murder and theft in acquiring a vineyard, then was denounced. (2 Kings 8:18; 2 Chr. 22:3, Micah 3:16)

<<< *King David* by van Honthorst

King Rehoboam by Hans Holbein the Younger

This gives Torah a special character because non-Israelite kings changed laws or ignored them as they wished. The Sinai law lasted for centuries and across the Diaspora, augmented by legal decisions and exegesis, but all harked back to Torah. Torah is not the king's law, and no king of Israel or assembly of elders engaged in law-giving. They were all subject to the law. And the law had the approval of the people, who chorused, "We will obey "(Ex. 20:16, 24:4-7; 2 Kings 23;3, Chron. 16:36, Nehemiah 8:6; Esther 3:8). But there was room for change and accommodation for evolving legal challenges in Torah. New circumstances required working from a beginning point from what can be called the Hebrew constitution, and drawing conclusions through the work of priestly, scribal, and, later, rabbinic decisions. (Walzer, *Legal,* 107- 118)

^^^ King Ahab *portrait published in 1553 by Rouile.*

Holy guidance for business

32 Behar Leviticus 25:1-26:2 בהר On the Mountain (The Lord Spoke)

Who would think that the Holiness Code set up standards for business? Who would think that there is anything holy or religious about business?

It turns out that moral business practices make for good business. Trust in business transactions and products make for long-term relationships and peace, while gross theft and misrepresentation amount to non-violent plunder and results in confrontation. Hebrews were in the best of positions to appreciate this reasoning. Almost 1,000 years before Sinai, Hebrew/Apiru managed donkey caravans in order to trade between regimes often hostile to one another. Their women manufactured textiles for sale and may have participated in other areas of the business. ((William Albright, *From the Patriarch to Moses,* pp. 5-33).

The Hebrew business model had to be good because kings and warlords had the option to obtain items they desired by ordering slaves to produce products or ordering troops to steal and plunder what they desired. Trading with Hebrews could prove less risky. In order to build such an elaborate trading system, an infrastructure of contracts, arbitration, acquisition, partnerships, investment banking, animal management, and armed protection was required. Added to this was the need for honesty and reliability (Wolfe, pp. vi-20; Gary Thompsom, pp. 31-34; Bottero, pp. 145-159; Albright, *From Patriarch to Moses, p.6*).

Honest shops attract customers (Carmel Market Tel Aviv by author.) ^^^^

A number of commands within the Holiness code pertain to business:

Do not steal	Do not deal falsely	Do not rob
Do not lie	Pay a laborer quickly	Pay for damages
Righteous judgments	Equality under law	No gossip
Keep scales true	Fair value for barley etc.	Limits of servitude

Keep the statutes of the Lord, which includes the Ten Commandments.

To be clear, Torah does not include a guide of how to succeed in business or how to market a new idea.

The Hebrew tradition realizes that commercial undertakings can be deceptive, "A merchant can hardly keep himself from wrongdoing and a storekeeper will not be acquitted of sin." (Ben Sira 26:29)

But business is indispensable and has aspects of holiness. "Character is tested through business." (from Avot D'rabi, Natan, ed. Schechter, version B, Chap. 31, p. 68) " 'If you will heed the Lord diligently, doing what is right in His eyes' (Exodus 15:26). This refers to business dealings. A famous interpretation of Hebrew rules (called a Midrash) lies in the *Mekhilta*. This work teaches us that "whoever trades in good faith, it is accounted to him as though he had observed the entire *Torah*." (Lauterbach, vol. 2, p. 96)

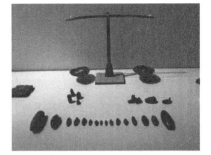

Rabbi David Golinkin summarized the Biblical basis of business ethics and law. He began with, *You shall not falsify measures of length, weight, or capacity. You shall have an honest balance…* (*Lev.* 19:35-36) In various times, rabbis would inspect scales just as they inspected kitchens for kosher compliance.

Weights from time of Sinai (Israel Museum by author) >>>

Secondly, there is monetary deception which can take the form of gouging, bait and switch, or ambiguous pricing. *When you sell anything to your neighbor or buy anything from your neighbor, you shall not deceive one another.* (Lev. 25:14) A series of laws and commentaries on monetary deception appear in *Talmud* and elsewhere.

A third category refers to verbal deception, from Lev. 25:17, *Do not deceive one another, but fear your God…* Rabbis have interpreted this as also related to verbal abuse in places like the *Mishnah Bava Metzia* 58b, which is in the *Talmud*.

Laws against stealing (*Ex.* 20:15) are interpreted as including the stealing of one's mind,

or false packaging, labeling, and misrepresentation. This would include placing unrepresentative fine potatoes on the top of a bushel full of blemished potatoes.

You shall not curse the deaf nor put a stumbling block before the blind… (Lev. 19:14) forbids the selling of a product with important defects and not disclosing the same, or literally taking advantage of a blind person. (*above thought from Golinkin, The Basic principles of Jewish Business Ethics*).

^^^^ *Tradable items from the Negev, Timna Mines, see Deut 8:9, picture by author.*

Now that *Torah* has established a level playing field, we can feel confident to shop, even online, when we know the dictums of *Torah* are followed.

The history of Hebrews and then Jews as providers of commercial services continued throughout history, although others, including Phoenicians, Greeks, Christians, Muslims, Venetians, Dutch, and British recognized the value of trade and participated. An alternative to military dominance was accepted. This in turn opened more possibilities to advancement for people who could not swing a sword or shoot an arrow, but had other skills. Increased use of other skills could open new kinds of human endeavor.

The basic ethics of business as proposed in Torah has heavily influenced all business standards.

Every man under his vine and fig tree

33 Bechkotai Leviticus 26:3 – 27:34   בחקתי   My statutes

The end of Leviticus promises wheat, fruit, and peace to those who follow the Lord's commandments rather than desolate land and plague for those who disobey. It sounds Jeffersonian.

Does this promise square with history? The answer is yes and no. A Torah document made in the desert recorded by Hebrew scribes 3,000 years ago leaves itself open to criticism by modern researchers. Although Torah gives scant instructions on how the abundance of food is to be produced, Israelites did not wait for the details and set about establishing small family farms on the rocky hills and in the dry desert regions of their country. Extensive use of retaining walls, cisterns, and terraces to control water combined with water saving plants brought forth dates, vineyards, olives, and fruit trees. Even in the patriarchal era, Hebrews produced wheat and a type of "corn"; Jacob made a profit from his gardens, and grain from the

area supplied the Egyptian army. As long as peace prevailed, Hebrew agriculture prospered and "Judah and Israel dwelt safely, every man under his vine and fig tree from Dan to Beer-Sheva."   Israeli agriculture had a certain ebb and flow, according to the degree of peace in the land. (Main; *Jewish Virtual Library agriculture in Israe*l; Gen 26:12, Deut 1:7, I Kings 5:7, Judges 1:19, 27-36; *Gezer Calendar*)

<< Israelite terraces restored by JNF

Peace in the land is the sticking point in the *Leviticus* promise. Israel always had Jewish residents but not always did it have peace (Verlin). Just as Torah lacked details on horticulture, so did it lack details on exactly how to insure peace in the country. Surrounding nations did not agree to love their neighbor, to trade with fair weights, or grant property rights, but instead they came in waves as conquerors to steal and enslave: Assyria, Babylonia, Greece, Rome, Persia, Arabs, the Crusaders, Mongols, Mamluks, and Turks came one after the other (Verlin). In earlier pre-Israel times, settlers in the major river valleys increased wealth rather than steal it. They created vast irrigation projects in Sumer and the Nile Delta. For instance, the water projects of Joseph opened new land to agriculture and population increases (see chapter 43 on on Joseph).

^^^Ancient military empires aspired to the same land. Shown are Assyria, Rome, Persia, and Ottoman lands. Among those not included are Byzantium, various Islamic, and Mongol conquerors, who took control of empires with violence.

So what strategies did Israelites and Jews employ, strategically or by default, in order to bring peace to their country?

<u>Military Action and Defensive Structures</u>: Many countries employed their strength for expansion and defense. In fact, a combination of armed rebellion and military liberation created Israel itself; David put Israel firmly on the map with military victories against Philistines and other enemies. Force of arms also did the job when the Maccabees defeated the Seleucid Greeks. However, an ill-advised resistance of the Northern Kingdom of Israel failed against Assyria, which disbursed the population and put some of the defeated Hebrews on the slave market (Sayce, p. 88), while a combination of negotiation and, later-on, defense allowed Judah to survive. Walled defensive cities were the standard of the day.

<u>Alliances or Negotiation</u>: From early Hebrew times, Abraham allied with Egypt to stop incursions by Elam. On-again, off-again partnerships with Assyrians, Persians, and Arabs helped local Israelites at different times (see chapter 3 on Abraham; Coogan, pp. 242-298).

<u>Following Commandments</u>: The decisive defeat of Assyria, the vicious enemy of Israel, was predicted by the Prophet Nahum as just retribution for all the oppression wrought by that regime. The hideous nature of the Assyrian war machine, as well as those of Egypt and Rome, earned these regimes untold hatred and deserved defeat. They engaged in the most extreme forms of torture and dehumanization -- impalement, flaying, and burning, to name a few. This resulted in loud condemnation from people like the Prophet Nahum. (Timmer; Sayce, p. 84; Nahun, p. 1-3; Hershkovitz; Matic). Torah demands humane behavior for female captives (*Deu.* 21:10-15); stands against evil things in war (*Deu.* 23:10); states that civilians may escape a siege (Maimonides, *Mishneh Torah, Kings and Wars 6*); imposes limits on punishment for a civil offense (Deu. 25:3); does not accept confessions from torture, the basis for the US fifth amendment (Greenwald; Maimonides, *Mishneh Torah Book 14*; *Sanhedrin* 18:13); and limits vengeance, because "vengeance is Mine" says the Lord." (Deu. 32:35).

However, in a more general sense, the Hebrew/Jewish attachment to Israel remained intense over the millennia, and their residence there remained consistent, even when the majority of their population scattered. Judaism remained closely identified with Israel (*Tanakh; jewishvirtuallibrary*).

 *Desert Farming and Tel Aviv skyline. (stock)*

In summary, Israel deserves an uncertain review when it comes to protecting the country. Disastrous decisions by the Northern Kingdom of Israel against Assyria and all of Israel against Rome could have been avoided by realistic analysis. Persian occupation turned out to be temporarily acceptable, as evidenced by permissions allowing exiled Hebrews to return. However, Israel has always existed as a small player in a world of great politics and power. Nevertheless it has always existed, even as Egyptians were reduced to an oppressed minority in their country, as Assyrians were reduced to a few villages in isolation, and as Rome was swallowed by Italy.

After all the centuries, Israel exists as a small nation with innovative agriculture, with a strong defense, and with a dedication to its Covenant. That's what Moses strived for.

Tent of Meeting position as a clue to tribal history

34 Bamidbar במדבר Numbers 1:1 – 4:20 in the Desert

As the *Book of Numbers* opens, various lists are disclosed including a tribal census, marching orders, additional sacrifices, details of battles, and recitation of some laws. These lists reflect the process of separate tribes voluntarily ceding rights in order to form a nation rather than forming a nation through conquest. This in itself represents a monumental departure from the formation of other nations such as Egypt, Hattusa (Hittites), or Assyria.

Torah condenses and simplifies the history of the nation into the story of Jacob and his sons because Torah serves purposes different than history.

In the deserts (Bamidbar or במדבר) of Sinai and Negev, a remarkable coalescence of the Israelite tribal tradition yielded to a national purpose for a people sharing a history of both trade and shepherding, monotheism, common moral ideas, a sense of equal rights, and connection with the land of Israel.   The Tent of Meeting mirrors this national unity. Each tribe had an equal seat around the Tabernacle according to Torah. The placement of the tribes around the Tabernacle reflects future land allotment in Israel and clues to tribal history.

Re-creation of Tent of Meeting size, not decorations, from evidence at Timna National Park (photos by author); Timna Park representation of actual Tabernacle; Tabernacle placement of tribes as compared to their land portions.

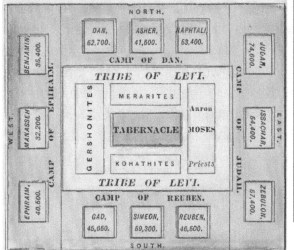

Gad, Simeon, and Reuben are positioned south of the Tabernacle. Their lands were to be located in the south of Israel. Evidence from Egypt, Torah, and Israel has helped uncover the evolution of these tribes. As will be seen, these tribes were pastoral Bedouins concentrated in the Negev and Sinai, but following desert trails from Egypt through Israel and into Syria and Lebanon. They were the earliest and possibly the most fervent worshippers of YHWH.

Torah introduces Simeon as the second son of Jacob with Leah, along with brothers Reuben, Levi, Gad (with handmaid), and others. Simeon and Levi took control of the town of Shechem after disputes with its ruler (Gen. 29, 34:1-29). This led to another dispute, because Jacob admonished his sons for their military action, which may have partially resulted in Joseph leaving for Egypt (Gen. 37-50).

Evidence supports continuous Hebrew occupation of the Shechem area from the time of Jacob. Egyptians may have helped in the fight for Shechem. (Brested, Vol. I #680-681; Wright, p. 16; Pritchard, James tr. W modification; Grimal, p. 169; Mourad, *Asiatics*, p. 34; Mourad, *Rise, pp.* 100-101; Wright, 5). One interpretation is that Simeon and Levi settled in Shechem before Jacob (Noth, *Pentateuchal*, pp. 86-87). The tomb of Amenhotep III about 1370 BCE attests to the continuing presence of Simeon near Shechem In Dotham, the area of Joseph's sale to traders and transport to Egypt (Giveon, pp. 22-24; Inscription at funeral temple at Thebes for Amenhotep III; *Gen.* 37:12-17). This reference also points to Simeon as part of the Beduion Shosu tribes. This is important because the Shosu are the first attested to worship of YHWH. A number of attributes of Judaism trace to Shosu:

YHWH in land of Shosu. Sier in land of Shosu – Ramesses inscription in Nubia, duplicated elsewhere. In Torah and Egypt, Sier is Negev or Sinai.

Long before the leadership of Moses, Shosu, and by extension, Simeon, wore tassels now known as tzitzit; skull caps like today's kipot, and most importantly worshipped YHWH. Pharaoh Amenhotep III has also identified the Samath, Simeon clan, in the land of Shosu as Kenite scribes and YHWH as worshipped in that land of the Shosu, aka Seir. Some of the most import concepts of Hebrew monotheism can be traced to the desert tribes. (Giveon, p. 26; toponyms at Soleb; Fleming, Yahweh, pp. 23-53, 67-161). Torah agrees with Adonai coming from Seir. "Adonoi came from Sinai, and shone upon them from Seir. O Lord, when You came forth from Seir… " (*Deu.* 33:2; *Judges*, 5:4).

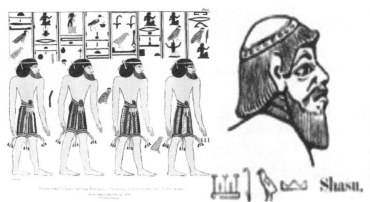  

Shosu from Thebes by Belzoni, head from Thutmose IV (wikia.com), Simeon flag w Shechem, stele @ Soleb

The name Simeon and the name Samath come from the same root as "hear," shema שמע . Because of the early worshipping of YHWH by Simeon or Samath. Samath persons, aka Shimeathites, performed duties such as teaching Hebrews the law (I Chron 2.55, Sanherin 106a:2-4, 11.83, Midrash Tanchuma, Vayakhel 8.2, Ginzberg) If scribes wrote Torah at Sinai, these might be Samath or Simeon. Now that Simeon is connected with the larger Shosu tribe and primarily lived in Seir and was connected with Kenite scribes, a further connection is possible. Simeon was part of the southern Shosu federation that early on worshipped YHWH. Torah does not mention the Shosu directly, but does mention Esau. It makes sense that Shosu and Esau are the respective Egyptian and Hebrew pronunciations for the same word. The Hebrew for Esau is עֵשָׂו while the Hebrew interpretation of the Egyptian Shosu is שׁשׁ. The Aramaic שׁ in Shosu שׁשׁ is the same as the Hebrew ע in Esau עשׁו (Giveon 3-1). Shosu and Esau are the same.   The conclusion is that the three tribes on the south side of the Tabernacle, plus Levi, were from the Esau branch of Hebrews. More later.

The other Hebrews, desert tribes collectively called "Shosu."

35 Nasso Numbers 4:21-7:89 נשא Carry

The second section, or parashah, of the *Book of Numbers* is called "נשא, *Nasso*," or "carry." It continues with a census of Israelites and the duties and contributions they carry to the Tabernacle. More questions arise as to as to the history of Gad, Simeon, and Reuben whose station was on the south side of the Tabernacle. Tribes on this side have been shown to be derived from the legacy of Esau, known as Shosu by Egyptians.

Also, some special duties assumed by a group identified as Nazarites are introduced. Nazarites take a special vow of holiness. The characteristics of a Nazarite are brought forth suddenly without much description (Num. 6:1-21). Earlier, Joseph is described as a nazir by Jacob (Gen. 49:26), but that description is generally translated as someone special or a leader. Later, Samson and Samuel are so designated, while still later, the concept is used in Christian scripture referring to John the Baptist. The concept has been defined or recognized as a monk or devoted abstinent in Judaism, Christianity, Hinduism (swami), and Buddism.

This portion presents an example of how people living in a civil society that includes women's rights can misinterpret Torah without appropriate study. We know that even today, abuses against women are tolerated in some societies and can include honor killings, denial of education, mandated clothing, forced marriage of children, and spousal abuse. In the ancient times, such abuses also included the purchase or gifting of wives. The laws of Moses took enormous steps in protecting women, steps which are still not practiced in some parts of the world, but have been greatly surpassed in other parts such as western democracies.

The first step is the recognition of Eve as the beginning of knowledge, as opposed to the expectation of services in a utopia (see chapter 30.). Later, God commanded Moses to insure inheritance rights to Zelophehad's daughters (Num. 36) and women possessed other rights of inheritance per Judges 11:30-35. Women are compared to military actions such as "an army with banners," or a wall with "battlements." (See Solomon Song of Songs 1:9; 4:4, 8; 6:4, 10; 8:9-10). Still later, Deborah assumed duties as head of the State of Israel. Women were prophets such as Miriam, the unnamed partner of Isaish (Isa. 8:3; No'adiah, who defeated the attempt of prophet Nehemiah to establish rules of ethnic purity (Neh. 6:14); Huldah, who validated the discovered Torah scroll in the time of Josiah, and, of course, Deborah. Then, because of the Hebrew alphabet, many women were literate. There were other examples.

This brings us to the question of Numbers 5:11-31, the "law of jealousy." In this law, a man cannot arbitrarily discipline or abuse his wife if he is jealous and thinks her unfaithful. Instead, he must take his case before a priest and proclaim his suspicions. This requirement alone is designed to stop any outrage and block the abusive husband from harmful action because he must present his case to a higher authority and be shamed if he has no cause for anger.

Thereafter, the woman must drink a bitter potion and expect her belly to swell if she is guilty. No doubt, this ceremony saved many a woman and prevented undue violence. In some select countries, notably in Europe, North America, and elsewhere, there are modern protections for women.

Referring back to the Esau/Shosu tribes, that network can be traced from the time of Esau. This group was desert oriented and the first to be recorded as worshipping YHWH, which appears in extra-Biblical sources. While Joseph and his followers moved to Egypt, Esau and other Hebrews followed different trajectories.

Desert Bedouin including Shosu were described as dangerous, unkempt rogues in early Egyptian records: (1) Instructions ~ 2070 BCE to Pharaoh Merikare, "*The* [Asiatic sandweller] *neither conquers nor can he be conquered.... But is like a thief whom society has expelled*"; (2) A Ramesses era father wrote to a son enamored of Shosu lifestyle, "*You have consorted with Asiatics* [Shosu], *having eaten bread with your own blood! You have lost your wits! .... The horses were loosed... and your clothes were stolen. Your groom... took the rest. He has wholly gone over to a life of evil. He mixes with the tribes of the Shosu, having adopted the guise of an Asiatic.*" (*Papyrus Petersburg* 1116A, tr Tobin); (3) Pharaoh Amenhotep II's mortuary reported Shosu still in the area of Shechem around 1370 BCE, even though Egypt attempted to control the area.

In the period after the ten plagues, the relationship between Esau/Shosu and Egypt remained peaceful even though Egypt wanted control of more territory. New pharaohs were determined to pacify the coastline of the Mediterranean extending into Syria where Hyksos had gone after being ejected from Egypt. The pharaohs were also increasingly interested in the mineral deposits of the Sinai. All of these areas were adjacent to Shosu, whose influence stretched from their homeland in Seir or the Negev, north into Syria, and south to the edge of Egypt, constituting a tribal confederation, even a Bedouin nation (Redford, pp. 269-272). Biblically speaking, Shosu represented a national creation of Esau. Not much interaction took place involving Egypt and Shosu for quite a while aside from a minor squabble with Thutmose II in the Negev in about 1485 BCE. Then came the Napoleon of Egypt, Thutmose III, who demolished and pillaged Canaanites, Mitannis, Hurrians and their allies. He campaigned clear up the Mediterranean Coast, well into Lebanon and Syria, and across the Euphrates. Then in another thrust, he conquered Nubia in about 1465 BCE. Egypt became an empire. In Israel, the actions of Thutmose eliminated some enemies of Hebrews and allowed them a better chance at forming a nation. Hebrew land was spared the Egyptian army thrust. (Redford, p. 153; Giveon, pp. 9-10).

<<< Mt. Lebanon range from ASOR

On his campaign of pillage into Syria and the Euphrates, Thutmose III either could not or did not try to subdue an enclave of Shosu and Apiru occupying a mini city-state called Amurru including a city called Ibirta, east of ancient Byblos or the modern Tripoli coastline near the base of Mount Lebanon, a name of the mountain derived from the Hebrew for "white" as in the snow at the top. (Cline and O'Connor, p. 335; Na'aman, *Ibirta*, pp. 27-29). That would be about 200 miles north of the Hebrew Shechem mini city-state in Israel. Thutmose and other Pharaohs avoided all but inconsequential encounters with the Israel hill country, where the new Hebrew nation percolated (Fletcher; Kozloff; Na'aman, *Shephela, p.* 281).

Thutmose III inscribed details of his campaigns through Lebanon and Syria. This stele proclaims his victories across the Euphrates: "Now, brought there for his majesty upon the shore of the Euphrates. Never had the like been done. His stele was brought back from the end of the earth." University of Penn Museum Saplinger, translation..

Hebrews were forming the country of Israel. It happened that the main enemies of Egypt at the time, namely Canaanite states, were also Israel's enemies. (Redford, pp. 269-272.) When The forces of Thutmose conquered the Mediterranean coast and destroyed those Canaanites, Israel gained a free hand to establish a new country. There are no accounts in this period of battles in the Negev or Sinai between Egyptians and Hebrews.

Shosu did, however, irritate the imperial ambitions of Egypt during the reigns of the next several pharaohs with Amenhotep III publicizing the Shosu as worshippers of YHWH, as prisoners, as occupants of Shechem, as Samath Kenite scribes, and as one of his "nine bows" consisting of the enemies of Egypt. Skirmishes with these pharaohs did not amount to much, with Shosu continuing as princes of the desert. Egypt continued with its empire, and the boundaries of each reached the empire of the Mitanni on the Euphrates and parts of Syria.

Pharaoh Akkenaten (Amenhotep IV) ascended to the Egyptian throne just after 1350 BCE and promptly surrounded himself with foreign troops that he could trust for a special mission. Police Chief Mahu and Royal Chancellor Ahmes commanded troops that included Nubians and Shosu. A number of new officials were appointed, many from the Delta including Aper-el,

a Hebrew who served as vizier, perhaps providing a reason for later oppression of the Delta and Hebrews. (Hornung, pp. 48-58; inscriptions in the tombs of Mahu and Ahmes; Zivie).

Royal Guard of Ahkenaten, mainly foreign: Egyptian (red); Syrian (blue); Nubian (green); Shosu with tassles (yellow circle); Egyptian officer (white), in Tomb of Ahmes, explained by artehistoriaegipto blogsspot & author.

Under Akhenaten, establishment priests and their entourages were rounded up and either killed or dismissed; separated from their temples of power, secrecy, and perversion; and their funds diverted to Akhenaten. Priests had much available for confiscation. The Temple of Amen at Karnak employed (or owned) some 81,000 people for its vast operations. (Tyldesly, *Hatchepsut,* p. 84). Thereafter, only the sun stood above all people as their god, and only Akhenaten served as priest. Akhenaten removed himself from the active political and commercial centers of Egypt to build an isolated holy city where he ensconced himself. He replaced much of the Egyptian hierarchy with new deputies that included some Hebrew advisors, presumably from the group that remained in Egypt after the ten plagues and served other pharaohs in that particular dynasty (Watterson, pp. 51-52, 59-6481-90; Hornung, pp. 49-56, 87-88; Tyldesley, *Ramesses,* pp. 22-27; Mendenhall, p. 11)

It seemed as though Joseph Hebrews and Esau Hebrews reached a peaceful co-existence with Egypt while Hebrews in Israel continued to build their own nation (more on this later). The peaceful situation did not last. Akhenaten did not build structural relationships with the old guard. He died with only a young heir who was persuaded to reverse sun worship. A very confusing and dangerous period of about twenty years followed until a military general took over the reins of government and reinstated the old order of priests. Egypt quickly became an even more dangerous place and the world was to become engulfed in new wars.

At this time, the heirs of Esau and the heirs of Jacob seem to have begun reconciliation, thus providing a path to the gathering before the Tabernacle and revelation at Sinai. More on Esau and Jacob heirs to follow, but first, *Numbers* introduces the Nazirites and blessings. Anyone can decide to become a Nazirite or to give these blessings, relating to God individually, without a priest.

> *When either man or woman shall clearly utter a vow, the vow of a Nazirite, to consecrate himself unto the Lord, he shall:*
>> *abstain from wine and strong drink… neither shall he drink any liquor of grapes.*
>> *there shall no razor come upon his head… shall let locks of the hair of his head grow long.*
>> *he shall not come near to a dead body.*
>> *All the days of his Naziriteship he is holy unto the Lord. – Num. 6*

A Narzarite was self-proclaimed and did not require special training. These instructions are followed by blessings announced to the children of Israel, perhaps with emphasis towards the Nazirites, and repeated today in synagogues and churches:

> *The Lord bless thee, and keep thee;*
> *The Lord make the Lord's face to shine upon thee, and be gracious unto thee;*
> *The Lord lift up the Lord's countenance upon thee, and give thee peace.*
> *So shall they put My name upon the children of Israel, and I will bless them. –Num. 6*

The characteristics of a Nazarite are brought forth suddenly without much description (Num. 6:1-21). Earlier, Joseph is described as a nazir by Jacob (Gen. 49:26), but that description is generally translated as someone special or a leader. Later, Samson and Samuel are so designated, while still later, the concept is used in Christian scripture referring to John the Baptist. The concept has been defined or recognized as a monk or devoted abstinent in Judaism, Christianity, Hinduism (swami), and Buddism.

The Narzarite concept gripped the world beyond Israel. The implication is that Nazirites already existed before Sinai. The notion that anyone can pledge him/her self to God inspired, to name a few, Samson (*Judges* 16), parents of Samson (*Judges* 13), Banns, tutor of Josephus, *Antiquities*, 20:6; Samuel (*1 Samuel* 1:11), John the Baptist (*Luke* 1:13-15), and Paul (*Acts* 18:18). Regardless of who actually takes the Nazirite vow, many attempt to follow the ideal.

Conquest within Israel before Joshua

36 Behaalotchah Numbers 8:1 – 12:6 בהעלתך You Raised

Numbers continues with the process of travelling the desert with the Israelite tribes. The tribes feast on quail, which stop in the Levant on their migration between Europe and their southern winter home. Some of the desert tribes probably knew about the migrations. After centuries of minimal contact, both the Joseph tribes and the Shosu had some representatives serving the rebel sun-worshipping pharaoh Akhenaten in Egypt (chapter 35).

migrations of quail   (Bruce sound blog)>>>

Notwithstanding the Midianite opposition to Israel, no doubt a dispute over land, the Kenite division of Midianites was according to Torah and Egypt, Instrumental in Israelite success by hosting Moses, providing scribes, and dwelling in Timna. *Numbers* explains that they were offered a place in Israel alongside the tribes, but for a time declined.

Torah positions the Hebrews as moving towards a home in Israel and a Joshua conquest. However, history reveals that the major battles for possession of Israel took place before the arrival of Moses. This is not to detract from the telling of the tale in Torah. During the time of Akhenaten and his father, about 1350 BCE, a flurry of correspondence took place between the various rulers of greater Canaan, which includes Lebanon and Syria, and Pharaoh.   The correspondence was stored at the palace of Akhenaton in his royal city, Amarna.   The letters show that Hebrews, referred to as Apiru, were in the process of expanding their base in Shechem with its ruler Labayu and also in the Syrian valley near Mount Lebanon referred to as Amurru with its ruler Abdi-Ashirta (Redford, p. 179). The expansion took place at the expense of Canaanite Amorite and Hurrian mayors or lords known for abusing their serfs and slaves with oppression and high taxes. Canaanites continued their hierarchy of sharp division with a nobility of largely non-Semitic lords, serfs bound to the land, and outright slaves (Albright, *Biblical, pp.* 25-26). No wonder that rulers in the areas of Hebrews worried about rebellion at the instigation of Apiru.   Across the land, Canaanite chieftains surrounded themselves with patrician

kinsmen and retainers. The rest the population lived as half-free serfs surviving wretchedly, judging from the contrasts between the estates of the nobles and the hovels of the commoners (Albright, *Archaeology, p.* 91)

The Apiru continued their age-old practice of over 1,000 years of accepting runaway slaves (Gottwald, p. 216). The various taxes and oppressions of Egyptian and Canaaite lords produced economically disadvantaged people who decided to run away to Apiru (DeMagistris, pp. 26, 31-35) The Hebrew revolution attracted rural inhabitants to its cause (Na'aman, *Shephela, p.* 295). These actions took place long before Moses and Joshua. They involved cities not conquered by Joshua. A small but independent Israel was formed.

Ironically, the Canaanite and Hurrian leaders targeted by Apiru for expansion complained to Pharaoh for help. The Canaanites and Hurrians were descendants of the same rulers who invaded Egypt and were thereafter crushed by Thutmoses III. Notable in these letters are the successes of Apiru; their alliances with peasants; continued payment of tribute to Egypt by Apiru; and the lack of interest by Pharaoh in the Apiru aggression. By the era of Moses, a small Israel had formed. Here follows sample letters to pharaoh from a cache of letters discovered at the city of Akhenaton, Amarna:

EA 70 (from Byblos): *The war of the Apiru forces against me is extremely severe*
EA 71 (from Byblos): *What is Abdi-Ashirta [*Hebrew leader from Amurru]*, servant and dog that he take the land of the king? Through the Apiru his auxiliary force is strong.*
EA 73 (from Byblos): *Abdi-Asirta (Amurru) messaged… "Kill your lord and join the Apiru" … All land will go Apiru."*
EA 74 *Ruler Rib-Addi of Byblos said, "My villages are joined to the Apiru… the entire country be joined to the Apiru."* Abdi-Asirta said, *"Let us fall upon Byblos… let us drive out the mayors from the country that the entire country be joined to the Apiru."*
EA 76 (from Byblos): *Your 5-garrison city is joined to the Apiru. You have done nothing.*
EA 77 (from Byblos): *I am afraid the peasantry will strike me down.*
EA 85 (from Rib-Hadda of Jerusalem*): I would drive Abdi-Asirta from the land of Amurru… the lands have been joined to the Apiru.* [Showing emergence of the Hebrew city-state of Amurru around the center of Ibirta, Syria.]
EA 89 (from Byblos): Abdi-Asirta (Amurru) has taken the city of Tyre.
EA 90 (from Byblos): *You have been negligent of your cities so that the Apiru takes them.*
EA 104 (from mayor of Jerusalem): *They will attack me and Byblos will be pinned to the Apiru. They have gone to Ibirta* [Shosu/Apiru city in Syria], *and made an agreement with the Apiru.*
EA 114 (from mayor of Jerusalem): *My peasantry long to desert me.*
EA 286 (mayor of Jerusalem): *Why do you love the Apiru but hate the mayors? The sons of Labayu* [Shechem] *have given the land of the king to the Apiru.*
EA 288 (mayor of Jerusalem*): Apiru have taken the very cities of the king… all are lost…Silu… Lachish…the king did nothing.*
EA 244 (mayor of Megiddo): *Since the archers returned Labayu has shown me enmity. We*

are not able to go out of the gate because of Labayu. If it be known that you have not given archers, then behold he will certainly set his face to take Megiddo

However, Apiru said that they were helping pharaoh in their letters:

EA 195 (mayor of town close to Damascus): *I am indeed ready together with my troops and chariots, … together with my Apiru …wheresoever the king shall order me to go.*
EA 252 (from Labayu the Hebrew at Shechem): *I am slandered before the king. When an ant is struck, does It not fight back.? Another city of mine will be seized.*
EA 253 (from Labayu): *I am a servant of the king like my father and my grandfather.*
EA 254 (from Labayu): *I have not held back my payments of tribute.*

All the while, this is what interested pharaoh:

EA 99 (from pharaoh to unknown mayor): *Prepare your daughter for the king, your lord, and prepare the contributions: 20 first class slaves, silver, chariots, horses.*
(translations by Youngblood and Albright; Wright, pp. 191-207; Moran, ed. *Armana Letters*; Murnane; Also see Albright, *Patriarchs*, p. 51; on emergence of Hebrew Amurru also see EA 73, 74, 85, 86, 91, 101, 103, 114, & 117; Mendenhall, *Message*)

Ruins of Ibirta, base city of Abdi-Ashirta whose name roughly means servant of Ashira or Ashira/YWVH in a time before Sinai and codification of Torah (Thulman; Emerton).

In chapter 42, the Amarna campaign will be compared with the Joshua campaign, and there is much in common. Joshua is credited with winning Jericho, Bethel, Gibeon, Shiloh, Mizpeh, and Debir. Just as explained in Joshua, some cities could not be taken by Hebrews, such as Gezer and Jerusalem, so Canaanites continued to live among Israelites.

These letters found at Amarna also shed some additional light on the tribe of Dan/Danites/Danuna/Danoi/Dana/Denyen/DNNYM/Daunian, whose history is difficult. Letter EA 151, from the ruler of Tyre to Pharaoh Akhenaten, in describing events in the area, refers to the "king of Danuna." Danuna was located on the Mediterranean at the extreme north of ancient Syria; aka Lukka in reference to the Sea People; aka Lycia in Greek epics; and Antalya in today's Turkey. The name of one king of Danuna who was part of a long dynasty appears to be Semitic. Caution mush be exercised to not assume that all of the references to Dan are exactly the same group of people, but could be related to one another. Dan and cognates of Dan were located in many places of the eastern Mediterranean. The Hebrew Nile

Delta, early proto-Greek Islands, Syria, Lebanon were closely connected by trade and cultural exchange. A discussion of Dan leads to the intersection of Hebrew and Greek beginnings, but this search is beyond the scope of this book (Simon; Kempinski; chapters 14 & 42 herein; Bryce; Gordon, Greek; Gordon Ugarit; EA 151, 38, Martin, pp. 21-35; Bohstrom). The tribe of Dan ended up as part of the Hebrew coalition.

Israelites delivered a religious message: Seek voluntary submission to the will of God, which commands ethical behaviors that are binding beyond any social or territorial boundary. The idea that religion exists to keep a king in power is false (Mendenhall, p. 25). Peasants, Hebrew and other, welcomed that call and stood ready to throw their support to the cause of Israel. (Isserlin, p. 58) "In the case of Yahwistic Israel we see fully formed the marks of a conscious, organized, broad-scale social egalitarian movement..." Israel accomplished a coalition of many anti-statist social sectors. (Gottwald, pp. 474-492; Albright, *Biblical, pp.* 25-26; Albright, *Archaeology, pp.* 91) Add to that, the humanistic thrust of the Hebrew religion, which is that people are free to live according to the moral law, and in so doing, can form their own dreams, whether that be skills, wealth, spirit, leadership, or study.

Serfs and slaves belonging to Canaanite kings stood up and rejected the abominations of their overlords. They joined the Apiru. The lord king of Jerusalem lamented, "The Apiru capture the cities of the king. There is not a single governor remaining to the king – all have perished.... The townsmen of Lachish have smitten him, slaves who had become Apiru." (EA 288)

What a difference between the Israelites and neighbors both in Canaan and in Egypt ! True, the Israelites did make accommodations to live together with these peoples in many aspects. However, the differences, fundamentally driven by religion, were immense. Canaanite practices offended Israelites. Ritual prostitution of both sexes, divination, snake worship, human sacrifice, and rape constituted various professions, some with temple guilds. In Egypt,

the universal worship of animals and the purchase of a lovely afterlife via gifts to temples and elaborate tombs shielded those with pecuniary means and low morals. An astonishingly high proportion of the wealth of Egypt found its way into the constructions of tombs and the maintenance of temple cults. Hebrews stood up and rejected these abominations (Muhlestein).

Their revulsion extended to the trading of people. Pharaohs and kings, in order to express friendship, gifted their daughters to be, perhaps, the fourth or tenth wife of the other. Also, these gifts might end up as an addition to the harem or house or temple. Akhenaton had five wives, while Ramesses married eight but fathered dozens of children from his harem. Akhenaton's father wed kings' daughters

(Cline, 1177, pp. 56-57).

But the revulsion of Hebrews regarding some Egyptian habits did not prevent Egyptians and Hebrews working with each other. Akhenaton and his father Amenhotep III continued the close relationship with Hebrews that their entire dynasty had experienced. Both pharaohs enjoyed the services of the Hebrew Aper-el, or Abdiel, vizier, general of the horses [chariots], and father of the god [close adviser to pharaoh] (Zivie).

The intersection of scripture pertaining to the rise of Israel as a country, archeology, and countless interpretations is explored in many papers and books including that of van Bekkum (Van Bekkum).

Aper-el possessed a large tomb for his family
(Zivi;, Wikipedia)

The Vanities of Ramesses II Destroy Egypt

37 Shelach Lecha Numbers 13:1 – 15:41 שלח Send (Spies)

We read in Shelach Lecha that Moses sent representatives to observe the Israelite landscape. They returned with reports of difficulties to be encountered in making Israel their home. As reviewed in the previous section, some of Israel had already been settled by Hebrews who were stymied in advancing further. These could be the areas observed by Israelite spies. Moreover, in this portion Torah commands that the tassels worn by Shosu should be worn by all Hebrews in recognition of God's laws. The history preceding the Moses exodus explains why and how Hebrews departed from Egypt.

Preceding enslavement, Sinai, and the spies episode, Hebrews lived peacefully in Egypt. The era of Pharaoh Akkenaten and his father saw tolerance, if not friendship, between Egypt, its Hebrew subjects, and Hebrews in Israel. Israel gained traction as a country. Hebrews had long been serving various pharaohs. The rise of Ramesses II after 1303 BCE introduced slavery of Hebrews, setting the stage for the second exodus.

Chapters 12 to 16 review the events of the ten plagues and the **first** Israelite exodus from Egypt, then briefly introduces the **second** exodus with Moses that led to travels in Sinai. Details of the second exodus started with the death of Akhenaten. About 40 years and several pharaohs later, Ramesses II gained the throne and erased the memory of Akhenaten (Dodson, *Amarna, pp.* 75-80, 136-138). Friends of the old dynasty such as Hebrews and Nubians were oppressed. The people of the Egyptian Delta were restive under the ecclesiastical tyranny of the priests of Amun and resisted their restoration after Akhenaten's death as shown in the subsequent civil war. (Albright, *Biblical*, p. 15; Assman, *Moses, p.* 54)

A Ramesses II administrator reported on *the Apiru (Hebrews) who drag stones for the great pylon of the building Ramesses II Beloved of Truth.* He instructed his servants to *distribute grain rations to the soldiers and to the Apiru who transport stones to the great pylon of Ramesses.* In addition they are also mentioned as brick-makers, as residing near the royal harem, and as having a country in Israel. (*Papyrus Leiden* 348; Ben-Sasson, p. 42; *Exodus* 1.8-14, Grimal, pp. 258-259).

Whipping Shosu (at Luxor) >>>

Ramesses bankrupted Egypt by enslaving a productive class, fruitless wars, and ordering wasteful monuments. His sixteen years of war to annex Syria failed. The major battle in those years was a loss to Hatti at Kadesh, Syria. On the way to his loss, Ramesses intruded on Shosu and Apiru lands in Amurru, Syria (Kuschke). Then he blamed Shosu for the loss. (Kitchen, *Triumphant, pp.* 53-56; Cline, pp. 80-83; Giveon, p. 227).

After the Egyptian loss, Hebrews in the City of Ibirta and the mini-state of Amurru remained independent under the protection of Hatti (Redfprd. Pp. 176-177).

Ramesses II made a career of attacking Hatti and Shosu, exhausting both sides with little to show. Many of his claims are lies or exaggerations (Hasel; Kadesh; Kuschke; Tyldesley, *Ramesses, p.* 58; Drew, pp. 138, 182). He avoided Israel, where settlement continued (Lemche, *Israelites pp.* 69-73). Below are just a few of the claims made by Ramesses II (Inscriptions located by Giveon) :

Shosu to the east that I can loot. (inscription on statue at Boubastis).
The fierce lion Ramesses II full of rage, has plundered the land of Shosu and captured Sier (stele at Tanis).
(Ramesses II) *ruined the inheritance of Shosu, and they bring tribute to Egypt* (2nd stele at Tanis).
The valiant Ramesses II …. made a massacre of the Shosu and made them all pay (Stele V Tanis).
Ramesses who loves Re has conquered the Shosu (Also at Tanis).
Victory over Hatti and Shosu (Stele IX at Tanis).
The Shosu are taken captive (sanctuary at Tanis).
Beware traveling with troops in Israel…. narrow clifts are infested with Shosu (Papyrus Anastasi I).

Over the course of many years Egyptian documents show the evolution of the Shosu from a small irritating group to a people cited alongside the most powerful enemies of Egypt, collectively known as the "nine bows." (Giveon, p. 224-225)

Shosu Soldiers (below)

As the end of the Ramesses II term (1213 BCE) approached, the strength of Egypt stood at a perilous state of decline due to failed military adventures; profligate spending on self-aggrandizing monuments; oppression of subjects, especially Hebrews and Nubians; the strength of intrusive Libyans; and lack of allies in the world. An astonishingly high proportion of the wealth of Egypt found its way into the construction of tombs and the maintenance of temple cults. Hebrew values rejected these inclinations.  (Albright, *Biblical, pp.* 16-19). Despite the Ramesses wars, Shosu remained in the desert and in Syria and in Israel.

161

The situation of other Hebrews was different. Certainly some tribes were enslaved in Egypt including the Joseph tribes of Manassah, Ephraim, and Benjamin. Southern tribes, probably including Simeon, Levi, Gad, and Reuben lived in desert areas and were observed also in Israel and Lebanon. The tribal affiliations of the Labayu Hebrews from Shechem are not totally known. The same can be said for the Hebrews in and around the Lebanon city of Ibirta in the land of Amurru. Parts of any tribe could have been located not only in Israel but elsewhere (Isserlin, pp. 56-58; Gottwald, pp. 176-219; Yeivin, pp. 41-42; Redford, pp. 263-280).

Then, suddenly, the world changed. A violent force made its appearance, beginning with an attack on the Nile Delta by Aegean pirates, quickly neutralized by Ramesses II. This incident introduced the beginning of what became a rolling offensive against the major Mediterranean powers. A combination of natural disasters, drought, the rise of piracy, new iron weapons, and outright famine stirred up a number of Aegean peoples

Rameses III - Medinet Habu, Thebes.
The Battle against the Sea Peoples   Clarendon Press, Oxford

known as Sea Peoples, that included Philistines (Cline, pp. 139-152). Trade decreased precipitously. The supply of copper from places like Cyprus dried up. Copper was an essential ingredient to the Bronze Age, as it was combined with tin to make bronze. Shosu controlled a safe supply of copper from their mines in the Timna area of the Negev. To trade for that copper or to form an alliance with Hebrews against Sea People was beyond the imagination of Ramesses II. Instead, he compromised Egyptian

interests by sending his army to steal copper, as did his successor. Ramesses wrested control of the Negev Copper mines at Timna for Egypt, and a temple for Hathor was erected. By the time of Moses, that temple was destroyed and a Hebrew Tabernacle built (Rothenberg; Neilson, pp. 9, 12; Bury, pp. 19,35-36)

<<< Phillistine relief at Medinat Habu.

In rapid succession over the course of a few short-lived pharaohs, established governments in Greece, Cyprus, the Aegean, Hatti, Amurru, and Lebanon were destroyed. The Egyptian country teetered but took longer to fall than its neighbors. However, the large Egyptian empire quickly disappeared as its possessions along the Mediterranean were taken by Sea Peoples, especially Philistines. Egyptians were thrown out of the Negev and Sinai by troops such as Shosu, leaving a path along the King's Highway across the desert open and available for migration such as the Moses exodus shortly to come. Egypt, having squandered its resources, having fomented internal dissent by its oppression of Nubians and Hebrews, eventually succumbed. Native Egyptians became subservient to new masters: first Lybians, then Nubians, then Ptolemy Greeks, then others (Cline, p. 9; Drew; Redford, pp. 241-256).

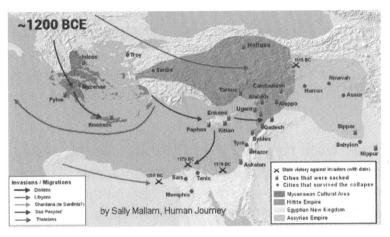

With turmoil in the world came change within the Hebrew community. The Lebanese Amurru state evaporated along with its Hatti protector. Consequently, Ugarit, located in Amurru and home of a Hebrew trading community, was destroyed. (Cline, pp. 105-107). Israel held fast, but with new challenges

In Egypt itself, internal discord brewed. A scribe wrote that peasant farmers were beset by taxes, thieves, and abuse (Kitchen, *Pharaoh, p.* 183). Hebrews in particular looked for freedom. It came. *Exodus* relates how God intervened on behalf of the Israelites.

That liberation gained momentum with the leadership of a person who was a prince of Egypt, in line for the throne, a viceroy of Nubia, willing to challenge the military dictatorship of Egypt. Efforts to suppress his name did not succeed, for his identity is known in rare surviving Egyptian records as Amenmesse/Messuy/Amunmoses or Moses born of Amun. Hebrews called him Moses.

<<< *Moses as a prince of Egypt, and a royal cup with his name.* (Metropolitan Museum of Art with his Egyptian name Amenmese, from Karnak, by author)

Civil War in Egypt

38 Korach Numbers 16:1 – 18: 32 קרח

Numbers reveals a dispute within the Israelite community wherein the leadership of Moses is challenged. This should not be surprising because the Hebrews, although sharing an abundance of values, combined a few independent groups into a new nation. Moses, as a prince of Egypt, had the most international and political experience. He also led a war against Egypt's establishment. He was not, however, the only one responsible for establishing the rise of Israel and the downfall of Egypt. Many had a hand in the demise of Egypt. Torah presents Moses as a religious leader par excellence with an ability to explain and teach the values of freedom, tolerance, and YHWH. The rebels Korah, Dathan, and Abiram came with their own credentials by representing the tribes of Reuben and Levi, and presumably also Simeon and Gad, of the South or the Esau Shosu. The earliest recorded worshippers of YHWH were Shosu, who had successfully battled Ramesses II and indeed Egypt for centuries; had captured Shechem for Hebrews in the time of Jacob; had hosted Israelites in the deserts of Negev and Sinai; and had been custodians of the copper mines where Moses rested the Hebrew congregation.

In this section of *Numbers* the rebels were consumed with fire and Moses continued in undisputed leadership. Actually there is evidence for a political compromise. *Numbers* and history descibe how different traditions and beliefs of southern tribes merged with those of other tribes in order to share knowledge and tradition in a manner consistent with divine worship. With Shosu/Esau contributions to the Hebrew cause so great, the Shosu traditions and beliefs inevitably became part of the conclusions at Sinai. It was the Levites who were guaranteed permanent control of an entire branch of government, namely as judges for the new country. Monotheism was a given for all tribes and a unifying religious duty, but it was the Shosu worship of YHWH emanating from Seir that Israel formally adopted. Hebrews would thereafter wear skull caps, now known as kippot or yarmulkes, and tassels, known as tzitzit, all in the Shosu tradition. The Shimeathites mentioned in multiple Torah and Jewish sources as important scribes over the centuries originated within Shosu culture. On the other hand, the extensive covenantal laws adopted by Hebrews fit in well with the Moses group, given their history as caravan traders and administrators in Egypt. (Deu. 22:12; Num. 15:38-39; Giveon, pp. 24-26,26a, & doc 6; temple at Soleb; I Chron. 2:55; *Sanhedrin,* 104a:2)

Moses, an Egyptian prince with military and administrative experience, then gained religious inspiration in the desert. With this background, he was the right person to forge Hebrews into a people. But first he had to free Hebrews from the oppression of Pharaoh. During the turmoil in the world and in Egypt around 1200 BCE, two princes stood in line to inherit the crown from Pharaoh Merneptah, son of Ramesses II. One of those, Seti II, was well documented as a son of the pharaoh, but served as a military general not recognized in his father's monuments (Gilmor, pp. 8-11). The other, Amenmesse, or Moses born of Amun, lacked firm parental documentation. *Exodus* 6:20 declares the father of Moses to be Amram, a possible corruption of Amun Ra, the putative father of all pharaohs. Moses seems the more accomplished son as vizier of Kush and viceroy of Egypt, controlling the anti-Theban anti-military areas of Egypt (Callender, pp.28-30; Dodson, 42; Tyldesley, *Ramesses*). Perhaps he became involved in forbidden political ideas, because Pharaoh Merneptah fired him and his staff, whereupon Amenmesse disappeared for some years (Dodson, *Poisoned, pp.* 42-44, 58-59). This disappearance is compatible with Torah's narrative of an exile for Moses where he met the burning bush.

Exodus and Egyptian court records seem to verify an incident involving Moses. The incident can be described as an excuse to fire a prince of Egypt rather than a root cause, but the recitations are important. In *Exodus*, Moses strikes and kills an Egyptian slave master for beating a Hebrew and must leave the country. In Egyptian court records, the trial of a certain Paneb took place in the same time of turmoil, when food and supplies were not delivered to tomb workers. The workers knew the plans of the tombs and stole from them. The case revolved around accusations of the murder of a supervisor, favoritism in promotions, and appeals to higher authorities, including Moses. The case may be tied to the dismissal of Moses (Callender, p. 28; *Papyrus Salt* 124; Dodson, *Poisoned*, pp. 33-59). It is possible that the case was only a peripheral excuse for dismissal and that Moses actually became too

friendly with oppressed Nubians and oppressed Hebrews. <<Tom*b of Rekhmire*

Moses's base in the north and south was with the discontents of Egypt (Schneider; Dodson all 5 references; Yurko; Callender). After a period of exile, Moses returned to Egypt and claimed the throne. Seti II claimed the throne for a short while before his early death at about age 25 (Callender). Each destroyed the tomb of the other. Needless to say, there has been no body found in the tomb meant for Amenmesse. Each spent a few short years on the throne, a couple of them probably simultaneously, with each ruling a different area. The history of the two brothers may be told in the Egyptian "Tale of Two Brothers." The civil war that ensued was neither short nor restrained (Tyldesley, *Ramesses*, p. 190; Schneider; Dodson pp. 46—67; Tyldesley, *Ramesses,* pp. 189-192; Kitchen, *Pharaoh, p.* 216; Callender). At a place on the Nile opposite the abandoned City of Akhenaten, the eastern side, stands a small area called T-en-Moshe, the island or river bank of Moses. (Brugsch, 182).

The civil war was as intense as any civil war in recorded history (Callender, Dodson, *Poisoned,* pp. 69-131). There came a time of death of a country, of a population, and of an era. A scribe named Ipuwer witnessed it and committed it to writing, excerpts from which follow:

The face is pale. The bowman is ready. The wrongdoer is everywhere. There is no man of yesterday as all is full of confederates. A man goes out to plough with his shield. The door-keepers say let us go and plunder. The confectioners.... the bird catchers draw up in line of battle. People of the Marshlands carry shields.... A man looks upon his son as his enemy. A man smites his brother, the son of his mother. What is to be done? A man is slain by the side of his brother. He tries to save his own limbs. He who has a noble lady as wife, her father protects him. He who has not they slay him. Men's hearts are violent. The plague is throughout the land. Blood is everywhere. Death is not lacking. The mummy cloth speaks before ever one draws near to it. The river is blood. Men drink of it, and shrink from the taste of people. Men thirst after water. ... A foreign tribe from abroad has come to Egypt. The Delta is overrun by Asiatics. ... The tribes of the desert have become Egyptians everywhere. There are no Egyptians anywhere.. Tents are what the Egyptians have made like the desert tribes. (Ipuwer is with the Theban side.)....

Men eat grasses, and wash them down with water. No fruit or herbs are found for the birds have taken away food even from the mouth of the swine. Corn has perished on every side. People are stripped of clothes, spices, and oil. Everybody says there are none for the storehouse is ruined with its keeper stretched on the ground. Noble ladies have their limbs in sad plight by reason of rags, all of which sinks their hearts in greeting one another. Men are like game birds. Squalor is throughout the land. There is none whose clothes are white in these times..... Thus serfs become lords; officials are slain; and their writings taken away. Woe is me because of the misery in this time. Scribes see their writings destroyed. The corn of Egypt became common property and so the poor man has come into the estate of the divine Ennead (family of nine deities).

The brothers disappeared from the scene. A Syrian, called "Bay" rose to prominence. Bay brokered the rise of the child Siptah of uncertain parents.

<<< Bay and Siptah - from Aswan, by Malatkova

Queen Twosret, possibly sister of one brother or wife of the other became regent for the child pharaoh, who soon died at age 16. Tworset became pharaoh. The fragile peace did not last. (Callender). Civil war resumed. A royal scribe presented the Theban side of what happened next:

The land of Egypt was overthrown from without and every man was thrown out of his right; Egyptians had no leader for many years. Each town possessed a warlord; one slew his neighbor, great and small (Callender).

166

An obscure Egyptian military man, Sethnakht, took control of the country. Then, with his opponents vanquished, the victor proclaimed himself Pharaoh Sethnakht and his son as successor. In a short uninformative stele located in the city of Elephantine, he claimed:

This land was in disorder. Egypt had fallen into a state of neglect of the gods. To His Majesty Life ! Flourishing ! Health ! Sethnakht is like his father Seth who stretches out both arms around Egypt to purify it through this expulsion of him who attacks, as his strength is around Egypt as a protection. His adversary falls before him, as he has put fear into their hearts…. (Sethnakht) set in order the entire land, which had been rebellious (Callender).

Hebrews were defeated. Torah emphasizes the military nature of the second Hebrew Exodus, this one with Moses: "Israelites went up armed out of the land of Egypt. (Ex. 13.18). "the angel of God … had been going ahead of the Israelite army," "a cloud … came between the army of the Egyptians and the army of Israel." (Ex. 14.19-14.20). Manetho, the Egyptian priest quoted by Josephus agreed with the interpretation of two events of exodus. With regard to the second, he said:

After those that were sent to work in the quarries had continued in that miserable state for a long while, the king was desired that he would set apart the city Avaris, which was then left desolate of the shepherds. [Manetho introduced a priest who,] *called himself Moses," and "First ordained that they [Hebrews] should neither worship the gods, nor abstain from those animals that were worshipped by the Egyptians…. they built a city in that country which is now called Judea, and that large enough to contain this great number of men, and called it Jerusalem.*

Many people were "disappeared" but may have departed for Israel. Evidence was destroyed:
- **Pharaoh Tutankhamen** – erased from records until discovery of his tomb, was a manipulated, and possibly murdered youth.
- **Pharaoh Ay -** no body in his tomb and his tomb was desecrated, his name suppressed, possible refugee to Israel or merely disposed of. (Harwood, pp. 44-46)
- **Pharaoh Amenmesse** – no body, accused of usurping the throne, his tomb taken by his rival, no death reported, may have exited, participated in insurrection and stands as a candidate for Moses leading Hebrews to Israel.
- **Bakenkhonsu** – no body, second prophet of Amun under Amermesse, his figure mutilated on Pylon VIII at Karnak. (Dodson, *Poisoned*,p. 74), possible refugee to Israel.
- **Pharaoh Siptah** - short-lived youth with deformed foot, erased from records.
- **Pharaoh Twosret** - monuments defaced, tomb used by her successor, temple destroyed, generally discredited and erased. (Wilkinson)
- **Chancellor Bay** – kingmaker, behind the scenes ruler, tomb fit for a pharaoh but used by a subsequent prince, memory erased – He might have exited despite a claim he was executed.

Egypt is a de facto suicide while Israel is born in the desert

39 Chukat Numbers 19:1 – 22:1 חֻקַּת statute - Deaths of Miriam and Aaron

In *Numbers 19-22*, as Hebrews approach the last days of wandering before entering Israel, several   items are folded into the record. It is the end of days for Miriam and Aaron and the period of mourning follows.   The ancient fear of death and spirits emerges with rules on how to cleanse a person who comes into contact with a corpse by using ashes from a sacrificed red calf. The mourning lasts for thirty days. Those, thirty days of mourning, called *shloshim*, שלושים , follow the death of a Jewish person even today. During this time, depending on a person's observance, daily activities are restricted. So the "statute" in *Chukat* is the law of handling a corpse. (*Num.* 19; Plaut, 1148).

The practical matter of proceeding to the Israel hill country from the Negev is then addressed. Problems arise when a number of kingdoms refuse to allow the Israelite community to pass through on the most direct route. The refusal is not surprising given the presence of soldiers within the Israelite group, replete with arms and troops. In the case of Edom, Moses tactfully chooses a alternative route, while other uncooperative kings are dispensed with militarily. Moab and Midian are still a problem.

Along the route, the community recites songs and poetry that sometimes refer to some ancient unknown documents and which often highlight their concerns about water and help from God in war, all reminiscent of the earlier songs of Moses and Miriam (*Num.* 21:14-16, 21:17-18, 27-30). This is interesting to history because poetry was a way for a population just getting acquainted with literacy to remember their traditions.

Sometimes ironies and representations are all too obvious in history. As Miriam and

Aaron, then shortly Moses approached death, Egypt itself reposed on a deathbed, for Egyptians will have shortly ceded rule to their enemies, one after another.   The misadventures of the 19th Ramesside Dynasty brought on this decline. As a final straw, the civil war brought on by Hebrews wishing for freedom put an ignoble end to the Ramesside era. Ramesses II had squandered the wealth and power of Egypt.

Broken stature of Rameses II at his mortuary. *Look on my Works, ye Mighty, and despair !* *Nothing beside remains. Round the decay of that colossal wreck, boundless and bare the lone and level sands stretch far away.*   From the poem *Ozymandias* by Percy Bysshe Shelley

As the partnership of Hebrews, Egyptians, and other foreigners came to an end, it is instructive to review the beginnings of that partnership. From the start there were aristocrats who opposed friendship with non-Egyptians, preferring to conquer, enslave, and exact tribute from them.

The Asiatic is a crocodile on its shore,
It snatches from a lonely road,
It cannot seize from a populous town
by Pharaoh Khety, *Teaching of Merykara* , 2150 BCE

<< *The Egyptian crocodile instills fear and demands respect – World Tribune*

All happiness has departed, flung down in the land of hardship,
from those supplies of the Asiatics who are throughout the land.
Men of violence have emerged in the East,
Asiatics are coming down into Egypt,…. [There are] *Walls of the Ruler which were made to repel the Asiatics and crush the Sand-farers* *Prophecy of Neferti* (written circa 1900 BCE.), Excerpted from R.B. *Parkinson*)

But Amenemhat I won a civil war with help of Asiatics, probably Hebrews, as Hebrew inscriptions from that time, the era of Abraham, prove. (ref. proto-Hebrew alphabet in Egypt at this time, Petrovich; Darnell; Himelfarb).

It is I who acted as a fortress when there were no people with me except for my retainers, the Medjay (Sudan tribes), Wawat (Nubians), and the Asiatics (Hebrews). Upper Egypt and Lower Egypt being united against me (Amenemhat I stele).

Thereafter for almost 1,000 years, Asiatics participated in Egyptian government, especially Hebrews from Abraham to Joseph to the viziers Aper-el and those with unverified homelands like Yuya and Bay. They largely lived in the Delta; introduced "commoners" into the aristocratic ruling class, and preferred policies differing from those of Egypt, such as distaining Egyptian gods or emphasizing trade (Legacy of Abraham, Hebrews of Ugarit).

Hebrew officials largely came from the Delta while friends of Hebrews in Nubia also contributed administrators. These are the very areas repressed by Ramesses II. Officials like Moses had many perks such as elaborate tombs and power. But they did not side with the Ramessides (short-lived 19th dynasty) and as a result were "disappeared."

It is possible that Moses could have rectified the errors of Ramesses, but he never got the opportunity. He had the help of others in his quest, people who may have ultimately journeyed to Israel. Egypt has no known records of individual oppressed Hebrews. However, sparse records of individuals who may have aided Moses in the civil war are available, inevitably defaced, suppressed, and denied.   Some notable persons mentioned in the previous chapter who "disappeared," were all somehow commoners, all with uncertain ancestry. Here is more information on some:

Pharaoh Ay: Brother of Queen Tiya who was married to Amenhotep III in an Egyptian golden age of harmony with Hebrews. He was replaced by the military.
Pharaoh Sitptah: Somehow related to Moses and his rival Sety II, but parentage is in question. Mother was "Canaanite." He died and disappeared at age 16..
Pharaoh Twosret: Female pharaoh until the end of the civil war, then "disappeared."
Chancellor Bay: King maker and deal maker, but "disappeared."

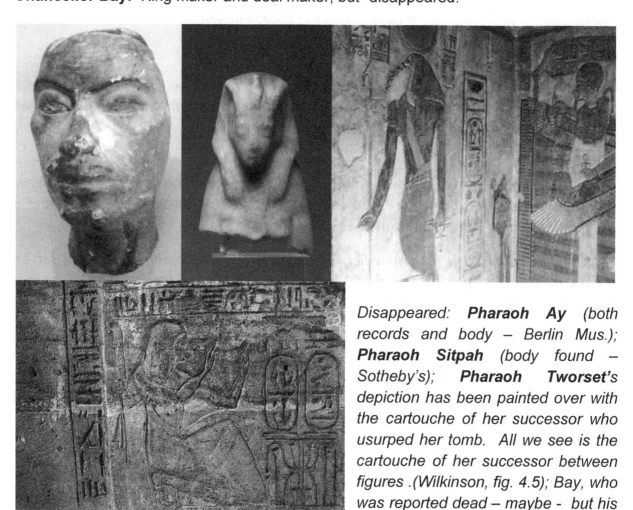

Disappeared: **Pharaoh Ay** *(both records and body – Berlin Mus.);* **Pharaoh Sitpah** *(body found – Sotheby's);* **Pharaoh Tworset's** *depiction has been painted over with the cartouche of her successor who usurped her tomb. All we see is the cartouche of her successor between figures .(Wilkinson, fig. 4.5); Bay, who was reported dead – maybe - but his*

records and body are missing. Some think he surfaced as a leader during the civil war (Adora Temple Nubia). Others are missing.

And so the groups represented at Sinai and in Israel were a diverse lot of Hebrews with varying knowledge of YHWH. They included privileged newly minted foreigner nobles with unused tombs; desert tribes of Shosu; long established as well as recent arrivals within Israel; and other unidentified Hebrews or sympathizers such as runaways. This group formed the nucleus of a new country Israel in the midst of a violent world, a country that has lasted thousands of years, often under the rule of foreign conquerors (Avner; Desert).

What these Hebrew groups created was much more than extraordinary. First among themselves, and then among others, they demolished the credibility of human, animal, stone, and wind or rain gods, replacing them with only one legitimate God. They received a code of morals that respected human dignity and proposed the notion that people should be free to live under universal laws rather than the laws of monarchs. They codified laws of commerce so that people could create ideas and crafts for trade rather than go to war and plunder.

Many leaders were present in the desert, but also craftspeople, soldiers, and scribes arrived at places like Timna. By that time the Hebrew alphabet existed and was used by Hebrew scribes including the scribe Az Romam.

Signature of Hebrew scribe at Timna (Wimmer).

Both Hebrew and Egyptian scribes identified the southern desert, or Seir, as the home of YHWH.

In stitching together the sequence of events that led to Sinai, it is probable that the enslaved population of Hebrews and royalty with Hebrew roots had lost much of their connection with details of monotheism and the worship of YHWH. It is doubtful that Moses, as a prince of Egypt, was totally engaged in the worship of YHWH. To become both a political and religious leader, Moses needed an education. Torah suggests his time in Seir with the Kenites, also known as a subgroup of Shosu, was when Moses became fully introduced to God and accepted a mission to free Hebrew slaves. Egyptian records show that Pharaoh Minerptah dismissed him from his powerful positions, after which his record goes cold for a while. Both recitations are consistent with the proposition that Moses learned to worship YHWH from Shosu Kenites and to acquaint himself with the desert.

What does milk and honey really mean?

40 Balak Numbers 22:2 – 25: בלק Balak, prince of Moab

The history of Balaam, the diviner who intends to curse Israel but instead blesses Israel, is not unique to *Numbers* in Torah. It has also been discovered in the archeological excavation located at Deir Alla in Jordan (Levine; *jewishvirtuallibrary.org/balaam*). Both Torah and the Deir Alla document identify Balaam, son of Beor, the diviner, then portray his activities in the style of Biblical poetry. In both documents God, or El, comes to Balaam at night. The circumstances are so similar that the Torah incident seems the same as the one described at Deir Alla, certainly each with common themes. At Deir Alla, a council of gods commands El to cause darkness and distress. Death will abound, but through his powers, Balaam saves his people in Moab by oracle. In Torah, the darkness for Moab would come from battle with Israel. In both presentations, Balaam is "condemned for what he has said and banned from pronouncing words of execration" Which is a curse of death (i.e. to Israel). This part mirrors the Torah version, that Balaam was condemned by Moab for his words of praise for Israel but he had been forbidden by God to curse Israel.

Coming from opposite sides of a tense situation, the people of Jordan, which was Moab, and the people of Israel faced a dark situation. Through skills in negotiation, rather than divination, Balaam could have arranged for Israel to pass and not harm Moab. He did not threaten Israel (execration), but found a mutually satisfactory solution. Israel passed through and a conflict was averted. This interpretation reconciles both accounts of the incident. Later we see in *Joshua* 13.22 that Balaam was still involved with Israel and killed in a battle between Midian and Israel. It can be inferred that he extricated Moab from conflict but may have been involved on the side of Midian in subsequent conflict. There is no independent verification of the Midian battle.

Torah description of Israelites weaving around Edom and Moab on the way to Israel. The Midianites were further south. From Atlas of the Bible Lands >>>

While both Torah and Moab, in their respective documents, recite the same incident, each believes in Divine coordination which is presented with poetic verse. In Torah, Moab is warned that Balaam will only speak what God commands. "Thus spoke Balaam, How can I damn whom God has not damned? . . . There is a people (Israel) that dwells apart . . . . My message was to bless. When He blesses, I cannot reverse it. No harm is in sight for Jacob, no woe in view for Israel (Num. 23-24.) The threat from Moab is dissipated as far as Israel is concerned.

No battle ensues.   A modern reporting of the incident would rely more on the geopolitics at play.   Any recognition of Divine involvement would be more subtle, but more likely non-existent.

The Balaam incident provides an opportunity to understand the mind set of Hebrews over 3000 years ago. After their stunning observation that human gods, idols, and diviners offered false explanations of how the world works, Hebrew revelation at the time showed a very direct relationship between conformance to the dictates of God and a person's success and health.

An example of the difference in ancient and modern interpretation comes from medicine. Torah did employ quarantine, disinfection, avoidance of dangerous foods, and disposal of excreta (*Ex.* 29:14; *Lev.* 7:24, 13:47, 14.8-9, Num. 19:15; *Deut.* 14:21, 23:13). That was the limit of science at the time, but it was not sufficient to ward off all illness. So Torah also says that ethical behavior, i.e. conformance with the dictates of God, will prevent sickness. Furthermore, sacrifice will help healing.   Also sacrifice done as an act of expiation will encourage morality. (*Plaut*, pp. 750-756; *Lev.* 1-7; *Deut.* 7:15). With regard to medicine, civilization has looked deeper into nature than sacrifice or behavior in order to better understand health.   Of course, this is the same nature created by God.   Medicine has improved by exploring nature more deeply, thereby discovering antibiotics, vaccines, and various medicines. The same is true for other areas of physical science, military science, and social science.

In the Balaam incident, both sides appear to tell the same story. Both sides believe that a divine force has taken a detailed interest in how the situation unfolds, even though the two explanations do not exactly comport.   This leaves us with unanswerable questions as to the beliefs of Torah scribes:
a) Are events controlled by God in order to affect the behavior of Hebrew individuals and the Hebrew nation?
b) Are many events seemingly arbitrary, unpredictable, and uncontrolled as related in Job?
c) Are Hebrew events a result of knowledge, study, and planning?
d) Does Torah teach that the progress of Hebrews is a combination of God's will, arbitrary happenings, and hard work of Hebrews? Torah provides evidence of all three options. From instructions to Abraham to the ten plagues to Sinai, Torah relates how God has nurtured the Hebrews. Then in Job and later in Ecclesiastes, the possibilities of bad things happening to good people, the search for meaning, the abuses of power, and the vanities of life are exposed. Torah gives credit to personal initiative. Abraham accumulated a large retinue and master-minded the defeat of King Chedorlaomer (see chapter 3) and his allies. Isaac founded a large business and following in the south. Joseph advanced to administer "all the land of Egypt."

> *Vanity of vanities, says Koheleth, vanity of vanities, all is vanity.*
> Ecclesiastes 1.2 (Gordis Tr.)

Torah handles religious, philosophical, historical, legal, and moral questions, in five very short books. It accomplishes this as an advanced document, even by today's standards, using many techniques. These techniques include metaphor, representation, hyperbole, and symbols. In doing so, one message can relate to people of various skills and learning at the same time. For instance, the Hand of God strikes Egypt; brings out the sons of Israel from Egypt; causes the earth to swallow Pharaoh's soldiers; executes law; redeems Israelites from slavery; and more. Torah continually refers to a pillar of cloud that protects and guides Israelites.

Scheuchzer Bible   1731 >>>

A pillar of cloud guided, protected and enveloped Israelites. Paintings representing the hand of God or a pillar of cloud are often not taken as paintings of reality but symbols of ideas like guidance, protection, or control (Ex. 3:20, 6:10, 13:21-22, 14:19-20, 24, 33:9-10. 15:12, Num 9:15-21, 14:14; Deut. 7:19, 6:21; 1 Sam 5:6-9). One interpretation would be that the hands and also the cloud of God are symbols for protection and comfort. A literal or metaphorical interpretation is available.

*Michelangelo ^^*

Writing techniques used and possible pioneered in Torah include poetry, hyperbole, narrative, metaphor, symbolism, allegory, personification, irony, wordplay, parallelism, history, and didactic delivery (Gabel, pp. 22-68). Also to be included are faith and condensation (combining multiple events or time spans into one short narritive). Great writers like Shakespeare used these techniques, as do politicians, scientists, historians, and teachers.

The above writing techniques can aid in looking behind various chapters of to reveal something akin to modern history, realizing that Torah was written as a guide to life rather than as a history. A number of researchers have done just that, with William F. Albright being the dean of this approach. He combined Torah study with archeology and ancient documents.

Keeping the above discussion in mind, many common interpretations can be revisited with a result of better history. Etan Levine (see bibliography) has explained how the common Biblical phrase, "a land of milk and honey," has been misunderstood and improperly used:

A land of milk and honey is **not** a land of abundance, is **not** a land of luxury, is **not** a sign of cultivated rich farmland. Part of the misunderstanding comes from an incorrect translation of "midbar מדבר," which is often interpreted as uninhabitable desert or wilderness. Although this can sometimes be the case, just as often, the word refers to a land of meager, uncultivated grazing ground; ground suitable for animals that provide milk and meat; and ground where honey can be found in the bushes and thickets. According to Levine, "milk and honey" is a code phrase for shepherding.

The conclusion with this insight is that Egypt produced food as a result of an agricultural strategy requiring hard work, often from slaves. Alternatively, a grazing strategy produces food as a result of allowing animals to roam and requiring the grace of God to provide rain from heaven, not from canals and labor.   This would be the attraction of a life seemingly free of oppression presented by the roaming tribes of Israel, who inhabited a wide swath of scrub land in the southern belt between Egypt and Syria; who freely worshipped God far from the

controlling god rulers of Egypt and Canaan; and who exhibited some military success against ambitious pharaohs.

The land of milk and honey (Author) >>>

Deuteronomy 11:9-21 puts it all in place: "a land flowing with milk and honey…. For the land whither thou goest in to possess it, is not as the land of Egypt, from whence ye came out, where thou didst sow thy seed, and didst water it with thy foot, as a garden of herbs; but the land, whither ye go over to possess it, is a land of hills and valleys, and drinketh water as the rain of heaven cometh down; a land which the Lord thy God careth …   if ye shall harken diligently unto My commandments which I command you, to love the Lord your God, and to serve Him with all your heart and with all your soul, then I will give the rain in its season…."

In conclusion, while reading about Balaam, there are many obstacles obscuring the actual history such as speech from a donkey and manipulations of a diviner. But then, Torah is not history.

Ingredients for a new nation

41 Pinchas Numbers 25:10 – 30:1 פינחס Pinchas aka Phineas

This portion of Torah begins with a census of the tribes and clans; then with the refinement of Hebrew law into a code; and establishes the right of an individual to appeal a decision or law. When completed, this code will influence the world almost as much as the monotheism revolution.   An issue arose with regard to inheritance, which is a lively topic for all the ages. Addressing this issue shows an advance beyond the basics of monotheism, no stealing, no lying, and no jealousy.   Inheritance laws led to things like the rights of women and others.   Few societies of the time concerned themselves with equality under the law.

Starting with the new rights for women in the area of inheritance, we review all the diverse elements put together to form Israel as a religion, a people, a nation, and a land. Cobbled together are a God that can't be seen, outcasts, serfs, refugees from Egypt, a humanistic morality, government without a king, and an expanding area of land under Hebrew control stretching out fom Shechem.

The case regarding inheritance has to do with the daughters of the deceased Zelophehad. He had no son. The daughters pled to be granted the inheritance of their father, a request that breaks tradition and could put the land into play should they inherit and then marry outside of their tribe. Most modern societies allow for a person to write a will and to have wide discretion as to how an estate will be distributed, with some protections for a widow.   Much later, even in medieval England where land formed the backbone of wealth, the practice of primogeniture insured that land would be passed to the eldest son.   Other assets were less restrictive (Shammas).   In deciding the case of Zelophehad, Hebrews decided that the daughters could inherit, albeit with some restrictions in order to keep property in the tribe (Num. 27, 36). Hebrews were not totally unique, but were advanced; women in some other societies of the time could inherit under certain circumstances.

<<< *Ancient Hebrew fabric with dye from snails, frequent item of trade, Israel Antique Auth., Clara* Amit, Times of Israel 1/1/2014

Inheritance has to do with assets, income, power, and wealth.   Hebrews pioneered alternative sources of income such as trade and craft. Some women engaged in such businesses.   Hebrew women early on participated in money lending, trading, and property ownership, both with spouses and independently (Tallan and Taitz).   Hebrews were not the only group that allowed women to conduct business, but permissions granted to Hebrew women were of a high standard for the time (see Chapter 31, Kedoshim).

For Hebrews, the extension of rights, responsibilities, and privileges went not only to women but to the entire congregation, adding to the strength of the group as a whole. This practice extended to the age-old habit of accepting cast-offs into the community, provided they obeyed Hebrew law (see ch. 1; *Lev.* 17:8, 10, 13, 20:2). The community of Israelites was liberal in its inclusiveness, welcoming desert tribes, tribes from Israel, tribes that had stayed in Israel, oppressed people, and others. Phineas, aka Pinchas, is a personal example. His Egyptian name suggests that he came with those from Egypt and may very well have been a scribe (Avner *Desert*, pp. 35-41).

The narrative of Pinchas, grandson of Aaron, represents the difficulty in Biblical interpretation without additional reference. At the time, Torah relates that Israelite men were cavorting with Moabite women who worshipped Baal thereby bringing the wrath of God. Pinchas observed such an Israelite man and his Moabite consort, then proceeded to impale them both. Was Pinchas an overly zealous murderer or a hero who observed an act of espionage and saved the Hebrew army? More than likely, a person's answer will depend on his/her relationship with Torah.

As seen from the Amarna letters in the time of Akhenaton, peasants wanted to join Hebrews. There is also evidence that entire clans may have joined the Hebrew movement. Fluidity did exist within the tribal system across the Mideast with clans going from one tribe to another, or splitting so that part of a clan might join another tribe. There is some extra-Biblical evidence for this occurring (Avner *Desert*). Torah describes complicated tribal evolution and entanglements by using literary techniques such as simplification, condensation (compressing events over a long time to a short summary), and bifurcation. An example of bifurcation is the description in *Joshua* of military settlement in Israel. *Judges* describes peaceful settlement of the same land. Here is how these literary techniques work, and this shows how complications can obfuscate the Torah message:

Torah introduces us to Kenites/Kenaz as grandsons of Esau and an Edomite, then the Kenite clan priest Jethro, a member of the Midianite nation, became the father-in-law of Moses. When invited to join the Israelite nation, Jethro initially declined. Kenites were extremely important to the development of Israel, not only as instructors in the religion of YHWH, but as scribes. In this position, they are mentioned not as Midianites, but as Hebrew Shosu tribes by Egyptians (Giveon, 26; Amenhotep III toponyms at Soleb). Then, soon afterwards, Jethro's Kenites became part of the tribe of Judah. (Gen. 26:11, 36:15; Ex. 2; Num. 10:29-30; Judges 1:16). A Kenite woman, Jael, kills the general of the army arrayed against Deborah (Judges 24-27). Another example is that the town of Kain (Kenites were purportedly descended from Cain) was established within Judah (Joshua 15:57). Judah, in assembling its Israeli land, absorbed, rather than fought, tribes such as Nahash (known for copper) and Harashim (copper smiths; Avner , *Desert* 13; *Joshua* 15:7; Hirsh et al).

Then there was the clan of Zerah, which, either from splits or changing affiliations, appeared associated with different tribes or clans, starting out in Edom as a ruler (Gen. 36:17, 33), but then as a son of Judah (Gen. 38:27-30; Num. 26:20), and also with Simeon. The infamous Korah, if it is a clan, known to have challenged Moses for leadership of Israel, appears as a Levite then later as a keeper of the Tabernacle under David still as a Levite. Earlier, Torah introduces this clan as a son of Esau or an Edomite, and, later, as a son of Judah. Some Korahites ended up with

Benjamin and others became Temple doorkeepers (Gen. 36:5, 14-16; Ex. 6:21; Num 16, 26; 1 Chron 1, 2: 3-43, 6, 12:6, 26).

Amarna letter from Gezer needing help against Apiru from the British Museum

The broad drawing power of the Israelite movement in a time of tyranny may have attracted clans and people not only from the obvious Houses of Jacob and Esau, but also limited numbers of Hittites, Hurrites, Canaanites, and Amorites. The tribe of Dan had its own unique history (see Chapter 12). *Joshua* gives the impression of a steamrolling Israelite military. *Judges* backs away from that. A close look at the mixing of people and tribes, combined with the turmoil of the era, suggest ethnogenesis, or, to use a Biblical term, a "mixed multitude." This is a process well known to Americans. (*Jewish Encyclopedia.com*; Avner, *Desert*; Num. 19-22)

Sometime after 1200 BCE the ingredients coalesced for Israelites to claim a national home for its people.

Israelites already had a foothold in the land they sought. History has seen this in the Amarna letters. Torah confirms that Manasseh was already in the land, as they had a clan of Shechemites (*Num.* 26:29). Moses reveals as much in an address, mentioning that Esau had disposed Horites "just as Israel did in the land they were to possess." (*Deut.* 2:12)
Just as Israel gathered freedoms for the oppressed including women, it also gathered cultural and statutory pledges for new freedoms and a safe land to form a new society.

- Israel was recognized as a nation, even if its boundaries were small before the arrival of Moses. Egypt admits this in the Pharaoh Merneptah Stele. Both Torah and Egypt recognize Esau/Shosu as inhabiting the land of Negev, also called the land of Seir (Deut. 20:12, inscriptions at Soleb). Shechem had been a Hebrew outpost at the time of Amarna letters and before.
- Israel had an army.
- The YHWH religion had a priesthood and a priestly code.
  - The YHWH religion had a holiness code that mixed civil and religious obligations.
  - The YHWH religion was based on monotheism.
  - The YHWH religion showed people how to live together.
  - The YHWH religion worshipped God as One, and thus was unique.
  - The YHWH religion had its set holidays: Passover, Unleavened Bread, First Fruits (Shavuot), self denial (now Rosh Hashanah), Atonement (Yom Yippur), Shemini Atzeret (Num. 28-29).

<< Merneptah Stele refers to Israel circa 1210 BCE prior to Moses in Cairo Museum(Times of Israel)

A long list of national requirements stood in front of the Hebrew people: expanding Israel's territory, settling the expanse of open land in the highland, including pastoral Hebrews' desert lands, routing out oppressive mini-kings of Canaan, fending off aggressive neighbors such as Philistines, accepting refugees, some of whom were Hebrew already and some Hebrew sympathizers, and getting an economy going.

History and Torah agree on the unfolding of many subsequent developments in general. Torah and history agree that Israel, over time, established itself on both sides of the Jordan River to the Mediterranean and from Egypt to Lebanon (Joshua: *1 Samuel* through *1 Kings*; Megan Moore, pp. 96-106). Shortly after 1200 BCE the population of Galilee, the central hills, the Judean hills, and Trans Jordan increased from a combination of new people from within and without the country, from military activity and from immigration. The Hebrew nature of the population created a new society (Moore, pp. 114-122).

The new society did not eat pig, favored particular ceramics, inhabited the Israelite house model with four rooms for residence and sometimes livestock, and utilized terracing for hillside agriculture. The One God was worshipped with increasing conformance. (Moore, pp. 129 - 133; Finkelstein Bible, 119-120)

Foundation of iconic Israel house in Hazor National park (Amit) >>>

The great influence of desert tribes on the emerging Israelite religion and nation has been discussed, with the original worshippers of YHWH coming from the desert, the tassels hanging from their sides, and the skull cap. Tradition from the desert also had its effect.

> *The desert tribal origin of groups in Israel may explain the egalitarian ethos, ideology of simplicity, and the primitive democracy of the Judges Period, as it is studied from both Biblical sources and material culture…. The ideology of simplicity is best demonstrated by a desert clan, the Rechabites, who preferred the simple lifestyle as a source of longevity and quality of life…. For them, simplicity was a way to protect their freedom. However, the tribes were not simple country folk. They controlled and ran an extensive copper mining and smelting operation, conducted trade, developed philosophy with religion, and demonstrated military prowess. (Jeremiah 35:6-9; De Vaux, 14-15; Avner, Desert, pp. 8, 46-47).*

> *Go and tell David My servant: Thus saith the Lord, "Thou shalt not build Me a house to dwell in; for I have not dwelt in a house since the day that I brought up Israel, unto this day; but have gone from tent to tent, and from one tabernacle to another. (1 Chron. 17.1-5)*

Israel formed a nascent country before birth of Moses

42 Matot Numbers 30:2 – 36:13 מטות Tribes

By the time Torah brings Moses and the Israelites to the edge of Israel, the tribes are organized en masse to settle the Promised Land. Of course, Hebrews had been there continuously from the time of Abraham. However, Torah describes an obstacle in this final step of the journey to Israel: the Midianites.

Balaam of Peor, the diviner who became involved in the Israelite–Moabite encounter, returned to the scene, this time as an agent of Midian, and, according to Torah, was up to all sorts of trickery and deception. Unlike the incident with Balaam and Moab, this event with Balaam and Midian is not referenced outside of the Bible. Pinchas, aka Phineas, an Israelite, kills a Simeonite chief and the chief's lover who is a daughter of a Midianite chief. The act leads to war between Israel and Midian, successfully executed by Israel, resulting in the death of Midianite men and the capture of their women (Num. 31).

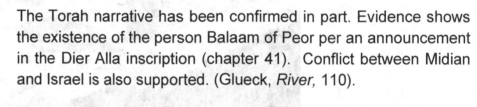

The Torah narrative has been confirmed in part. Evidence shows the existence of the person Balaam of Peor per an announcement in the Dier Alla inscription (chapter 41). Conflict between Midian and Israel is also supported. (Glueck, *River,* 110).

Torah explains later in Judges that the Midianites actually were still present and posed an even more serious problem, one that was resolved by the Israelite Gideon, who defeated the Midianites. Historians have weighed in on the later conflict.

^^ *Midian fr Wikipedia*

At harvest time, the Midianites and other Bedouins made rapid raids across the Jordan, carried off crops from Israelite threshing floors, and drove off whatever livestock they could lay their hands on. "The struggle between the Desert and the Town is continuous." (Glueck, *River,* 110)

The account of Israel slaughtering all Midianite men is hyperbole at its peak. The story served as a warning to those who would attack the Hebrew nation. Readers of Torah should understand that a victory only applies to those soldiers within sight. The desert area known to Midianites was vast. Only the uninformed, like a modern reader, would lack the knowledge of how to interpret the boasts of the ancients. This hyperbolic technique was continuously used by various pharaohs, especially Ramesses II, who, time after time, slaughtered the Shosu and drove them out of their homes, only to have to repeat the battle again and again, until it was the Egyptians themselves who were utterly defeated and the Shosu who went on to help found Israel.

Torah describes a confederation of Hebrews coming together in the desert at the Tent of Meeting. Evidence at Timna National Park in Israel's Negev shows that such a tent did exist. At that time, however, a nascent Israel already had been formed (see chapter 36). A meeting of tribes could very well have been convened consisting of the desert Shosu, the refugees from Egypt, those in Israel already, refugees from Lebanon (see below) and new adherents (Gottwald; Albright, *Patriarchs of Yahweh*; Moore & Kelle, pp. 117-126). More Hebrews were in Israel before Moses than is obvious in Torah. A close look at events in Israel some 150 years before Moses suggest that the Joshua campaign took place during the Pharaoh Amenhotep III and Akhenaten administrations, around 1350 BCE.

Archeological evidence does not support a Joshua rebellion at the time of Moses in the 12th - 11th century BCE. At that time, for instance, Jericho was already resettled after having been reconstructed by Hyksos, who invaded Egypt and then were destroyed at the time Egypt defeated and wiped out the Hyksos. Resettlement took place around the 14th century BCE, compatible with when the tribe of Benjamin could have occupied the city and named it Jericho after a Benjamin clan (Kenyon, "Jericho"; Kenyon, "Excavations,"; Kenyon, "Oldest Walled Town;" McConville & Williams, p. 4; Na'aman, "Conquest of Canaan;" Redford, pp. 263-269; Na'Aman, "Conquest;" chapter 12). Also, the extra-Biblical Amarna Tablets discovered in Egypt as discussed in chapter 36 supports the earlier date of the Joshua campaign, while describing a legitimate peasant revolt aided by Hebrew agitators. Reconciliation of these tablets and the *Book of Joshua* reinforces the proposition that two events of exodus took place and the Joshua campaign occurred between the two as described here:

- After the first exodus, many Hebrews arrived in Israel, joining whatever others were already present from as far back as Abraham. Egyptian and Mari records show Apiru or Shosu throughout the area. A large number of Apiru appeared in Israel at that time (Albright, *Abraham*, p, 32).
- The first exodus, at the time of the Santorini eruption (16th century BCE, see Chapter 14), not only caused many Hebrews from the Delta to evacuate, but also all of the Hyksos who had controlled a large part of Egypt for many years (chapters 12,14,15.16,36).
- A series of pharaohs captured the Hyksos territories along the coast of Israel. Hyksos included Canaanite, Amorite, Hurrian, and other powers. The defeated powers were enemies of Egypt and of Israelites. Hebrews in the hill country and in the Lebanon area took advantage of the situation in order to expand their influence.
- The trove of clay tablets found in the palace of Akhenaten represents about 400 letters between the mayors and rulers of lands from Hebron to Syria. They depict active campaigns of Hebrews centered in Shechem, Lebanon, and Syria, to support the oppressed peasantry and overthrow various Canaanite kings.

- The tablets describe the Joshua campaign and fit the Biblical script, placing Joshua about 150 years before Moses. Archeological findings show that no mass destruction took place at the purported time of Joshua after Moses. Biblical writing presents a commentary of events and not necessarily the timing of events. Placing Joshua after the two events of exodus made the Biblical commentary compelling and succinct.
- The Amarna tablets clearly describe two theaters of Apiru operation: one, described in the Joshua campaign, saw Hebrews expand from their base from Shechem, south to the gates of Jerusalem and north past Megiddo to Acco. The leader of this operation was Labayu, third generation ruler of Shechem. The *Armarna Tablets* are perhaps the only extra-Biblical reference to a Joshua, one "Yisuya" (Joshua, Yehoshus, Hoshea, Yusha, or Yehoshua bin Nun, as referenced in Armarna EA 256), who is called upon to vouch for the whereabouts of a man sought by pharaoh. Joshua perhaps was a legendary hero who masterminded the wishes of rulers like Labayu. The real-life campaign described in the *Amarna Tablets* is full of determined battles but not wholesale destruction and slaughter. *Amarna Tablets* and the Book of Judges make it clear that the blood-letting of the *Book of Joshua* is hyperbole and metaphor.

The Amarna letters, the descriptions of Israelites living together with other Canaanites in *Judges*, various documents, and the lack of archeological evidence for the violent campaign of Joshua depicted in *Joshua* show that the *Book of Joshua* is largely hyperbole. Jericho was occupied by the Tribe of Benjamin, but not in the manner or at the time suggested in the *Book of Joshua*. (Kenyon, "Jericho,"; Kenyon, "Excavations," Redford, pp. 179, 263-265; Stern, Philip; McConville, pp. 31-32).

What is a proper reconciliation between history and the *Book of Joshua*? Firstly, the *Book of Joshua* is not part of Torah, and hence does not make the claim of holiness associated with Torah. Israel was prohibited from changing Torah (Deut. 4:2), but no such prohibition prevailed for later books, particularly the *Books of Joshua* and *Judges*. Therefore, one idea to explain the contradictions between *Joshua, Judges*, and archeology is that the two books were edited for political purposes with uneven results (Goff).

Even though *Judges* rectifies some of the aberrations in *Joshua*, other history is not addressed. After Egyptians cleaned out remnants of Hyskos rule in the 16th-15th century BCE, parts of Israel, including the eastern Negev, were largely uninhabited, making for an easy transition to the Israelite period. New towns were not fortified in the Negev nor did they need to be. There is no evidence of a King of Arad in the Negev, who smote the Israelite tribes. (Aharoni)

At the time of the Hebrew campaign described in chapter 36, which we consider to be the "Joshua" battles, there was a parallel theater of Apiru operation. In this parallel operation, Hebrews expanded their enclave in the Beqa Valley of Lebanon into Syria and Damascus, an area known as Amurru. It involved defections of peasants to the Hebrew side. This effort is given oblique mention in *Joshua* 12:2 reference to Amorites but extensive coverage in the

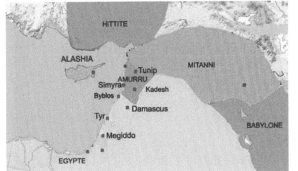

Amarna letters (EA 53-187: *EA numbers are in the book by Moran*). The Hebrew leader in Amurru was Abdi-Ashirta and his son Aziru.

*Amurru fr cuphistory^^*

Aziru roused his troops to subdue the Lebanese Port of Byblos:

"Assemble in Bit NIN.URTA and let us fall upon Gubla (Byblos). If there is no man who will deliver it from the hand of the enemy, then let us drive out the governors from the lands, and let all the lands join the Apiru and let an alliance be formed for all the lands in order that the sons and daughters may have peace forever. And even if the king should come out then all the lands will be hostile to him, and what will he (be able to) do to us?" (EA 74, Mendenhall, Message).

At the same time, other forces in the area were either allied with or sympathetic to Hebrews. For instance, King Idrimi, put on the throne of Alalah NW of Aleppo by Apiru, operated between the major powers as did Israel at that time. Idrimi also had friendly relations with Suteans, another confederation comprising some Hebrews. (Luciano, Edgar, chapter 2).

Torah gives credit to Joshua for the victory in Amurru (*Joshua* 12:2). Here follow some correlations between the Book of Joshua and the Amarna Letters:

	CH OF JOSHUA	TRIBE	COMMENTS	AMARNA LETTER	VICTOR
Lachish	10:1-27, 31-32, 1:.41		Zimredda ruler	97,234, 254, (Petrie)287, 328, 329,332	Apiru
Jerusalem	10:1-27	Judah	defeated king Abdi Heba but city contested	287, 289, 290,	
Gezer	10:33, 1:.13	Judah	captured by Joshua	253, 254, 287, 290, 298, 300, 369, 378	Apiru

Hazor, Hasura	11:1, 15:23-25, 19:36	Naphtali	captured by Joshua	148, 227, 228, 364	Apiru
Shimron	11:01	Asher	near Hazor. Ally also Madon,		
Madon	11:01	Asher	near Hazor. Ally also Madon, Shimron		
Ashshaph	11:1, 12:20, 19:25	Asher	near Hazor. Ally also Madon, Shimron	223, 366, 367	draw
Amurru, Amorites	12:02		Syria, Lebanon, Beqa Valley ruled by Aziru	60, 61, 70, 73, 82, 85, 82, 91, 95, 101, 103, 114, 115, 117, 127, 142, 145, 156, 158, 162, 165, 166, 167, 178,	Apiru
Meggido	12:13, 12:21, jdg 1:27	Menassah	Menassah could not hold	234, 242, 243, 244, 245, 246, 247, 248	draw
Taanach	12:21	Levites	SW of Meggido	248	Apiru

Kedesh, Qadesh	12:22	Levites (Barak)	S. of Beersheva ruler was Etakkama claimed by Joshua	189	Apiru
Ashkelon		Judah	Gaza coast Joshua won it from Philistines	287, 320, 321, 322, 370	Apiru
Byblos, Gubla, Gebal	13:03 13:05		won by joshua, Apiru	67, 68, 70, 72, 74, 75, 78, 79, 81, 84, 85, 88, 90, 94, 98, 103, 104, 106, 109, 116, 123, 124, 126, 128, 129, 131, 132, 133, 136, 138, 139, 140, 142, 152, 162, 362,	Apiru
Acco	19:30 jdg 1:31,32	Asher	Asher could not posses shared with canaanites	8,88, 232, 233, 234	Apiru
Batruna,	jdg 1:31		N. Lebanon	89	Apiru

It is not possible to present a one-on-one reconciliation of the cities captured as per the *Book of Joshua* with the Amarna Tablets. One reason is that the tablets found represent only a portion of an unknown number of tablets. The battles of some cities and areas are lost. In addition, the tablets only cover cities beholden to Egypt. The *Book of Joshua* relates battles with cities not in the Egyptian orb such as Gilgal, Jericho, Ai, and Eglon.

The *Book of Judges*, describing a time period after the arrival of Moses, makes another suggestion: that the Joshua campaign was not given to slaughter. This is because, as *Judges* makes clear, numbers of Hittites, Hurrites, Canaanites, and Amorites were absorbed by Israel as neighbors. They integrated into Hebrew society through intermarriage.

 This description is entirely consistent with the Amarna Letters to Akhenaten and Amenhotep that narrated the revolt of the serf class against Canaanite lords in order to join
Hebrews. (*Judges* 3:4-6; Avner). Additionally, many of the Joshua cities were not totally conquered or burned because, according to Judges, they needed to be battled again in order to gain control. These included Hazor, Askelon, and Midians "defeated" by Moses.

No longer powerful – Hazor, Ashkelon, (Israel National Parks), and Meggido (site: conhecendo Israel)

Judges goes further to explain that a number of cities devastated by Joshua actually became cities where Israelites lived with purportedly conquered people including Megiddo, Tanaach, Gezer, Acco, and Askelon. In another group of cities, at least a dozen, including Rehob, Beth Shean, and Beth Shemesh, a mixed population lived together (*Judges; Joshua*; Avner; *Exodus* 12:38).

Evidence thus shows that the Joshua campaign did not slash and burn towns, but instead accepted existing residents in sizeable numbers, some of them serfs who revolted according to the Amarna Letters. In addition, the Amarna evidence shows that, between the exodus of plagues and the Moses exodus, Hebrews expanded in Lebanon and Syria to form an influential country and established themselves in Israel to form another country recognized by Egypt as per the Merneptah Stele.

"The Hebrew settlement of Canaan ... was successful thanks to a series of small battles with the petty kings of Canaan who held authority over some little piece of ground. This occupation presupposes a state of affairs in which the authority of the pharaoh had disappeared." (Dhorme, p. 167) The Apiru success was that of the native against the foreign overlords. (Greenberg, p. 8; Dhorme)

Subsequently, catastrophic events that occurred around 1200 BCE, including draught, famine, and invasion, led to the disintegration of major powers including Hatti, the Hebrew Amurru, Cyprus, Mycenae, and various Canaanite regimes (Cline; Dodson). Invaders known as Sea Peoples, which included Philistines and Denyen, disrupted the Mediterranean and brought Egypt to its knees. The civil war of Moses brought an effective end to the Egyptians and triggered exodus from Egypt. Moses was about to enter the Israel hills at a time when Hebrew Shechem had about the only stable government in Canaan. The old powers, Egypt, Hatti, and Mitanni, desirous of controlling Israel, were either gone or failing.

The Moses entrance into Israel resulted in the formalization of Israel as a unity of tribes. Some development of the country had already taken place, but final steps were needed. We mention, for example, the late arrival of the Dan tribe and references to it as having, at least in part, separated from other Israelites due to their migration to Greece. (chapters 14 and 36). The Sea Peoples also included Greek tribes such as the Danites/Denyen/DNNYM who were reviled by Egyptians. Pharaohs fought them and lost control of a large area along the Mediterranean. The tribe of Dan, who Torah mentions as being oppressed by Philistines for 40 years, evidently separated from the Philistines and founded their own tribal area in the north

of Israel, thereupon reuniting at least one part of Dan with Israel. (Yadin, Dan; Korpman, Judges 13, 14, 15; Gordon)

<<< Denyen as prisoners of Egypt shown on wall at Medinet Habu. Notice they have tassels like the Hebrew Shosu tribe. (see ch 34; pic. From widipedia)

1000 + 40 years of travel about to end by claiming a homeland

43. Massei Numbers 33:1 – 36:14 מסעי Journeys

The last chapter in the *Book of Numbers* provides an entrée into an entirely new phase of Hebrew development. This portion of *Massei* in the *Book of Numbers* recalls the journeys of Israelites from Egypt into the Desert of Sinai. With instructions from God, the tribes decide which parcels of land each will possess. This prevents bickering later on. The Levites understand that they will possess certain cities but no larger parcels of land. Those cities are to be refuge cities.

Of course, any number of Israelites already possessed land in Israel, and that was recognized by allowing those in Israel to retain their residences. References to Israelites already in the land have been made herein Chapters 6, 7, 36, 42, and elsewhere. The references cover the Hebrew battles reflected in the *Amarna Letters* to Pharaoh Akhenaten in the 14th century BCE. In that period, both the *Amarna Letters* and proto-Israelite sites suggest pastoral occupants such as Shosu Beduoin. (Finkelstein & Mazar, pp. 80-81) Settlements in suspected Hebrew areas have included no pig bones but did have other animal bones. In that same hill country and to a lesser extent in Trans-Jordan, northern Negev, and Galilee, open villages with Israelite architectural design sprouted before and after Moses. The villages often included a typical Hebrew four-room house. The hill country was available for pioneers. Joshua

states to Ephraim, "Go up into the forest and clear land for yourself there." In chapters 36 and 42 herein, we posit that much activity ascribed to Joshua in Torah occurred before Moses (Finkelstein & Mazar, pp. 80-81, 86-88; *Josh.* 17:15).

Excavation of ancient part of Beersheva (guggarji @ Wikipedia, cropped)

Pig bones are a reliable indicator of Israelite presence in the early period of Hebrew settlement. Excavations in Israel and Western Jordan show a scarcity or total absence of pig bones from the 12th century BCE except in Philistine areas. In Israelite areas conquered by Philistines, the incidence of pigs bones increased dramatically. After Philistines were defeated, pig bone evidence declines to a great extent. To the extent that pig bones might appear in an Israelite area, it is possible that other ethnic groups also lived there (*Bible History Daily* 5/12/22; Sapir-Hen).

Another example is the site of Khirbet Qeiyafa, settled before the Bronze Age that became fortified during the emergence of Israel as a country. The site is located 30 km. southwest of Jerusalem, which would be in the western part of the plain sloping down to the coast. Khirbet Qeiyafa is near the Philistine city of Gath, only 12 km. to the west. The excavated portion is estimated to be from about the time of Moses to the time of David, when the city experienced total destruction. No pig bones were found (Munger).

Khirbet Qeiyafa in 2011, the site where pro-Hebrew inscription was found on a shard with words regarding slaves, rulers, and God. (Photo from report of Garfinkel, Ganor, and Hasel).

Genesis and *Exodus* cover some 1,000 years and are packed with action while Hebrews developed their culture, religion, and morality. These years culminated with the receipt of God's law by Moses at Sinai. Not so long a time is ascribed to the events of the final three books comprising Torah. *Leviticus, Numbers*, and *Deuteronomy*, by their own reckoning, occupy about forty years of wandering. Those years as well present quite a story of action and law-giving that include the receipt of the *Priestly Code*, assigning ritual to the new religion, and the *Code of Deuteronomy*. Both add to the existing codes and form them into a national constitution.

The number 40 in Torah has a mystical dimension since it is the time all

otted to a number of events:

Years of desert wandering	Years under Philistine terror
Years of eating manna	Years that clothes and sandals did not wear out
Years of Ezekial's curse on Egypt	Years land rested before Othniel died
Saul's tenure as king	Moses' years in desert before burning bush episode
David's tenure as king	Years under Philistine terror
Solomon's tenure as king	Jehosphat's age at death
Joash's tenure as king	Isaac's age when he married Rebecca
Eli's tenure as judge	Esau's age when he married Judith and Basermath
Period of peace under Gideon	Period of peace after death of Sisera

With the journey of the Egyptian refugees over, an unverifiable timespan, Torah does some accounting as well as some recollection of speech from Moses. New refugees were about to join those already in Israel. A census was taken.

The focus of Torah is then about to change from from action to words. In fact, the Hebrew name of the *Book of Deuteronomy* is "*Devarim*," meaning "words."

Devarim describes a convention of parties coming together over an unknown period of time to forge a new nation, a new morality, a new people, and a new religion. The convention drew together over a thousand years of cultural development. Something akin to the process might be the forming of the United States from a new spirit and culture to a revolution to a declaration of independence to a confederation to a constitution connecting some 13 independent states. As a help, the United States had looked to the Enlightenment and to the Bible for guidance, and drew on example from both.

Torah narrates Moses listening to God and relaying instruction to the people of Israel. The physical event behind that presentation is not available. However, the results are available. In the next book, *Deuteronomy*, the *Shema*, the central affirmation of Judaism, is presented: "Hear, O Israel: The Lord our God, the Lord is One." Also, *Deuteronomy* reveals an epic poem of God's enduring relationship with Israel and the end of days for Moses, called the *Song of Moses*, or *Ha'azinu*."

We can turn the page and enter *Deuteronomy*, the blueprint for Hebrew society that became the plan of modern civil society.

The Hebrew obligation to rescue Israel

44 Devarim Deuteronomy 1:1 – 3:22 דברים Words

Perhaps more influential and spell-binding than the incredible story of patriarchs in Torah is the manual for a civil society presented to the world by the Israelites. *Deuteronomy* presents this set of instructions, relying on previous history such as the Holiness Code and the Priestly Code. More than the giants of the ancient world: Egypt, Babylon, Sumer, Hatti, Assyria, Mycenae, Phoenicia, and Persia, to name a few, little Israel demonstrated a way for human beings to live together without the need for plunder, idols or sorcery, murder, and the like, thereby defining a humanistic concept of morality. Thus did Torah influence the development of civil society in the world. This process is enumerated in countless books and in many actions, including the founding documents of the United States. Three things were needed by Hebrews: a body of moral law, a monotheistic religion and land on which to enact it all.

At the beginning of *Deuteronomy*, Israelites receive orders that their freedom is dependent on their not duplicating the abominations they have witnessed and been subjected to. The timing of these orders correlates to the imminent entry into Israel by the Hebrews. Moses sears into the minds of his followers the necessity for judges to:

> *Hear the causes between your brethren and judge righteously between a man and his brother, and the stranger that is with him. Ye shall not respect persons in judgment; ye shall hear the small and the great alike; ye shall not be afraid of the face of any man; for the judgment is God's* ... (Deut. 1:16-17)

This call to equal justice rang true to the Hebrew cause; was a reason for its popularity across ethnic boundaries; and has resonated across Jewish and Judeo-Christian congregations throughout centuries. Given the state of the Mediterranean world at the time, the statement of Moses seems idealistic, quixotic, and unrealistic.

At the time of the Moses exodus, any semblance of civilization had disintegrated. Ruthless pagan tribes like Philistines, Tjekkers, and Pelesets hacked their way through the tyrannical kingdoms of the day, bringing even more depravity to the greater Mediterranean. Starvation, murder, plunder, and refugees blanketed the area. Hebrew communities in Israel needed help to survive attacks from the Philistines, who had little opposition. The only available force to combat the onslaught, the only available force to introduce an alternative to tyranny,

Philistine warrior fr. Luxor

and the only force available to unite many of the disparate governments of Canaan was Hebrew. Hebrews had incentives to organize and protect Israel. More than incentives, they had obligations:

- To protect the many Hebrews already in Israel from attackers like Philistines
    - ~ Including those who never left for Egypt until the time of Moses such as parts of Judah, Benjamin, Ephraim, and Manasseh (Albright, *Yaweh, p.* 155).
    - ~ Including the Shechemites who expanded their area during the Joshua battles previously described in the Amarna Tablets and in the *Book of Joshua*.
    - ~ Including an unknown number of peasants and serfs who joined the Hebrew cause, together with some of their leaders. Only the Canaanite political exploitive class were enemies of Israel, not the common people (*Amarna Tablets*, Gottwald, pp. 430-431, 586-587).
    - ~ Including an unknown number of refugees from the destroyed country of Amurru, described as Apiru during the Amarna period
    - ~ Including an unknown number of Hebrew refugees fleeing the disasters of the world.
- To find a home for the Hebrew escapees from Egypt.
- To establish a defendable home for Hebrews against the fierce tyrannies of the world.
- To establish a home for the Torah and its followers.
- To establish a zone free of the iniquities abominable to God.

Torah made mention of those iniquities at the time that Abraham was recovering from battle with the king who invaded Sodom. A divine message came to him in a deep sleep: "Know well that your offspring shall be strangers in a land not theirs, and they shall be enslaved and oppressed four hundred years; but I will execute judgments on the nation they shall serve, and in the end they shall go free with great wealth . . . . And they shall return here in the fourth generation, for the iniquity of the Amorites is not yet complete." (*Gen.* 15.13-16)

Does the concept of indigenous rights apply to any Canaanite group at the time of Moses? The land known as Canaan experienced swarms of rulers with no one unifying group. Human beings who originally inhabited Canaan consisted of stone-age populations, Neanderthals, and elephant hunters.

<<< 9000 year old settlement West of Jerusalem

They were all replaced by ambitious overlords who became absolute rulers. The land was continuously coveted and frequently conquered by strangers. The older population mixed in with newer populations and were dominated by them. In some cases, like Neanderthals, older groups were eliminated. The migration of Abraham represented the westward expansion of West Semites, Amorites, Indo-Europeans, Anatolians, Syrians, Hittites and Hurrians. Torah remarks that Abraham bought a gravesite for Sarah from Hittites. (Glueck, pp. 21- 24, 115; Ben-Sasson, p. 6-7). In addition, the patchwork of people and states covering Canaan pushed out one another. Areas settled by early Apiru/Hebrew had rapidly thinned out and so the Apiru part of the West Semitic population settled in undesirable essentially vacant land. (Eben, p. 5; Noth, *History of Israel, pp.* 10-16; Albright, *Biblical Period From Abraham*, pp. 3-4) and Hebrews could therefore establish themselves without challenge. Hence, Israelites at the time of Moses had a claim to be one of the surviving indigenous peoples, and, later, the only early group remaining. Consequently, they could lay claim to being the only indigenous people of Israel. Israel was not the heart of Canaan. The jewels of "Canaan" were Lebanon and Syria because of valuable cedar trees, minerals, agricultural products and coastline. In the southern part of Israel, the Negev and beyond, the Hebrew Shosu were entrenched from early times as documented in Egypt and Torah, which explains that God "gave Esau the hill country of Seir…." (Joshua 24:4).

As described, Israelites were coming home.

They planned to form a country unlike those that had abused them. Stretching back 1000 years as donkey caravan traders, Hebrews learned to accommodate the high, the mighty, and the imperial. The Hebrew nation would have none of that for itself. Indeed, after the instruction from Moses to treat the small and great alike, came another instruction,

> When you enter the land that the Lord your God is giving you, you shall not learn to imitate the abhorrent practices of those nations [Egypt and those in Canaan]. Let no one be found among you who consigns his son or daughter to the fire, or who is an augur, a soothsayer, a diviner, a sorcerer, one who casts spells, or one who consults ghosts or familiar spirits, or one who inquires of the dead. For anyone who does such things is abhorrent to the Lord, and it is because of these abhorrent things that the Lord your God is dispossessing them before you. … Those nations that you are about to dispossess do indeed resort to soothsayers and augurs: to you, however, the Lord your God has not assigned the like.

The list of abominations practiced by tyrants in Egypt and Canaan constitute a veritable guide to unlimited control and abuse by dictatorships and oligarchies practiced from ancient times to today. These abominations are antonyms to the instructions in Torah.

<<< Syrian mermaid godess on coin, photo public domain

In addition to the standard oppressions employed by various kings, oligarchs, and emperors, many Canaanite city-states added other layers of iniquity such as child sacrifice, rape, and prostitution. These abominations were practiced in concert with the worship of the storm god Baal, king of heaven and earth, "enthroned" on Mount Zephon in Lebanon. Baal fought the god of death. He raped his sister dozens of times. The sister took pleasure in murdering humans.   In both Egypt and Canaan, the word "sister" and "wife" were synonymous, and in both locations, a long array of gods received worship.   To Hebrews, one of the most horrific practices in Canaan was human sacrifice. (Albright, *Yaweh*, pp. 124-152; Henry Smith; Lucian).

<<< Baal: photo public domain

Upon the arrival of Hebrew refuges, the hilly dry area from which so many had departed still remained hilly and dry. The mini kings had not changed their tyrannical ways including sacrifice of children and abuse of serfs. Torah recited time and again a promise to Hebrews to return to Israel. The time was not always ripe for the return. Many hundreds of years before, Abraham was told that Hebrews would be as "a stranger in a land that is not theirs and serve them." That sojourn would not be indefinite. After a time and when the abominations of Canaanite lords reached a certain level, Israel would return to home. "And in the fourth generation they shall come back hither; for the iniquity of the Amorite is not yet full." (Gen. 15:16).

Even though the Hebrew/Apiru appeared on the world scene before four thousand years ago, and established an outpost in Israel, they were in no position to begin nationhood or even to defend territory. Various Canaanite, Amorite, other Semites, and Hurrian tribes were too powerful. Hebrews were without a substantial military, without an administrative arm, without a developed religion, and without a sizable economy. All of that changed by the time of Moses. Canaanite lords were largely defeated by Egypt and Sea Peoples. Egypt itself had lost its colonies, and its independence wavered. Hebrews had the army of Moses, the army of Shosu tribes, the armies of Israel mini-states like Shechem, and forces in Syria.

The atrocities of Canaanite leaders gave them little legitimacy with their subjects, while the Hebrew culture offered an appealing option for serfs as proven by their willingness to attack leaders during the time of the Amarna Tablets when Hebrews expanded their domain (see Chapter 37). Miles of relatively open land still existed in the Israel highlands for immigrants to settle. At the same time, Hebrews held land around not only Shechem but also in the Negev, in the Timna area, and elsewhere (see Chapter 35). An explosion of population took place just after 1200 BCE in the Israeli Highlands (Finkelstein & Silberman, pp. 105-120).

Preserve your faith - live it & recite the commandments

45 Va'etchanan Deuteronomy 3:23 – 7:11   ואתחנן   I implore (you to follow)

Torah proceeds to relate the second great discourse of Moses, which emphasizes the benefits of a nation that worships God. He implores Hebrews to take his advice but then faces some hard facts.

MOSES: "Of all the peoples on earth the Lord your God chose you to be His treasured people." (Deu. 7:6)

FACT: Hebrews were the only people to embrace One God, but did so with much resistance. Other cultures vehemently rejected the notion and preferred multiple gods. Hebrews suffered scorn and exclusion for their attachment to monotheism. Therefore it makes sense that Torah devoted much attention to maintaining obedience to God.

MOSES: "It is not because you are the most numerous of peoples that the Lord set His heart on you and chose you – indeed you are the smallest of peoples." (Deu. 7:7)

FACT: Being a small minority in a neighborhood of aggressors and avaricious tyrants is dangerous. Better be careful and stay together.

MOSES: You must not bring an abhorrent thing into your house…   (Deu. 7:26)

FACT: To a large extent, this is the crux of Hebrew desires but also problems. Torah wanted Hebrews to live lives apart from idols, god-kings, state murder, human sacrifice, military adventurism, arbitrary laws, large state taxation, state ownership of land, temple prostitution, and state controlled business. Torah was a guide for how to achieve such a life for its adherents.

Idols Enki of Sumer (Pub), Ra of Egypt (Nefartari's tomb), Zeus of Greece (Louvre), and Jupiter of Rome (Hermitage) are all relics, as are the empires that spawned them.

Today's religions of the East and West show the far-reaching effect of the Hebrew Bible. They do not support idol worship; idol worship was eliminated in Israel, and subsequently in the world. Human sacrifice was eliminated. Temple prostitution was eliminated. To a lesser degree in the wide world, the practices of state murder, military adventurism, arbitrary laws, and state control of crafts or businesses was not practiced.

The ambition described in the Torah anticipated a sanctuary for "the smallest of peoples." That sanctuary needed to include a piece of land away from the great productive river valleys like the Nile or Euphrates where Hebrews could practice faith in God, laws and morals to live by. The discourse presented in this portion – *Va'etchanan* – I implore you – speaks to the issue of commitment. Many cults came and went, and the Hebrew cult had not stood the test of time even though various aspects of the teaching had proved popular, such as dispersion of government power, honesty in justice, and so on.

The speech attributed to Moses seems to recognize the problem, and hence, implores, even begs, Hebrews to give the laws of God a chance. Moses makes the case for commitment. There will shortly be a vote among Israelites on the matter, so one could say that Moses is doing some electioneering.

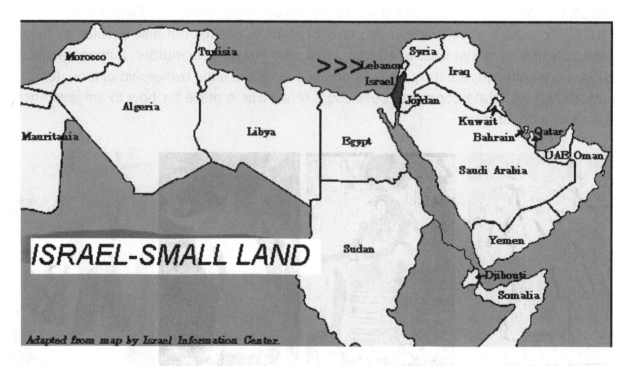

ISRAEL-SMALL LAND

Adapted from map by Israel Information Center.

Jumping ahead of the story, it is well-known that Israelites, some grudgingly, did accept the arguments of Moses. Four major Abrahamic religions and some smaller ones flourish today. Abraham indeed has progeny as numerous as the stars.

Israelites were the first to grapple with the admonitions of Moses. That religion is known today as Judaism, and the Judaism of today reflects the original teachings, but not without adjustments. Looking only from an historical viewpoint, a few sample aspects of Judaism in all its denominations show ancient and present religious practices in concert with each other.

Jewish congregations read the Torah over the course of a year in weekly segments. Judaism keeps the Sabbath as the day of prayer and rest, and recognizes the special days mandated in Torah. In general, services include numerous quotations in song or recitation from Torah, and Torah is always close to the Apiru/Hebrew/Israelite story. Here is a small sampling of Hebrew Bible quotations used in Jewish liturgy:

Reading of Torah

Deut. 6"4: **Shema**   Hear O Israel, the Lord is our God, the Lord is One. **...** שמע 'שראל 'הוה אלה'נו

Nehemiah 9:5 **Blessed** Blessed is God's glorious majesty forever and ever. ברוך שמ כבוד מלכותו

Ezekiel 38:23 **Kaddish**   Magnify and sanctify **....** יתגדל ויתקדש

Deut. 6:5-9 **V'ahavta**   love Adonai your God with all your heart ... ואהבת את " אלה'ך בכל לבבך

Ex. 1:18, 15:11, 15:2, *Jeremiah* 31:10 **Mi chamochah** Who is like You..This is our God... Adonai will reign...Adonai redeemed   מ' כמכה באלם " ... זה אל' ... " 'מלך ...' פדה "כ

Num. 24:5, *Psalms* 5:8, 26:8, 6914 **Mah Tovu** How fair are your tents, O Jacob ...מה טבו אהל'ך 'עקב

Psalm 84:5, 144:15 **Ashrei yoshvei** Happy are those who dwell... אשר' 'ושב' ... אשר' העם

Ex. 20:2-14 **Anochi Adonai**   I am Adonai, Your God ... " 'אנכ

Num. 15:37-41 **Adonai said to Moses** Speak to the Israelites and instruct them to make fringes on the corners of their garments... ....ו'אמר " אל משה לאמר דבר אל בנ' 'שראל ואמרת על כנפ' בגד'הם לדרתם

Num. 6:24-26 **Y'varech'cha** May God bless you and keep you... ... 'ברכך " ו'שמרך

Deu. 4:44, *Num.* 9:23 **Vzot haTorah al pi Adonai...** Torah Moses placed   before the people of Israel, God's word through the hand of Moses.וזשת התורה אשר שם מושה לפנ' בנ' 'שראל על פ' " ב'ד משה

Gen 1:31, *Gen* 2:1-3 **There was evening** and there was morning... ...ה'ו ערב ו'ה' בקר'

Ex 31:16-17 **V'shamru v'nei Yisrael** people of Israel keep Shabbat . שמרו בנ' 'שראל את השבת

Christianity, Islam, and Bah'a'i are also Abrahamic religions in that they are monotheistic, recognize Abraham and Moses, and, to a varying degree, have adopted Hebrew concepts. It is not the purpose here to trace the development of the religions stemming from Abraham in any religious or historic context past the Hebrew settlement in Israel. Below are just a very few comments to highlight the thread from Abraham.

In the case of Christianity, holy scriptures have adopted the entire Hebrew Bible as part of those scriptures.

Some observations on come commonalities of the four Abrahamic religions:

1. There is one God.
2. Abraham is the father of all those religions.
3. God has revealed the essentials of each religion, recorded in holy script.
4. Each religion has codes of morality, being the Ten Commandments and other guiding principles in Judaism, and therefore in Christianity. Islam has its own code of morality. Bah'a'I' emphasizes the unity of all humankind.
5. All four religions credit God with creation of the universe.

There are other aspects of the religions with commonality and also great deal of difference.

Voting, Branches of Government, Rights, and the Hebrew Republic

46 Eikev Deuteronomy 7:12 – 11:25 עקב Because (you obey)

In *Deuteronomy*, the important history research no longer concerns the activity of the Israelites, but rather the activity of Torah itself, specifically the ideas embedded in Torah and what happened to them, how they influenced the development of Western - then Eastern - civilization. What evolved is civil society, democratic society, religious society, and humane society, all in one. Crime, injustice, and other abhorrent events still take place on a regular basis. However, the ideas that individuals have some control over their lives and also have some moral responsibility have changed the world.

"If you do obey these rules and observe them faithfully.... "(wonderful things will happen)" (Deu 7:12) The opening stanza of *Eikev* sounds like a political speech, and indeed it is. Promises and responsibilities roll off the tongue of Moses: bless you, multiply you, be free of Egyptian diseases, defeat enemies. You must, however, consign craven images to flame, and not bring abhorrent things into your house. Furthermore, remember, the lord has brought you out of Egypt to a good land... Moses goes on in great detail about how well Israelites have been treated in light of their past enslavement and their wonderful future with God. The electioneering begun by Moses is completed by Joshua.

One reason for the election-type speech could be that, indeed, an election was coming. Torah recognizes the benefits coming from consent of the governed, and hence Hebrews conducted seven elections.

Torah records that Hebrew leaders Moses and Joshua conducted votes on whether to worship God and obey God's laws (Holman 1890 bible)   >>>

First: Ex. 19:5-9 "All the people answered as one, saying, 'All that the Lord has spoken we will do !' " Torah's statement of such a vote has to be one of the most extraordinary descriptions of the astounding Hebrew legacy. A people voting for their God and concomitantly for the laws they will live under ? Unheard of ! Not permitted ! But they did it anyway. In addition, the vote can be inferred to be honest in many ways. All voters were present, so only eligible voters participated, no tampering with voter rolls. The issue was so popular that it passed by acclamation, without the need to trade favors or buy votes.

Second: Ex. 24:3-4, 7-8 "All that the Lord has spoken we will faithfully do!"

Third: Deu. 1:14 "You answered me and said, 'What you propose to do is good.'" (Organize political divisions into chiefs of thousands, hundreds, fifties, and tens.)

Fourth: Deu. 5:24 "You go closer and hear all that the Lord our God says, and then you tell us, 'everything that the Lord our God tells you, and we will willingly do it.'"

Fifth: Josh, 24:15-27 "Now, therefore, revere the Lord and serve Him with undivided loyalty; put away the gods that your forefathers served beyond the Euphrates and in Egypt, and serve the Lord. Or, if you are loath to serve the Lord, choose this day which ones you are going to serve..."

In reply, the people declared, 'Far be it from us to forsake the Lord and serve other gods ! . . . We too will serve the Lord, for He is our God.'

Joshua, however, said to the people, 'You will not be able to serve the Lord, for He is a holy God... And the people declared to Joshua, 'We will serve none but the Lord our God, and we will obey none but Him.'"

Sixth: 2 Kings 23:2-3 "All the people stood to the covenant."

Seventh Nehemiah 10 "an oath, to walk in God's law, which was given by Moses."

With the introduction of "voting" to Israelites, another new idea for humanity was instituted, what was to be called the Hebrew Republic (Nelson). Torah became a monumental inspiration to the ages. In a sense, we are all – all of humanity – Hebrew. Torah is open to all and was not restricted to Israelites. The religious, moral, legal, and now political lessons, to name a few revelations, have been adopted in various degrees throughout the world. As explored below and above in this book, the world has benefitted from this remarkable ancient document.

Assyrian wall from Ninevah showing deportation of Lachish residents (British Museum by author) >>>

Over the course of time, Israelites were scattered due to lost wars. Whether this was a divine idea or an unintended result of aggression, Hebrews then spread their ideas. "Adonai will scatter you among the peoples, and only a scant few of you shall be left among the nations.... But if you search there, you will find your God...." (Deu. 4.27-29) The world slowly learned Hebrew ideas, which expanded beyond the confines of Israel. The Roman Empire allowed the spread of monotheism while attempting to harness religion to its imperial purposes. The result was the spread of the one God of Abraham, but inhibition regarding the laws of God from Moses. Roman defeat of Israel and suppression of religious and personal freedom pushed the instruction of Moses underground for centuries. But out of sight was not out of mind. Hebrew communities and Hebrew minds, then defined as Judaism, did survive, often under extreme duress. Great leaders such as Maimonides, Nachmanides, and Rashi kept those ideas alive under the protection of particular monarchs such as Visigoth King Theodoric, French Charlemagne, Spanish Caliphs Rahman I through III, and Jaime I of Aragon Spain. (Crane).

During the medieval period, land constituted the basis of wealth. Roman oligarchs and European aristocrats assembled enormous tracts of land, worked by serfs and slaves while allowing only a tiny middle class of traders, priests, and craftspeople. Manors, feudal estates, nobles, lords, divine kings, papal leadership, and vassalage were the rules of the day (Cantor, pp. 214-223, 447-455).

Then came the Renaissance and Reformation. New ideas flooding intellectual circles challenged existing precedent, especially long-held notions about concentrating land ownership, power, and privilege. Up for consideration was the political order of the day. With idols gone and God in, these intellectual circles searched for inspiration involving political systems. But wait! Did they believe in God? Did God have a divine political system? Where was it described? One only needed to look at God's own words, words which were recorded in the *Five Books of Moses*, and, to understand the Hebrew Bible, a person needed to learn Hebrew, consult with Jews, and read related works from Talmud to Maimonides. New discoveries of old knowledge followed.

In 1566 the *Status et conversions imperii Hebraeorum* by Jean Bodin was printed; it was followed by *De politia judaica tam civiliquam ecclesiastica* by Bertram in 1574; then came three separate works by the same title – *De Republica Hebraeorum* by Sigonio in 1582, by Menochio in 1648, and by Cunaeus in 1617; and in 1611 Henry Ainsworth wrote *Annotations upon the five books of Moses*; over 100 such volumes were published before 1700.

These works brought forth ideas antithetical to the rulers of the day. It was suggested that any claim that a monarch was selected by divine order is false, that agrarian redistribution according to the laws of God was required, that a monarch or political aristocrat is subject to the same laws as the general population, and that the practice of toleration is both political and also pious.

Rather than consult with philosophers for political wisdom, one should refer to the political constitution of God as revealed in Torah. Hebrew sources of all sorts were examined in order to discern the wishes of God regarding government approved by the Divine. The process of Biblical examination led to a glimmer of hope for toleration through the agency of religion, not through secularization (Nelson, pp. 16-136). The following were ancient Hebrew ideas rediscovered by Reformation Christians and those that followed? (Berman)

1. Commoners are not servants of the king, but the king is a servant of the commoners. Also, religiously, In *Genesis* 2, humans are created to till the ground for their own nourishment and pleasure, while in other traditions like Akkadian, humans are created to engage in labor on behalf of the gods. Kings in Egypt and Babylon were gods. Hebrews are not servants, but made in the image of God to have dominion on Earth (*Gen.* 1:26-29, Psalms 8:5-6). Israel and Hebrews are not subjected to arbitrary laws of god kings, but to their covenant with God, except to honor local law per Maimonides. Hebrews voted to accept laws of God rather than have them dictated These ideas slowly made their way toward democratic forms of government.

2. Hebrews instituted constitutional government that separated powers into an executive branch; a judiciary; a priesthood, an assembly of tribal leaders, and prophets from the commoners (Deu, 1:2; Num. 35:12, 24-25; Josh, 22:16, Judges 21:10; Samuel: 1,2 Kings). Legal curbs were put upon the size of the military, the treasury, the ability to control debt or land ownership, ability to change law, and the possessions of the king. All Israelites are equal under God, and it is God, not a king, in charge of Hebrew settlement in Israel. This idea of constitutional government is now wide-spread.

3. Hebrews installed a number of asset laws to prevent the buildup of a large class of landless peasants. A modern economy has evolved in many ways different from the ancient economy, but biblical ideals persist: debt release in the form of bankruptcy; laws to protect workers from serfdom and insure payment for labor; a new form of debt that can help a person buy a house; and breakup of large manors and estates through economic incentive, taxation, grants of public lands; the emancipation proclamation; the American Homestead Act; and insurance to protect against loss.

4. The Hebrew alphabet and emphasis on education made knowledge more universal.

The Hebrew Republic that foreshadowed American democracy and European civil society received renewed interest and commentary during the seventeenth century "in the full fervor of the Reformation, [when] political theology reentered the mainstream of European intellectual life. ...." (Nelson, p. 2)

World's First Modern State

47 Re'ei Deut 11:26 – 16:17   ראה see, or behold – blessing or curse

In Torah, Moses sets a blessing of land, crops, and peace before a people who will obey the commandments of God, and a curse for those who disobey. If Hebrews do not obey despite all that has been done for them, a curse of plague and misery will descend. The Israelites accepted the challenge. However, their obedience was flawed, but improving. Likewise, their lives did not return to Eden, if that was what they had in mind. Hard work and danger lurked around every corner. That is life. However, they gained freedom and access to knowledge.

After the time of Moses Israel, as a country and as a people, increased population quickly. The size of the existing Hebrew population and the type of governance in place before this increase are not known. In any case, a large influx of people was anticipated, not only from the Egyptian refugees, but from those fleeing from turmoil of the Mediterranean. So many factors were in play: Philistines ravaging the coast, serfs abandoning lords, and established empires collapsing.

Ancient cities once key to Israelites, now ruins: Jericho and Shiloh - center for the Tabernacle, Joshua, and Samuel. (Wikipedia and biblical Israel tours)

Principles of practical government were recorded in Torah. The government of ancient Israel did not follow norms of the day. In Egypt, Hattusa, Babylonia, Ugarit, and new entities emerging out of the world's turmoil, a hierarchical political and economic structure served at the pleasure of a king and the king's retinue. Israel turned this order of entitlement around.

In the books of Moses we find a blueprint for a social and religious order that is more egalitarian in nature. Before Israel, social and political hierarchy in the ancient Near East received legitimization from idols and monarchs, because the heavenly order was construed as paralleling the terrestrial one, featuring gods behaving with human traits. In this scheme, the common person emerged as a servant, the lowest rung in the hierarchy, as is evidenced in Mesopotamian creation epics, and echoed elsewhere as well. The theology of covenant in *Torah* rejects this model. (Berman, pp. 5, 9).

The *Deuteronomy* government of Israel 3,000 years ago included a number of novel laws:

- System of magistrates and officials shall govern with justice. (16:18)

- Law against taking of bribes. (16:19)
- Law against partiality in administration of courts and ordinary governance (16:19).
- Prohibition of worshipping idols like the sun, the moon, or heavenly bodies (17:2-6).
- A supreme court shall decide appeals (17:8-12)
- Constitutional limitations on a king and a king must obey the law. (17:14-20).
- Justice, justice shall you pursue (Deu. 16:20).

This sounds like a modern civil society.

An executive branch with layers of leaders.

A judicial branch with local magistrates and an appeals court.

A moral branch with Levites.

People's advocates consisting of prophets.

Various departments:

1. **Internal Revenue Service for taxes.** Torah distinguishes between voluntary contributions and taxes, which are compulsory payments enforced by government or other authorities. Contributions for assembly of the tabernacle are presented in Torah as free will offerings. The first tax is described as a 10% tithe. Apparently, during the tenure of Joseph, the tax rate was 20%, and even more later. The 10% was in addition to the command to leave the corners of field unharvested so the poor could gather some of the crop. (Gen. 47: 26, Ex. 35:4-35; Lev. 27:30-34; Num. 18:26-28; Deu. 14:22-29; Manuel & Moore.)

Then came the kings, with the warning by Samuel (I *Samuel:8*) that kings would tax heavily. He was correct. Solomon and his son used corvee labor and so increased taxes that Israel split into two nations. (*I Kings: 5*) Under its kings, Israel's taxes gradually increased to a repressive level. Johoiakim instituted a tax on land after his father's unnecessary war was followed by defeat at the hands of Pharaoh Neco (II Kings 23:28-35; II Chronicles 35:20-24) II Chronicles 24:5 mentions a special assessment tax to repair the Temple. Also a poll tax started with Moses continued with *Nehemiah* (*Ex: 30.12, Neh.* 10:32). Taxes continued to cause problems with rulers like Romans. *Samuel warned about kings but anointed David (William. Hole)* >>>

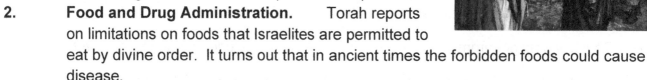

2. **Food and Drug Administration.** Torah reports on limitations on foods that Israelites are permitted to eat by divine order. It turns out that in ancient times the forbidden foods could cause disease.

   a. No pork (*Deu.* 14:6-8).– undercooked pork is prone to spread trichinellosis

    b. Fish must have fins and scales (*Deu.* 14:9-10), meaning no shellfish, shark, or eel. Mud burrowing or undercooked fish or shellfish can have disease.

    c. Do not cook meat with milk (*Deu.* 14:21). The bacteria mycobacterium avium is transmitted through milk, and beef and can affect the digestive system. Heat promotes the development of mycobacterium.

    d. Eat animals that have split hoofs and that chew the cud. (*Deut.* 14:4-7). The ox, sheep, goat, deer, gazelle, ibex, and antelope normally are not diseased.

    e. In slaughter, drain the animal of blood (*Deu.* 12:15-16, 20-24)
    This makes it less likely to contract blood borne illnesses including hepatitis and norovirus. (Anderson)

    f. Do not eat birds of prey such as vultures that eat corpses. (*Deu.* 14:11-20)

    g. Strict laws of slaughter. Unclean slaughter invites many types of bacteria.

3.   **Department of Education.** *Torah.*

4.   **Commerce Department.**

    a. The Lord your God May bless you in all the enterprises you undertake.

    b. There shall be no needy among you.

    c. Allow the Levite, the fatherless, and the widow to eat their fill.

    d. Open your hand to the poor.

    e. Set a Hebrew slave free in seven years, and don't send him away empty-handed.

    f. Follow the laws of business, including honest scales, no fraud, pay laborers quickly, and do not steal (See Chapter 33).

5.   **National holidays.**

    Passover, Atonement, Shavuot, Sukkot. Rosh Hashanah, Shemini Atzeret.

6.   **National Science Administration**

    a. Creation: Torah immediately addresses the question of existence. "In a beginning": by using the indefinite article "a," the reader knows that many beginnings, either in sequence or parallel, can be or could have taken place. This interpretation of "beginning" is compatible with the "big bang" theory, but also compatible with a much more expansive view of the beginning. It opens the possibility of continuous beginnings. *Genesis* imbues creation with a concept of God, YHWH – I am that I am – something beyond the ability of a human mind to totally comprehend. This is also a theological and philosophical issue outside of the intentions of this document.

    b. Infinity is approached as a concept, but again, a precise definition is avoided, perhaps being not understandable. Torah explains that God made heaven, but also the heaven of heavens (Deu. 10:14, I Kings 8:27, Nehemiah 9:6).

    c. Celestial objects are not deities (NASA photo), but bodies given for light (Gen. 1:14-19, Psalms

104:19, Avodah Zarah 54b.12:14)

Torah Geography

d. Some Torah scientific assumptions might have been adequate for ancient times, but Torah study permitted refinements to the original dictates. For instance, Torah geography was short on the world outside of the Mediterranean and military science included sacrifice. The Hebrew tradition of wrestling with God seems to have given permission to update God's commandments while retaining respect for those commandments. The treatment for illness involving sacrifice gave way to treatment by medicine. The obligation to maintain a temple in one place gave way to rabbinic Judaism. The openness to questions and study gave rise to new science including the description of blood circulation by Maimonides and the theory of relativity by Einstein.

e. Blood is the source of life (*Lev.* 17:11)

7. **Bureau of Immigration.**

   a. From the earliest times, pre-Hebrew people known as Apiru had the tradition of admitting the outcast, the runaway slave, and the misfit (see Chapter 1).

   b. Many Hebrews migrated to Egypt, and later in the Amarna period, serfs and slaves joined the Hebrew cause (See Chapters 9-11, 43).

   c. Torah in numerous places advises Hebrews to "welcome the stranger."

   d. Welcoming the stranger, however, is not a carte blanche for the welcomed people to do as they please. The stranger must obey the laws of Israel (Ex.12:43, 49, 20.10, 22:20, 23:9,12;   Lev. 16:29,17:8, 19:10, 33, 34, 23:22; Deu. 10:19, 16:14,1:.15, Num. 9:17, 15:15,30 and others).

      i. The stranger cannot work on forbidden days, marry the wife of a deceased husband, eat of Passover provisions unless he/she has become a citizen, become an Israelite ruler, do any abhorrent things, offer incense, sacrifice children, approach the Mishkan.

      ii. The stranger must participate in festivals, obey the law, offer sacrifices, and obey God's laws and rules.

      iii. Not obeying them is to be cut off from the community of Israel (*Ex.* 23:12, Num. 15:30)

      iv. Strangers with evil intent are attacked (*Judges* 6; *Gideon*)

8. **Department of Defense.** Joshua heads the army. Each tribe has a division.

9. **Property Rights.** Do not steal, Do not move neighbor's landmark (*Ex.* 20:15, 22:1-31; *Num.* 27, 33:53-54, 36: *Deu.*19:14, 27:17)

10. **Representative Government.** Moses chose capable individuals out of all Israel, and appointed them heads over the people, chiefs of thousands, hundreds, fifties, and tens... Ex 18:19-26.

11. **Democracy.** See chapter 46.

Hebrew liberation and an unintended world revolution

48 Shoftim Deuteronomy 16;18 – 21:9   שפטים Judges

Shoftim begins by reminding Israelites to avoid the oppressive practices of Egypt and Canaan. By repeating a few of the Hebrew laws and regulations, this portion reminds us today of the enormous changes wrought by this small group of people. It also reminds us that the governments of Canaan and Egypt were at the end of their existence.

While Egypt declined, Hebrews strengthened their presence in Israel, though it was a small nation surrounded by aggressive powers including Philistines, Midianites, Hittites, Amorites, miscellaneous Canaanites and a waning Egypt. Torah adds Girgashites, Perizzites, Hivites, and Jebusites to the list of adversaries. As history shows, Hebrews, maintained their presence in Israel throughout all the centuries (Verlin). That little piece of land was used to keep the ideas expressed by Abraham and Moses alive. Without that land to call home and nurture their culture, the people of Israel might well have lost the laws of Moses and the monotheism of Abraham. The exile of northern Israelites by Assyria caused that group to lose their much of their relevance in the world.

Another example of losing Hebrew culture almost happened to Falasha Jews formerly in Ethiopia. "Falasha" is a word in the Ethiopian language of Amharic that means "outsider, exile."

<<< Beta Israel in Israel (Wikipedia).

Calling these people "outsiders" fits right into the names given to Jews, Hebrews, Israelites, and their predecessor Apiru. Ethiopian Jews, however, did not call themselves "outsiders," bur rather "Beta Israel" – House of Israel.   Religious persecution forced many of the Beta Israel to convert over the course of many centuries. Areas of modern Ethiopia and Sudan are loosely related to the Kush – or Cush - and Nubians mentioned in Biblical and Egyptian documents. They were allies of Hebrews over a long period of time and specifically connected to a time of Moses the vizier (Chapter 39, Unseth). The very word "Amharic," the name for the Ethiopian language, means "people of the mountains, עמ הרים or "am harim." *Amharic is an offshoot of Hebrew and not an African language.* The vast majority of Beta Israel now reside in Israel with complete freedom of religion.   Their experience adds to the argument that Jews require a defendable homeland in order to survive.

Beta Israeli Yityish Titi Aynas, Miss Israel 2013 (Hadassah) >>>

The House of Israel from Ethiopia is no longer an oppressed group facing slow extinction, but now participates in the affairs of Israel.

But the Moses civil war in Egypt and the establishment of the small nation of Israel is not what has thrust Hebrews, Israel, and Judaism into prominent attention across the world. Torah, over the course of many centuries, changed the face of religion, politics, law, and morality. This small book for a small people was not written to change the world. It only concerns itself with establishing a Hebrew culture in Israel. Nevertheless, because of that book, the worship of idols and celestial bodies has been eliminated and most of the world practices monotheism. Torah morality is the undisputed benchmark of world ethics. Kings and monarchs with absolute power are diminished in number. Mosaic laws in varying degree apply everywhere. What Torah describes as the Sinai revelation ignited a global revolution.

"Freedom" is a universally understood and desired concept, and the Exodus story of deliverance and liberation has captivated billions of people.

Oliver Cromwell described the Exodus as "the only parallel of God's dealing with us that I know in the world."
Latin American Catholic priests used Exodus in their "Liberation Theology."
An African-American spiritual lyrics say, "Go down Moses / Way down in Egypt land / Tell old Pharaoh / Let my people go."
Ezra Stiles, President of Yale, 1783, said America is "God's American Israel."

Exodus has inspired and consoled countless people while also guiding many to liberation. Liberation, however, is no guarantee of liberty. The French Revolution culminated in bloodshed and misery. Not surprisingly, the French leaders of that revolution were distinctly hostile to the Jewish and Christian concepts of history. (*Walzer*, 5) Likewise, the Russian Revolution, wrapped in the cloth of anti-religious atheism, did not follow any ideas of Torah, and merely traded one tyranny for another (*Waltzer*, 5).

Israelites received instructions on how a free people can live together. The answer was service to each other, or covenant, which Waltzer describes: "Slavery is begun and sustained by coercion, while service is begun and sustained by covenant." Covenant is different than the many historical contracts with rulers, for it is a moral and legal

208

directive in which all people are morally equal. Men and women accepted their covenant through several "votes." Seven votes are referenced in Chapter 46 of this series. (Waltzer, pp. 74-98, Chapter 46).

> "Ye are standing this day all of you before the Lord our God: your heads, your tribes, your elders, and your officers, even all the men of Israel, your little ones, your wives, and thy stranger… that you shouldest enter into the covenant of the Lord thy God as He spoke unto thee – and into His oath – which the Lord thy God maketh with thee this day (*Deu.* 29:9-14).

While true liberation movements have the goal of freedom from repression, and are therefore similar, not all are based on Torah. Ghandi's opposition to British rule shared some Torah concepts, but used its own rationale and techniques.

Four of the world's major religions have followed the inspiration of Abraham, and are thus called the Abraham religions. Judaism, Christianity, and Islam have all

adopted monotheism as a central part of their worship and so have direct affinity to Torah, recognize Moses, and show concern about poverty. Torah presents the need not only for monotheism and worship of God, but also for the laws of Moses. Concerning the laws of Moses, the four religions and political bodies spawned from them have different interpretations on how to apply those laws. Concepts involving freedom of religion and separation of church and state have also yielded new interpretations. Nevertheless, principles expressed in Torah still guide much of the Abraham culture. Many of those principles transcend the Abraham cultures and are expressed in other parts of the world, including honoring parents, practicing humility, respecting individual freedoms, conducting economic matters in a good-faith manner, extending forgiveness, and practicing public health.

The Torah revolution is by no means accomplished, and counterrevolution knocks in every century. As enticing to the broad population as they may seem, principles such as equal justice, no murder, abandonment of idols, and fair-trade practices were slow to be adopted. In fact, right into "modern" times, wave after wave of autocratic invasions of peaceful countries have occurred, bringing with them various degrees of murder, theft, destruction, slavery, suppression of religion, and other type of abominations once practiced in Egypt and Canaan. A very few of these regimes that rejected peace in favor of conquest include Assyria, Babylonia, Persia, Rome, the Holy Roman Empire, various caliphates, Austria-Hungary, the British Empire, various khanates, various Chinese empires, African empires, Nazi Germany, czarist Russia, Soviet Union, multiple European states, and a host of others. There seems to be no lack of leaders desiring to pull all power to themselves.

But at the same time, over the millennia, there has also been a great increase in the constituency favoring Biblical morality, law, and humanity. Many nations have some form of justice for all such as voting. Even dictators realize the power of the Torah message and at least give lip service to justice rather than brag about exploitation. Changes such as these took several thousand years. The next 1000 years should be interesting.

Who gets to speak?

Rome against Moses in five rounds

49 Ki Teitzei Deuteronomy 21:10- 25:19 נ' תצא When you go (to battle)

Torah introduces some additional ethical standards which deal with a range of subjects, all of which are new protections for persons in situations that could lead to abuse, and so this section has been called a love parashah.   As per the title of this section, the first pertains to war, giving permission to Hebrew soldiers to marry captured women and giving those women protections.   Hebrews are forbidden to return escaped slaves and cult prostitution is also forbidden.   Other rules protect inheritance for children, show compassion for animals, and prohibit incest .   One rule is generally misunderstood. It protects sons from honor killings or abuse.   While allowing parents to punish or stone a "stubborn and rebellious son," such extreme punishment can only be executed with the approval of a court of elders. As a result, no such punishment was ever recorded as having taken place.

The necessity for Hebrews, Israelis, and Jews to "battle against their enemies" has never ended. Yet today, the Hebrew legacy has survived many a tyranny, usually not because of military prowess but rather because of the strength of the Hebrew message to rally lovers of freedom.   One of the most serious enemies was Imperial Rome.   Rome took aim at non-conforming cultures in several great waves. An untold but fascinating story is the journey of Mosaic law through the Roman tyrannies to eventually guide the Renaissance.

From the time of the Babylonian exile in 586 BCE to the first century CE first Jewish-Roman War, the Jewish population in the Roman Empire increased dramatically to 7 million or about 10% of the empire because of many conversions to Judaism including among the ruling class.   Judaism was popular and fashionable. (Louis Feldman).   Rome suddenly wanted to impose increased oversight.   Jews revolted.   Clearly the decision to revolt against Rome was ill-conceived and disastrous.   This constituted the **first** wave of Roman violence against Israel. So disastrous was this first wave that

*Jewish Roman Catacomb ~ 200 CE Haaretz ^^*

in the year 325 when Emperor Constantine nationalized independent Christianity and unleashed the **second** wave of religious oppression, Jews had no power to object. Neither did numerous other Christian denominations and pagan cults.   Not since the days of ancient Egypt had the state exercised such power for such a long period of time. Enormous estates filled with slaves were owned by aristocrats and approved religious orders.   One by one, religious competitors to the state religion were suffocated and eliminated. The second wave of

Roman repression had begun. The Great Library of Alexandria, or Shrine of the Muses, was sacked and burned (Carroll 187-191. This 1000-year period has justifiably been called the Dark Ages. Only the areas controlled by Rome truly repressed freedom in the way a dark age would suggest. A more accurate definition of the Dark Ages would be the time periods and areas controlled by Imperial (not Republican) Rome and its ideological successors. (Lewis - *The Jews* 107-109, Bridbury).

How did the teachings of Moses survive? The answer is that an array of Christian and Muslim allies stood in partnership with Jews to preserve the teachings of Torah. Tracing the history of these partnerships increases appreciation of how the concepts of a civil society developed.

Rome ruled against independent religious thought and authorized the execution of minority Christians like Docetists, Donatists, Nestorians, and Arians. Rome ruled against freedom for slaves. Rome ruled against the taking of a "barbarian' wife by a Roman or a Roman woman taking a "barbarian" husband, on punishment of death. Rome ruled against the assemblage of "heretics." These laws directly affected Germanic tribes – once allies of Rome -- because they were among the minority Christians. (Carroll 206)

No wonder, then, that the Germanic tribes had no love for Romans. Unlike Romans, many of those tribes respected both the monotheism of Abraham and the laws of Moses. They followed one of the Christian religions that was remarkably close to the Judaism of the era but banned by Rome. This was the Arian religion, not to be confused with the "race" spelled with a "y," Aryan promoted by Nazi Germany.

German Visigoth Christian Arian Spanish Church

Observing Roman weakness and decadence after the year 400, Visigoths crossed the Rhine and sacked Rome, followed by Vandals, other Goths and Alans. The serfs and other oppressed classes considered these Germans to be liberators. In no time, the Vandals swept through France and Spain to Gibraltar and Carthage, where Berbers, Jews, and various Christians welcomed them. Vandals reversed the Roman laws of discrimination and ruled with tolerance and equality. Trade increased. While Roman propagandists and apologists referred to the German tribes as "barbarian." In fact it was the Romans who deserved that appellation.

Germanic tribes ruled the European part of the Roman Empire, so when they instituted new laws around year 450, they looked to Israel and not to the Rome that discriminated against them. Theft of land was no longer allowed. Widows were entitled to a portion of available inheritance. Perjury became illegal, as did murder, and judges needed to become impartial. Everyone was equal under the law, and even the elite needed to pay damages for cause.

Visigoths set a new standard for civil society. This standard came from the laws of Torah, not Rome.

Hence Hebrew law survived the early Roman assault through the channel of early Visigoth law. Hebrews sometimes provided communications between Goths and Romans. (Chapter 46-48; Crane, pp. 41-56; Sidonius Vol. I, pp. xxvii-xxx, 335-345; Vol. II, pp. 83, 181-182, 315-323; Scott, who presents a corrupted version of laws.)

Other events would yet threaten the Mosaic foundation. When a Visigoth king converted to Roman ideology, he corrupted Visigoth law, and initiated the **third** Roman repression. This resulted in a civil war between newly converted Visigoths against a coalition of traditional Visigoths allied with Jews (Chapter 46-48; Crane; Scott's corrupted version requiring redaction; Sidonius Vol. I, pp. 335-345; Herwig, pp. 159-182).

That third assault on Biblical morality was brought to an abrupt end in 711 with the invasion of the Iberian Peninsula by Islamic forces who established a comparatively tolerant government for three religions called the "Convivencia." The Islamic period, although not without problems, produced a "golden" age that respected such Jewish luminaries as Maimonides, Samuel Ha-Nagid, Moses ibn Ezra, Solomon ibn Gabirol, Moses ben Enoch (Cordoba Talmudic center), and Judah Halevi. Christians and Jews of all types received this tolerance, albeit limited, in early Islamic Spain. Notable Christians were Abu Uusuf al-Kindi (author of

Polemic for Christianity), Serapion the Elder (medicine), and Rabi ibn Zaid al-Usquf (bishop of Cordoba and political advisor). Besides many relatively tolerant Spanish Andalusian caliphs, Muslim notables included the poet Princess Valada, the architect Ahmad ibn Baso, and the vizier and

Muslim Alhambra rebuilt by Jewish vizier >>>

polymath ibn Tufail. During the tolerant phase of Islamic Spain, the country prospered. Cordoba supported a population of 500,000 with paved streets and lamps when Paris had a population of 38,000. (Ashtor; Gerber, pp. 24-89)

Remarkably, contemporaneous with Andalusian (Spanish) Islamic tolerance was French Christian tolerance under Charlemagne, his father, grandfather, and his son Louis. Although Charlemagne's family disdained a friendship with Spanish Muslims, they did form an alliance with the Bagdad caliph, Jewish counts, and selected Christians. This led to other tolerant Christian kingdoms in Castile, Lisbon, and Aragon/Barcelona (Crane, pp. 92-102; Yitzhak Baer, pp. 78-305; Lewis, *The Jews,* 1-62; Eban, pp. 150-160).

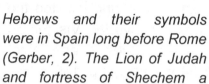

Hebrews and their symbols were in Spain long before Rome (Gerber, 2). The Lion of Judah and fortress of Shechem a symbol of the Simeon Tribe, is shown on a Toledo synagogue, coat of Catholic Castile-Leon; Hebrew text book; and tomb of Ferdinand III of Castile-Leon with Hebrew, Arabic, Latin, and Castilian as proof of tolerance.

The most historic and influential document to come out of this era was the legal code of the Catholic counts of Barcelona called Usatges, from the Hebrew word usot נוסו. Count Ramon Berenguer III the Great refined the Usatges, so, in the year 1064 they stood as a beacon of constitutional limitations and equal rights, reminiscent of Torah, in contrast to the Roman rules of dictatorship.

Each regulation, or usot, formed a part of the overall constitution of Spanish Aragon-Catalonia and followed the original uncorrupted Visigoth/Torah example. Some excerpts:

- Let townsmen and burghers litigate among themselves…
- Let the murder of a peasant or any other man… be compensated…
- Let Jews who are beaten, wounded, captured, …be compensated…
- Let every woman be compensated according to the rank of her husband…
- If a lord wishes to unjustly oppress his knight… the ruler must defend the knight.
- Let ships coming into and out of Barcelona be under peace and protection.
- The noble and ignoble kings and princes, magnates and knights, peasants and rustics, traders and merchants, pilgrims and wayfarers, friends and enemies, and princes shall be granted safety without any fear. (Kagay)

The oath of Catalonian citizens to their monarch went thus: "We, who are as good as you, swear to you, who are no better than us, to accept you as our king and sovereign lord, provided you observe all our liberties and laws, but if not, not." (Hughes, p. 119)

In 1492, a united Castile and Aragon/Catalonia under new monarchs Ferdinand II of Aragon and Isabella shut the door on any form of toleration and cooperation by initiating the Inquisition against Muslims, Jews, non-conforming Christians, and any other "heretics." Rome and France did the same. The **fourth** wave of Roman repression began, but it had been some time in coming. Murders, torture, and tyranny were the political acts of the day and no minority escaped brutality. (Stow, pp. 157-308)

The fourth wave of human destruction came to an end with the re-introduction of old ideas, ideas from antiquity, ideas of the value of reason, of humanism, ideas of questioning rather than obedience. Looking back to antiquity for inspiration meant looking back to Greek and Hebrew thought. The Renaissance arrived. A great many people contributed to breaking the intellectual ice including, to name just a few, Dante, da Vinci, Bacon, Michelangelo, Machiavelli, and Mirandola, most of whom studied Hebrew texts. One event of many demonstrates the magnitude of changes in a new era.

In 1215, King John of England signed the Magna Carta, which ceded a number of his absolute rights to rebellious barons, creating the first English document of constitutional law. It was not, however, the first, or even close to the first such document. The Magna Carta seems to copy a number of rights the lineage of which follows the rights practiced in Catalonia as reflected in the Usatges laws. The Usatges came from the more ancient original Visigoth law instituted by the Christian Germans who broke up the Roman Empire. In turn, the Visigoth Law derived its basics from humanistic laws of antiquity, namely the Laws of Moses.

A sampling: Both Magna Carta and Usatges had signatures of nobles; protected inheritances of orphans and widows; protected knights from assault; gave judgment of people to their equals; required regular court dates; protected ships of commerce; set standards for coinage; required vassals to aid lords. However, only Usatges, and not the Magna Carta, protected Muslims and Jews; declared public roads to be safe from theft and violence; said princes shall not do evil; made murder specifically illegal; punished rape; declared found items must be returned; said lords can be sued; disallowed perjury. (Kagay; J. G. Davis)

In the **fifth** round, Torah ideas on limited powers of monarchs came to England. Just after 1066, William the Conqueror established a Jewish community in England. Biblical ideas with an emphasis on Israelite interpretation could circulate. William's son Henry I proclaimed liberties for Jews as well as a Charter of Liberties that was a blueprint for the Magna Carta. Hebrew writers and luminaries such as ibn Ezra visited England (Jewish Virtual Library), and many from Paris emigrated to England. Many English Christians such as Roger Bacon studied with Jews. Jews represented 0.25 % of the population by 1200 and were lenders, merchants, smelters, and landlords. Taxes on them provided 8% of royal income and raised money to ransom Richard I. Jews played a significant role in the establishment of Oxford University and Balliol College (Abrams). Rome fell. Judaism lived.

One conclusion is that Moses directly or indirectly inspired the Magna Carta. *Henry I Liberties for Jews >>*

America – the new Israel?

50 Ki Tavo Deuteronomy 26:1 – 29:8 כי תבוא When you come (into the land)

This section of *Deuteronomy* presents one of the darkest outlooks in Torah. While promising great abundance and happiness if Israel follows the dictates of the Lord, it also threatens Armageddon if those dictates are not followed. The lecture in Deuteronomy explains what a country must do in order to become prosperous and have a satisfied population. Especially in this section, the meaning of the 3000 year old language protocols must be translated. Just as many people have trouble understanding 500 year old Shakespeare literature, the same difficulty is true for Torah. Adding to the problems of history, Torah was never meant to be a purely historical document.

Israelites are warned that certain behavior will doom them as a people and as a nation. Various types of negative behavior had often been discussed previously in Torah and examples of Egypt and Canaanite states have been offered as examples of offenders. In the case of Egypt, it is possible to say that Egypt enjoyed a long period of expansion, prosperity, and certain success, up until the Akhenaten and Ramesses period when oppression and profligacy increased while prosperity and freedom decreased, leading to the demise of the state. Of course, observations must be viewed relative to the times. Egypt was never freedom loving, and did not have the laws of Moses as a measuring stick. Another example is Rome, starting out as a Republic featuring an expanding state with opportunity, then a dictatorship, then an empire, then a murdering shell of post-Holy Roman instinct as in the Inquisition. Although this comparison is somewhat subjective and cannot be treated thoroughly in these short paragraphs, it does show that warnings in Torah are credible.

The concept of a civil society and a republican government began in Torah, then evolved ever so slowly to Greece, through Europe, to the Renaissance and the Enlightenment. In the late 18th century, the time was ripe for a country to put all of the teaching into practice on a large scale. A new country did just that. That new country was the United States.

Gutenberg Bible at NYC Library

In some sense, the American experience began in Europe with the printing of the Bible, first in German by Gutenberg right after 1450, then everywhere in Europe. In a very short time the Hebrew story of slavery and liberation became available not only in the libraries of Renaissance elites, but also in the homes of common people. The *Geneva Bible*, favored by Puritans, went through some 160 editions before the appearance of the *King James Bible*.

Ideas percolated in Europe that flowered in America. Various writers sharpened the Biblical arguments to more modern ears. John Locke wrote treatises against the theory of the divine right of kings, for the necessity for consent of the governed, and the existence of natural rights. Puritans held fast to observing the Sabbath and other dictates of Torah. Rousseau produced his *Contract Social* in 1762 about proposals for an ideal political community and that monarchs did not have divine rights, but only the people have sovereign rights. 3,000 year-old teaching of Torah made it into the mainstream. The Bible itself, and in particular the first five books, had achieved celebrity status. (Katsh; Straus, *Pilgrims*)

Colonial codes of law referred to Biblical instruction for justification. States from Virginia to Massachusetts enacted legislation that embodied Biblical propositions including representative government, consent of the governed and fair trials. The New Haven code of 1655 contained specific Biblical references in half of their 79 statutes. The New York Colonial Congress of 1765 adopted the human rights of liberty, property, pursuit of happiness, and trial by jury. Bible reading became a required text for school and for the moral guidance of ordinary people. Not only the English but also other immigrants like Germans and Swedes participated in liberated politics (Sweet). Waves of refugees undertook arduous journeys to escape the grip of various pharaoh-like kings so they could live under the rules of God as described by Moses. They arrived with a minimum number of possessions, but always a Bible.

Higher as well as lower education, put great emphasis on Biblical studies. The attitude of the secular Miami University president was typical, "The Bible is the source of all intellectual as well as moral strength...." (Sweet, Katsh, Fowler).

Colonists, fleeing from absolute rulers, looked to the Israelite system of government without a king and also to the warnings of Samuel concerning the powers of kings (*I Samuel* 8:7, 9). Colonists regularly required Biblical justification for their actions, and so Benjamin Rush, in his editorials denouncing the British Tea Act, pointed to the "holy men of old,"

Benjamin Rush's house in Philadelphia

"What did not Moses forsake and suffer for his countrymen! What shining examples of Patriotism do we behold in Joshua, Samuel, Maccabeus, and all the illustrious princes, captains and prophets among the Jews" (Katsh).

America was primed for revolution. It was quite natural that the American Declaration of Independence states that government is to uphold the rights of man as ordained by divine law, and that the duty of the citizen is to defend the same against any encroachment – even by his own government. That divine law is Torah. Thomas Paine argued in *Common Sense* that "These portions of the Scripture… admit of no equivocal construction. That the Almighty hath here entered his protest against monarchical government is true, or the Scriptures are false."

Thus we see that the Five Books of Moses, more than other books or other parts of Bible, provided the model for Colonial America to assert itself as independent. Thus we see that the most basic difference between a republic and a monarchy is the natural political equality of citizens, a concept also basic to Mosaic Law and the Declaration of independence. In this spirit, the Confederacy of four New England Colonies 1643-1684 was modeled on the confederacy of the twelve Israelite tribes, and afterwards inspired the confederation of the thirteen states (Katsh, Fowler).

Benjamin Franklin and Thomas Jefferson proposed a seal for the United State with the words, "Rebellion to Tyrants is Obedience to God" and a picture of Pharaoh's demise at the hands of Moses. The Continental Congress promptly passed a resolution for the publication of an American Bible in 1780.

The framers of the American Constitution then went shopping for models on which to write the law of the land. They immediately rejected the European models. They immediately considered the Hebrew model. They immediately went to their libraries and consulted a book they all possessed, namely *Discourses Concerning Government* by Algernon Sidney. Sidney's book was read throughout the colonies and became the guide of the Founding Fathers. In his description of the Hebrew Commonwealth, he states,

Having seen what government God did not ordain, it may be reasonable to examine the nature of government He did ordain and we shall find it consisted of those parts, besides the magistrates of the several tribes and cities: They had a Chief Magistrate, who was called Judge or Captain, as Joshua, Gideon, and others; a council of seventy chosen men, and the General Assembly of the people. The first was merely occasional, like to the Dictators of Rome… The second is known by the name of the Great Sanhedrin, which, being instituted by Moses, according to the command of God, continued till they were all, save one, slain by Herod. And the third, which is the Assembly of the people, was so common that none be ignorant of it, but such as never looked in the Scripture (Katsh).

So there it is: a president, a senate, and a house of representatives. In addition were advocates for the law of God including prophets, Levite judges, and Nazarites.

Joshua was succeeded by a line of elected Judges (shoftim) from Othniel to Samuel. The presidential responsibilities of these judges were to serve as commander-in-chief, act as chief magistrate, and convene the General Assembly. This person was accountable to the Seventy Elders, or Sanhedrin. They all had to include the congregation of Israel.

Samuel Langdon, President of Harvard, addressing the Massachusetts Congress on the eve of the Revolution, said, "The Jewish government, according to the original constitution which was divinely established, if considered merely in a civil view, was a perfect republic. And let them who cry up the divine right of kings consider, that the form of government which had a proper claim to divine establishment was so far from including the idea of a king, that it was a high crime for Israel to ask to be in this respect like other nations, and when they were thus gratified, it was rather as a just punishment for their folly…. The civil polity of Israel is doubtless an excellent general model…." (Straus, *The Origin*, pp. 77, Straus, *Pilgrims*).

In certain areas, America did not rise to Biblical teaching. Most egregious was the treatment of slaves. Torah places limitations on slavery, provides for their freedom, prohibits abuse, forbids return of escaped slaves, and in general, bondage was more like an indentured servant.

Biblical exhortations weren't the only inspiration for America. Along with Biblical teaching are the pioneer spirit; the practical conclusion that America should not be a theocracy; and the philosophies of various Greeks, Hobbes, Locke, Montesquieu, Rousseau, and Spinoza - all of whom employ biblical references. Here are famous American words that could have been spoken by Moses:

"We hold these truths to be self-evident, that all men are created equal, that they are endowed by their Creator with certain unalienable Rights, that among these are Life, Liberty and the pursuit of Happiness.--That to secure these rights, Governments are instituted among Men, deriving their just powers from the consent of the governed, --That whenever any form of government becomes destructive of these ends, it is the Right of the People to alter or to abolish it, and to institute new Government, laying its foundation on such principles and organizing its powers in such form, as to them shall seem most likely to effect their Safety and Happiness..... But when a long train of abuses and usurpations, pursuing invariably the same Object evinces a design to reduce them under absolute Despotism, it is their right, it is their duty, to throw off such Government, and to provide new Guards for their future security...."

The painting by Trumball represents the signing of the Declaration of Independence.

Moses makes his case to Israel and the message goes global

51 Nitzavim Deuteronomy 29:9 – 30:20 נצב' מ standing (before God)

This is a special parashah, part of which is recited during many services on the Day of Atonement Yom Kippur. Moses announces the dramatic Hebrew departure from other religions so that God's covenant and words of Torah shall be open to all people, present and in the future, common and exalted, not hidden behind temple walls.

A very simplified abstract of this portion might be that good things happen to good people. This can be true enough, but it is fair to refer to the story of Job and conclude that the desired result might not always happen, even when behavior is commendable.

As it happened, Israel did suffer greatly from foreign invasions, and the North was scattered. While there were transgressions worshipping idols and excesses under some of the kings, it is debatable whether defeat and suffering came as a direct result of transgressions. Some of the enemies were empires that conquered vast tracts of land far and wide; they were not going to exempt Israel from imperial designs. Hebrews did manage to maintain a continuous presence in Israel despite military losses, sometimes under leniency from empires and sometimes under duress. Unlike many other defeated peoples, Israelites survived.

In managing that continuous presence, Israel did eventually gain its independence as the State of Israel once again in 1948. Some historical processes take long periods of time to show results. It took a thousand years from Abraham for Israel to establish a state. Another thousand years until idols or worship of god kings disappeared. A thousand years more and the idea of the Hebrew republic took root in Europe.

That brings us to today with not only Israel but a large part of the world, perhaps more than half, practicing politics and religion based to some degree on the ideas of Torah. Depending on interpretation, at least half of the Ten Commandments can be practiced as secular law and not monotheism. Parts of the world can practice parts of Hebrew law or pay lip service to Hebrew humanism separate from monotheism. It is possible to follow many of the laws and not the religious dictates. For instance, an atheist country may find it in its interest to observe the laws of business, of public health, of false witness, of property rights, of immigration, of defense, or of science.

Once the teachings of Moses spread from the exclusive domain of Israelites into the greater world, there was no stopping their dispersal and adoption in one form or another by most cultures. Chapters 30, 32-35, and 45-50 herein address the results.

There is discussion that nation-to-nation violence has decreased in the world in an incremental fashion. Much of that theory has to do with proportion. Certainly individual violence still occurs. Certainly terrible war and genocide still occurs, but less continuously and affecting a less portion of the world's population. Armies are smaller compared to populations. Many enhancement for peace come right out of Torah, such as freedoms of speech, religion; democracy; individual rights; equality before the law; private property; respect (if not love) for neighbors; democratic capitalism; and trade. (Pinker, Blattman of Modern War Inst., Kleinfeld, Doyle @ nobelprise.org., Coleman & Fry.)

The dissemination of Hebrew ideas did not bring peace to the Hebrews. As time passed, torments again appeared from time to time. In each of those thousand year periods, acts of oppression and exile are well documented. Partial acceptance of ideas means that it is possible to follow some, but not all of Torah.

The commandment to not murder has made murder a crime but has not eliminated it. Painting by Sabastiano Ricco depicts the murder of Able by Cain.)

Torah seems to grant latitude to humans in putting its laws into practice, although that latitude has been stretched very far in some instances. According to *Nitzavim*, the Torah is not in heaven (Deu. 30:12), which can be interpreted in several ways: (1) That excessive obsession with heaven detracts from life on Earth. (2) That following the law lies in the interpretation of people here on earth and that interpretation will decide the efficacy by the results. "According to the law which they [Levites] shall teach thee, and according to the judgment which they shall tell thee... (Deu. 17:11) (3) That the laws are plain and people can follow them without constant reminders. (4) That the commandments remained out of reach to humans, in heaven, until they were revealed to Moses. This is for clergy to explain further. Was the law of relativity residing out of reach until revealed to Einstein? There are many more truths beyond the capabilities of the human mind. (5) It is possible to abuse the teaching of Torah by faulty interpretation.

Torah has spread its message globally, but that message may be incomplete because of differences in adaptation. However, Bible has taken its place in our language and hence into our sub consciousness.   The names in Torah: Abraham, Sarah, Isaac, Rebecca, Leah, Esau, Jacob, Joseph, and Moses, are well known. The Biblical stories are subjects of books, plays, musicals, discussion, names for babies, and archaeological searches.

"Our Jewish Bible has implanted itself in the table-talk and household life of every man and woman in the European and American nations." *Ralph Waldo Emerson in Representative Man.*

The chart below gives some phrases, only a sample, from Tanakh, or Hebrew Bible, that are in wide-spread daily use:

A fly in the ointment   Ecclesiastics 10:1

He is known by the company he keeps   Proverbs 13.20, Psalms 1:1

A drop in the bucket   Isaiah 40:16   *Beating a sword into*
                                                                                                              plough @ UN garden
                                                                                                              by Yevgeny (below)

Craven image   Deu. 5:8

You shall beat swords into plowshares   Isaiah 2:4

Can a leopard change its spots?   Jeremiah 13:23

A man after my own heart   I Samuel 13:14

Am I my brother's keeper?   Genesis 4:9

Scapegoat   Lev. 16

Song of Songs   Song of Songs

Amen   Num. 5.22, Deu.
                                                                        27, Neh. 5.13,
                                                                        (confirmed in NT)

Behemoth   Job 40:15-24

His heart is as hard as a stone   Job 41:16 (41:24 some tr.)

Peace offering   Exodus 24:5

A gentle response yields wrath;
A harsh word provokes anger.   Proverbs 15:1

A thorn in the flesh   II Corinthians 12:7

A two-edged sword	Proverbs 5:4
A voice crying in the wilderness	Isaish 40 (confirmed Mark 1:3, Luke 3:4)
Love your neighbor as yourself	Leviticus 19:18 (confirmed New Testament, repeated by Hillel with change)
This too shall pass.	Genesis 8:6, 13 (It came/shall to pass Deu. 28:1; Proverbs 29:25; Isaiah 65:24)
An eye for an eye…	Exodus 21:22
Thou shall not murder.	Exodus 20:13
Old as the hills	Job 15:7
What you sow you shall reap	Job 4:8, Proverbs 22:8 (confirmed Galatians 6:7)
Ashes to ashes, dust to dust	Genesis 3:19; Ecclesiastes 3:20
Be fruitful and multiply	Genesis. 1:22
By the sweat of your brow	Genesis 3:19
By the skin of your teeth	Job 19:20
For everything there is a season	Ecclesiastes 3
Feet of clay	Daniel 2:31-33
Fire and brimstone	Genesis 19:24-26
Forbidden fruit	Genesis 2:9
Heart's desire	Psalms 21:2
Lamb led to slaughter	Jer. 11:*19*
Nothing new under the sun	Ecclesiastes 1:9
Pride goes before the fall	Proverbs 16:18
Leave part of harvest for the poor	Leviticus 19:9-10

Ruth, David's great-grandmother cuts grain left for the poor (Women of the Bible)

223

Torah meets challenges from pagans, science, and philosophers

52 Vayelech Deuteronomy 31:1 – 31:30 וילך (Moses) went (to speak)

Moses announces that he will not live to enter Israel, that Joshua will succeed him, and that the children of Israel will shortly possess their homeland. Israel will have to face uncertainly and be prepared to adjust.

A new world is about to open for Israelites who will shortly have a homeland, a nation home, not the most desirable land in the Mideast, but suitable for a small people. They have a new monotheistic religion and a cultural and spiritual heredity designed for a small people. Their new humanistic laws are rejected by their neighbors. The remarks by Moses presented in Torah show he realized the existential problem of keeping his people together. His previous remarks offer strategies to enable Israel the people, Israel the land, and Israel the religion to survive despite being enmeshed in difficulties. Moses was correct. Difficulties have abounded inside and outside Israel. Yes, other countries adopted many of Israel's principles in religion and law, but that did not make Israel the land, the people, or the religion safe.

There was another set of challenges to Israel over the years, namely challenges from critics and propagandists. We are talking here about criticism, not anti-Semitism, which is the domain of propagandists and not a subject for this book. We are examining the ability of Hebrew and Jewish thought to adapt to legitimate critical challenges.

Early printing of ancients Hecataeus 1730, Philo 1886, and Aristotle ~1495

Early Egyptian and Greek commentators criticized Hebrews for not worshiping idols. Pagans, starting with Egyptians, disrespected all other worshippers. According to

Torah, Egyptian hosts refused to eat with Joseph (*Gen.* 43:23) and it did not help that Hebrews ate beef and Egyptians worshipped cows (Hathor). Later religious pagans aimed criticism at all religions that recognized a divine authority. Still later, these pagans worshiped only one God.

The pagan Greek Hecataeus wrote (~310 BCE):

> Moses said heaven that surrounds the earth is alone divine, and rules the universe. The sacrifices that he established differ from those of other nations, as does their way of living, for as a result of their own expulsion from Egypt he introduced an unsocial and intolerant mode of life. He picked out the men of most refinement and with the greatest ability to head the entire nation, and appointed them priests; and he ordained that they should occupy themselves with the temple and the honors and sacrifices offered to their God. These same men he appointed to be judges in all major disputes and entrusted to them the guardianship of the laws and customs. For this reason, the Jews never have a king, and authority over the people is regularly vested in whichever priest is regarded as superior to his colleagues in wisdom and virtue.

This type of Greek criticism disappeared when pagans ultimately adopted the Hebrew ideas. Aristotle (circa 350 BCE), another Greek, did not concern himself with the divine but rather with more philosophical and theoretical thinking. Thus his works were deemed compatible with or even evolutionary from Hebrew thinking by the likes of Jewish philosophers Aristobulus (200 BCE), Philo Judaeus (25 CE), and Maimonides (1100) (*Jewish Encyclopedia*). These Jewish thinkers confirmed the compatibility of science, Judaism, and rational thought. Torah accommodated new scientific developments. One of the first such accommodations was the evolution of Hebrew medicine. Torah included a mixture of science and sacrifices to cure certain illnesses, but early on Hebrews utilized the services of physicians and medicine. As the science of medicine emerged, Jews realized that as creation was a divine activity, the study of creation, including medicine, was not only permitted, but holy. In a short time, Jewish medicine caught up with the most advanced medicine and surpassed some of it.

Maimonides in Cordoba >>>>

Science requires a number of tests to prove theorems, the best known being the scientific method by which the results of a test should be predictable and repeatable. For example, every time a piece of iron is exposed to the weather, it develops rust – iron oxide.

Torah has proved open to new thought as new discoveries or questions surface. This process is called exegesis, using the basis of Torah to solve unanticipated problems, or even anticipated but unresolved questions. Exegesis is a very large topic, so in this space we will only introduce part of the conversation.

Rather than looking at physical science, let us take an example of evolving Biblical commentary in associating moral behavior with rewards in life. What follows is the thinking of a few notable commentators and philosophers.

QUESTION: IS IT POSSIBLE TO GUARANTEE A SATISFYING HAPPY LIFE ?

EVOLVING ANSWER:

- 1000 BCE: Do good and you will receive good things.
  "And if you do obey these rules and observe them carefully, your God will …. favor you and bless you and multiply you – blessing your issue from the womb and your produce from the soil, your new grain and wine and oil, the calving of your herd…" (*Deu* 12:13)
- 500 BCE: Do good and usually, not always, you will receive good things.
  "(Job) was whole-hearted and upright, and one that feared God, and shunned evil."

<< *Job by Repin 1869*

Very quickly he lost his vast possessions, his family, his health, and the strength of his conviction towards God. A friend of Job advised, "Behold, God is great, beyond our knowledge." He created light, water, food, animals, humans, the sun. Then God questioned the knowledge base of Job, "Where wast thou when I laid the foundations of the earth?" (*Job* 1-3, 36-38) (limits of knowledge)

- 500 BCE: <u>Life is uncertain, so rejoice in what God grants you.</u> Ecclesiastes   "Vanity of vanities, saith Koheleth; vanity of vanities, all is vanity (1:2). The race is not to the swift, nor the battle to the strong, neither yet bread to the wise, nor yet riches to men of understanding nor yet favor to men of skill, but time and chance happeneth to them all" (9:11-12). "I saw under the sun, in the place of justice, that wickedness was there" (3:16). "There is nothing better than a man should rejoice in his works (3:22), for... all go unto one place, all are of the dust, and all return to dust" (3:20). "The end of the matter, all having been heard: fear God, and keep His commandments; for this is the whole man." (12:13)   So said Koheleth aka Qoheleth.

- 300 CE: <u>Some things are unknown</u>
  Rabbi Yanai   "We don't have the ability to explain the success of the wicked or the suffering of the righteous." Pirkei Avot 4:15

- 1000 CE: <u>Chance can remove one's pleasures and materials possessions, but not the soul.</u>
  Maimonides: "He who thinks that he can have flesh and bones without being subject to any external influence, or any of the accidents of matter, unconsciously wishes to reconcile two opposites, viz., to be at the same time subject and not subject to chance.... The evils ... that befall man are very few and rare. Difficulties arise from the desire for superfluous things. The more necessary a thing is for living, the more easily it is found and the cheaper it is." God has given us existence and provided what is needed. There is nothing wrong with rubies and emeralds, but they are superfluous.
       (*Guide to the Perplexed*, sec. III, Ch. XII)
       -- Saadia, Ibn Tibbol, Gersonides: Suffering can teach the soul or the world, as Abraham and Isaac taught everyone that sacrifice is wrong. God has purpose. God may grant prophecy.

- 2000 CE   <u>God has provided Creation, beauty, life, humanity, morality, Sinai laws, prophets, love, freedom, and nature, but not immunity, for immunity is incompatible with nature.</u>
  Harold Kushner: *When Bad Things Happen to Good People* - Religion offers comfort, strength, community, courage, self-worth, inspiration, and intelligence to combat challenges. God has created a world in which many more good things than bad things happen. God does not send illness, accidents, or crime, and most of those are surmountable.

Song of Moses and other Torah commentary

53 Ha'azinu Deuteronomy 32:1 – 32:52 האזינו Give ear

In this end-of-life poem dedicated to his people Israel, Moses recalls the special relationship that Israel has developed with God. Moses knows only too well the difficulties in keeping Hebrews focused on the One God they cannot see or touch. He expresses his fears with the language of poetry and knowledge of the Covenant. This important final instruction of Moses is recited either on the Shabbat between Rosh Hashanah and Yom Kippur, or on the Shabbat following Yom Kippur. The "give me your ear" is another version of the word *sh'ma,* listen!

In this portion and the next, Moses closes Torah and the last episode of his own life, and therefore an important place for reflection and summation. And so a reference to divine greatness, divine righteousness, divine gifts to the children of Israel, and divine care follows. Moses then opens his heart to his disappointments with his followers and their lack of religiosity, for they are undeserving of the divine gifts. If taken in isolation, this portion, Ha'azinu would imply a failure in religious instruction and a warning of punishments to come. We know that Apiru, Hebrews, the Abrahamic religions, and other worldly groups have only followed and learned the teachings of Torah and Moses very imperfectly and that will continue.

The Moses plea to "give an ear" to his oration is only part of the long teachings of the leader and accomplishments of the Hebrews, who have evolved from a ramshackle group of outcasts to a cohesive people with a nation and a religion amidst a crumbling world. The Hebrew nation and people have endured in various modes throughout the rise and fall of many other powerful empires, while the teachings of Abraham and Moses also endure and grow. Therefore the dark side of this portion, namely the disappoints of Moses, do not represent the entire picture, either historically or in scripture.

Ha'azinu is a song of Moses. The Songs of Moses in <u>Exodus</u> 15, <u>Deuteronomy</u> 32, and <u>Psalms</u> 90 are excellent displays of the mannerisms of Torah. Poetry, metaphor, hyperbole, condensation (combining many occurrences into one narrative), and parallelism are front and center. In <u>Exodus</u> "Who is like unto Thee מי כמכה," thanks to God for freedom is offered. The rousing <u>Deuteronomy</u> song, "Give me your ear האזינו " can only be compared to speeches of Lincoln, Churchill, and Patrick Henry. It aligns with the tradition of the Exodus song, the *Song of Deborah,* the *Song of David, Song of Moses* in <u>Psalms</u> – a "Prayer of Moses תפלה למשה, " *Ecclesiastes, Job,* and *Song of Solomon.* It is estimated that a third of Tanakh in Hebrew is poetry (Smith's Bible dictionary). All three of the Songs of Moses are used in synagogue services.

The Songs of Moses give an opportunity to explore a few of the linguistic traditions and commentaries of Torah, being among the oldest compositions. The oldest known copy of the text is the Dead Sea Scrolls, written approximately 2,000 years ago. There are

only fragments prior to those scrolls. Only small phrases have been discovered in the paleo-Hebrew that was in place at the time of the Moses Exodus.

Israelite women were known to use tambourines in songs (Songs of Joy Tissot 1902)

In Biblical literature, the subject of the divine nature of God is critical, but how to write about it? How to write about an entity that defies definition and limits? This necessitates the use of poetry, metaphor, hyperbole, and the like. Here are a few of the most telling references to the Almighty:

> In a beginning, God created heaven and earth.
> The earth was vacant and void.
> The face of the void was dark; On the face of water hovered the spirit of God.
> God said, "Let there be light," and there was.
> > "Let the light separate from darkness," and there was day and night.
> > There was the first day. (Ex. 1:1-5)

We see that our Creator fashioned our universe, and perhaps others, but we are only creatures of creation, uninformed as to the process of creation and endowed with extremely limited powers of understanding it. Unlike other creation stories, there is no birth of a creator; this creator configured nature and is not an aspect of it such as wind or rain; this creator is not the result of a union of forces or planets. So, perhaps in simple verse we learn more about God than is later explained anywhere.

> They shall say, "What is his name. What shall I say?"
> You shall say, "I am that I am."
> Thus you shall say, "I am that I am sent me." ...
> Thus you shall say, "The God of Abraham, Isaac, and Jacob sent me."

Message from burning bush (Cecil DeMille film)>>>

In this verse, we are granted further information about God, however enigmatic. The only explanation understandable to humans is that God is beyond our comprehension and any description or name is ineffable. Some people solve this problem by simply referring to the divine as "Hashem," the name.

However, the history of monotheism is not satisfied with merely using the appellation "Hashem," "The Name," or the like. Other references are made throughout Torah, but none comes any closer to explaining the unfathomable. These references to God form another category of literary description, namely attributes. A few examples follow:

> *For the Lord will vindicate His people. (Deu. 32:36)*
> *Do you not know? Have you not heard? The LORD is God from of old,*
> > *Creator of the earth from end to end, He never grows faint or weary,*
> > *His wisdom cannot be fathomed. (Isa. 40:28)*
> *Can I escape from Your spirit? Can I flee from Your presence?*
> *If I ascend to heaven, You are there; if I descend to Sheol, You are there.*
> *If I take wind with the dawn to come to rest on the western horizon,*
> *Even there Your hand will be guiding me, Your hand holding me fast.*
> *(Psalms 139:8-10)*

In addition, Torah describes many communications between mortals and the Divine. These communications are not meant to be anything like everyday conversations. They display the special relationship between God and His people.

> *God said, "Hear these My words: When prophets arise among you, I make Myself known to them in a vision, I speak with them in a dream. Not so with My servant Moses.... With him I speak mouth to mouth, plainly and not in riddles," (Num. 12:6-8)*

Here we have yet another literary form and another method for describing the relationship between humans and an unfathomable creator. Prophets get their instructions or inspirations through visions. The use of visions is a metaphor for the gift of a prophet to tap into the vastness of unknown wisdom. Moses' channel is more direct and far greater. The phrase "mouth to mouth" surely is a metaphor.

The Lord said to Abram, "Go forth from your native land.... "(Gen. 12:1)
That very day the Lord spoke to Moses. (Deu. 32:48)

The concept of speaking through visions is further developed in later commentaries, such as those of Rabbi Jonathan Sacks (see Chapter 15 & 17), who discuss the concept of the bat kol בת קול - an echo, whisper, or daughter's voice –not a spoken word, but an entree into the depth of wisdom or spirit of the divine for those so prepared and inclined.

You heard the sound of words but saw no shape, other than voice . (*Deu.* 4:12)

A still small voice and a voice addressed him. (*I Kings.* 19:12-13)

In thought-filled visions of the night, When deep sleep falls on men... I heard a murmur, a voice. (*Job* 4:13-16)

Just as Torah's many concepts later received more definition, so it was with the small voice and discussion of bat kol or spirit in Talmud, or in comments of Rashi, Tosafot, Kuzari and Rabbi Sacks.

A core instruction of Torah is to study it, and, in doing so, to extrapolate, to extend as in exegeses, and to further define. The many people who now believe in monotheism have various interpretations of the Sinai laws. How faithful these interpretations are to the original is open to debate. *Chart below from slife.org/abrahamic-religions*

Small Abrahamic religions

Religions	Yazidi	Samaritanism	Mandeans	Druze	Babism	Baha'i Faith	Rastafari
Symbols	☀	🕎	⊕	★	✮	✴	🏴

A body of priests, Levites, and judges may decide matters too hard or controversial for local officials (Deu. 17:3-11) *because they have been given the wisdom already from Torah.* Keep the commandments and statutes which are written in Torah. *"It is not in heaven, that thou shouldest say, 'Who shall go up for us to heaven, and bring it unto us, and make us to hear it..."* (*Deu.* 30:12, Baba Metzia 59)

One is able to innovate in Torah matters that Moses himself was not permitted to reveal (*Zohar* V1, p. 175 D. Matt, tr.).

The Deuteronomy Song of Moses, rich in commentary, brings up the questions of Torah commentary in general. Is the *Song of Moses*, and possibly most or all of Deuteronomy, a commentary on the other four books of Torah? That would make Moses the originator of Torah commentary. There are a number of arguments for that conclusion. The first reference would be the Torah itself where Deuteronomy is introduced as words spoken by Moses.

These are the words which Moses spoke unto all Israel beyond the Jordan; in the wilderness, the Arabah [after leaving Sinai]… according unto all that the Lord had given him in commandment unto them.

Moses speaks (Philippoteaux) >>>>

Perhaps that is why *Deuteronomy* is referred to as the *Mishneh Torah*, repeated *Torah*. Moses adds some commandments and detail to his commentary. New laws added by Moses include the law of a king and the law of captive women. One small change refers to Exodus 20:11, which explains that God rested on the seventh day, Shabbat, but Moses suggests that Shabbat is to celebrate freedom from slavery (Deu. 5:15). In Numbers 13, God commanded that spies scout the Holy Land, but Moses remembers that it was the people who requested it of Moses (Deu. 1:22). Moses presents a subtle difference in his rendition of the Ten Commandments, thus making a codification of Torah. For example, the Ten Commandments in *Deuteronomy* adds a vav (meaning "and") between each commandment. (D. Hartman; Rachel Sabath; Palvanov)

Monotheism, Laws, and Culture Formed modern civil society

54 Habrakha Deuteronomy 33:1–34:12 רואת הברכה Blessing (of Moses)

This week's presentation is the finale of so much: the final words of Moses in the form of a blessing; the end of Hebrew wandering and searching; the ending passages of Torah; and a defining moment in Hebrew history, when the monotheism of Abraham, the Laws of Moses, and the eminence of God converge in a place called Israel.

Moses confirms the revelation of God at Sinai/Seir (near or in the Negev), and the convocation of the tribes at that location. He blesses each tribe individually except for

Simeon, whose travelled areas lie in Sinai and Seir, but who later was absorbed by Judah. Moses climbs Mount Nebo and gazes upon the land of Israel that he will not enter but has brought his people to. Upon his passing, Israel mourns for thirty days (tradition called shoshim - 30).

Mountt Nebo (B. Werner Widipedia)
>>>

Israelites set in motion great changes in the world, even though they only intended a small corner of it for their worship and obedience to the laws of God. But Torah reflects the personality of Hebrews a thousand years before the world paid much attention. From a history view the position as outsiders from the time of donkey caravans is embedded in Torah and somewhat in a modern Jewish mind. This has allowed the freedom to enlist a critical eye towards the inside elite and their tightly controlled central governments. Continual questioning first depicted by Jacob "wrestling with God" (*Gen.* 32:22-32) and the curiosity born of freedom to investigate became Torah hallmarks. In addition, torah relates a number of "wonders or miracles" and then recognizes them as amazing but not cornerstones of religion. Some other points regarding the Hebrew personality follow:

Torah and the rest of scripture is peppered with wonders, now usually called "miracles," as well as events of communication with the Divine. Miracles define some of the most dramatic moments of the Hebrew story and manifest the might of God: the flood; the destruction of Sodom and Gomorrah; the ten plagues, and the destruction of Jericho. Miracles can also show God's love: the parting of the Sea of Reeds; manna from heaven; meat of quail from the sky; water from a rock. Finally, miracles can serve as signs of God's will – the burning bush; Aaron's rod becoming a serpent; and the sun and moon stayed in their orbits.

Many opinions allow for miracles but do not consider them essential to religion.

If a prophet or dreamer performs a miracle, then says to worship other gods, do not listen.	-- *Deu*. 13.2-4.
Miracles are revelations from God.	–Judah HaLevi.
A miracle cannot prove what is impossible. Some are allegories or metaphors.	– Maimonides.
Miracles are not to be cited as an argument	-- *Talmud Berachot* 60a.
Miracles do not necessarily conflict with nature	-- Nachmanides.
Believe in God through faith, not miracles	-- Nachman of Bratslav.
The created world admits of no alteration of nature	-- Kedushat Levi.
The truth of a religion cannot be maintained by miracles	-- Moses Mendelssohn.

(references fr R. Isaacs 103-117)

Miracles that involve natural phenomenon such as manna, the burning bush, the ten plagues, can often be explained in terms of historic events or scientific evidence. Documentation shows a great many of these miraculous occurrences did happen or could have happened, supporting the twin beliefs that either a divine presence made arrangements or that coincidence was involved. Metaphor and hyperbole cannot be discounted in some narratives of miracles.

Moses Mendelssohn by Anton Graff >>>

As dramatic and spectacular as these miracles are in print, for Torah, they are only attention getters. "One is forbidden to rely upon miracles." (Talmud Taanit 20b).
Events that cannot be explained [miracles]… have never been the major preoccupation of Jewish thinkers. Judaism and its thinkers have been much more interested in the miracles that are evident each day: the air we breathe, the fact that the sun rises and sets each day, the beauty of nature's creations (flowers, plants, streams rivers, and lakes). Life itself is considered a hidden miracle, so often taken for granted (R. Isaacs p. 2).

234

This conclusion is famously proposed by Abraham Joshua Heschel who looked around at all the wonders of existence, nature, human capabilities, stars, flowers, wind, and finds himself immersed in "radical amazement" of these miraculous proofs of God.

Thus we can see that many methods of recognizing an all-encompassing creator, God for most people, have been presented throughout history, constituting what can be called the an over-riding miracle of Torah. The most basic idea generated by the Hebrews was the Abrahamic concept of divine monotheism, as further developed by later Hebrews, then Judaism, then by Christianity and Islam. Starting in *Exodus* 19:5 and thereafter, God chose Hebrews for a covenantal relationship. It can also be said that the Abrahamic religions chose God and defined their own respective relationships. From the earliest time that Hebrews adopted the One God, the days of idols and god kings were marked for extinction.

Another astounding miracle: revelation, or insight from the depths of unknown wisdom, is the body of morals and laws that can guide humanity toward a better way of living together. These are the laws of Moses.

Still another astounding miracle: is much more subtle than the others. The commitment of Hebrews in general and Torah in particular to create a culture of thought, curiosity, and correction allowed them to propose new interpretations not only to Torah, but to problems in general. Science benefitted. Societies adopting the Hebrew republic model benefitted most (Cahill, Isaacs).

> ... *science has generally flourished in democratic periods of history.....many (antifascist intellectuals) rallied around a set of classically liberal values associated with that tradition. The liberty, equality, and fraternity of individuals was to be defended and expanded without regard to race, nationality, or religion; the free march of the human mind was to be obstructed by no sacred cows, vested interests, or other particularisms. Susceptible as these commitments were to divergent political application, they were specific enough to be contrasted to fascism, and it was in the name of these general commitments that English-speaking antifascist intellectuals of the late 1930's and early 1940's affirmed and sought to clarify the bond between science and democracy.* (Hollinger p. 88)

The result of "Abraham and Moses" includes most of what we call modern civil society, feared by tyrants of old and of today. The theory of civil society offers many components previously discussed, including a day of rest to relax, create, and give thanks; the Ten Commandments with the Holiness Code; and justice with responsible freedom.

In conclusion, we can say that the Torah, created thousands of years ago by a small minority, sparked an immeasurable advance in civilized culture and religion.

Besides inspiring much of modern civil society, the Torah preserves and reflects Jewish character. The early Apiru, Shosu, and Falasha predecessors all had appellations signifying they were outsiders, that they did not believe in the idols, temples, and structures of their times. Even though the designation as outsiders came with a negative perception, it also freed their  minds to question, to create, and to build alternative models, many of which eventually became accepted. And so it is today.

With direct and indirect influence and inspiration from Torah, countries in Europe, the Americas, and Israel have improved the lot of their populations.

It started with a group of independent-thinking donkey caravan operators.

Summary

Torah wants us to be moral free people

The history of the Biblical patriarchs encompasses a vast panorama of human drama, struggle, search for truth, and belief. As a result of their efforts, we are presented with a path to peace and freedom that eschews a lust for central unrestrained power.

Events described in Torah did happen. They were recorded in archaic Hebrew using the newly invented alphabet with a flourish that made the story of the Hebrews a universally understood and admired record of faith, hope, and humanity. With tools of critical thinking, archeology, and chronological research, inquiries are made today into the exact nature of Hebrew development. Because history as we know it today is not an objective of Torah, such inquiries Require examination of countless extra-Biblical objects and the result will not be Biblical but rather a parallel narrative. With proper transitory explanations, we can understand how events helped to mold Hebrew opinion and how modern history and Biblical writing are compatible. The astounding circumstances and results are completely compatible with divine will and revelation, a matter to explore separate from this book.

The Five Books speak in a unique language or style. This should come as no surprise as the text most used is the ninth century Hebrew Masorete text, which comports well with the Dead Sea Scrolls of a thousand years prior. The first Torah writing came another thousand years before the Dead Sea Scrolls, at a time when Hebrews had recently invented the alphabet to accompany their language. The newly introduced alphabet at the time allowed a virtual exposition of literary technique that includes poetry, metaphor, and didactic lecture, to name a few. Common people could read and write without the services of a scribe. Nevertheless, diction and references known to people 3000 years ago are not common today. Shakespeare and Coleridge are hard enough to comprehend, but with the Bible, the additional barrier of translation is mounted for English and other non-Hebrew speakers. Study with others, preferably trained clergy, and use of references is required to gain maximum benefit from the wisdom of Moses.

Chronology and geography are given only tepid respect. A search for dates related to events simply will yield nothing. The location of Laban's house, a map of Goshen, and details of desert locations are sketchy............

Torah presents a very succinct sketch of actual history only as necessary for purposes of teaching. The formation of the Jewish people and the background of the patriarchal period show many additional chapters. These include the proto-Jews often referred to as Apiru who entered history as outcasts; learned to trade; and united with pagan tribes before accepting God. There is the story of the desert Shosu Tribes that included Simeon and who were recognized by Egypt as worshippers of YHWH.

The Five Books of Moses have deeply influenced the development of civilization. Giving the world an alternative to pagan beliefs, a moral compass, and a set of moral laws gave individuals and whole nations a new modus operandi that is not yet followed everywhere, but is certainly respected and given lip service everywhere. It is for good reason that this work has been the hand-down global best seller for some 3000 years.

Some of the best literature and writing known to humans comes to us via the stories of Abraham, Jacob, Joseph, and Moses.

Prescriptions for many religious practices

BIBLIOGRAPHY WHEN BIBLE MEETS HISTORY

Aboelsoud, N.H., "Herbal medicine in Ancient Egypt," in Journal *of Medicinal Plants Research Vol.* 4(2) pp. 82-86, 1/18/2010 https://academicjournals.org/article/article1380374686_Aboelsoud.pdf .

Abraham, Kathleen, and Michael Sokoloff. "Aramaic Loanwords in Akkadian – A Reassessment of the Proposals." *Archiv Für Orientforschung* 52 (2011): 22–76. http://www.jstor.org/stable/24595102

Abrams, Rebecca, *The Jews of Medieval England,* London: BBC History Extra, 2018. https://www.historyextra.com/period/medieval/the-jews-of-medieval-england/ .

Aderet, Ofer,"Two 3800 year old cuneiform Tablets found in Iraq Give First Glimpse of Hebrew Precursor," in *Haaretz* 6/20/2023. https://www.haaretz.com/archaeology/2023-01-20/ty-article/two-3-800-year-old-cuneiform-tablets-found-in-iraq-give-first-glimpse-of-hebrew-precursor/00000185-ca23-d3a8-a3cf-cf3326430000.

Aharoni, Yohanan. "Nothing Early and Nothing Late: Re-Writing Israel's Conquest." *The Biblical Archaeologist* 39, no. 2 (1976): 55–76. https://doi.org/10.2307/3209354.

Albright, W. F., *"The Early Alphabetic Inscriptions from Sinai and Their Decipherment,"* in *Bulletin of the American Schools of Oriental Research*, No. 110 (1948): pp. 6-22. doi:10.2307/3218767.

Albright, W. F. "Abram the Hebrew a New Archaeological Interpretation." *Bulletin of the American Schools of Oriental Research*, no. 163 (1961): 36–54. https://doi.org/10.2307/1355773.

Albright, W.F., "From the Patriarchs to Moses Part I: From Abraham to Joseph," in *The Biblical Archaeologist* 36, no. 1 (1973): pp.5–33. https://doi.org/10.2307/3210978.

Albright, William F.. "From the Patriarchs to Moses Part II. Moses out of Egypt," in *The Biblical Archaeologist* 36, no. 2 (1973): 48-76. doi:10.2307/3211050.

Albright, William, *The Archaeology of Palestine*, Baltimore: Pelican, 1960.

Albright, William F., "Jethro, Hobab and Reuel in Early Hebrew Tradition" in *Catholic biblical Quarterly, 25*, 1963, pp. 8-9.

Albright, William, "Northwest-Semitc Names in a List of Egyptian Slaves," in *American Oriental Society* Bulletin 74, No. 4, 10/11 1954 pp. 222-233.

Albright, W. F. The "Smaller Beth-Shan Stele of Sethos I (1309-1290 B. C.)," in *Bulletin of the American Schools of Oriental Research*, no. 125 (1952): pp. 24–32. ttps://doi.org/10.2307/1355937.

Albright, W.F., *The Biblical Period From Abraham to Ezra*, New York: Harper, 1963.

Albright, William, *Yahweh and the Gods of Canaan*, New York: Doubleday, 1968

Allan, Nigel, "The Physician in Ancient Israel," in *Medical History*, Vol. 45, Issue 3, 7/2001, pp. 377-394, Cambridge: Cambridge University. https://doi.org/10.1017/S0025727300068058.

Anderson, Trevor, "What Are the Health Benefits of eating Delicious Kosher Food?" In *Lifestyle*, 6/16/2022, https://blog.stamfordadvocate.com/lifestyle/2022/06/16/what-are-the-health-benefits-of-eating-delicious-kosher-food/

Annus, Amar, :Sons of Seth and the South Winds," in *Mesopotamian Medicine and Magic*, eds. Strahil Panayotou and Ludek Vacin, Leiden: Brill, 2018.

Arnold, Dorothea. "Amenemhat I and the Early Twelfth Dynasty at Thebes," *in Metropolitan Museum Journal,* 26 (1991): pp. 5–48. https://doi.org/10.2307/1512902.

Assman, Jan, *Moses the Egyptian*, Cambridge: Harvard Press, 1997.

Assman, Jan, To Moses from Akhenaten, New York: American University in Cairo, 2016.

Ashtor, Eliyahu, tr. Aaron & Jenny Klein, *The Jews of Moslem Spain, Vol. 1, 2, 3,* Philadelphia: JPS, 1992.

Athanassiadi, and Michael Frede, eds, *Pagan Monotheism in Late Antiquity*, Oxford: Clarendon Press, 1999.

Avner, Uzi, *The Desert's role in the formation of Early Israel and the Origin of Yhwh*, Bochum: Universitatsbibliothek der Ruhr, 2021. https://www.academia.edu/82059233/The_Desert_s_Role_in_the_Formation_of_Early_Israel_a nd_the_Origin_of_Yhwh

Avner, Uzi, *Egyptian Timna: Reconsidered*, in *Unearthing the Wilderness*, Supplement 45 of Ancient Near Eastern Studies, Juan Tebes ed., Walpole, MA: Peeters, 2014, https://www.academia.edu/33143899/Egyptian_Timna_Reconsidered_2014?email_work_card= view-paper

Baer, Klaus, "The Low Price of Land in Ancient Egypt," *in Journal of the American Research Center in Egypt* Vol. 1, 1962 , pp. 25-45

Baer, Yitzhak, *A History of the Jews in Christian Spain* Vol, I, II, Philadelphia: JPS, 1961

Bedkerath, J.V., "Notes on the Viziers Ankhu and Iymeru in the thirteenth Egyptian Dynasty," in *Journal of the Near Eastern Studies Vol. 17 No. 4:* 10/1958 pp. 263-268.

Baines, John, "The Stela of Emhab," In *The Journal of Egyptian Archaeology* Vol. 72 pp. 41-53, 1986.

Barako, Tristan, "Coesixtence and Impermeability: Egyptians and Philistines," in *Contributions to the Chronology of the Eastern Mediterranean*, Bietak, Manfred, and Hermann Hunger,e es., Vol. IX, pp. 509-516: Wien, Osterreichiche Akademie der Wissenschaften, 2007

Bar-Ron, Michael Shelomo, *The Seal of Joseph in His Palace*, academia.edu

Bar-Ron, Michael Shelomo, *Hebrews Smelting with Hobab are Reminded of those who Strayed to a Golden Cow-deity.* Academic. Edu. http://www.torathmoshe.com/wp-content/uploads/Sinai-361-Another-Exodus-Inscription-Confirms-the-Torah-Narrative.pdf.

Bar-Ron, *The Exodus inscriptions at Serabit el-Khadim* https://www.academia.edu/45153790/The_Exodus_Inscriptions_at_Serabit_el_Khadim_NOTE_I n_light_of_new_evidence_I_recant_my_reading_of_Sinai_361_A_new_draft_will_be_uploaded _in_March_2022_

Bart, Anneke, Saint Louis Universityweb page on Egypt, https://mathstat.slu.edu/~bart/egyptianhtml/kings%20and%20Queens/Viziers.html#Middle_King dom

Bart, Kathryn *An Introduction to the Archaeology of Ancient Egypt,* Chichester: Wiley & Sons: *2015.*

Barton, George A., *"The Place of the Amorites in the Civilization of Western Asia." in Journal of the American Oriental Society ,* vo. 45 (1925): pp. 1–38. https://doi.org/10.2307/593461.

Bauer, Robert, "Still the Fertile Crescent?" in *The Ozark Historical Review*, Vol. XXXIIX, Spring 2009. https://fulbright.uark.edu/departments/history/_resources/pdf/ozark-historical-review/ohr-2009-3.pdf

Beit-Halachmi, T. Rachel Sabath, The *Most Radical Book of Torah*, NY: Reform Judaism.org, 7/22/2022, D'varim, *Deu.* 1:1-3.22 https://reformjudaism.org/learning/torah-study/torah-commentary/most-radical-book-torah-and-necessity-interpretation

Ben-Sasson, H., ed . *A history of the Jewish People*, Cambridge: Harvard, 1976

Ben-Tor, A. Do the Execration Tests reflect an accurate picture of the Contemporary Settlement Map of Palestine? In Essays on Ancient Israel in its Near Eastern Context, Amit, Y. et al. eds, Winona Lake: Eisenbrauns, 2006 63-87.

Ben-Yosef, Erez, *The Architectural Bias in Current Biblical Archaelolgy*, in *Vetus Testamentum* 69-3 London: Brill, pp. 361-387. 2019, https://www.academia.edu/39789332/The_Architectural_Bias_in_Current_Biblical_Archaeology _Vetus_Testamentum_69_3_2019_361_387_

Berlin, Adele, & Brettler, Marc, *The Jewish Study Bible*, based on the JPS translation, Oxford: Oxford: Oxford U. Press, 2014.

Berman, Joshua A., *Created Equal*, Oxford: Oxford U. Press., 2008

Bertalanffy, Ludwig von, *Perspectives on General Systems Theory*, NY: Braziller, 1976

Biblical Archaeological Society Review and online https://www.biblicalarchaeology.org

Bienkowski, Piotr, "The Edomites," in *You Shall Not Abhor an Edomite*, Atlanta: Scholars Press, 1995, pp. 41-92.

Bietak, Manfred, *Avaris*, London: British Museum, 1996.

Bietak, Manfred, "From where came the Hyksos and where did they go," in M. Maree ed., *The Second Intermediate Period: Current Research, Future Prospects*, Leuven: Orientalia Lovaniensia Analecta, 192, 2010: pp. 139-181, https://www.academia.edu/10074987/_From_where_came_the_Hyksos_and_where_did_they_ go_in_M_Mar%C3%A9e_ed_The_Second_Intermediate_Period_Thirteenth_Seventeenth_Dyna sties_Current_Research_Future_Prospects_OLA_192_Leuven_2010_Peeters_139_181

Bietak, Manfred, "Harbor Towns of the Bronze age: the Examples of Avaris and Byblos," in *The City Across Time*, Grangipane, Marcella, ed., Rome: Bardi Edizioni, pp. 207-251, 2022.

Bietak, Manfred, "The Hyksos Enigma," Review Article, in *Archaeopress Egyptology, 11,* Bibliotheca Orientalis LXXV/3-4, Oxford, 2015, 2018, pp. 229-248.

Bietak, Manfred," Israelites found in Egypt," *in Biblical Archaeology Review* 29:5, 9-10/2003.

Bietak, Manfred, "On the Historicity of the Exodus," in T.E. Levy, T. Schneider, & W.H.C. Propp, eds., *Israel's Exodus in Transdiciplinary Perspective*, Heidelberg-NY, pp. 17-36.

Bietak, Manfred, "The Many Ethnicities of Avaris," in J. Budka & J. Auenmuller,. *From Microcosm to Macrocosm,* Leiden: Sidestone Press, 2018, pp. 73-92

Bietak, Manfred, "A Thutmosid Palace Precinct" in M. Bietak & S. Prell, eds., *Palaces in Ancient Egypt and the Ancient Near East* Vol. I : *Egypt, Contributions to the Archaeology of Egypt*, Vienna,: Austrian Academy of Sciences, 2018, pp. 231-257.

Bietak, Manfred, "The Unexpected Origin of the People Behind Hyksos Rule in Egypt," Prepublication, 2023, https://www.academia.edu/108987214/Bietak_The_Unexpected_Origin_of_the_People_Behind _Hyksos_Rule_in_Egypt?email_work_card=view-paper

Bietak, Manfred, "Der Ubergang van der G\Fruhen zur Mittleren Bronzezeitkultur im Vorderen Orient anhand von Wandbildern in Grabern des agyptischen Mittleren Reiches," in <u>Mitteilungen der Anthropologischen Gesellschaft in Wien</u>, CXXIII./CXXIV.Band, Wien: Verlag Ferninand Berger & Sohne Horn, 1993/94

Billington, Clyde E., "The Name Yahweh in Egyptian Hieroblyphic Texts," Washington: *Biblearcheology*, 3/8/2010. https://biblearchaeology.org/research/exodus-from-egypt/3233-the-name-yahweh-in-egyptian-hieroglyphic-texts.

Blackman, Aylward, and R. Eric Peet, trs., "Papyrus Lansing," in *The Journal of Egyptian Archaeology Vol. 11 No. 3/4* 10/1925, pp. 284-298.

Blasweiler, Joost, "The kingdom of Hurma during the Reign of Labarna and Hattusili," in *Bronze Age Archaeology*, 2020, Arnhem, from https://www.academia.edu/42931706/The_kingdom_of_Hurma_during_the_reign_of_Labarna_and_Hattusili_Part_1

Bienkowski, P., & A. Millard, *Dictionary of the Ancient Near East*, Phila., U of P : 2000.

Blattman, Christopher, "The Five Reasons Wars Happen," Modern War site at West Point, https://mwi.usma.edu/the-five-reasons-wars-happen/

Blum, Erhard, "The Jacob Tradition" in *The Book of Genesis. Composition, Reception, & Interpretation*, Boston: Leiden-Boston, pp. 181-211.

Bodi, Daniel, "Is there a Connection Between the Amorites and the Arameans?" in *Zoroastrianism in the Levant and the Amorites,* Oxford: ARAM Vol 26, 1 & 2, 2014, pp. 383-409, https://www.academia.edu/26464713/_Is_There_a_Connection_Between_the_Amorites_and_the_Arameans_ARAM_26_1_and_2_2014_383_409?email_work_card=view-paper

Bohstrom, Philippe," Tribe of Day: Sons of Israel, or of Greek Mercenaries Hired by Egypt?" in *Haaretz*, 12/4/2016 https://www.haaretz.com/archaeology/2016-12-04/ty-article-magazine/tribe-of-dan-sons-of-israel-or-of-greek-mercenaries-hired-by-egypt/0000017f-f2fa-d497-a1ff-f2fac60a0000

Bonar, Andrew, *The Biography of Robert Murray M'Cheyne*, Paris: Adansonia Publishing, 2018 reprint of 1844 book.

Bos, Gerrit, "Maimonides' Medical Works and their Contribution," in *Maimonidean Studies*, Vol. 5, NY: Yeshiva U., 2008, pp. 243-266.

Bottero, Jean, *Le Probleme des Habiru*, Paris: Imprimerie Nationale, 1954.

Bradbury, Louise, "Nefer's Inscription," *in Journal of the American research Center in Egypt Vol. 22* pp. 73-95 1985.

Brazier, Yvette, "What was ancient Egyptian Medicine Like?" In *Medical News Today*, 11/16/2018, https://www.medicalnewstoday.com/articles/323633

Breasted, James Henry, *Ancient Records of Egypt Vol.I*, Chicago: U. Chicago, 1906.

Breasted, James Henry, *Ancient Records of Egypt Vol.III*, Chicago: U. Chicago, 1906.

Breasted, James Henry, *Ancient Records of Egypt Vol.IV*, Chicago: U. Chicago, 1906.

Breasted, James Henry, *Ancient Records of Egypt Vol.V*, Chicago: U. Chicago, 1906.

Bridbury, A. R. "The Dark Ages." In *The Economic History Review* 22, no. 3 (1969), pp. 526–37. https://doi.org/10.2307/2594125.

Brugsch, Henry, *The True Story of the Exodus of Israel*, Boston: Lee & Shepard, 1880.

Bryce, T. R. "The Lukka Problem-And a Possible Solution." *Journal of Near Eastern Studies* 33, no. 4 (1974): 395–404. http://www.jstor.org/stable/544776.

Bury, J.B. and Meiggs, Bussell, *A History of Greece*, NY: St. Martin, 1980.

Bryan, Cypil P., *Ancient Egyptian Medicine The Papyrus Ebers*, Chicago: Ares, 1930.

Bryan, Betwy, *The Reign of Thutmose IV*, Baltimore: John Hopkins, 1991.

Bryner, Jeanna, "Wild Ass Tamed," in livescience.com, Washington: Wild Ass Tamed, Buried with Egyptian King, Live Science : National Academy of Sciences, 2008.

Bryson, Maggie, *Man, King, God? The Deification of Haremhab*, Paper at the 66th annual Meeting of the American Research Center in Egypt, April 2015

Bryson, Maggie, *A New Look at the Coronation Inscription of Horemheb*, paper at the 63 rd annual Meeting of the American Research Center in Egypt April 2012

Burke, Aaron, "The Amorites and the Bronze Age Near East," Cambridge: Cambridge U., 2021.

Burke, Aaron, "Canaan under Siege," in *Studies on War in the Ancient Near East,* Gottingen: Hubert & Co., 2010, pp. 43–67.

Butzer, Karl W., *Early Hydraulic Civilization in Egypt,* Chicago: U. Chicago, 1976.

Cahill, Thomas, *The Gifts of the Jews*, NY: Anchor Books, 1998.

Callender, Cae, "Female Horus: The Life and Reign of Tausret," in Wilkinson, Richard, *Tausret,* Oxford: Oxford U., 2012 file:///C:/Users/Office1/Downloads/02_Wilkinson_Ch02recorrected.pdf

Cannon, Ray, "Tamarisk: the manna tree," in *Ray Cannon's Nature Notes*, Cannon, https://rcannon992.com/2015/05/18/tamarisk-the-manna-tree/ 2015.

Capek, Fillip, "The Shephelah in the Iron Age I and Iron Age IIA," in *Oriental Archive 80*, Prague: John Benjamin, via Academia.com, pp. 475-505, 2012

Carroll, James, *Constantine's Sword*, Boston: Houghton Mifflin, 2001.

Caton-Thompson, Gertrude, and E. W. Gardner. "Recent Work on the Problem of Lake Moeris" *in The Geographical Journal* 73, no. 1 (1929): 20–58. https://doi.org/10.2307/1782277.

Cawson, Warren R., "Anastasi, Sallier, and Harris and Their Papyri" in the *Journal of Egyptian Archaeology* Vol. 35, 12/1949, pp. 158-166

Cerny, Jaroslav, "Papyrus Salt 124," in *Journal of Egyptian Archaeology*, Vol. 15 no 3/ 4, 11/29, pp. 243-257, Sage Publisher.

Chace, Arnold Buffum, "The Rhind Mathemaical Papyrus V I," Oberlin: Mathematical Association of America, 1927

Chace, Arnold Buffum, "The Rhind Mathemaical Papyrus V II*,"* Oberlin: *Mathematical Association of America*, 1929.

Chesney, Francis Rawdon, *Narrative of the Euphrates Expedition*, London: British Government, 1868.

Christian, David. "Silk Roads or Steppe Roads? The Silk Roads in World History," *in Journal of World History* 11, no. 1 (2000): pp. 1–26. http://www.jstor.org/stable/20078816.

Cilliers, Louise, "Mesopotamian Medicine," in *South African Medical Journal*, 2/2007, https://www.researchgate.net/publication/6429561_Mesopotamian_medicine

Clapp, Frederick G. "The Site of Sodom and Gomorrah. Diversity of Views" *in American Journal of Archaeology* 40, no. 3 (1936): 323-44. doi:10.2307/498693.

Clay, Albert, *The Origin of Biblical Traditions*, San Diego: Book Tree, 1997.

Cline, Eric H. & O'Connor, David, *Thutmose III*, Ann Arbor: Michigan Press, 2006.

Cline, Eric, *1177 BC*, Princeton: Princeton, U. Press, 2014

Cohen-Weinberger, *Anat, Tell el-Yahudiay Ware,* Israel Antiquities Authority, unpublished.

Cohen, Susan. "Interpretative Uses and Abuses of the Beni Hasan Tomb Painting," in *Journal of Near Eastern Studies*, vol. 74, no. 1, 2015, pp. 19–38. *JSTOR*, www.jstor.org/stable/10.1086/679590. Accessed 29 Jan. 2021

Colemen, Peter, Douglas Fry, "What Can We Learn From the World's Most Peaceful Societies?" in *Greater Good Magazine,* June, 7, 2021, https://greatergood.berkeley.edu/article/item/what_can_we_learn_from_the_worlds_most_peaceful_societies

Colless, Brian., "The Proto-Alphabetic Inscriptions of Sinai," *in Ancient Near Eastern Studies*, 28, pp. 1-52, 10.2143/ANES.28.0.525711, 1990.

Collier, Mark, "More on Late Nineteenth Dynasty Ostraca Dates, and Remarks on Paneb," in *Ramesside Studies*, M. Collier and S. Snape eds., Great Britain:Rutherford Press, 2011, pp. 111-123

Collins, Billie Jean. "Ḫattušili I, The Lion King," in *Journal of Cuneiform Studies*, vol. 50, American Schools of Oriental Research, 1998, pp. 15–20, https://doi.org/10.2307/1360028.

Conder C.R. "Exodus, the Route," in James Orr. Editor, *The International Standard Bible Encyclopedia*, 1915.

Coogan, Michael, D., ed., *The Oxford History of the Biblical World*, Oxford: Oxford U., 1998.

Cooper, Kenneth R., "The Shasu of Palestine in Egyptian Texts, Part One," in *Artifax*, Vol. 21, No. 4 2006, Autumn, pp.22-27.

Coote, Robert B. (2000). "Hapiru, Apiru" In David Noel Freedman and Allen C. Myers (eds.). *Eerdmans Dictionary of the Bible*. Grand Rapids: Eerdmans. ISBN 9789053565032.

Crane, Lee (Stephen) Jewish German Revolution: Saving Civilization in 400, Philadelphia: Pavilion Press, 2010.

Cross, Frank M., and David Noel Freedman, "The Song of Miriam," *in Journal of Near Eastern Studies,* 14, no. 4 (1955): 237–50. http://www.jstor.org/stable/543020.

Cross, Stephen W. "The Workmen's Huts and Stratigraphy in the Valley of the Kings." *The Journal of Egyptian Archaeology* 100 (2014): 133–50. http://www.jstor.org/stable/24644967.

Dagan, Y., *The Settlement in the Judean Shephelah in the Second and First Millennium B.C.,* (Ph.D. dissertation, Tel Aviv University, 2000,(in Hebrew)

Darnell, J.C., F.W. Dobbs-Allsopp, M.J. Lundberg, P.K. McCarter, Bruce Zuckerman, "Two Early Alphabetic Inscriptions from the Wadi el-Hol," *The Annual of the American Schools of Oriental Research*, vol. 59, The American Schools of Oriental Research, 2005, pp. 63-124. https://www.jstor.org/stable/3768583?searchText=Two%20Early%20Alphabetic%20Inscriptions%20from%20the%20Wadi%20el-Hol&searchUri=%2Faction%2FdoBasicSearch%3FQuery%3DTwo%2BEarly%2BAlphabetic%2BInscriptions%2Bfrom%2Bthe%2BWadi%2Bel-

Hol&ab_segments=0%2Fbasic_search_gsv2%2Fcontrol&refreqid=fastly-default%3A7ca9d9f096e554cc5744c56d3e662395

Darnell, J.C, "Wadi el-Hol," in Willeke Wendrich (ed.) *UCLA Encyclopedia of Egyptology*, LA: UCLA, 2013, Pernalinkhttp://digital2.library.ucla.edu/viewItem.do?ark=21198/zz002dx2tj

or https://www.academia.edu/19068407/Wadi_el_H%C3%B4l?email_work_card=view-paper

Davis, D., R. Maddin, J. D. Muhly, and T. Stech. "A Steel Pick from Mt. Adir in Palestine" *in Journal of Near Eastern Studies* 44, no. 1 (1985): 41-51. http://www.jstor.org/stable/544369.

Davies, J.G., *The Early Christian Church*, NY: Barnes & Noble, 1965.

Davies, Vanessa, "The Treatment of foreigners in Seti's Battle Reliefs" in *The Journal of Egyptian Archaeology* 98 (2012): 73–85. http://www.jstor.org/stable/24645004.

Dearman, J. Andrew, "Edomite Religion," in *You Shall not abhor an Edomite for He is Your Brother*, Atlanta: Schlors Press, 1995, pp. 119-136.

DeMagistris, Francesco, *The Apiru and the Egyptian Domination of Late Bronze Age Israel*, Edinburgh: U. Edinburgh dissertation: 2014, https://www.academia.edu/8639555/The_Apiru_and_the_Egyptian_domination_of_Late_Bronze_Age_IsraelDeMagistris, Francesco, *The Apiru and the Egyptian Domination of Late Bronze Age Israel*, Edinburgh: U. Edinburgh dissertation: 2014, https://www.academia.edu/8639555/The_Apiru_and_the_Egyptian_domination_of_Late_Bronze_Age_Israel

Demsky, Aaron. "An Iron Age IIA Alphabetic Writing Exercise from Khirbet Qeiyafa." *Israel Exploration Journal* 62, no. 2 (2012): 186–99. http://www.jstor.org/stable/43855624.

Demsky, Aaron, Joseph Reif, and Joseph Tabory eds., *These are the Names*, Ramat-Gan: Bar-Illan, 1997.

De Vauz, R. *The Early History of Israel*, Tr D. Smith, London: Darton, Longman and Todd, 1971.

Dhorme, E., Les Habiru et les Hebreux, in JPOS, Vol. IV, pp. 162-168, 1924.

Di Teodoro, Micol, "The scribes of the hnrt wr Senebeni and Sobekhotep," in *Studien Zur Altagyptischen Kultur,* eds Herausgegeben von Jochem Kahl und Nicole Kloth, Hamburg: Helmut Buske Verlag, 2018.

Dodson, Aidan, *Amarna Sunset*, NY: American University, 2009

Dodson, Aidan, "Amenmesse *in Kent, Liverpool, and Thebes,*" in *Journal of Egyptian Archaeology*, Vol. 81 pp. 115-128, Sage, 1995

Dodson, Aidan, "Messuy, Amada, and Amenmesse,*" in Journal of the American Research Center in Egypt* Vol 34, pp. 41-48, 1997

Dodson, Aidan, *Poisoned Legacy*, NY: American U. in Cairo, 2016

Dodson, Aidan, *"The Takhats and Some Other Royal Ladies of the Ramesside Period."* in *The Journal of Egyptian Archaeology* 73 (1987): 224–29. https://doi.org/10.2307/3821541.

Dorma, Peter F., *Introduction of Innovation*, in *Creativity and Innovation in the Reign of Hatshesut*, Chicago: U Chicago, 2014 pp. 1-6.

Dorman, Peter F., "The Origins and Early Development of the Book of the Dead," in Scalf, Foy ed., *Book of the Dead Becoming God in Ancient Egypt*, Chicago: Oriental Institute, 2017.

Edzard, D.O., "Die Tontafeln von Kāmid el-Lōz," in D.O. Edzard, et al., eds., *Kāmid el-Lōz - Kumidi. Schriftdokumente aus Kāmid el-Lōz.* (Saarbrücker Beiträge zur Altertumskunde 7; Bonn: Rudolf Hablet Verlag, 1970) pp. 55–60.

Drews, C. W., "Could wind have parted the Red Sea?" in *Weatherwise, 64,* pp. 30-35. doi:10.1080/00431672.2011.536122, 2011

Doyle, Michael W., "Liberal internationalism: peace, war and democracy," in *The Nobel Prize,* partially from *Doyle's Ways of War and Peace,* NY: W.W. Norton, 1997, https://www.nobelprize.org/prizes/themes/liberal-internationalism-peace-war-and-democracy.

Dudhane, Rahul, "Concept of God in Hinduism," in *Hinduism Facts,* https://www.hinduismfacts.org,   https://www.hinduismfacts.org/concept-of-god-in-hinduism/

Dunn, Jacob Edward, *A Land Whose Stones are Iron and from Whose Hills You May Mine copper: Metallurgy, Pottery, and the Midianite-Qenite Hypothesis,* Athens, GA, 2015, Thesis at University of Georgia, sourced in academia.edu.

Eason, Perri, Basem, Rabis, and Omar, Attum, *Hunting of Migratory birds in North Sinai, Egypt,* Cambridge: Cambridge U. online, 2015.

Eben, Abba, *The Story of the Jews,* NY: Random House, 1968

Edelman, Diana ed., *You Shall Not Abhor an Edomite,* Atlanta: Scholars Press, 1995.

Edgar, Paul, A Most Ancient Statecraft: The Idrimi Statue Inscription, in Classics of Strategy.com, Washington D.C.: Hillsdale College Van Andel School,   12/22/2021 https://classicsofstrategy.com/2021/12/22/a-most-ancient-statecraft-the-idrimi-statue-inscriptio

Ehrlich, Carl S. Ed., *An Introduction to Ancient Near Eastern Literature,* NY, W

Rowman & Littlefield, 2009.

Emerton, J. A. "Yahweh and His Asherah," in *The Goddess or Her Symbol*? in *Vetus Testamentum* 49, no. 3 (1999): 315–37. http://www.jstor.org/stable/1585374.

Eusebius, "Chronicle," Tr. Robert Bedrosian, in *Sources of the Armenian Tradition,* Long Branch: NJ, 2008

Fadl, Sherwet Mostafa El-Sayed, "Natural and Human Impacts on the Egyptian Northern Lagoons between the Ptolemaic and Roman Eras in the Light of Greek Sources Mareotis and Sirbonis," in *The Egyptian Journal of Environmental Change,* 2016 https://www.academia.edu/94161578/Natural_and_Human_Impacts_on_the_Egyptian_Northern _Lagoons_between_the_Ptolemaic_and_Roman_Eras_in_the_Light_of_Greek_Sources_Mareo tis_and_Sirbonis_A_Case_Study

Fariman, H.W. and Bernhard Grdseloff, "Texts of Hatshepsut and Sethos I," in *Journal of Egyptian Archaeology,* Vol. 33 12/47, pp. 12-33.

Falconer, M.A., Ed., The Geography of Strabo, Book XVI, http://www.perseus.tufts.edu/hopper/text?doc=Strab.+16.2.42&fromdoc=Perseus%3Atext%3A1 999.01.0239

Faust, Avrahem, and Katz, Hayah, "A Canaanite Town, A Judahite Center, and a Persian Perior Fort" in *Near Eastern Archaeology ,* Vol. 78, No. 2 (June 2015): The American Schools of Oriental Research: Chicago, https://www.jstor.org/stable/10.5615/neareastarch.78.2.0088#metadata_info_tab_contents

Feldman, Louis H. "Conversion to Judaism in Classical Antiquity," in *Hebrew Union College Annual* 74 (2003): 115–56. http://www.jstor.org/stable/23509246.

Feldman, Steven, *Biblical History: From Abraham to Moses, 1850-1200 BCE,* Center for Online Judaic Studies, 2017

Feinman, Peter, "The Tempest in the tempest", in Bulletin of the Egyptological Seminar Vol. 19, NY, 2015

Finkelstein, Israel, and Amihai Mazar, *The Quest for the Historical Israel,* Atlanta: Society of Biblical Literature, 2007

Finkelstein, Israel, "Hazor and the North I the Iron Age," in *Bulletin of the American Schools of Oriental Research*, No. 314: American Schools of Oriental Research, 1999, pp. 55-70. From http://www.jstor.org/stable/1357451

Finkelstein, Israel, *The Forgotten Kingdom*, Atlanta: Society of Biblical Literature, 2013

Finkelstein, Israel & Thomas Romer, "Comments on the Historical Background of the Jacob Narrative in Genesis," in Zeitschrift für die alttestamentliche Wissenschaft, 126:317-338, 2014

Finkelstein, Israel, and Nadav Naʾaman. "Shechem of the Amarna Period and the Rise of the Northern Kingdom of Israel. " In *Israel Exploration Journal* 55, no. 2 , 2005, pp. 172-93. http://www.jstor.org/stable/27927106.

Finkelstein, Israel, Neil Asher Silberman, "David and Solomon,*" In Search of the Bible's Sacred Kings and the Roots of the Western Tradition*. Simon and Schuster, 2007.

Finkelstein, Israel, and Neil Asher Silberman, *The Bible Unearthed*, NY: Free Press, 2001.

Fleming, Daniel E., "Mari and the Possibilities of Bilblical Memory," in *Revue d'Assyriologie et d'archéologie Orientale* 92, no. 1, 1998, pp. 41–78, http://www.jstor.org/stable/23282083.

Fleming, Daniel E., *Democracy's Ancient Ancestors*, Cambridge, Cambridge U. Press, 2004.

Flemin, Daniel E., *Yahweh before Israel*, Cambridge: Cambridge University, 2021.

Fletcher, Joann, *Chronicle of a Pharaoh*, Oxford: Oxford U., 2000.

Foster, Karen P., *"Ahmose and the Eruption of Thera,"* American Research Center in Egypt , 171 (1996/1), pp. 9-10. https://library.arce.org/xmlui/handle/123456789/246?show=full#data-fancybox.

Foster, Karen Polinger, Robert K. Ritner, and Benjamin R. Foster. "Texts, Storms, and the Thera Eruption" *in Journal of Near Eastern Studies* 55, no. 1 (1996): 1–14. http://www.jstor.org/stable/545376.

Fowler, Henry Thatcher. "Influence of the Bible in American Democracy" *in Christian Education* 3, no. 1 (1919): pp. 22–25. http://www.jstor.org/stable/41174645.

Fracaroli, Diego A. Barreyra, *"The Chronology of Zimri-Lim's Reign,"* in Barcelona: *Aula Orientalis*, No. 29 vol. 2, 2011, pp. 185-198. https://www.academia.edu/5260717/The_Chronology_of_Zimri_Lims_Reign

Frank, Irene M., David Brownstone, *The Silk Road, a History*, NY: Facts on File, 1986.

Freed, John, *Near Eastern Archaeology bBog*, https://nearchaeology.blogspot.com/2015/12/steal-of-amenyseneb.html
12/25/2015

Freedman, David, ed., *The Anchor Bible Dictionary,* Vol 5, NY: Doubleday, 1992.

Frendo, Anthony J., "Two Long-Lost Phoenician Inscriptions and the Emergence of Ancient Israel,*"* in *Palestine Exploration Quarterly* 134, 200), pp. 37-43.

Friedman, Matti, "An Archaeological Dig Reignites the Debate Over the Old Testament's Historical Accuracy," in *Smithsonian Magazine*, 12/2021.

Friedman, Richard Elliott, *Who Wrote the Bible*, NY: Summit Books, 1997.

Frost, Stanley Brice, "The Death of Josiah: A Conspiracy of Silence," *in Journal of Biblical Literature* 87, no. 4, 1968, pp. 369–82, https://doi.org/10.2307/3263298.

Gabel, John B., andCharles B. Wheeler, *The Bible as Literature*, Oxford: Oxford U. Press, 1986.

Gafney, Wilda, *Daughters of Miriam Women Prophets in Ancient Israel*, Minneapolis, Fortress, 2008.

Galan, Jose M., ed., *Creativity and Innovation in the Reign of Hatshesut*, Chicago: U Chicago, 2014

Galil, G. "Most Ancient Hebrew Biblical Inscription Deciphered." In University of Haifa Phys.org https://phys.org/news/2010-01-ancient-hebrew-biblical-inscription-deciphered.html, *Science*

Daily https://www.sciencedaily.com/releases/2010/01/100107183037.htm , and *EurekAlert!*, American Assoc. for the Advancement of Science, AAAS, 2010.

Gardiner, Alan H., *The Admonitions of an Egyptian Sage*, Leipzig: Buchhandlung, 1909.

Gardiner, Alan H., "The Defeat of the Hyksos by Kamose," in *The Journal of Egyptian Archaeology* Vol 3., No. 2/3 4-7 1916, pp 95-110

Gardner, Alan, *Egyptian Hieratic Texts*, Series I, Part I, *The Papyrus Anastasi and the Papyrus Koller*, Leipzif: Hinrichs' Sche Buchhandlung, 1911.

Gardner, Alan, *Late Egyptian Stories*, Bruxelles: Bibliotheca Aegyptiaca I 1932.

Gardner, Milo, *Ahmes Papyrus*, unpublished paper, CA State U. Fullerton Campus.

Garzanti, Eduardo, "The Euphrates-Tigris-Karun River system," in *Earth-science Reviews*, Amsterdam: Elsevier BV, 2016.

Gee, John, "Overlooked Evidence for Sesostris III Foreign Policy," in J*ournal of American Research Center in Egypt Vol. 41*, 2004, pp 23-31.

Gelb, I.J., "Computer-Aided Analysis of Amorite," Chicago: Oriental Institute, 1980.

Gelb, I. J. "The Early History of the West Semitic Peoples." *Journal of Cuneiform Studies* 15, no. 1 (1961): 27–47. https://doi.org/10.2307/1359584.

Gerber, Jane, *The Jews of Spain*, NY: Free Press, 1992.

Gertoux, Gerard, *Abraham and Chedorlaomer*, unpublished, 2015. https://www.academia.edu/15710900/Abraham_and_Chedorlaomer_Chronological_Historical_and_Archaeological_Evidence?email_work_card=abstract-read-more

Gertoux, Gerard, *Absolute Egyptian Chronology, a monograph*, Universitie Lyon, https://www.academia.edu/72228719/Absolute_Egyptian_chronology_From_Narmer_2838_2808_to_Nakhtnebef_II_360_342_?email_work_card=view-paper

Gertoux, Gerard, *Moses and the Exodus: what evidence?* Thesis, Paris: L'Harmattan, 1999.

Gideon, Tsur, *The Ostracon from Khirbet Qeiyafa*, 8/2019, Open University, Natanya https://www.academia.edu/40180212/The_Ostracon_from_Khirbet_Qeiyafa_Correction_of_the_letters_in_Ostracon_due_to_errors_in_their_identification.

Gilmour, Garth, and Kenneth A. Kitchen. "Pharaoh Sety II and Egyptian Political Relations with Canaan at the End of the Late Bronze Age," *in Israel Exploration Journal* 62, no. 1, 2012, pp. 1–21, http://www.jstor.org/stable/23214251.

Ginzberg, Louis, *The Legends of the Jews*, tr. by Henrietta Szold, Baltimore: John Hopkins U., Vol. 1 – 7, 1998

Giveon, Raphael, *Les Bedouins Shosou Des Documents Egyptiens*, Leiden: Brill, 1971.

Giveon, Raphael. "*The* Shosu of the Late XXth Dynasty." in Journal *of the American Research Center in Egypt* 8, 1969, :pp. 51–53. https://doi.org/10.2307/40000037.

Glueck, Nelson, "The Civilization of the Edomites," in *The Biblical Archaeologist* 10, no. 4 1947, pp. 77-84, doi:10.2307/3209256.

Glueck, Nelson, *The River Jordan*, NY: McGraw-Hill, 1946.

Gobiet, S. "The Gezer Stone." *The Biblical World* 34, no. 1 (1909): 57–59. http://www.jstor.org/stable/3141940.

Goedicke, Hans, "The Chronology of the Thera/Santorin Explosion," in *Ägypten Und Levante / Egypt and the Levant* 3, 1992, pp. 57–62. http://www.jstor.org/stable/23783686.

Goedicke, Hans. "Papyrus Anastasi Vol., pp. I 51-61." In *Studien Zur Altägyptischen Kultur* 14, 1987, 83–98. http://www.jstor.org/stable/44322889.

Goedicke, Hans. "'Irsu Kharu" in *Papyrus Harris, Wiener Zeitschrift Für Die Kunde Des Morgenlandes*, vol. 71, Department of Oriental Studies, University of Vienna, 1979, pp. 1–17, http://www.jstor.org/stable/23858901.

Goff, Beatrice L. "The Lost Jahwistic Account of the Conquest of Canaan." *Journal of Biblical Literature* 53, no. 3 (1934): 241–49. https://doi.org/10.2307/3259670.

Goldwasser, Orly , "How the Alphabet Was Born from Hierglyph," *in Washington: Biblical Archaeology Society*, March/April 2010 The BAS Library, https://www.academia.edu/6916402/Goldwasser_O_2010_How_the_Alphabet_was_Born_from _Hieroglyphs_Biblical_Archaeology_Review_36_2_March_April_40_53_Award_Best_of_BAR_ award_for_2009_2010_Discussion_with_Anson_Rainey_http_www_bib_arch_org_scholars_stu dy_alphabet_asp_

Goldwasser, Orly, "The Miners Who Invented the Alphabet," in Journal of Ancient Egyptian Interconnections, Vol. 4, No. 3, September 2012. https://egyptianexpedition.org/articles/the-miners-who-invented-the-alphabet-a-response-to-christopher-rollston.

Goldwasser, Orly, "King Apophis of Avaris and the Emergence of Monotheism," In *Timelines*, E. Czerny, ed., V II, Orientalia Lovaniensia analecta 149/II, pp. 129-133.

Goldwasser, Orly, *Goldwasser,* "First Rebuttal." *in Biblical Archaelogy Society, Bible History Daily*, August 25, 2010 https://www.biblicalarchaeology.org/daily/biblical-artifacts/inscriptions/goldwassers-first-rebuttal/

Goldwasser, Orly, "Out of the mists of the Alphabet," in *Agypten und Levante*, Jan., 2014. https://www.researchgate.net/publication/289616061_Out_of_the_mists_of_the_alphabet_-_Redrawing_the_brother_of_the_ruler_of_Retenu/link/5ab383bda6fdcc1bc0c28bcd/download

Golinets, Viktor, "Amorite," in Hasselback-Andee, Rebecca, Ed., *A companion to Ancient Near Eastern Languages,* Hoboken, NJ: John Wiley & Sons, 2020, pp. 185-202..

Golinkin, David, *The Basic Principles of Jewish Business Ethics*, Jerusalem: Schechter.edu, 10/11/2003 https://schechter.edu/the-basic-principles-of-jewish-business-ethics/?msclkid=f9492cfec5cb11ecbb7db9aea4143613

Gottlieb, Yulia, "The advent of the Age of Iron in the Land of Israel," in *Tel Aviv vo. 37*: Tel Aviv U., 2010, pp. 89-110, from Academia.edu.

Gordon, Cyrus H., *Ugarit and Minoan Crete*, NY: Norton, 1967.

Gordon, Cyrus H., *Greek and Hebrew Civilizations*, NY: Norton, 1965

Gottwald, Norman, *The Tribes of Yahweh*, NY: Orbis, 1979

Goyon, Jean-Claude, "Inscriptions Tardives Du Temple de Mout à Karnak," *in Journal of the American Research Center in Egypt*, vol. 20, American Research Center in Egypt, 1983, pp. 47–61, https://doi.org/10.2307/40000901.

Gray, Mary, "The Habiru-Hebrew Problem," in *Hebrew Union College Annual Vol. XXIX*, Cincinnati: Hebrew Union, 1958.

Grajetzki, Wolfram, *Court Officials of the Egyptian Middle Kingdom*, London: Bristol Classical, 2012

Greenberg, Moshe, *The Hab/piru*, New Haven: American Oriental society, 1955.

Grimal, Nicolas, *A History of Ancient Egypt*, Malden, Mass.: Blackwell, 2000

Gunneweg, Jan, Isadore Erlman, and Zeev Mishel, *The Origin of the Pottery of Kuntillet 'Ajrud in Israel Exploration Journal* 35, no. 4, 1985, pp. 270-83. http://www.jstor.org/stable/27926000.

Habicht, M.E., Bouwman, A.S., Ruhli, F.J., *Identifications of ancient Egyptians royal mummies from the 18th Dynasty reconsidered, American Journal of Physical Anthropology V 159 Issue 561,* 1/2016.

Halpern, Baruch, "The Sea-Peoples and Identity", in *Scripta Mediterranea* Zeev Vol. 27-8, Canadian Inst for Mediterranean Studies, 2005,   Retrieved from https://scripta.journals.yorku.ca/index.php/scripta/article/view/40119, pp. 15-32.

Hamori, Esther J. "Gender and the Verification of Prophecy at Mar*i," in Die Welt Des Orients* 42, no. 1, 2012, pp. 1–22. http://www.jstor.org/stable/23342110.

Har-El, M., הראל, מנשה, "'And They Dwelt from Havilah unto Shur" (*Genesis* 25: 18) / ' וישכנו מחוילה (בראשית כ"ה, יח ...'עד שור אשר על פני מצרים)." *Beit Mikra: in Journal for the Study of the Bible and Its World /* יז ועולמו המקרא לחקר כתב-עת :מקרא בית ,סח. 2–501 :(1972) (נא) ד. http://www.jstor.org/stable/23502959.

Hartment, David, *A Living Covenant,* Nashville: Jewish Lights 1985.

Harwood, Richard S., "The Western Valley of the Kings Project," in *Archeological Research in the Valley of the Kings and Ancient Thebes*, P.P. Creasman ed., Tucson: U Arizona, 2013, pp. 39-53.

Hasel, Michael G., *The Battle of Kadesh*, in *Egypt, Canaan, and Israel: History, Imperialism, and Ideology*, ed., S. Bar et al: Leiden: Brill, 2011, pp. 65-87, https://www.academia.edu/37321435/Michael_G_Hasel_The_Battle_of_Kadesh_Identifying_New_Kingdom_Polities_Places_and_Peoples_in_Canaan_and_Syria_Pp_65_85_in_Egypt_Canaan_and_Israel_History_Imperialism_and_Ideology_ed_S_Bar_D_Kahn_and_J_J_Shirley_Leiden_Brill_2011?email_work_card=title

Hasel, Michael G., "Israel in the Merneptah Stela," in *Bulletin of the American Schools of Oriental Research 296,* Chicago: U Chicago Press, 11/1994, pp. 45-61

Hasselback-Andee, Rebecca, Ed., *A companion to Ancient Near Eastern Languages,* Hoboken, NJ: John Wiley & Sons, 2020.

Hasson, Nir, *How was Iron Smelted in Ancient Israel?* In Haaritz, 2/19/2019.

Hayes, William C., *A Papyrus of The Late Middle Kingdom,* Brooklyn: Brooklyn Museum, 1955.

Hays, Brooks, "Modern DNA reveals ancient origins of Indian population," Washington DC: *Science News,* 5/2017, https://www.upi.com/Science_News/2017/05/08/Modern-DNA-reveals-ancient-origins-of-Indian-population/6721494272565/

Heltzer, M. "TheYaureans and the Yairites," in *Rivista Degli Studi Orientali* 56, 1982, pp. 17–20. http://www.jstor.org/stable/41880350.

Heltzer, M. *The Suteans*, Naples: Istituto Universitario Orientale, 1981.

Hendel, Ronald, "The Exodus in Biblical Memory," *in Journal of biblical Literature* Vol. 120 No 4, Atlanta: SBL Press, 2001, pp. 601-622.

Herodotus, *Histories*

Hershkovitz, Israel, "Assyrian Attitude Towards Captive Enemies," in *International Journal of Osteoarchaeology*, Philadelphia: Wiley-Blackwell, 2012.

https://www.academia.edu/78109965/Assyrian_Attitude_Towards_Captive_Enemies_A_2700_y
ear_old_Paleo_forensic_Stu.

Hertz, J.H., ed, *Pentateuch and Haftorahs,* London: Soncino, 1965.

Hertzberg, Arthur, *Jews,* San Francisco: Harper, 1998.

Himelfarb, Elizabeth, "First Alphabet Found in Egypt," in *Archaeological Institute of America newsbriefs* Vol. 53 No.1 /2 2000.

Hirsch, Emil G; Pick, Bernhard, Barton, George, A, Kenites, JewishEncyclopedia.com

Hoch, James, *Semitic Words In Egyptian Texts of the New Kingdom and Third Intermediate Period,* Princeton: Princeton U., 1994.

Hoffmeier, James, "A Highway out of Egypt," in *Desert Road Archaeology*, Forester & Reimer eds., Koln: Heinrich-Barth, 2013, pp. 476-510.

Hoffmeier, James K., *Israel in Egypt*, Oxford: Oxford U., 1996

Hoffmeier, James K., Thomas W. Davis, and Rexine Hummel. "New Archaeological Evidence for Ancient Bedouin (Shasu) on Egypt's Eastern Frontier at Tell El-Borg," in *Ägypten Und Levante / Egypt and the Levant* 26, 2016, pp. 285–311. http://www.jstor.org/stable/44243955.

Hoffmeier, James, "Sinai in Egyptian, Levantine and Hebrew Perspectives," in *The History of the Peoples of the Eastern Desert*, LA: UCLA, Ch 8, 2012.

Holdrege, Barbara A., *Veda and Torah*. Albany: State U. of NY, 1996.

Hollinger, David, *Science, Jews, and Secular Culture*, Princeton: Princeton U., 1999.

Hornung, Erik, David Lorton tr., *Akhenaten and the Religion of Light*, Ithaca: Cornell U., 1999.

Hughes, Robert, *Barcelona*, NY: Knopf, 1992.

Humphreys, Colin J., *The Miracles of Exodus*, NY: Harper Collins, 2004.

Isaacs, Ronald H., *Miracles, A Jewish Perspective*, Northvale, NJ: Jason Aronson, 1997.

Israel Nature and Parks Authority, *The Beer Sheva National Park*.

Isserlin *The Israelites*, London: Thames and Hudson, 1998.

Jacobovichi, Simcha, *Exodus Decoded*, film on The History Channel, 2016.

Jacobs, Joseph, *Jewish Contributions to Civilization*, Phila.: JPS , 2016.

Jensen, Victoria, *The Cemeteries of Deir el-Ballas*, dissertation U CA 2019.

Jhunjhunwala, Bharat, *Common Prophets of the Jews, Christians, Muslims and Hindus in the Indus Valley,* Presentation of Union Biblical Seminary, Pune, 8/16/2018
https://www.academia.edu/83801406/Common_Prophets_of_the_Jews_Christians_Muslims_an
d_Hindus_in_the_Indus_Valley_A_Hypothesis_for_Exploration.

Joshua, Judges, Samuel, and Kings, The Early Prophets, Schocken Bible V II, tr. Fox, Everett, NY: Schocken, 2014.

Josephus, Flavius, "Against Apion,", in Thackeray, *Josephus: The Life, Against Apion*, Cambridge: Harvard, 1926.

JPS, Jewish Publication Society, *The Holy Scriptures*, Philadelphia: JPS, 1916-1955.

Junkkaala, Eero, *Three Conquests of Canaan*, Vaajakoski: Abo Akademi University Press, 2006, https://www.academia.edu/35716749/Conquest_Canaan?email_work_card=view-paper

Kagay, Donald J., tr. The Usatges of Barcelona, Phila., U. of Penna., 1994.

Kahn, Dan'el, "Merneptah's Policy in Canaan," in G. Galil, A. Maeir, A. Gilboa, and D. Kahn, *The Ancient Near East in the 12th-10th Centuries BCE*, Conference at U. Haifa: Israel, 2010, pp. 255-268.

Kamrin, Janice, "The Procession of 'Asiatics' at Beni Hasan," in *Cultures in Contact*, Joan Aruz, Sarah Graff, and Yelena Rakic, eds., NY: The Met, 2013, brief in: https://www.academia.edu/30529730/The_Procession_of_Asiatics_at_Beni_Hasan_in_Cultures_in_Contact?email_work_card=view-paper.

Katsh, Abraham I. *The Biblical Background of the Political System in America, in Hebrew Studies* 17, 1976, pp. 30–48, http://www.jstor.org/stable/44898226.

Kelder, Jorrit, *From Thutmoses III to Homer to Blackadder*, at symposium at Getty: LA, 2018.

Keller, Werner, Neil, William tr, *The Bible as History*, NY: Barnes and Noble 1995.

Kempinski,, Aharon. "Some Philistine Names from the Kingdom of Gaza." *Israel Exploration Journal* 37, no. 1 (1987): 20–24. http://www.jstor.org/stable/27926047.

Kent, Charles, *Journal of the Victorian Institute*, Vol. XXVIII, p. 267, and Vol. XXVI, p. 12.

Kent, Charles Foster, *Biblical Geography and History*, NY: Scribner, 1914.

Kenyon, Kathlen M., *Amorites and Canaanites*, Oxford: Oxford U. 1963.

Kenyon, Kathleen M. "Excavations at Jericho." *The Journal of the Royal Anthropological Institute of Great Britain and Ireland* 84, no. 1/2 (1954): 103–10. https://doi.org/10.2307/2844004.

Kenyon, Kathleen M. "Jericho." *Archaeology* 20, no. 4 (1967): 268–75. http://www.jstor.org/stable/41667764.

Kenyon, Kathleen M. "Jericho: Oldest Walled Town." *Archaeology* 7, no. 1 (1954): 2–8. http://www.jstor.org/stable/41663196.

Kitchen, K.A., "Egyptian Evidence on Ancient Jordan," in Bienkowski, Piotr, *Early Edom and Moab*, Sheffield: Sheffield Press, 1992.

Kitchen, K.A., *Pharaoh Triumphant*, Warminster: Aris & Phillips, 1982.

Kitchen, K.A., *On the Reliability of the Old Testament*, Grand Rapids: Eerdmans, 2003. And Grand Rapids, 2006, 345-346.

Klein, Rabbi Charna, *Inside the Torah*, Bloomington, IN: Archway, 2020

Kleinfeld, Rachel, "No War, No Peace," in *Carnegie Endowment for International Peace*, 2019, https://carnegieendowment.org/2019/10/14/no-war-no-peace-healing-world-s-violent-societies-pub-80034.

Klenck, Joel, *The Exodus from Egypt*, FL: PRC Press, 2010.

Knauf-Belleri, Ernst, "Edom: The Social and Economic History", in *You Shall Not Abhor an Edomite for He is Your Brother*, Atlanta: Scholars Press, 1995, pp. 93-118.

Knohl, Israel, *The historical Joseph*, Hebrew U., unpublished paper, 2019.

Koller, Aaron, "The Diffusion of the Alphabet in the Second Millennium BCE," AZ: *Journal of Ancient Egyptian Interconnections,* Vol. 20, 2018, pp 1-14, https://journals.librarypublishing.arizona.edu/jaei/article/id/1355.

Korpman, Matthew J., "Dan Shall Judge," In *Journal for the Study of the Old Testament*, March 11, 2020, pp. 490-499- https://www.academia.edu/en/36376363/Dan_Shall_Judge_The_Danites_and_Iron_Age_Israel

_s_Connection_with_the_Denyen_Sea_People_Journal_for_the_Study_of_the_Old_Testament_44_3_2020_490_499

Kozloff, Arielle & Bryan, Betsy, *Egypt's Dazzling Sun*, Cleveland: Cleveland Mus. of Art, 1992.

Kramer, Samuel Noah, *History Begins at Sumer*, Philadelphia: U. Penn, 1956, 1981.

Krauss, Rolf, "Unterscuhungen zu Konig Amenmesse: Hachtrage," in *Studien zur Altagyptischen Kultur Bd*.24, Germany: Helmut Buske, pp. 161-184, 1997.

Kuschke, Arnulf, tr. by Mills, Donald Keith, "The terrain of the Battle of Qadesh and the approach Route of Ramses II," in *Zeitschrift des Deutschen Palasina-Vereins 95, 1,* 1979, pp. 7-35, https://www.academia.edu/34800528/The_Terrain_of_the_Battle_of_Qadesh_and_the_Approach_Route_of_Ramses_II.

Kurinsky, *The Glassmakers*, NY: Hippocrene, 1991.

Laboury, Dimitri, "How and Why did Hatshepsut Invent the Image of Her Royal Rower?," in *Creativity and Innovation in the Reign of Hatshesut*, Chicago: U Chicago, 2014, pp. 49-91.

LaMoreaus, P. and Hussein, I., *The Exodus: Myth, Legend, History*, Tudcaloosa: Word Way Press, 1996.

Langdon, S., "Tablets from Kish and Umma" *Revue D'Assyriologie Et D'archéologie Orientale* 34, no. 2, 1937, pp. 67-79. http://www.jstor.org/stable/23284110.

Lange-Athinodorou, Eva. "Palace Cemeteries of the Eastern Delta." In *Ancient Egyptian and Ancient Near Eastern Palaces: Proceedings of the Conference on Palaces in Ancient Egypt, Held in London 12th–14th June 2013, Organised by the Austrian Academy of Sciences, the University of Würzburg and the Egypt Exploration Society*, edited by MANFRED BIETAK and SILVIA PRELL, NED-New edition, 1., 157–68. Austrian Academy of Sciences Press, 2018. https://doi.org/10.2307/j.ctvrzgw3b.14, also https://www.academia.edu/36191866/Palace_cemeteries_of_the_eastern_Delta

Langgut, Dafna and Israel Finkelstein, "Dry Climate in the Middle Bronze I and its Impact on Settlement Patterns, *in the Levant and Beyond* in *Journal of Near Eastern Studies,* Vol. 73, No. 2, pp.219-234, Chicago: UC Press, 2014

Layton, Scott C. Archaic Features of Canaanite Personal names in the Hebrew Bible, Atlanta: Scholars Press, 1990.

Lawler, Andrew, "DNA from the Bible's Canaanites lives on in modern Arabs and Jews," in *National Geographic*, May 28, 2020,

Lederman, Zvi, and Slomo Bunimovitz, "Iron Age Iron: from Invention to Innovation," in *Studies in Mediterranian Archaeology,* Uppsala: Paul Forlag Astroms, 2012, pp. 103-112.

Lee, Sharen, Christopher Ramsey Christopher, Amihai Mazar, "Iron Age Chronology in Israel," in Arizona: *Journals of University of Arizona*, 2016 (Also online by Cambridge U Press, 2016) .

Lemche, Niels Peter, *Early Israel*, Leiden: E.J. Brill, 1985.

Lemche, Niels Peter, *The Israelites in History and Tradition*, Louisville: John Knox, 1998.

Lemche, Niels Peter. *Preludes to Israel's Past*, Peabody: Hendrickson, 1998.

Levine, Baruch A. Review of *The Deir 'Alla Plaster Inscriptions*, by J. Hoftijzer and G. van der Kooij. *Journal of the American Oriental Society* 101, no. 2 (1981): 195–205. https://doi.org/10.2307/601759.

Levine, Etan. "The Symbolism of Milk and Honey," in *A Review of General Semantics* 41, no. 1, 1984, pp. 33–37. http://www.jstor.org/stable/42576652.

Levy, Thomas E., and Augustin Holl, *Migrations,* "Ethnogenesis, and Settlement Dynamics," in *Journal of Anthropological Archaeology* 21, 2002, pp. 83-118 doi:10.1006/jaar.2001.0390, http://www.idealibrary.com or academia.edu 2992621.

Lichtheim, Miriam, *Ancient Egyptian Literature vol. I*, Berkeley: UC, 2006.

Lichtheim, Miriam, *Ancient Egyptian Literature vol. II*, Berkeley: UC, 2006.

Liszka, Kate. "Egyptian or Nubian? Dry-Stone Architecture at Wadi El-Hudi, Wadi Es-Sebua, and the Eastern Desert'" in *The Journal of Egyptian Archaeology* 103, no. 1, 2017, pp. 35-51, https://www.jstor.org/stable/26948550.

Lloyd, Alan B., Perseus and Chemmis Herodotus II 91 , journal of Hellenic Studies, Vol. 89, pp. 79-86, 1969.

Lucian of Samosata, tr. by Herbert A. Strong and John Garstang, *The Syrian Goddess*, London: Constable, 1913, http://lucianofsamosata.info/wiki/doku.php?id=home:texts_and_library:essays:the-syrian-goddess, composed ~ 150 CE .

Luce, J. V., and Kathleen Bolton. "Thera and the Devastation of Minoan Crete: A New Interpretation of the Evidence." *American Journal of Archaeology* 80, no. 1 (1976): 9–18. https://doi.org/10.2307/502934.

Luciani, M.," The Northern Levant during the Late Bronze Age Syria," in *The Oxford Handbook of the Archaeology of the Levant,* Oxford: Oxford U., 2014, pp. 509-523, https://www.academia.edu/17101671/Luciani_M_2014_The_Northern_Levant_Syria_during_the_Late_Bronze_Age_Syria_Small_Kingdoms_between_the_Supraregional_Empires_of_the_International_Age?email_work_card=view-paper .

MacGillivray, J. Alexander, "Thera, Hatshepsut, and the Keftiu," in *Dating the Minoan eruption of Santorinin*, Denmark: Danish Institute at Athens, 2009, pp. 154-170.

Magistris, Francesco, *The Apiru and the Egyptian Domination of Late Bronze*, Edinburgh: U. Edinburgh, 2014.

Main, Douglas, "Holy Land Farming Began 5000 years earlier than thought," in *Live Science Online*, https://www.livescience.com/28011-ancient-agriculture-israel.html 3/19/2013.

Malamat, Abraham. "The Danite Migration and the Pan-Israelite Exodus-Conquest: A Biblical Narrative Pattern." *Biblica* 51, no. 1 (1970): 1–16. http://www.jstor.org/stable/42609488.

Malamat, Abraham, "King Lists of the Old Babylonian Period and Biblical Genealogies in Journal of the American Oriental Society 88," no. 1, 1968, pp.163–73, https://doi.org/10.2307/597910.

Malamat, Abraham, "Mari." In *The Biblical Archaeologist* 34, no. 1, 1971, pp. 2–22, https://doi.org/10.2307/3210950.

Malamat, Abraham, "Origins and the Formative Period," in H. Ben-Sasson, *A history of the Jewish People*, Cambridge: Harvard, 1976

Malamat, Abraham, "Syro-Palestinian Destinations in a Mari Tin Inventory," in *Israel Exploration Journal* 21, no. 1, (1971, pp. 31–38, http://www.jstor.org/stable/27925249.

Manuel, Jose L.,and Charles K. Moore, "The Development of Taxation in the Bible,Improvements in counting, Measurement, and computation, in The Ancient Middle East," *in The Accounting Historians Journal* 25, no. 2, 1998, pp. 63–80. http://www.jstor.org/stable/40697526.

Maimonides, *Mishneh Torah*, trans. By Eliyahu Touger, Brooklyn, Moznaium, 2010.

Mark, Joshua J., "Trade in ancient Mesopotamia," in *World History Encyclopedia*, 11/22/2022

Mark, Joshua J., "*Women's Work in Ancient Egypt,*" in *World History Encyclopedia*. Last modified May 03, 2017. https://www.worldhistory.org/article/1058/womens-work-in-ancient-egypt/.

Martin, Geoffrey T. "The Toponym Retjenu on a Scarab from Tell El-Dabʿa." *Ägypten Und Levante / Egypt and the Levant* 8 (1998): 109–12. http://www.jstor.org/stable/23786957.

Martin, Thomas R., *Ancient Greece*, New Haven: Yale, 2000

Matic, Uros, "*To* Kill like a god and to Kill like a ma*n*," in *Conference on Violence, Punishment and Labour in Ancient Egypt and the Ancient Near East*, University of Bonn, 1/15/2019, 2018, https://www.academia.edu/37900251/To_kill_like_a_god_and_to_kill_like_a_man_Ontological_t urn_and_violent_treatments_of_enemies_and_prisoners_of_war_in_New_Kingdom_Egypt.

Mazar, Amihai, "The Egyptian Garrison Town at Beth Shean," in S. Bar, D. Kahn, and J. Shirley, eds., *Egypt, Canaan and Israel: Proceedings at U. Haifa* 6/2009, Leiden: Brill, 2011.

Mazar, Amihai, "Tel Beth Shean: History and Archaeology," in *One God – One Cult – One Nation*, Reinhard Kratz, and Spieckermann, eds, Berlin/NY: 2010 p.p 239-272.

McConville, J. Gordon, & Williams, Stephen N., Joshua, Grand Rapids and Cambridge U.K.: 2010

McCoy, Floyd W., and Grant Haiken. "ANATOMY of an ERUPTION." *Archaeology* 43, no. 3 (1990): 42–49. http://www.jstor.org/stable/41765836.

Mendenhall, George E. "The Hebrew Conquest of Palestine." *The Biblical Archaeologist* 25, no. 3 (1962): 66–87. https://doi.org/10.2307/3210957.

Mendenhall, George E. "The Message of Abdi-Ashirta to the Warriors, EA 74*" in Journal of Near Eastern Studies* 6, no. 2 1947, pp. 123–24. http://www.jstor.org/stable/542591.

Mendenhall, George,*The Tenth Generation*, Baltimore: Johns Hopkins, 1973

Meshel, .Ze'ev, "Kuntillet ʻAjrud" in *Expedition Magazine*, 1978, in. *Expedition Magazine*. Penn Museum, 1978, Web. 18 Aug 2021, http://www.penn.museum/sites/expedition/?p=4373.

MET Isis and Horus https://www.metmuseum.org/art/collection/search/545969

Meyers, Carol, *Discovering Eve*, Oxford: Oxford Press, 1988.

Milevski, Ianir, and Liora Horwitz, "Donkeys, Domestication and Early Bronze Age Society," in *The Ancient Near East Today*, Israel: ASOR May, 2020.

Mills, Andrew C., & Abdu Shata, "Ground-Water Assessment of Sinai, Egypt," *in NGWA the Groundwater Assoc.*, Vol. 27, Issue 6, 1989, pp. 793-801.

Misgav, H., Garfinkel, Y, and S. Ganor, "The Ostracon in Kirbet Qeiyafa,*" Vol. 1: Excavation Report 2007-2008*, Jerusalem: *Israel Exploration Society*, Institute of Archaeology, Hebrew University of Jerusalem, pp. 243-57.

Morris, Ellen, *The Architecture of Imperialism*, Leiden: Boston: Brill, 2005.

Moore, Megan Bishop, and Brad E. Kelle, *Biblical History and Israel's Past*, Cambridge: Eerdman, 2011.

Mourad, Anna-Latifa, *Asiatics and Abydos, Bulletin of The Australian Centre for Egyptology V 24*, 2013, pp. 31- 58.

Mourad, Anna-Latifa, "Foreigners at Beni Hassan: Evidence from the Tomb of Khnumhotep I (No. 14)," in Bulletin of the American Schools of Oriental Research 2020 384:, 105-132, https://www.journals.uchicago.edu/action/showCitFormats?doi=10.1086%2F710528&mobileUi=0

Mourad, Anna-Latifa, *Rise of the Hyksos*, Oxford: Archaeopress, 2015.

Muhlestein, Kerry, *Violence in the Service of Order*, Oxford: Archaeopress, 2011.

Muhlestein, Kerry, "Levantine Thinking in Egypt," in *Culture and History of the Ancient Near East*, V. 52, S. Bar, D. Kahn, and J.J. Shirley, eds, Leiden: Brill, 2011, pp. 190-235.

Manetho, W.G. Waddell, tr. *Manetho*, Cambridge: Harvard U. Press, 1964.

Maspero, G., *History of Egypt, Chaldea, Syria, Babylonia, and Assyria*, V. 4, M.L. McClure, tr., London: Grolier, recovered from Gutenberg.

McLaughlin, John L., *The Ancient Near East*, Abingdon Press 2012.

Megahed, Mohamed, "Archaeo-mineralogical Characterization of Ancient Copper and Turquoise mining in South Sinai, Egypt," in *Archeomatica* N 4, Dec 2018.

Moore, Megan, and Kelle, Brad, *Biblical History and Israel's Past*, Grand Rapids & Cambridge: Eerdman's, 2011.

Moran, William, ed. *The Amarna Letters*, Baltimore: Johns Hopkins, 1992.

Morris, Ellen," Mitanni Enslaved: Prisoners of War, Pride, and Productivity in a New Imperial Regime," in *Creativity and Innovation in the Reign of Hatshesut*, Chicago: U Chicago, 2014 pp. 361-379.

Mourad, Anna-Latifa, "Asiatics and Abydos: From the Twelfth Dynasty to the Early Second Intermediate Period, "Sydney*: Bulletin of Australian Centre for Egyptology*, Vol. 24, 2013.

Mourad, Anna-Latifa, "Foreigners at Beni Hassan: Evidence from the tomb of Khnumhotep I (No. 14)," in Bulletin of the American Schools of Oriental research 2020 384:, 105-132. https://www.journals.uchicago.edu/action/showCitFormats?doi=10.1086%2F710528&mobileUi=0

Munger, Stefam, *Khirbet Qeiyafa in the Shephelah*, Gottingen: Vandenhoeck & Ruprecht, 2017, https://www.academia.edu/32837388/Khirbet_Qeiyafa_in_the_Shephelah?email_work_card=view-pap.

Na'aman, Nadav, "The'Conquest of Canaan' in the Book of Joshua and in History," in Finkelstein & N. Na'aman (eds.), From Nomadism to Monarchy, Washington, Biblical Archaeology Society, 1994, pp. 218-281, https://www.academia.edu/13459417/The_Conquest_of_Canaan_in_the_Book_of_Joshua_and_in_History_in_I_Finkelstein_and_N_Na_aman_eds_From_Nomadism_to_Monarchy_Archaeological_and_Historical_Aspects_of_Early_Israel_Jerusalem_1994_pp_218_281

Na'aman, Nadav, "The Exodus Story*," in Journal of Ancient Near Eastern Religions*, 2011, pp. 39-69

Na'aman, Nadav, *The Jacob Story and the Formation of Biblical Israel*, Tel Aviv: TAU Vol. 41 2014.

Na'aman, Nadav, "Did Rameses II Wage Campaign against the Land of Moab?" In *Gottinger Miszellen 209:* Gottingen, from academia.com 2006, pp. 63-69.

Na'aman, Nadav, "The Shephelah According to the Amarna Letters," in I. Finkelstein and N. Na'amon, eds., *The Fire Signals of Lachish*, Winona Lake, Indiana: Eisenbrauns, 2011, pp. 281-299.

Na'aman, Nadav, "The Town of Ibirta and the Relations of the Apiru and the Shosu," in Gottinger Miszellen 57, Gottingen: Georg-August-Universitat, 1982 pp. 27-33.

https://www.academia.edu/13452231/The_Town_of_Ibirta_and_the_Relations_of_the_Apiru_an d_the_Shosu_G%C3%B6ttinger_Miszellen_57_1982_pp_27_33.

Neale, Sandra, *Akhenaton and the Amarna Period*, M.A. Thesis, U of Kent .

Newman, James R. *The World of Mathematics Vol. I,* NY: Simon and Schuster, 1956.

Nakhai, Beth Alpert, "A Landscape Comes to Life: The Iron I Period,*" in Near Eastern Archaeology*, via academia.edu, Issue 2, V 62, 1999, pp. 62-92, 101-127.

Nelson, Eric, *The Hebrew Republic*, Cambridge: Harvard, 2010

Nielsen, Joshua*, Egypt's Interactions with pastoral Nomads in the Sinai, Negev, and Transjordan,* research paper University of Alabama, 2010, https://www.academia.edu/38856768/Egypts_Interactions_with_Pastoral_Nomads_in_the_Sinai _Negev_and_Transjordan?email_work_card=view-paper&li=0

Nigro, Lorenze, "Hoteprbra at Jericho," in *Contributi e Materiali di Archeologia Orientale, XVIII*, 2018, https://www.academia.edu/38309062/HOTEPIBRA_AT_JERICHO_INTERCONNECTIONS_B ETWEEN_EGYPT_AND_SYRIA_PALESTINE_DURING_THE_13TH_DYNASTY

Nigro, Lorenzo, "Tell Es-Sultan 2015: A Pilot Project for Archaeology in Palestine." *Near Eastern Archaeology* 79, no. 1 (2016): 4–17. https://doi.org/10.5615/neareastarch.79.1.0004.

Noll, K.L., *Canaan and Israel in Antiquity: An Introduction.* A&C Black, 2001.

Noth, Martin, *The History of Israel*, NY: Harper & Row , 1958.

Noth, Martin, *A History of Pentateuchal Traditions*, Chico, CA: Scholars Press, 1981.

Ouaknin, Marc-Alain, *Mysteries of the Alphabet*, NY: Abbeville Press, 1999.

Panitz-Cohen, Nava, Mullins, Robert, David, Arlette, & Ariel Shatil, "A Late Middle Bronze IIB Burial from Tel Abel Beth Maaacah," in *Tell it in Gath*, eds. Shai, Chadwick, Hitchcock, Dagan, McKinny, and Uziel, Munster: Zaphon, 2018

Pappi, Cinzia, "Colapse in the Transtigrine Regioin,*" in Exploring 'Dark Ages' Archaeological Markers of Transition in the Near East*, Wiesbaden Germany: Studia Chaburensia issue 10, 2022, pp. 53-78. https://www.academia.edu/73949404/Between_Assyria_and_Adiabene_Discussing_Resilience _and_Collapse_in_the_Transtigrine_Region.

Palvanov, Efraim, Mayim Achronim blog, https://www.mayimachronim.com/tag/13-principles-of- exegesis/.

Parkinson, R.B.,*The Tale of Sinuhe and Other Ancient Egyptian Poems*, Oxford:Oxford 1997.

Parrot, Andre, tr. James Farley, *Abraham and His Times,* Philadelphia: Fortress Press, 1968

Peirce, Laura, *The Legacy of the Hyksos*, unpublished theses, Dept. Ancient History, Macquarie U, Sydney, 2015

Pentawer, *Quarrel of Apophis and Seqenenre*, Papyrus Sallier I in British Museum

Petrie, W.M.Flinders, *Syria and Egypt from the Tell El Amarna Letters*, NY: Scribner, 1898.

Petrie Museum of Egyptian Archaeology, *Digital Egypt for Universities*, https://www.ucl.ac.uk/museums-static/digitalegypt/Welcome.html

Petrovich, Douglas, *Origins of the Hebrews*, Nashville: New Creation, 2021.

Petrovich, Douglas, *The World's Oldest Alphabet*: Israel, Carta Jerusalem, 2016

Petrovich, Douglas, *The Reading of Sinai 115' Caption*,
https://www.academia.edu/30408017/_2016_The_Reading_of_Sinai_115s_Caption_An_Open_Response_to_Thomas_Schneider 2016

Philologos, "Daughter of a Voice" *in Forward*, issue 12/22/2021, written 7/16/2008,
https://forward.com/culture/13776/daughter-of-a-voice-02187/

Pinker, Steven, *Better Angels of Our Nature: The decline of Violence in History and Its Causes*, NY: Penquin Books, *2012.*

Pitard, Wayne T., "Arameans," in *Peoples of the Old Testament World*," Hoertb, Mattingly, and Yamancbi eds., Cambridge: Lutterworth Press, 1994.

Plaut, W. Gunther, ed., *The Torah*, NY: Union of American Hebrew Congregations, 1981

Pratico, Gary D., "Nelson Glueck's 1938-1940 Excavations at Tell El-Kheleifeh: A Reappraisal," *in Bulletin of the American Schools of Oriental Research*, no. 259 (1985):pp. 1-32, doi:10.2307/1356795.

Pritchard, James B., Ancient Near Eastern Texts, Princeton: Princeton University, 1955.

Pritchard, James B., The Ancient Near East Vol. I, Princeton: Princeton University, 1958.

Pritchard, James B., The Ancient Near East Vol . II, Princeton: Princeton University, 1975.

Procopius, *History of the Wars III & IV* (Vandal). Tr. H.B. Dewing, Gutenberg: 1916.

Rabinovich, Abraham, and Neil Silberman, "The Burning of Hazo*r*," in *Archaeology* Vol. 51, No. 3, 5/6 1998 pp. 50-55, *JSTOR*, www.jstor.org/stable/41771387.

Radday, Yehuda T., "*The Four Rivers of Paradise*," in *Hebrew Studies* 23, 1982, pp. 23–31. http://www.jstor.org/stable/27908758.

Rainey, Anson F. , "Amenhotep II's Campaign to Takhsi," in *Journal of the American research Center in Egypt,* 1973

Rainey, Anson F., "The Biblical Shephelah of Judah," in *Bulletin of the American Schools of Oriental Research* No. 251 (Summer, 1983), The University of Chicago Press on behalf of The American Schools of Oriental Research, *JSTOR*, www.jstor.org/stable/1356823 pp. 1-22.

Rangan, Haripriya and Bell, Karen, "Elusive Traces: Baobabs and the African Diaspora in South Asia *."in* Environment and History 21, no. 1, 2015, pp. 103-33. http://www.jstor.org/stable/43299719.

Redford, Donald B., *Egypt, Canaan, and Israel in Ancient Times*, Princeton: Princeton, 1992.

Redford, Susan, and Donald B. Redford. "Graffiti and Petroglyphs Old and New from the Eastern Desert." in *Journal of the American Research Center in Egypt* 26, 1989, pp. 3–49. https://doi.org/10.2307/40000700.

Renger, Johannes. "On Economic Structures in Ancient Mesopotamia: Part One." *Orientalia* 63, no. 3 (1994): 157–208. http://www.jstor.org/stable/43076166.

Ritner, Robert K., The Mechanics of Ancient Egyptian Magical Prectice, Chicago, U.Chicago, 1993,1995, 1997, 2008.

Ritner, Robert K., and Nadine Moeller. "The Ahmose 'Tempest Stela', Thera and Comparative Chronology," *in Journal of Near Eastern Studies*, vol. 73, no. 1, The University of Chicago Press, 2014, pp. 1–19, https://doi.org/10.1086/675069.

Robins, Gay, *Women in Ancient Egypt*, Cambridge: Harvard U., 1993.

Robinson, George L. "The Route of the Exodus from Egypt," *in The Biblical World* 18, no. 6, 1901, pp. 410–23, http://www.jstor.org/stable/3137178.

Rohl, David, *A Test of Time, London*: Random house, 1995.

Rollston, Christopher, "The Emergence of Alphabetic Scripts," in Hasselback-Andee, Rebecca, Ed., *A companion to Ancient Near Eastern Languages,* Hoboken, NJ: John Wiley & Sons, 2020, pp. 65-82..

Rollston, Christopher, *The Khirbet Qeiyafa Ostracon*, Tel Aviv 38, 2011, pp. 67-82, https://www.academia.edu/591966/The_Khirbet_Qeiyafa_Ostracon_Methodological_Musings_and_Caveats

Rom-Shiloni, Dalit, "When an Explicit Polemic Initiates a Hidden One: Jacob's Aramaic Identity," in *Words, Ideas, Worlds*, Brenner, Athalya, and Polak, Frank, ed., Sheffield: Sheffield Phoenix Press, 2012, pp. 206-236.

Ross, James F. "Gezer in the Tell El-Amarna Letters." *The Biblical Archaeologist* 30, no. 2 (1967): 62–70. https://doi.org/10.2307/3210955.

Rothenberg, Beno, "Pharaonic Copper Mines in South Sinai ,"in IAMS, London: *Institute of Archaeology*, Num. 10/11, June/Dec 1987.

Rothenberg, Beno, *Timna*, Great Britain: Thames and Hudson, 1972.

Rotstein, Andrea, "The Parian Marble and the Mnesiepes Inscription," Aeitschrift fur Papyrologie und Epigraphik, 190 2014 pp. 3-9.

Routledge, Carolyn, *The Balu's Stele Revisited*, Liverpool: University and World Museum, 2009 from Academia.com

Roux, Georges, *Ancient Iraq*, NY: Penguin, 1966.

Rowton, Michael B. "Economic and Political Factors in Ancient Nomadism." In *Nomads and Sedentary Peoples*, edited by Jorge Silva Castillo, 1st ed., 25–36. Colegio de Mexico, 1981. https://doi.org/10.2307/j.ctv233p9m.7.

Ruben, Brent, Kim, John, *General Systems Theory & Human communication*, Rochelle Park: Hayden Book, 1975.

Ryhold, Kim, "The Date of Kings Sheshi and Yaqubhar and the rise of the Fourteenth Dynasty," in *The Second Intermediate Period,* Maree, Marcel, ed. Leuven: U Peters and Dept Oosterse Studies, 2010.

Ryhold, Kim, *The Political Situation in Egypt during the Second Intermediate Period*, Copenhagen: CNI Publications vol.20, 1997.

Sacks, Jonathan, *The Great Partnership*, NY: Schocken Books, 2011.

Sacks, Johathan, *Morality: Restoring the Common Good in divided Times*, NY: Basic Books, 2020.

Sacks, Jonathon, *Vayikra – Between Destiny and Chance*, office conversation, 3/11/2013, https://rabbisacks.org/covenant-conversation-vayikra-between-destiny-and-chance/

Saffs, H.W.F., *Everyday Life in Babylonia & Assyria*, NY: Dorset, 1965.

Samuel, Rabbi Michael Leo, blog, https://www.rabbimichaelsamuel.com/what-does-josephs-egyptian-name-zaphenath-paneah-actually-mean/#:~:text=Some%20suggest%20that%20the%20name%20Zaphenath-

paneah%20is%20a,was%20pronounced%20Djed%20%28u%29en-
ef%20%28%E2%80%98he%20who%20is%20called%E2%80%99%29. 12/19/2009

Saretta, Phyllis, *Asiatics in Middle Kingdom Egypt*, London: Bloomsbury 2016.

Sapir-Hen, "Pigs as an Ethnic Marker? You are What You Eat*" in Biblical Archaeology Society*, 10/7/2016, https://www.biblicalarchaeology.org/?s=pigs+as+an+ethnic+marker.

Sanmartin, Joaquín. "ARS SYRA: How to do Things with Words." *Revue d'Assyriologie et d'archéologie Orientale* 107, 2013, pp. 111–18. http://www.jstor.org/stable/42771766.

Saretta, Phyllis, Asiatics in Middle Kingdom Egypt, Oxford, NY: Bloomsbury, 2016.

Sasson, Jack M. "The King and I a Mari King,*" in Changing Perceptions in Journal of the American Oriental Society* 118, no. 4, 1998, pp. 453–70, https://doi.org/10.2307/604782.

Sasson, Jack M, "About Mari and the Bible," in *Revue d'Assyriologie et d'archéologie Orientale* 92, no. 2, 1998, pp. 97–123. http://www.jstor.org/stable/23281695.

Sasson, Jack M., "Year: Zimri-Lim Dedicated His Statue to Addu of Halab," in *Editions Recherche sur les civilizations,* Paris: Vanderbilt, pp. 577-589, https://ir.vanderbilt.edu/bitstream/handle/1803/3702/Year%c2%a0Zimri-Lim%20Dedicated%20his%20Statue%20to%20Addu%20.pdf.

Sayce, A.H., *Assyria*, London: By- Paths of Biblical Knowledge, vol. VII, 1885, retrieved by Sandycroft Publishing, 2017.

Schreiner, David, *Pondering the Spade: The Kuntillet ajrud Pithoi in* Wesley Biblical Seminary, 9/27/2016 sourced in https://wbs.edu/pondering-spade-kuntillet-ajrud-pithoi/

Shammas, Carole, ",*" in The American Journal of Legal History* 31, no. 2, 1987, pp. 145–63, https://doi.org/10.2307/845880.

Sidebotham, Steve E., "Routes Through the Eastern Desert of Egypt," in *Expedition* V. 37 Issue 2, Philadelphia, Penn Museum, 1995.

Save-Soderbergh, T.*,* "The Hyksos Rule in Egypt," in *The Journal of Egyptian Archaeology* v. 37 pp. 53-71, 1951

Scherrer, Nathan H., *Yahweh of the southlands*, Denver Seminary, Theses, 2017 sourced from https://www.academia.edu/37551115/Yahweh_of_the_Southlands?email_work_card=view-paper

Schneider, Thomas, "Conjectures about Amenmesse," in *Ramesside Studies*, eds. M. Collier, S. Snape, Bolton: Rutherford Press, 2011, pp. 445-451.

Schreiner, David, "What are the Saying About Khirbet Qeiyafa?" TRINJ 33NS pp. 33-48 as in https://www.academia.edu/14459170/What_Are_They_Saying_About_Khirbet_Qeiyafa

Shirley, J. J., "The Power of the Elite: The Officials of Hatshepsut's Regency and Coregency,", in *Creativity and Innovation in the Reign of Hatshesut*, Chicago: U Chicago, 2014, pp. 173-245.

Shirley, J.J., "Crisis and Restructuring of the State," in *Ancient Egyptian Administration*, Juan Garcia, ed., Boston: Brill, 2013.

SIKER, JEFFREY S., "Abraham in Graeco-Roman Paganism," *in Journal for the Study of Judaism in the Persian, Hellenistic, and Roman Period* 18, no. 2, 1987, pp. 188–208. http://www.jstor.org/stable/24657910.

Simon, Zsolt, "Where Did the Kings of Danunna of EA 151 rule?" in *There and Back Again – the Crossroads II,* Prague: Charles University, 2015, pp. 391- 408. https://www.academia.edu/8427867/Where_Did_the_Kings_of_Danuna_of_EA_151_rule

Sivan, Gabriel, *The Bible and Civilization*, NY: NY Times, 1973

Sivertsen, Barbara J., *How Volcanoes, Earthquakes, and Plagues shaped the Story of Exodus*, Princeton: Princeton U. Press, 2009

Smith, Henry B.," Canaanite Child Sacrifice," in *Biblearcheology.org.* 2019, https://biblearchaeology.org/research/contemporary-issues/4375-canaanite-child-sacrifice-abortion-and-the-bible

Smith, Mark S., *The Early History of God,* 2nd ed., Eerdmans, 1990

Snell, Daniel, *Life in The Ancient Near East,* New Haven: Yale U., 1977

Snowden, Jorden, *The Sherden in His Majesty's Captivity: A comparative Look at the Mercenaries of New Kingdom Egypt*, Rhodes College paper, unpublished.

Snyder, Dave, Abraham of Ur – *a Critical Analysis of the Life and Times* of the Patriarch, iUniverse, Bloomington, IN: 2015.

Spalinger, Anthony J. "The Northern Wars of Seti I: An Integrative Study," *in Journal of the American Research Center in Egypt* 16, 1979, pp. 29–47. https://doi.org/10.2307/40000316.

Spalinger, Anthony. *A New Reference to an Egyptian Campaign of Thutmose III in Asia in Journal of Near Eastern Studies* 37, no. 1 (1978): 35–41. http://www.jstor.org/stable/544293.

Strabo, Geography, tr. Hamilton and Falconer, London: Bell & Sons, 1892

Stavig, Gopal., *INDIA AND THE PENTATEUCH in Annals of the Bhandarkar Oriental Research Institute* 80, no. 1/4 (1999): 77–94. http://www.jstor.org/stable/41694578.

Stern, Philip D. "Joshua-Judges" In *The Biblical Herem: A Window in Israel's Religious Experience*, 139–64. Brown Judaic Studies, 2020. https://doi.org/10.2307/j.ctvzpv53h.14.

Stol, Marten., *Women in the Ancient Near East,* Boston: De Gruyter, 2016, (pp.663-667)

Stol, M., *Women in Mesopotamia,* in *Journal of Economic and Social History of the Orient,* Brill academic Publishers, 1995, pp, 124-144. https://www.academia.edu/48737591/Women_in_Mesopotamia

Stow, Kenneth, *Alienated Minority*, Cambridge Ma: Harvard, 1992.

Straus, Oscar S., *The Origin of Republican Form of Government in the United States of America,* NY: Putnam, 1885 (reprinted by Hardpress 2013)

Straus, Oscar S., *The Pilgrims and the Hebrew Spirit, The Menorah Journal, 6, No 6,* December 1920 https://babel.hathitrust.org/cgi/pt?id=ien.35556034674150&view=1up&seq=17

Sweet, William W., *The English Bible in the Making of America in Christian Education* 19, no. 1 (1935): 9–13. http://www.jstor.org/stable/41176100.

Taking of Joppa, Egyptian tale in the time of Thutmose III, Harris Papyrus 500

Fallan, Cheryl, and Taitz, Emily, *Entrepreneurs: From Antiquity through the Early Modern Period,* in *The Shalvi/Hyman Encyclopedia of Jewish Women* https://jwa.org/encyclopedia/article/entrepreneurs#:~:text=From%20the%20Middle%20East%20to%20Northern%2C%20Southern%20and,were%20successful%2C%20and%20even%20expanded%20the%20original%20enterprise

Taubler, E. *Kharu, Horim, Dedanim,* in *Hebrew Union College Annual,* NYC: Hebrew Union College, 1924, pp. 97-123 https://www.jstor.org/stable/43301982

Tebes, Juan Manual, *A Land Whose Stones are Iron, and Out of Whose Hills You can Dig Copper in* The Exploitation and Circulation of Copper in the Iron age Negev and Edom, Buenos Aires: Univ of Buenos Aires, Davar Logos 6.1, 2007, 69-91 at

file:///C:/Users/Office1/Downloads/Tebes2007TheExploitationandCirculationofCopperintheIronA
geNegevandEdomDavarLogos6-1.pdf

Tebes, Juan Manual, *Yahweh's Desert Origins*, Washington: Biblical Archeology, vol. 48, # 3, fall 2022, pp. 32-40.

Tel Aviv University, A 6500 year old copper workshop uncovered in Beer Sheva, Tel Aviv: Tel Aviv U., 10/11/20 A 6,500-year old copper workshop uncovered in Beer Sheva | Tel Aviv University | Tel Aviv University (tau.ac.il)

Timmer, Daniel C., *"Ah, Assyria is no More!"* Ch. 7 in Theodicy and Hope in the Book of the Twelve, NY: Bloomsbury Publishing, 2021 pp. 157-172

Thalmann, Jean-Paul. *Tell Arqa: A Prosperous City during the Bronze Age in Near Eastern Archaeology* 73, no. 2/3 (2010): 86–101. http://www.jstor.org/stable/25754039.

Thomson, Gary Arthur, *Habiru: The Rise of Earliest Israel, 2011, Bloomington*

Thompson, Thomas L. *The Historicity of the Patriarchal Narrative*, 1974

Thompson, Thomas L. Shechem, Blaiklock & Harrison, eds., *The New International Dictionary of Biblical Archaeology,* 1983 Grand Rapids.

Tobin, Vincent Arieh, and Vincent A. Tobin. "The Secret of Sinuhe." *Journal of the American Research Center in Egypt* 32 (1995): 161–78. https://doi.org/10.2307/40000836.

Trigger, B.G., Kemp, B.J., O'connor, D., & Lloyd, A.B., *Ancient Egypt*, Cambridge: Cambridge U., 1994.

Trigger, B.G., Kerma: The Rise of an African Civilization, in *The International Journal of African Historical Studies,* Vol. 9, No. 1, Boston: BU, 1976, pp. 1-21 (21 pages), accessed from academia.com.

Toledo, Victor, A Cross, *Disciplinary Review of Biblical Desert-Dwellers,* in *Damqatum*, the CEHAD Newsletter, N. 13, Argentina: Catholic U. of Argentina, 2017, pp. 3-15, https://www.academia.edu/37459989/The_Southern_Border_of_Judah_A_cross_disciplinary_review _of_biblical_desert_dwellers.

Torah

    Berlin, Adele and Brettler, Marc Zvi, JPS, Philadelphia, 2014

    Eskenazi, Tamara Cohn and Weiss, Andrea L., Women of Reform Judaism, NY, 2008

    Fox, Everett, World Publishing, Dallas, 1983

    Hertz, J.H., Soncino, second edition, London, 1987

    JPS, Philadelphia, 1955

    Plaut, Gunther, Union of American Hebrew Congregations, NY, 1981

    Sefaria.org

Touger, Eliyaho, "Kings and Wars," in *Mishneh Torah*, Jerusalem: Moznaim, 1986, https://www.sefaria.org/Mishneh_Torah%2C_Kings_and_Wars.6.7?ven=Mishneh_Tora h,_trans._by_Eliyahu_Touger._Jerusalem,_Moznaim_Pub._c1986-c2007&lang=bi

Tsur, Gideon, *The Ostracon from Khirbet Qeiyafa*, 8/2019, Open University, Natanya https://www.academia.edu/40180212/The_Ostracon_from_Khirbet_Qeiyafa_Correction_of_the_ letters_in_Ostracon_due_to_errors_in_their_identification

Tsur, Gideon, "The Ostracon from Khirbet Qeiyafa Correction of the letters in Ostracon due to errors in their identification," *Academia.edu,* 8/2019, https://www.academia.edu/40180212/The_Ostracon_from_Khirbet_Qeiyafa_Correction_of_the_letters_in_Ostracon_due_to_errors_in_their_identification?email_work_card=view-paper

Tyldesley, Joyce, *Ramesses*, Middlesex, England: Penguin, 2001.

Tyldesley, Joyce, *Hatchepsut*, London: Penquin, 1998.

Tyldesley, Joyce, and Julian Heath. "The Story of Truth and Falsehood" In *Stories from Ancient Egypt*, 78–86. Oxbow Books, 2005. https://doi.org/10.2307/j.ctvh1dnrw.14.

University of Haifa, *Ancient Earthquake*, news release, Mt. Carmel: U Haifa, GW, N. Geographic, 9/11/2020

Unseth, Peter, *Hebrew Kush: Sudan, Ethiopia, or Where?* in *Africa Journal of Evangelical Theology*, 18.2, Biblical studies.org 1999, https://biblicalstudies.org.uk/pdf/ajet/18-2_143.pdf#:~:text=This%20article%20will%20explain%20that%20Hebrew%20kush%20does,translations%20of%20kush%2C%20according%20to%20their%20context%

Van Bekkum, Koert, *From Conquest to Coexistence*, Leiden: Brill, 2011, https://www.academia.edu/1991367/From_Conquest_to_Coexistence_Ideology_and_Antiquarian_Intent_in_the_Historiography_of_Israels_Settlement_in_Canaan?email_work_card=title.

Van der Veen, Pieter Gert, & Their, Christoffer, *Israel in Canaan*, in *Journal of Ancient Egyptian Interconnections* 2, 2010 pp. 15-25

Van Seters, John, *Abraham in History and Tradition*, 1975

Vassiliev, Alexandre, The Localization of the Shasu-Land of Ramses II's Rhetorical Texts, in *Current Research in Egyptology* 2006, Oxford, Oxford U., 2006 https://www.academia.edu/3834515/The_Localization_of_the_Shasu_Land_of_Ramses_IIs_Rhetorical_Texts?email_work_card=view-paper

Verlin, Jerome, *Israel 3000 Years*, Philadelphia: Pavilion Press, 2005

Vitalliano, Dorothy, *Legends of the Earth*, Bloomington: Indiana U. Press, 1945.

Von Bertalanffy, Ludwig. *The History and Status of General Systems Theory in The Academy of Management Journal*, vol. 15, no. 4, Academy of Management, 1972, pp. 407–26, https://doi.org/10.2307/255139.

Warker, Margaret, ed.: *Ancient Israel in Egypt and the Exodus,* biblicalarchaeology.org, 2012

Warin, Roger, *The Pharaoh "Who Had not Known Joseph,"* originally from "Le pharaon qui n'avait pas connu Joseph", in *Les Nouveaux Cahiers du Cercle Ernest Renan* no. 1 (July-September 2016), Paris, pp. 55-117.

Walzer, Michael, *Exodus and Revolution*, NY: Basic Books, 1985

Walzer, Michael, *The Legal Codes of Ancient Israel*, in *Yale Journal of Law & the Humanities vol.4:335*, 1992. http://www.jstor.org/stable/24219507.

Waterhouse, S. Douglas, Who are the Habiru of the Amarna Letters? In Journal of the Adventist Theological Society, 12/1 2001, pp. 31-42, https://digitalcommons.andrews.edu/cgi/viewcontent.cgi?article=1280&context=jats

Watterson, Barbara, *Amarna*, Charleston: Tempus, 1999

Weinstein, James M., *Egyptian Relations With Palestine In the Middle Kingdon.*Phila:Penn 1975

Weiss, Avi, *the Meaning of Tumah*, in *Jewish Journal of the South Florida,* Sun Sentinel, 3/2/2022 https://www.sun-sentinel.com/florida-jewish-journal/fl-jjps-torah-0422-20150421-story.html

Weld, A.G., *The Route of the Exodus*, in *The Expositor* v, 5, Cox, Samuel, ed., London, 1885.

Wenham, Gordon J., *Genesis 1-15*, Grand Rapids: Zondervan, 1987

Wenham, Gordon J*., Genesis 16-50*, Grand Rapids: Zondervan, 2000

Werner, Karel., *Symbolism in the Vedas and Its Conceptualisation in Numen* 24, no. 3 (1977): 223–40. https://doi.org/10.2307/3269600.

Whipps, Heather, "How the Eruption of Thera Changed the World,"

In LiveScience, 2/24/2008. https://www.livescience.com/4846-eruption-thera-changed-world.html.

Wilkinson, Richard, *Tausret*, Oxford: Oxford U., 2012

Wilson-Wright, Aren M., *Sinai 345 and Some Linguistic Features in Society of Biblical Literature*: Chicago, UC, 2012

Wilson-Wright, Aren M.," Mat Gets a Promotion: A Revised Reading of Sinai 349," in MAARAV, Vol 25, Num 1-2, 2021, https://www.journals.uchicago.edu/doi/10.1086/MAR202125113, *and* file:///C:/Users/Office1/Downloads/Ma_Gets_a_Promotion_A_Revised_Reading_o.pdf.

Wimmer, Stefan Jakob, A Proto-Sinaitic Incscription in Timna/Israel In Journal of Ancient Egyptian Interconnections, Vol. 2.2, 2010, pp. 1-12, also in https://www.academia.edu/36615699/PB?email_work_card=view-paper

World History EDU Horus: Birth Story, Famly, Eye of Horus, Powers, & Symbols 1/9/2020, 2/6/2022

https://www.worldhistoryedu.com/horus-the-ancient-egyptian-god-of-the-sky/

Woudhuizen, Fred, *The Ethnicity of the Sea Peoples*, Dissertation, U Rotterdam, 2006

Wright, G. Ernest, *Shechem*, NY:McGraw Hill, 1965

Worldhistory.biz, https://www.worldhistory.biz/ancient-history/61213-2-the-reign-of-yahdun-lim.html

Wolfe, Robert, *From Habiru to Hebrews*, Minneapolis, Mill City Press, 2011

Worschech, Udo. *Egypt and Moab in The Biblical Archaeologist*, vol. 60, no. 4, The University of Chicago Press on behalf of The American Schools of Oriental Research, 12/1997, pp. 229–236, *JSTOR*, www.jstor.org/stable/3210625

Wulf, Andrea, *The Invention of Nature*, NY: Vantage Books, 2015

Yadin, Y., *Hazor*, London: Oxford, 1972.

Yigael, Yadin, *Dan, Why Did He Remain In Ships*, in *American Journal of Biblical Studies* 1, 1968. https://biblicalarchaeology.org.uk/pdf/ajba/01-1_009.pdf

Yoon, Jong Yoo, *A Sociolinguistic Approach to the Proto-Sinaitic Writings*, academic paper for Pierson School of Theology, Pyeongtaek U., https://www.academia.edu/32598689/A_Sociolinguistic_Approach_to_the_Proto?email_work_card=view-pa

Yurco, Frank J. *Was Amenmesse the Viceroy of Kush, Messuwy*? in *Journal of the American Research Center in Egypt* 34 (1997): 49-56. doi:10.2307/40000798.

Zivie, Alain, *Pharaoh's Man, Abdiel inBiblical Archaeolg*y Review vol 44 # 4, 7/8, 2018

https://www.academia.edu/36784024/_Pharaohs_Man_Abdiel._The_Vizier_with_a_Semitic_Name

Index (Numbers refer to chapter numbers, not page numbers)

Index (Numbers refer to chapter numbers, not page numbers)

Index (Numbers refer to chapter numbers, not page numbers)